IND

IDEAS

OF

FREEDOM

Celebrating
30 Years of Publishing
in India

INDIAN
IDEAS
OF
FREEDOM

·

SWAMI VIVEKANANDA

AUROBINDO GHOSE

MAHATMA GANDHI

RABINDRANATH TAGORE

B.R. AMBEDKAR

M.N. ROY

JAYAPRAKASH NARAYAN

·

DENNIS DALTON

WITH A FOREWORD BY RAMACHANDRA GUHA
& AN AFTERWORD BY JAMES TULLY

HarperCollins *Publishers* India

First published in India by HarperCollins *Publishers* 2023
4th Floor, Tower A, Building No. 10, DLF Cyber City,
DLF Phase II, Gurugram, Haryana – 122002
www.harpercollins.co.in

2 4 6 8 10 9 7 5 3 1

P-ISBN: 978-93-5629-002-0
E-ISBN: 978-93-5629-007-5

Typeset in 11/15.2 Adobe Garamond at
Manipal Technologies Limited, Manipal

Printed and bound at
Thomson Press (India) Ltd

To
Sharron—
and the Force of Friendship

Contents

Foreword

RAMACHANDRA GUHA

In the early 1980s, as a doctoral student in Calcutta, I read a brilliant essay by Dennis Dalton on the evolution of Gandhi's views on caste. This was published in an edited volume entitled *India: Unity and Diversity*. Later in the decade, I came across other insightful essays by Dalton, among them an essay on the Salt March and a comparison of Gandhi and the Bengali radical M.N. Roy.

By now, I was reading a great deal of stuff about Gandhi, and saw that Dennis Dalton's work stood out in several respects. First, while Dalton had closely read Gandhi's own writings and speeches, he also incorporated other primary sources, such as newspaper reports of Gandhi's activities. Second, he paid careful attention not just to Gandhi's followers and acolytes, but also to his rivals and adversaries. Third, while a political scientist by training, unlike others of his academic discipline he had a deeply historical approach to his subject.

In 1993, Dennis Dalton brought together a lifetime of research and writing on Gandhi in his book *Mahatma Gandhi: Nonviolent Power in Action*. The book was published by Columbia University Press in

1996. I remember picking it up in a New York bookstore shortly after it was published, reading it closely and with fascination, underlining passages and writing comments in the margin as I went along. Once I had finished the book, I wrote a letter to Rukun Advani, then with the Oxford University Press, urging him to publish an Indian edition (which the OUP did). I have returned to the text several times since; it remains one of my favourite books about Gandhi.[1]

It was much after I read Dalton on Gandhi that I was made aware of an earlier book of his, which dealt with a quartet of thinkers, rather than just one. That work, called *Indian Idea of Freedom*, was first published in 1982, and is here issued in a greatly expanded edition. The eight chapters of the original text have been prefaced with a long personal memoir, where Dalton describes, with sensitivity and feeling, his lifelong engagement with India and with Indian thinkers, and followed by new chapters dealing with three remarkable individuals not featured in the first edition of the book, these being B.R. Ambedkar, M.N. Roy and Jayaprakash Narayan. The inclusion of these three thinkers has necessitated a small but subtle change in the title, which has now become *Indian Ideas of Freedom*.

The four thinkers whom Dennis Dalton had originally focused on were Vivekananda, Aurobindo, Gandhi and Tagore. The first was a spiritual leader, the second a revolutionary-turned-mystic, the third a politician and social reformer, and the fourth a poet. None were 'political theorists' in the way Western academics define the category; that is to say, their professional and personal trajectories were rather different from that of canonical thinkers like Hobbes, Locke, Kant and Mill. Yet the contributions to Indian political thought of Vivekananda,

---

1   Interview with Sophie Roell, 'The Best Books on Gandhi: Recommended by Ramachandra Guha', FiveBooks. Available at: https://fivebooks.com/best-books/gandhi-ramachandra-guha/. Accessed 6 May 2022.

Aurobindo, Gandhi and Tagore were far greater than those made by any number of academic philosophers or theorists. As for the three thinkers Dalton has added for this new edition, while B.R. Ambedkar had not one but two PhDs, like M.N. Roy and Jayaprakash Narayan, he was for much of his life an active politician. Though Dalton himself does not make the point, none of these seven individuals saw themselves principally as scholars or thinkers. Their lasting contributions to political theory were made while they were functioning as activists, social reformers, writers or seers.

The key thesis of this book is that Indian ideas of freedom drew deeply on indigenous traditions of thought, especially religious thought. Dalton argues that these thinkers all saw the quest for freedom as both individual and political, as a deeply personal search for spiritual liberation that was linked to, and indeed preceded, the transformation of society as a whole. They were all also concerned with the ethical dimension of public life, with the relationship between ends and means, for example. Hence the emphasis of several of these thinkers on nonviolence.

The thinkers profiled in *Indian Ideas of Freedom* are perhaps best characterized as 'critical traditionalists' (to use a phrase of Ashis Nandy's). 'There were many elements in the Indian tradition,' writes Dalton, 'which Vivekananda emphatically rejected, and his idea of growth meant that India must not merely recall her past, but improve upon it.' This assessment broadly holds true of Aurobindo, Gandhi and Tagore as well. These individuals were culturally grounded as well as open-minded and innovative. They drew deeply on their cultural resources while recognizing the need to adapt to the challenges of the modern world. They thus incorporated Indic traditions in their focus on inner freedoms, on the spiritual liberation of the individual; at the same time, they were unafraid to acknowledge the importance of Western concepts of political and social liberty.

B.R. Ambedkar's intense admiration for Buddha is well-known. In a fascinating passage of the book, Dalton points to the less noticed impact of the Buddha on Vivekananda, Aurobindo and Gandhi as well. This constellation of Indian thinkers, argues Dalton, 'viewed life, and Buddha's example especially, as a quest for spiritual liberation and thought. They actualized this ideal within a common intellectual tradition. The archetype of Buddha's lifetime transformation and search for enlightenment served as exemplary for the evolution of their intellectual journeys.'

The book draws the reader into the narrative through vivid, well-chosen quotations from the thinkers themselves. Here, for example, is Tagore explaining the difference between the spirit and the form of religion:

> The spirit of religion says that disrespect for man confers no benefit on him who insults and on him who is insulted, but the form of religion says that failure to obey scrupulously the detailed rules for treating man with cruel contempt is apostasy. The spirit teaches us not to destroy our own souls by inflicting unnecessary suffering on our fellow creatures, but the form warns parents that it is sin to give food and drink on specified days of the month to their widow daughter even to relieve her of the worst suffering. The spirit tells us to atone for evil thoughts and deeds by repentance and by performance of good deeds, but the form prescribes bathing in particular rivers at the hour of solar or lunar eclipse. The spirit advises us to cross seas and mountains and develop our minds by seeing the world, but the form puts an expiatory ban on sea voyage. The spirit tells us to revere all good men irrespective of their caste, but the form enjoins respect for the Brahmin, however unworthy. In sum, the spirit of religion leads to freedom, its form to slavery.

And here is Ambedkar, writing in *The Buddha and his Dhamma* on how humans can make themselves free:

When the appropriate motives arise, the will can be awakened and set in motion. With the coming of just enough light to see in what directions to guide the motions of the will, man may so guide them that they shall lead to liberty. Thus though man is bound, yet he may be free; he may at any moment begin to take the first steps that will ultimately bring him freedom. This is because it is possible to train the mind in whatever directions one chooses. It is mind that makes us to be prisoners in the house of life, and it is mind that keeps us. But what mind has done, that mind can undo. If it has brought man to thralldom, it can also when rightly directed bring him to liberty.

And here, finally, is a remarkable passage chosen by Dalton from Aurobindo's 1949 book *The Human Cycle*, demonstrating the parallels between Communism and Fascism:

> The essential features are the same in Russia and in Fascist countries. … There is the seizure of the life of the community by a dominant individual leader, Fuhrer, Dux, dictator, head of a small active minority, the Nazi, Fascist or Communist party, and supported by a militarised partisan force: there is a rapid crystallisation of the social, economic, political life of the people into a new rigid organisation effectively controlled at every point; there is the compulsory casting of thought, education, expression, action into a set iron mould, a fixed system of ideas and life-motives, with a fierce and ruthless, often a sanguinary repression of all that denies and differs; there is a total and unprecedented compression of the whole communal existence so as to compel a maximum efficiency and a complete unanimity of mind, speech, feeling, life.

In showing the striking similarities between left-wing and right-wing forms of authoritarianism, Aurobindo is anticipating the later (and very influential) formulations of the German-American thinker Hannah Arendt in her 1951 book, *The Origins of Totalitarianism*.

While Dalton has a fine eye for the telling quotation, his own judgements are themselves richly illuminating. This, for example, is what he says about Gandhi's early work, *Hind Swaraj*:

> As a statement of political thought *Hind Swaraj* has considerable limitations: it is a brief polemical tract more than a logical development of a serious and measured argument; written hastily, in less than ten days, it suffers from occasional disjointedness and egregious overstatement. Yet the essence of Gandhi's political and social philosophy is here...

And here is Dalton explaining the significance of Gandhi's multipronged approach to social reform: 'His campaign against untouchability was, above all, a movement to create a common feeling among castes and untouchables; his struggle for Hindu–Muslim unity sought a harmony of religious sympathies; and his attempt to advance the use of khaddar and the spinning wheel was an effort at bridging the gulf between groups of educated Indians and the majority in the villages.'

And, on Gandhi's lifelong campaign against untouchability in particular, Dalton writes: 'No single attempt in modern Indian political thought to establish social equality is more significant than Gandhi's attack on caste. The social innovation that Gandhi hoped to achieve was achieved; yet he continually couched his pleas for reform in traditional language and themes.'

Finally, here is Dalton on why, and in what manner, Tagore stands out from the three other thinkers profiled in the original edition of the book:

> Many of the ideas which Tagore voices ... are in profound agreement with those of Gandhi, as well as with Vivekananda and Aurobindo. All agree, ultimately, on the primary need for social reform in India, as well as on the supremacy of moral or spiritual freedom. Tagore's unique contribution rests with his early and emphatic assertion that

though India's adoption of nationalism might further the struggle for independence, it could only thwart the essential quest for moral and spiritual freedom.

Indian Ideas of Freedom is the work of a political theorist keenly interested in history and in biography. Dalton provides us a close study of the writings and speeches of his chosen protagonists, but also a profound understanding of the times they lived in that shaped their ideas and arguments. The intellectual and philosophical influences on each of his chosen thinkers are carefully traced. His readings are sympathetic but by no means uncritical.

Dalton himself was influenced by three intellectual cultures: the American, the British (he took his PhD at the School of Oriental and African Studies in London), and the Indian. Among the mentors he so generously acknowledges in his introductory memoir are the American intellectual historian Stephen Hay, the British political theorist Hugh Tinker and the Indian anthropologist Nirmal Kumar Bose. Dalton himself is a scholar of learning and compassion, whose moral orientation was shaped by his first-hand encounters with the American civil rights movement. The knowledge and the empathy are manifest in how the structure of this book is constructed and how its narrative proceeds.

Dennis Dalton's work is both interdisciplinary as well as comparative in orientation. It demonstrates that Indian political thought was anything but a derivative discourse. *Indian Ideas of Freedom* is a work of great scholarship as well as of deep humanity, and it is a privilege to introduce this wonderful book to a new generation of readers.

Memoir of India

DENNIS DALTON

John Lewis, American civil rights activist, statesman and national icon, wrote that his moment of truth came with the lynching of Emmett Till in August 1955. This tragedy traumatized many people because of its sheer brutality: a fourteen-year-old boy tortured and murdered by two white men in Money, Mississippi, for allegedly whistling at a white woman. The men were promptly acquitted by an all-white male jury. Till's mother insisted that his mutilated body be shown to the world in an open casket, so a photo of it was displayed on the cover of *Ebony* magazine. I have a vivid memory of that sight, so like John Lewis, it became a moment imbedded in my consciousness of why racism must be resisted.

The direct response to this act of hideous violence came four months later, that December, when Rosa Parks refused to yield her seat on a segregated bus in Montgomery, Alabama. Immediate support came from a large group of both women and men, black and white, to start the historic bus boycott that electrified the United States in 1956. It culminated in complete success when it was vindicated by a Supreme

1

Court decision to desegregate buses. This event proved a lesson coming when I was only eighteen, that remained with me throughout my life, guiding it in principle and practice. I learned that the worst act of violence could be effectively countered by collective nonviolence, although I didn't realize then that this bus boycott would become the purest nonviolent movement that I'd ever witness. In retrospect, it was right that such a perfect moment in the history of civil disobedience should have prompted the decision I made to join the civil rights movement and adopt the theory and practice of nonviolence.

As I studied political movements in college until graduation in 1960, it became clear that three main agents of change were necessary to ensure their efficacy: stellar leadership, a unifying ethos, and a tight organization from top to bottom. As the American civil rights movement gained momentum, the first two of these appealed to me instantly, while the third came only later when I joined in organizing it. Martin Luther King, Jr. stunned the nation with his charismatic oratory and message of nonviolence. His voice was incomparable, and it was reinforced by his writing—most significantly, his account of the bus boycott. This instant classic, entitled *Stride Toward Freedom*, was published in 1958. I had just turned twenty, eager for a belief system and political action. Therefore, for me, the requisites of leadership and creed came together in this book. It remains the single finest account of King's 'pilgrimage to nonviolence' (as he titled the most important chapter, composed when he was only twenty-nine). The succinct six principles written here of his 'philosophy of nonviolence', quickly became the lodestar that would guide my personal and professional life. I have never been a religious person in any formal sense, but the spirit and ethic of that book served as my first and enduring sacred text.

King explicitly pronounced his indebtedness to Gandhi's example and teachings as his inspiration. Therefore, when King went to India in early 1959, and then sermonized about it later in 'My Trip to the Land of Gandhi', my own journey there was determined. He spent six weeks talking with Gandhi's associates and delivering innumerable speeches. A year later, I was living in the villages of South Asia, in 1960–61, on an agricultural exchange programme that predated the Peace Corps. I gave a few speeches, attracted no large audiences, but I did discuss Gandhi with more people than King ever met. This was because, living and working in the villages, I discovered that the Mahatma was a popular topic. The other exchange delegate with me was Sharron Scheline, and we were married soon after our return home. Her background was nutrition, so if I'm indebted to King and Gandhi for going to India, then I owe the excellence of my vegetarian diet to Sharron, throughout our last sixty years together.

Although I would eventually be named a 'professor of politics' at Barnard College, Columbia University, my real designation should have been 'student' because I couldn't have become a teacher without a lifelong experience of learning from a series of Indian influences, starting with those who knew Gandhi. In 1960, only twelve years after his assassination, there were literally legions of those who claimed to have met him; Gandhian enthusiasts from villages and towns soon led me to extended interviews in four cities, Delhi, Bombay, Calcutta and Madras. My most rewarding informants, who eventually became guides and friends, were Nirmal Kumar Bose, who had served not only as Gandhi's Bengali interpreter, but also his keenest critic, and the brother–sister team of Pyarelal and Sushila Nayar, his personal secretary and physician, respectively.

Yet, there were many others to record who represent diversity in views ranging from followers of M.N. Roy—like Sibnarayan Ray, V.M. Tarkunde, G.D. Parikh, V.B. Karnik, Philip Spratt, K.K. Sinha, Amlan Datta, Abu Sayeed Ayyub, and his close friends, such as Richard Park—to Gandhians, most notably Vinoba Bhave, Acharya Kripalani, C. Rajagopalachari (Rajaji), Jayaprakash Narayan, Chhaganlal Joshi and Maurice Frydman. There were personal interviews abroad with Mirabehn in Vienna, A.D. Lazarus in Durban, relatives or friends of

Gandhi in India, South Africa or the US, Kantilal Gandhi, Arun Gandhi, Horace Alexander and Marjorie Sykes; and eventually, many of those who accompanied him on the Dandi March, the most informative (aside from Pyarelal) being Haridas Muzumdar. These extraordinary women and men became my passage to and around India.

This narrative of life in India during the 1960s may start with impressions of Nirmal Bose. He was then, at age sixty, Director of the Anthropological Survey of India (1959–1964) and would later hold the high office of Commissioner for Scheduled Castes and Tribes (1967–1970). A single afternoon in Calcutta, at our first meeting in his home, remains in my mind most vividly. I sought his personal and scholarly insights not into his field of anthropology but chiefly from his extraordinary experience of having worked closely with Gandhi and written the most critical and riveting among the books that I had studied. It is easy now, over six decades later, to marvel at his humanity. But at only twenty-two years old, I had come naïve and relatively uneducated in recent Indian history. I wanted to know about Gandhi's final months when Bose knew him best. He greeted me with the warmest of welcomes, an instant, instinctive embrace, and offer of tea and homemade biscuits. Then and now, my main impression was of his civility. He conveyed a sense of quiet dignity and a total absence of pretentiousness as we talked all afternoon and into the twilight.

My principal topic was his view of Gandhi's Calcutta fast in September 1947. I knew of Bose being with Gandhi then, and earlier in Bengal. Somehow, it recalled the example of King's movement, of extreme violence being overcome by nonviolence through stellar leadership and courageous collective action. The staunch dedication to an ethic of nonviolence impressed upon me as the key to success, as confirmed by this initial interview with Bose, and later, by conversations with Rajagopalachari. Thus, the Calcutta fast became the particular moment in Gandhi's satyagrahas, staged only five months before his assassination, that intrigued me so much that four years later, it would become a subject of my PhD dissertation at the School of Oriental and African Studies (SOAS), University of London, followed by a case study of it in my book on Gandhi. Bose served as the powerful inspiration for this choice, as I interviewed him about this 'miracle of Calcutta'. Seldom have I ever had a single conversation determine the direction of my subsequent study, not only about the 1947 fast but the consequences of my relationship with Bose.

Even then, in my earliest stages of research, I had at least come prepared with Bose's own writings so we could focus on these in the context of his recollections. He had chosen in *Selections from Gandhi* (1948, with my original marked copy before me now) to discuss the relationship of fasting to practising strict self-control, and Bose quoted Gandhi at length: 'Everyone must remember that his most secret thoughts have an influence on himself as well as on others. He should, therefore, practice self-control, so as to put all evil thoughts out of his mind, and give room only for thoughts that are noble and great.'[1]

Nirmal Bose discussed with me the reasons for Gandhi's success, from his theory of fasting to fascinating personal anecdotes of key players like H.S. Suhrawardy (Muslim Prime Minister of Bengal Presidency in 1946) and later enhanced by Rajaji, at the time of Gandhi's fast, the governor of what was then the state of West Bengal in independent India. Bose saw that I had read his most controversial book, *My Days with Gandhi* (1953, and again, my prized original copy is in my hand now). Moreover, he had been a visiting scholar at the University of Chicago, so he was well aware of the intense examination that this narrative of his personal experiences with Gandhi prior to the Calcutta fast had provoked. The question that I had then was about the well-known episode of Gandhi's sleeping with young women,

---

1   M.K. Gandhi as quoted in Nirmal Kumar Bose, 'The Life of the Satyagrahi', in *Selections from Gandhi* (Ahmedabad: Navajivan Publishing House, 1948), p. 215.

his grandniece, Manu Gandhi and his personal physician, Sushila Nayar.[2] Not incidentally, Manu wrote three pamphlets relating to this period, *The Lonely Pilgrim: Gandhi's Noakhali Pilgrimage*, *The Miracle of Calcutta* and *Bapu, My Mother*. Sushila Nayar became, with Pyarelal, Gandhi's most prolific biographer, as evidenced by their joint publication of *Mahatma Gandhi: 1958–1989*, in ten volumes.

It was a natural segue in my conversation with Bose from what Gandhi had written about fasting to what Bose had witnessed and recorded in *My Days with Gandhi*. His manner at this point maintained the calm and congenial countenance evident from the start of our meeting, but as he explained it, there was a sense of weariness, derived, as he said, from many American students or scholars focusing on Gandhi's behaviour in Noakhali, without viewing it in the context of the Calcutta fast that we had just discussed. That is, from his viewpoint, the whole matter must be related to Gandhi's gaining more self-control. Gandhiji (as he always called him) was steadfastly determined to gather all of his forces of 'soul strengthening' before a supreme testing ground like a fast, which Bose was sure that he anticipated.

As I recall this crucial conversation, it's remarkable how it corresponded to Ramachandra Guha's account of it much later. The singular instance of this comes with Guha's quoting the very same passage from *My Days with Gandhi* that I chose to press. This is Bose's honest confession of severe doubts about one aspect of the experiment when he wrote: 'Whatever may be the value of the *prayog* [experiment] in Gandhiji's own case, it does leave a mark of injury on the personality

---

2   For those unfamiliar with this event, the fairest, most accurate account of it has been given by Ramachandra Guha in 'The Strangest Experiment', in *Gandhi: The Years That Changed the World, 1914–1948* (New York: Penguin Random House, 2018), pp. 777–92.

of others who are not of the same moral stature as he himself is, and for whom sharing in Gandhiji's experiment is no spiritual necessity.'[3]

The question in my mind was how he felt about this now, over twelve years after. He replied by pointing to his comment on the next page, which he felt hadn't been noted much before, though written in a letter dated 16 March 1947, shortly after leaving Noakhali: 'Gandhiji himself invited public opinion on this subject twice in his prayer meetings in Noakhali. He expected the public to express an opinion even when they did not know the entire details of the situation.' Then Bose paused to say that he only wished in retrospect that he had italicized the next sentence: 'But, even if after knowing everything, the public thought that Gandhiji was in the wrong, while he considered himself to be right, I would stand by him.'[4]

Bose said that this was the answer to my question, as he often gave it to those like me who focused on this specific issue. He explained further that he was convinced that the mutual intentions of all parties concerned were the crucial determinant. When I saw Bose again, after the publication of Manu's *The Lonely Pilgrim,* I was surprised that he recalled our discussion about Gandhi's 'experiment' in Noakhali. Bose said that he wanted to emphasize that her book, published three years after our Calcutta interview, had further convinced him of his opinion that motives mattered, and asked me to check especially her reflection there, written about Srirampur (Noakhali), that she realized in retrospect, even more, the 'great power of the mind in influencing

---

3 N.K. Bose, *My Days with Gandhi* (Calcutta: Indian Associated Pub., 1953), p. 174 and Guha, *Gandhi: The Years That Changed the World; 1914–1948,* p. 792.

4 Bose, *My Days with Gandhi,* p. 175.

the thought and behaviour of a whole nation'.[5] This confirmed that
Manu had indeed viewed her own conduct as (by his own criterion)
a 'spiritual necessity'. This was not an innocent teenage girl unaware
of the import of the Noakhali episode, but a person very cognizant
of her mission. Bose admitted that he had underestimated her insight
then but was now fully convinced that all parties involved knew the
implications of the purpose that they shared. He had gained respect in
this sense not only of Manu but especially of Sushila Nayar.

Our next meeting occurred at the India International Centre (IIC)
in New Delhi. He urged me to return soon to Calcutta, recalling
fondly our long talks there, and now how much he missed his home.
He wanted to know if I remembered how he had paused there for a
moment to gaze in silence out the window while listening to a sitar
player outside. I replied that I couldn't forget this because he vowed
then that he would die in Calcutta (which he did in 1972). His only
wish was that he be able to fulfil a lifelong ambition to get a jeep and
visit outlying villages to examine little-known incidents of satyagraha
unrecorded by historians or anthropologists.

Another memorable encounter that I had with this man of such
extraordinary mind and character was when we were together at the
IIC in Delhi in March 1967. Sharron was with me, and we chatted
in the Fellows Flat, where we stayed with our young children for six
months. It was an amiable occasion, and then the next day, he visited
again for more conversations and also to ask a favour. It was to borrow
one of his own books, *Selections from Gandhi*, that he had noted was
in my library there. He needed it for the conference. A surprise came
when he returned it later to say that he was astonished at how I had
underlined or marked with marginal notes numerous passages. He
asked with genuine sincerity in his voice and eyes, 'You actually use
this so much as a source?'

---

5   Manu Gandhi, *The Lonely Pilgrim*, in Bose, *My Days with Gandhi*,
    p. 60.

If only I had the presence of mind then, I would have tried to convey to him the profound influence he had on me. Instead, I had weakly murmured, 'Of course.' I've reproached myself since for not finding the right words. Sharron did, later, when after overhearing our exchange, she said, 'Such elegance with so much humility!' I was thinking more of his wisdom, poise, experience and insights into Gandhi, yet these had to be combined with the sterling qualities that impressed her.

These few anecdotes and recordings of conversations can't convey my indebtedness to Nirmal Bose. In concrete terms, he had a direct and unexpected impact on my professional choices. At our first meeting, he casually mentioned his extensive contacts in the US as a prominent anthropologist. These were formed in part by having been at the University of Chicago in the formative stages of the Committee on Southern Asian Studies, a leading centre for such scholarship in America. He showed me correspondence with Milton Singer and Robert Redfield, eminent anthropologists but previously unknown to me. Solely on the basis of his recommendation, I was accepted to pursue graduate work there and subsequently completed an MA degree with a thesis on modern Indian political thought.

Yet, this account of his influence on my academic career doesn't end here. In 1962, he wrote to me in Chicago to enquire about my graduate study and, knowing that I had visited Vietnam (on a mission under the auspices of the US Department of Agriculture), asked about my opinions on American intervention there. When I expressed my strong opposition to it, he recommended that I might prefer further graduate study at SOAS. This would enable me to work there in their newly created Economic and Political Studies Department. I had learned well the wisdom of following his advice, and in this case, I did so to the letter, being supervised by scholars whom Bose had known in India. These were Hugh Tinker and W.H. Morris-Jones, who had both served in the mid-1940s throughout India, in various capacities. They soon became my mentors at SOAS. After earning a PhD in 1965, writing on the four Indian thinkers who became the basis for this book, I subsequently lectured in South Asian Politics until 1969, corresponding regularly with Bose as we anticipated our next meeting in Delhi for his lecture series, as related below.

In 1966–67, I participated in an ongoing seminar at SOAS on Partition, organized by C.H. Philips, then professor and director. The paper that I submitted was on the Calcutta fast (and published later in a collection edited by him). A close colleague of mine there was S.R. Mehrotra, who remained an intimate friend after he left SOAS to become an esteemed historian of the Indian National Congress at the Indian Institute of Advanced Study (IIAS), and then at the Himachal Pradesh University, both in Shimla. Mehrotra shared and valued my connection with Nirmal Bose, especially on this subject of the fast, so the correspondence among us continued as Bose served as a long-distance adviser until his death. Yet, there was a final consequential conversation with him in Delhi in 1970. I will save that account until the end of this memoir because it incisively signifies his exceptional grasp of Gandhi's thought.

The dissertation that I wrote at SOAS, being republished here in an expanded form, is dedicated to the 'Force of Friendship', and Bose ranks among the finest of these forces in my early career. As I reflect on him now, I think of the opening sentence of Marcus Aurelius's classic, *Meditations*: 'From my grandfather Verus I learned good morals and the government of my temper.' Lacking any biological grandfather when I knew Bose, forty years my senior, he and Pyarelal fulfilled this role together. I only regret not accepting his invitation to take that jeep he wanted, to tour India, discovering the satyagrahas that only he could have detected and recorded. He knew of my living in villages and knowledge of agriculture (albeit American, not Indian techniques), so he believed that I was qualified to accompany him. This mutual promise was unfulfilled at my loss because it could have ranked as among the most memorable experiences in India or anywhere else.

Among American academics who guided me in Indian studies, most came from the University of Chicago. Professor Stephen Hay, a Gandhi/Tagore scholar, foremost among them. Another, Richard Park, taught at Berkeley, and I met him in Delhi while he directed the Asia Foundation there from 1962–64. He had an extraordinary range of contacts and had been an intimate friend of M.N. Roy's. He introduced me to many Royists, whom I interviewed throughout India, from V.M. Tarkunde and G.D. Parikh in Bombay to Philip Spratt in Madras, with innumerable others in Calcutta. The most prominent scholar on Roy was S.N. Ray, who lectured at Columbia in 1974, stayed at our home in New Jersey, and eventually collected Roy's writings during his career as a professor at the University of Melbourne in Australia.

I felt closest to Roy in Dehradun in April 1967, researching at his Indian Renaissance Institute (IRI). He lived and wrote there for fifteen years before he died in January 1954, at age sixty-six. I found a vast, well-preserved and efficiently catalogued repository of his private correspondence, publications and extensive personal library. It was the most pleasant place in which I've ever researched. R.L. Nigam, a Royist and secretary of the IRI, gave me unrestricted access to the whole collection, allowing me to read and photocopy whatever materials I wished.

Such freedom of access to private letters may carry its costs to a young scholar as I was then, enamoured of great leaders. Disappointments may come from revelations in their personal letters. In Roy's case, there were marked discrepancies between public pronouncements and private correspondence with friends. I recall my shock at discovering how, when writing to a former communist comrade, Jay Lovestone, in 1937, he confided that 'Our real fight is against the right wing which is still very powerful thanks to the popularity of Gandhi ... I am striking at the very root. Gandhist ideology must go before the nationalist movement can develop its enormous revolutionary potentialities. And

Gandhi has recognized in us his mortal enemy. As a matter of fact, in his inner circle I am branded as the enemy No.1.'

I had already known from studying Roy at Chicago about his vehement opposition to Gandhi, but what distressed me here was that he wrote this to Lovestone at precisely the same time that he was claiming earnest 'appreciation' of Gandhi's leadership to one of the 'great Mahatma's' followers. Roy repeatedly expressed in private his determination 'to destroy the curse of Gandhism' while professing unqualified admiration of his leadership in public.

As evidenced in my article on Roy included in this volume, he made his basic differences with Gandhi clear in the 1920s, so the contradiction over public 'appreciation' a decade later was not as surprising as his overestimation of being ranked as 'enemy No. 1'. Richard Park had strongly recommended that I speak with Philip Spratt because of his long association with Roy. Their mutual respect came from a wide range of intellectual discourse, conversant in western authors from ancient Greek philosophers to Spinoza, Montaigne, Pascal and Nietzsche, and including poets like Blake, Goethe, Wordsworth, Shelley and Whitman.

There were brief essays in appendices devoted to each of these authors in the book that Spratt published in 1966, entitled *Hindu Culture and Personality*. Although Royists at that time were proud of their own ability to emulate Roy's familiarity with Western giants like these, they were not fond of Spratt anymore, even though he had known Roy longer than most of the followers. Spratt's unpopularity came from the twists and turns in his theories, having moved from being an orthodox Marxist to an ardent advocate of Freudian psychoanalysis. He was also, by this time, an advocate of free-market economics and pro-Americanism in foreign policy. It was a remarkable ideological journey, even by Roy's own standards.

Unlike Roy, who was mostly self-taught, Spratt had a solid academic background with a Natural Science Tripos at Cambridge. Like Roy, though, he embraced Communism in theory and practice. In 1926, at age twenty-four, he moved to India, to help organize the Communist Party there. A parallel career with Roy ensued, as they were eventually both arrested and imprisoned for sedition. After Spratt was finally released in 1936, he joined Roy's Radical Democratic Party until 1948. When the party was demolished in the national elections, he followed Roy into Radical Humanism. The break with this group came when Spratt settled in Bangalore to serve as the editor of the pro-American and capitalist weekly *MysIndia* until 1964. He welcomed me to his Madras home in May 1967, when he was editor of another strongly anti-Communist newspaper. By this time, he wanted mainly to discuss his new book on East–West cultures that he called his magnum opus.

He thrust in my hands a predictably favourable review of it in *Swarajya*, the paper where he served as deputy editor, and read aloud from it a couple of passages that he deemed most pertinent: 'The key to the understanding of the differences or contrasts [between "oriental" and "occidental" civilizations] is the nature of the Hindu which is introverted, passive, non-violent, self-absorbed, while Western man is extroverted, aggressive and violent.' The review ended with the acclamation that this 'is the first modern book to treat Hindu culture totally on its own right and as the source of the Hindu personality which it contains and reflects'. Turning to the book's opening chapter entitled 'The Narcissistic Personality', Spratt declared that 'The thesis of this book is that the Hindu psyche differs radically from the occidental', because of early childhood development, where a powerful strain of aggressiveness is induced by the father, in direct contrast to the Indian paternal relationship where 'in the narcissistic type, the superego is weak'. Hence, in Freudian terms, the entire personality type becomes directed at 'love for himself'.[6] When I

---

6   Philip Spratt, *Hindu Culture and Personality* (Delhi: Prakashan, 1966), pp. 5–6.

subsequently wrote to Spratt in 1969 asking him to contribute to a special issue of *Modern Asian Studies* on Gandhi that I edited, he reaffirmed the book's argument. He became, at the end, as much a Freudian as he had been a Marxist.

Spratt also pronounced his support of the American side in Vietnam, citing this as evidence of the Western culture of aggression. He included in this correspondence another favourable review by A.D. Moddie in the anti-Communist weekly published on 18 February 1967 in Delhi called *Thought* that characterized:

> Spratt's contribution as being unique, significant and revealing; hardly ever dogmatic, and always suggestive and informative. In a sense, he has produced a Hindu 'Golden Bough', with a wealth of evidence going deep into the heart of the Hindu psyche, drawing not only from its vast and ancient store of philosophy and ethics, but from its limitless mythology and the infinite variety of its religious beliefs and practices.

Moddie was impressed by Spratt's perceptive 'psychoanalytical study of Gandhi, who, too, he believes was of the Narcissist type, attracted early in life to the eminently Narcissistic subjects of health, diet and sex'.

In my conversation or correspondence with Spratt, I asked about his interpretation of Gandhi as well as of Roy. He pointed to his analysis of Roy, where he had written, in a foreword to Roy's *New Orientation* (1946), that Roy 'has never tried to get under the skin of the Mahatma or his admirers and see where that extraordinary power comes from'. Since this came as his foreword to one of Roy's own publications, it seemed like a fair enough comment. Yet when I pressed Spratt about Roy's hyperbolic estimate of his importance to Gandhi, he reverted to his penchant for psychoanalysis by diagnosing Roy as having a delusional obsession over the Mahatma, contradicting his rational and empirical theory.

Spratt's analysis of such delusions is confirmed by Gandhi's few dismissive references to Roy. Addressed to 'Dear Friend', Gandhi responded to Roy's request for advice about how he 'can best serve the Congress', with this counsel: 'Since you are new to the organization, I should say you would serve it best by mute service.' Gandhi's half a dozen other mentions of Roy express no open hostility but professed bewilderment over his meanings and motives, asking colleagues like J. Nehru for explanation. Whatever Gandhi's real views of Roy were, he certainly didn't see him as a threat.[7]

While I regard Roy's theory of Radical Humanism as a significant contribution to modern Indian political thought, it appears that only a few scholars agree with me. If I am wrong in this estimate, then I still retain vivid memories of the devotion that Roy elicited from his followers, no less than that of the Gandhians for their leader. I recall most vividly interviewing Justice V.M. Tarkunde at his elegant home on Malabar Hill, overlooking Mumbai, as he generously gave me an afternoon and evening recalling his life with Roy. Tarkunde was a Judge of the Bombay High Court from 1957–1969, and then became an advocate in the Supreme Court of India, until he resigned in 1977. He was then in the middle of his distinguished career, and his intellect was razor-sharp, his emotional demeanour under tight control—until we got to his relationship with Roy. He had joined Roy's Radical Democratic Party in 1942, founded the Indian Radical Humanist Association in 1969, edited *The Radical Humanist* after 1970, and was among the signers of the *Humanist Manifesto*. Among the oft-quoted lines from this document is 'No deity will save us; we must save ourselves'. Tarkunde claimed not to be a political theorist, but he clearly possessed a total grasp of the tenets of Radical Humanism. For

---

7   M.K. Gandhi, *Collected Works of Mahatma Gandhi* (Delhi: Publications Division, Government of India, 1994), 65:436, 445–46. Hereafter *CWMG*.

example, when I told him that I had written my MA thesis on Roy's Radical Humanism, he examined me like a professor of the subject.

As our conversation continued, however, it became apparent that he wanted mainly to relate his intimate relationship with Roy, so my vivid memory of this interview, in contrast to Nirmal Bose, was decidedly not of a solemn and self-possessed judge. As he described his life with Roy, especially at the Dehradun retreats, he lost control, bursting into tears over a particular moment when Roy showed fatherly affection towards him. I confess that he stunned me, so there we were together, complete strangers to one another, a brilliant jurist confiding his innermost feelings to a youth lost in admiration, especially of the enduring influence that Roy could exercise. I kept thinking of how different this occasion was from my conversations with Nirmal Bose.

On the one hand, both were intellectual powerhouses, gentle and kind persons who gave generously of their time. The personality trait that I identify with them was civility—they were never rude, abrupt or arrogant. On the other hand, Bose never came close to losing his self-control when talking about Gandhi; the idea of him breaking down into tears was unimaginable. Of course, there's nothing wrong with weeping at such times. The point is that Bose didn't show the subjective involvement with Gandhi that Tarkunde revealed over Roy, nor would the latter allow any criticism of Roy, in direct contrast to Bose's published objections to Gandhi's behaviour in Noakhali. So much for all the claims of objectivity versus hagiography, at least as revealed in leader–follower relationships.

I was especially fortunate to have extensive conversations with Sibnarayan Ray because he was not in India during our tours, and our discussions extended to his invitation that I contribute a chapter on Roy and Gandhi to his edition entitled *Gandhi, India and the World* (1970). Like Tarkunde, he claimed complete adherence to the humanist's core doctrine of rationalism. I trust that these contrasts between these three outstanding intellectuals—Bose, Tarkunde and Ray—will not be interpreted as critical of Tarkunde's magnificent contribution to the Indian justice system and to the Indian civil liberties movement, or of Ray's incomparable scholarship on Roy, much less their unfailing kindness towards me. As indicated above, my indebtedness and affection for Bose are inestimable because he shaped my whole professional future. Royists exhibited little interest in me as a person, and it honestly remains a mystery to me why the Gandhians like Bose, the Nayars and Maurice Frydman, could have, from the start, invested such unlimited time and sustained effort to meet the needs of a youth like me with no reputation.

As I indicated in my book, *Mahatma Gandhi: Nonviolent Power in Action* (2012), the theme of self-transformation has been an enduring subject of fascination, that is, what Gandhi termed the 'pilgrimage to swaraj'.[8]

In this context of the personal and political quest for swaraj, what follows is a comparison of three seekers, all devoted Gandhians whom I met and befriended. As a group, they could not, in most respects, be more different. Yet, they were united not only in their commitment to Gandhi's creed and practice of nonviolence but also in their quest for self-realization. It's no coincidence that the first, Mirabehn (Madeleine Slade), entitled her autobiography *The Spirit's Pilgrimage*. The next two, Maurice Frydman and Jayaprakash Narayan (JP), each chose markedly diverse paths to pursue.

Frydman was an expat like Mira, but with a completely different family and national heritage. JP, by further contrast, studied in the United States (like Ambedkar), and adopting Marxism like Roy, served long terms of imprisonment, pursuing at the end, a Gandhian vision of a nonviolent 'total revolution', and ultimately suffering from unjust regimes more than the others. Mirabehn and Frydman were both self-exiles from Europe who joined Gandhi as members of his ashrams and then settled in India after his death. Mirabehn ultimately returned to Europe in 1959, but she lived with Gandhi the longest of

---

8   *CWMG* 27:134.

all, having met him in 1925, while Frydman arrived a decade later. No one, not even Kasturba or Sushila, became as emotionally entwined with Gandhi as his adopted daughter, Mira. Their extensive and intimate correspondence amply reveals this, and we are indebted to two prominent Gandhi scholars for having collected it.[9]

Mira was twenty-three years younger than Gandhi, so their loving relationship was conveyed by their mutual account of that first meeting, when Gandhi took her into his arms, saying, 'You shall be my daughter.' He had four sons, no biological daughters, so her calling him 'Bapu', or 'father', although shared by millions of Indians, proved particularly apt in their case. Their abundant love, mixed with acute anxiety, was unrestrained, shown in Mira's intense expression of these feelings. In her reproach of Gandhi, she could be no less open than Bose, while still in awe of him, yet without his restraint.

In August 1975, when she welcomed my family and me to her home near Vienna, it was seven years before she died; she was healthy of mind and spirit. Since we had only recently left our Gandhian friends in India, she wanted news of their well-being, and I handed her letters from both of the Nayars and Frydman. As she read them and asked questions, I couldn't help but notice the obvious differences between her and the others. She was as warm as the Nayars, and had Frydman's twinkle in her eye, but Mira (as she insisted we call her) still carried the English patrician bearing of her family heritage. Her father, Sir Edmond Slade, was an admiral in the Royal Navy, Director of Naval Intelligence, and ten years Gandhi's senior. Mira had been raised with aristocracy, with a specialized training in classical music. In 1921, her profound passion for Beethoven led her to arrange a concert in London that featured his music. Through an uncanny circumstance of connecting with Romain

---

9   See Tridip Suhrud and Thomas Weber (eds.), *Beloved Bapu: The Gandhi-Mirabehn Correspondence* (New Delhi: Orient Blackswan Private Limited, 2014).

Rolland, an expert on Beethoven, she met him at precisely the moment when he was completing a book on Gandhi. This involvement with Rolland and his hagiographical account of Gandhi produced that fateful future with the Mahatma.

I had been following Rolland's writings as well, so I started my interview with her by asking a question that had puzzled me since I read his correspondence. This was a remark that Rolland wrote to his friend, reflecting on a dispute with Gandhi. However enamoured Rolland appeared in his biography of Gandhi, he had major issues with him, especially with their strong disagreements over Gandhi's inexplicable support of the British in WWI, to the point of actively recruiting Indian soldiers for the war effort. Rolland confided in his friend that Gandhi is 'infinitely more attracted by people who resist or criticize him than by those who acquiesce in his judgement'.[10] I prefaced my question to Mira that Rolland could have been thinking of Gandhi's sharp disputes with Charles Andrews, Mira's British acquaintance and contemporary, who, in 1915, joined Andrews by arguing fiercely against Gandhi, yet like Mira, they remained lifelong friends. I had thought that if anyone could satisfy my question, it would be Mira, because of her intense quarrels with Bapu. Was this somehow a pattern of behaviour with Gandhi? After all, she had observed his interactions with Nirmal Bose, who had challenged Gandhi in the most personal terms.

She first seized on my reference to Bose because he, among all people she had ever met through Gandhi, was a model of civility, a virtue that she prized. In fact, she asked if I knew why no one had written a biography of Nirmal Bose and if I would do it. I concurred that this was important, but beyond my current capacities, looking forward to the time when I could return to India and devote more time to him. It struck me then, as now, that everyone who knew Bose well, praised his singular trait of civil and decent conduct.

---

10 Cited in Ibid., p.26.

Mira then confirmed Rolland's view as accurate and perceptive, but with the crucial qualification that Gandhi's intention was always constructive and aimed at ultimate reconciliation. Bitterness, vengeance or malice were all alien to him, and she cited my references to both Andrews and Bose as proof. In her own experience, Gandhi was so eager to attain rapport with a person that he would not let a dispute rest without pressing on, even if it seemed irreconcilable.

Mira had an exhaustive command of Gandhi's writings that rivalled Pyarelal, so she reached for a copy of his autobiography to read aloud a relevant passage (for the benefit, too, of our two preteenage sons, who were listening).

The context was Gandhi's early attempt in South Africa to resolve a law dispute, so when his efforts were successful, he wrote:

> It was there I learnt the secret of success as a lawyer ... I felt that my duty was to befriend both parties and bring them together. I strained every nerve to bring about a compromise ... My joy was boundless. I had learnt the true practice of law. I had learnt to find out the better side of human nature and to enter men's hearts, to unite parties riven asunder. The lesson was so indelibly burnt into me that a large part of my time during the twenty years of my practice as a lawyer was occupied in bringing about private compromises of hundreds of cases. I lost nothing thereby—not even money, certainly not my soul.[11]

As it happened, this initial question inspired Mira so much that our subsequent afternoon and long evening of conversation prompted a flood of ideas. But first, Sharron interrupted us by saying that this was also a good lesson for our two young boys to learn because they had had their full share of arguments on our journey. Compromise was crucial, as Hugh Tinker, in an insightful essay on Gandhi, emphasized as the

---

11 *CWMG* 39:111, *Autobiography*.

key to understanding his power. Mira had no children herself, but she got the point. Then she proceeded to explain at length how Gandhi had dealt with his adversaries or those engaged in any sort of dispute with him. She welcomed this question, having directly witnessed many major players in the Indian Independence movement. Her analysis of Gandhi's attempts at conflict resolution reflected those instances that she had seen herself and discussed with him.

First, she recounted his contrasting encounters with British viceroys. She had firsthand knowledge of some of these meetings, closer than any of Gandhi's other associates. He liked Lord Irwin, who, after the Salt Satyagraha, had entered into earnest negotiations with him. Gandhi conceded that although he hadn't achieved his purpose of abolishing the salt tax, theirs had been a meeting of minds and, especially, mutual respect. This vindicated his belief in the beauty of compromise. The worst encounters were with subsequent viceroys, Linlithgow and Wavell, who cared little about his survival, much less entering into mediation. He allowed for Churchill's hatred, but since he had never met him, there was no chance of reconciliation, however unlikely. Mountbatten and his wife were definitely his chosen couple, and Mira laughed over whether Gandhi or Nehru was fonder of Lady Mountbatten. She quipped that there was no question about whom Edwina preferred.

Then she moved on to her direct observations of others who tested Gandhi's approach to compromise. I asked about Ambedkar, the Bose brothers (Subhas and Sarat), and M.N. Roy. She ranked them quickly, declaring that he had tried and failed to connect with Ambedkar and Subhas, agreed with Sarat over the Partition, and barely thought about Roy because they had had no personal encounter. I might have extended the list to include Nehru, Rajaji, Patel and many others, including Gandhi's sons, but instead, Mira wanted to talk about Gandhi's troubling argument with Margaret Sanger over the issue of birth control. Gandhi and Sanger met in Wardha on 3–4 December

1935. The dispute between them had become so adamant, with Gandhi insisting on the viability of abstinence and Sanger rejecting it, that his commitment to compromise utterly failed.

As Mira tried desperately to empathize with his frustration, stressing her own agreement with his position, it was hopeless. She worried about Gandhi's hypertension and insisted that his blood pressure be tested (Sushila hadn't become his doctor yet). As Mira suspected, it was extremely high and remained so for weeks. It would return during his imprisonment in 1942–44, when Mahadev Desai and Kasturba died, yet she insisted that never in his lifetime was it worse than during the days after Sanger left. Even in his historic disagreements with Jinnah over the Partition, much less with Ambedkar or Subhas Bose, did his distress ever approach the level of that irreconcilable conflict with Sanger.

Later, I asked the Nayars about this, and both concurred with Mira.[12] Sanger herself wrote later to Gandhi that she had left him 'with warm feelings' presumably due to his unfailing civility. Later, though, Sanger diagnosed him as having a lifelong neurosis over sex. Ramachandra Guha, after incisively relating the encounter with Sanger, notes that 'Shortly after Mrs. Sanger left Wardha, Gandhi was diagnosed as having high blood pressure. He was advised bed rest, and told to stop writing altogether.'[13]

It must be said that if Sharron were composing this memoir (rather than just correcting it), then she would insist on featuring Maurice Frydman, not only because so little has been written about him (discounting Ved Mehta's perverse account), but more importantly due to her singular relationship with him. He was undoubtedly a superstar observer and candid critic of our family relations during the time he

---

12 For Gandhi's own account, see 'Interview to Margaret Sanger', in *CWMG* 62:156–60.

13 Guha, *Gandhi: The Years That Changed the World*, pp. 584–87.

resided for weeks with us in Delhi, Dehradun, and when we were guests at his home in Bombay. In fact, he became a constant companion, providing ample anecdotes about life with Gandhi.

I'll try to do justice to his role, but first explain the dramatic difference between Mira and Frydman before they met Gandhi. In a brief narrative based on interviews with Frydman, David Goodman rightly describes his extraordinary background. After being born into a poor family in a Jewish ghetto in Krakow, Poland, then because of intellectual gifts reminiscent of Ambedkar in that same period of time, he rose from poverty and underprivilege to excel in academic distinction. Unlike either Ambedkar or any others who met Gandhi, Frydman's field of expertise was engineering, so he brought new practical skills to Gandhi's ashram and elsewhere throughout India.

Like Mira, he had an awesome command of several languages and enjoyed music. His teaching of Polish folk dancing at Sevagram became so famous that villagers from all around came to watch or learn (Gandhi was a bemused onlooker). He lived in this ashram from 1936 until Gandhi's assassination, and then served throughout the country in various programmes of social reform. When he stayed with us in 1966–67, he came with a blind Tibetan teenage boy whom he had adopted, and when Frydman died in 1977, he was still promoting the cause of Tibetan refugees. Gandhi gave him the name 'Bharatananda' (lover of India), which was apt; yet when he related to me comparisons between exiled Tibetans and the entire family that he had lost in the Holocaust, his empathy extended, like Gandhi, to all humanity.

He also grew vegetables or fruits that Gandhi sought for new experiments in agriculture. When Gandhi determined that better eggplants could be raised, he asked Frydman to try, and within a month, Sevagram was converted into what its members called 'Bapu's brinjal (eggplant) ashram'. Yet, for every request that Gandhi would make of Frydman, the latter would demand a satisfactory response. Sharron learned that this was Frydman's habit, that is, to contend with those he cared about, to compete in knowledge or practice. So their ceaseless exchanges on why a particular food contained one presumed nutritious value, as opposed to another, formed a dynamic of their dialogue. If the science of nutrition changed, as was often the case, then Sharron had to explain, to his satisfaction, that this was the essence of the scientific method. Frydman accepted this as a process of dietary experimentation. This was a signal trait that bonded him with Gandhi, a conviction that food experiments (within the confines of vegetarianism) comprised a crucial branch in his 'banyan tree' of satyagraha.

Sharron has always had a genius for repairing whatever broke down, whether an old stove or burnt-out fuse, and Frydman delighted in this similarity between them. When we stayed at Sevagram with him, the common praise of his talents was 'Bharatananda not only prays, he can fix anything'. Here, he rivalled Sharron, albeit she wasn't much of a gardener. Frydman's legacy in this respect was formidable because at one point, when Gandhi challenged him to improve on Sevagram's eggplants, he produced improved varieties so that eventually it would become known far and wide as the place to go for high-quality brinjals. When Sharron cooked an eggplant dish with tomato sauce and an exact blend of spices, Frydman appeared more impressed than with any of my disquisitions on satyagraha. We could never agree with him on the merits of brahmacharya in marriage. Mira did, later, but not on a taste for eggplant.

As much as fixing or planting things, Frydman relished telling stories. He had a favourite that admitted of so many variations that it served like his signature theme song. It related to his first arrival in Sevagram after an arduous trek. (Frydman could walk as fast and far as Gandhi; at this time, he was only thirty-five compared to Bapu, who was sixty-six.) He then pronounced that his purpose was to claim the prize of Rs 100,000 advertised by Gandhi for the person who could invent an improved spinning wheel. Gandhi's preoccupation with spinning was both famous and notorious. So when Frydman arrived late that afternoon on 25 August 1936, he introduced himself as an engineer who could do it. According to the official account in the *CWMG*, 'all joined heartily in the laughter' when Gandhi reneged, announcing that the contest date had closed. Mira didn't witness this memorable event, but she confirmed that Frydman was disappointed, if not outraged, and demanded that Gandhi at least answer one question to his satisfaction. Gandhi gave his usual conciliatory smile, so Frydman asked:

> Mr. Gandhi, explain why you are here in this godforsaken, poverty-stricken, snake-ridden, mosquito-infested hovel [the place was alive with both snakes and mosquitoes as we later discovered], with everyone complaining of malaria or dysentery (or both)? Do you honestly imagine that you can save these people or, as I suspect, are you trying to prove martyrdom?

Frydman said that Gandhi's response as it later appeared in *Harijan*[14] seemed more eloquent and cohesive in print than he recalled, but since it has been published in several versions, let it be given here as in the *Collected Works*:

> I am here to serve no one but myself, to find my own self-realization through the service of these village folk. Man's ultimate aim is the realization of God, and all his activities, social, political, religious, have to be guided by the ultimate aim of the vision of God. The immediate service of all human beings becomes a necessary part of the endeavor simply because the only way to find God is to see Him in his creation and be one with it. This can be done by service of all. And this cannot be done except through one's country. I am part and parcel of the whole, and I cannot find Him apart from the rest of humanity. My countrymen are my nearest neighbors. They have become so helpless, so resourceless, so inert that I must concentrate

14 See *CWMG* 63:240.

on serving them. If I could persuade myself that I should find Him in a Himalayan cave, I would proceed there immediately. But I know that I cannot find Him apart from humanity.

Frydman's inquisition on that day didn't stop here; those who are interested may pursue it further in the *CWMG*. But he told me that this exchange was enough for him to devote the rest of his life to sarvodaya ('upliftment of all').

Mirabehn usually followed Gandhi to prison in civil disobedience campaigns, but Frydman focused solely on social reforms, especially through crafts and agricultural development or the 'constructive programme'. Here, he pursued the work of some Americans who came to India specifically to join Gandhi in his ashrams or elsewhere for months or years to concentrate on village improvement. Foremost among these was Richard Gregg, so a brief comment on him is appropriate. Fortunately, Gregg's life and contributions to Gandhi's thought are finally being published—thus far the most prominent being a new edition of Gregg's classic *The Power of Nonviolence*, edited by James Tully.[15] Since I never met Gregg, I will not include personal accounts of him in this memoir, although he played a vital role by living and learning personally from Gandhi in the Sabarmati Ashram from 1925–29. This was before Frydman arrived at Sevagram. Gregg's writings are voluminous, having authored sixty-six works in 339 publications and seven languages. At least three aspects of his remarkable contribution may be mentioned briefly here because Gandhi adopted him as a trusted and long-time exponent of his thought and practice.

First, the emphasis on Gandhi's 'constructive programme' as indispensable for the creation of a nonviolent society. Gregg's brilliant

---

15 Richard Bartlett Gregg, *The Power of Nonviolence*, edited and introduced by James Tully (Cambridge: Cambridge University Press, 2018).

writing on this started as early as 1928 with his publications *A Preparation for Science* and *Economics of Khaddar*. Second, his effective communication of Gandhian thought to the United States, evidenced in his demonstrable influence on Martin Luther King, Jr. Gregg's detailed explanation of the training necessary for satyagraha campaigns became essential reading in the American civil rights movement. Third, the connection forged between Gregg's thinking about satyagraha and the essential analysis of it by James Tully. The latter has provided exceptional philosophical depth as a distinguished political philosopher who is renowned as well for his original work on the indigenous peoples of Canada, which would surely be close to Gandhi's heart. Tully's introduction to this new edition of Gregg's *The Power of Nonviolence* presents a systematic concept of 'integral nonviolence' that should serve as its foundation in this century and beyond.

There is now something of a renaissance of philosophizing about nonviolence among scholars based in North America, with Akeel Bilgrami, Karuna Mantena, Uday Mehta, Judith Butler, Martha Nussbaum, Erica Chenoweth, Partha Chatterjee, Leela Gandhi and Sudipta Kaviraj in the US. This follows the earlier work there of Ronald Terchek, R.N. Iyer, Joan Bondurant, Gene Sharp, or A.J. Parel in Canada, Thomas Weber in Australia, and, in England, Bhikhu Parekh. The knowledge or interest in Gandhi varies among these writers (and professors); they have in common a focus on nonviolent theory and practice.

Returning to the trio of Gandhian friends mentioned above, and the distinctive life paths that they chose to follow, I'll consider now the last of this group, J.P. Narayan. We became acquainted in 1966–67 through our mutual friend, Professor Bimal Prasad, who later sponsored my fellowship with the IIAS and served as an indispensable consultant in my writing about JP. We all talked together again in 1975.

In between these interviews, Sushila Nayar had introduced me to JP's wife, Prabhavati Devi, who had lived in Gandhi's ashram and died there in 1973, so when I saw JP again, I expressed my sympathies over his loss. Bimal Prasad had shared with me manuscripts of JP's writings that would eventually be collected, compiled by him into eight volumes and published as his complete works. I had also been inspired by Geoffrey Ostergaard and Melville Currell's *The Gentle Anarchists* (1971), with their analysis of JP and Vinoba Bhave as anarchists. I initially researched and published on this subject while at SOAS, and will return to it in the conclusion to this book.

Unlike Vinoba but like Gandhi and many Gandhians, JP formed intimate friendships with Westerners, as seen in his tight bond with an Australian couple, Wendy and Allan Scarfe. Whatever disagreements existed among these various people, JP, like Gandhi, seemed to thrive on them. JP firmly believed that the sharpest disputes with Gandhi over the efficacy of nonviolence versus the permissibility of violence enhanced his own personal and intellectual development.

While I never established the strong personal relationship with JP enjoyed by the Scarfes,[16] my long and searching interviews with him in May 1975 proved fortuitous because his arrest came less than a month later. What impressed me then was his unfortunate and, in retrospect, inexplicable naiveté about the dictatorial motives of Indira Gandhi's government. He had plenty of prior experience facing the Raj that had imprisoned him. Yet, despite his strident call for 'Total Revolution' against Indira's regime the previous year, he never realized the imminent danger to his freedom. When I asked at that time if he didn't anticipate arrest after publication of two rebellious declamations that week,[17] his response was to cite his May 'Manifesto for Bihar':

---

16 See their biography of JP, *Remembering Jayaprakash* (Delhi: Siddharth Publications, 1997), with its heart-wrenching final chapter about his imprisonment in pp. 306–16.

17 See interviews with him on May 10 and 11 in *The Economic Times* and *The Sunday Times*, respectively.

There is no doubt that had Gandhiji lived for only five years more, he would have awakened and mobilized the masses and the youth to compel the new rulers of India to cut out their high-sounding but empty verbiage and face the reality of India that lived and still lives in her villages and stinking urban slums.[18]

Therefore, with full confidence, he asserted that if the Congress dared to seize him and other revolutionary leaders, then the people would rise up instantly in revolt.

In fact, JP was sadly mistaken; not only did the masses submit to Indira's dictatorship but even the media folded in fear of punishment. JP subsequently spent 139 days in brutal incarceration until his health broke from untreated diabetes and appalling medical neglect as a result of inhumane imprisonment that even the Raj wouldn't have inflicted, as Sushila Nayar exclaimed in outrage. Thus JP, whose courage was unmatched among Gandhians or anyone else during this crisis, was finally released on 12 November. His prison letters were published a year later, and the first, dated 21 July 1975, began:

My world lies in shambles all round me … Where have my calculations gone wrong? I went wrong in assuming that a Prime Minister in a democracy would use all the normal and abnormal laws to defeat a peaceful democratic movement, but would not *destroy* democracy itself and substitute for it a totalitarian system. I could not believe that even if the Prime Minister wanted to do it, her senior colleagues and her party, which has had such high democratic traditions, would not permit it. But the unbelievable has happened.[19]

18 J.P. Narayan, Chapter 30, in *Towards Total Revolution*, Vol. 4 (Delhi: Popular Prakashan, 1978), p. 165.

19 J.P. Narayan, *Prison Diary, 1975* (Delhi: Popular Prakashan, 1977), p. 1.

This message carries an uncanny prescience today, as prophetic as from any political leader of that time. Because he foresaw a wave of what political theorists have termed 'totalitarian democracy'. Throughout his unbearable months in prison, JP suffered as much as Gandhi or any of his followers, yet his personal belief in nonviolence as a creed and method never wavered. As we face the alarming scourge of authoritarianism in democracies worldwide, his courageous example should speak to us of how easily democratic institutions or a free media may be lost and the price that may be demanded to defend them. Silence is complicity, and JP would not comply with despotic rule. This commentary on JP is not finished since I will return to him in the new introductory chapter and more extensively in the concluding chapter on his theory of sarvodaya.

For over six decades I have researched and lectured on Indian political thought throughout the world, at universities in North America, South Asia, Europe, Israel, South Africa and New Zealand. We often hear of students coming to the United States to earn degrees and build careers. In my case, I've studied and learned most from universities and thoughtful people abroad, especially the freedom fighters in India. As I've related, this began when Sharron and I arrived in Mumbai in 1960, and friendships were rapidly formed as I talked about Gandhi and Martin Luther King throughout India and Nepal, whether in big cities or villages as remote as in the Himalayas and Terai of Nepal. Did villagers in Nepal really want to compare Gandhi with B.P. Koirala, their newly elected (and swiftly imprisoned) prime minister? Yes, and I remember well their engaging comments. Although these unlettered peasants are not discussed in this book on political theory, their conversations remain indelibly imprinted on my mind from those first impressionable months spanning 1960–61.

In all of these encounters, usually with Sharron and our children, never have we found hospitality comparable to that extended by Pyarelal and Sushila Nayar, mentioned above.[20] If hyperbole and hagiography appear anywhere in this book, then they are in references to them. In striving for fair and balanced judgement, sometimes thinking in terms of contrasts serves well. For instance, when I remember their treatment of my family and me, I can also recall by contrast the rejection and denial I received from the Martin Luther King estate when trying to investigate the extent of his plagiarism on his PhD dissertation (since revealed by his more fortunate biographers). Or another example of being shut out of my research into B.P. Koirala in Kathmandu, when, as a Fulbright Scholar to Nepal, I attempted to write about his life. On the basis of how I had been welcomed by Gandhians or Royists in India, I had thought that I might receive assistance from the Koirala family and associates, but the contrary happened, and I gave up the project.

The point is that in my scholarly pursuits, I've learned never to take gracious hospitality or helpful assistance for granted. But when it happens, I know that my work cannot succeed without it. Generosity of this sort came throughout our years in India in many forms. The Nayars rank at the top. Sushila not only housed my family but treated our son when he suffered from cholera and me through hepatitis. All of this while conversing about Gandhi and collaborating on an article on nutrition with Sharron. No critic or reader of my writing could rival Pyarelal's scrutiny by giving literally hundreds of hours to our discussions and analysis of Gandhi. When I was ill, he walked miles to be at my bedside and apply his own type of treatments, not always consistent with his sister's. Engagement with him in historic events— such as being at Gandhi's side throughout the Salt March or attending to him during the Calcutta and Delhi fasts—was magnificent to hear

---

20 See also my essay in *Remembering Pyarelal: Mahatma Gandhi's Secretary and Biographer*, ed. D.C. Jha (New Delhi: K.W. Publishers, 2014).

in detail, especially given his unfailing openness and patience since we first met.

An aspect of Gandhi's life that deserves special emphasis is the high quality of people from all countries that felt a profound need to join him. Richard Gregg was a Harvard-educated lawyer and critical thinker from America. Then, from the land of the Raj, there came Quakers like Reginald Reynolds, Horace Alexander and Marjorie Sykes, all choosing to stay with him at his ashrams. Others from England were personified by Charles Freer Andrews, who met him first in South Africa and became a lifelong friend; he was the only one who called him 'Mohan'. What we may term the 'force of friendship' has been captured best by the British historian Hugh Tinker in his unique biographical study of their relationship, aptly entitled *The Ordeal of Love*. While Andrews performed the vital role of mediating between Gandhi and official representatives of the Raj, others from England became vigorous activists in the nationalist movement for decades, notably Catherine Mary Heilman, whom Gandhi named Saralabehn, with Mirabehn, one of his two 'English daughters'.

Yet, among all those around him, Gandhi was most fortunate to have the Nayars. If Sushila was his dedicated physician, then Pyarelal, along with Mahadev Desai, became his prolific biographers as well as gifted personal secretaries. Pyarelal joined him soon after Desai in 1920, and together, they were earnest and penetrating minds. Pyarelal, having lived longer, could write a magnum opus chronicling the life of the Mahatma, working ceaselessly on it until the month of his death in October 1982. Obituaries commonly called him 'Gandhi's Boswell', but Pyarelal spent decades longer with his subject than Boswell did with Dr Johnson, and one can't imagine Pyarelal debauched and dying of syphilis.

Pyarelal, as I knew him from 1966–82, as a mentor, indefatigable correspondent, scrupulous critic of what I wrote on Gandhi, and a compassionate caregiver like his sister, impressed me as any other person

I met. Even more than Nirmal Bose, Pyarelal could say from decades of experience, 'I was there.' While my instinct was to wish that I might have been there, too, I had second thoughts about it when Sharron and our boys barely reached the first village of the Dandi March (in 1975, in an attempt at emulating the great event of 1930). Unlike the energetic Gandhi scholar Thomas Weber, who walked the entire route of the March, we did reach Dandi but cheated by taking the train for most of the over 200 miles. As amply documented from his prolific writings on Gandhi, Weber did it and charted the exact route, correcting, as he often has, previously incorrect Gandhi scholarship.[21]

I first met Pyarelal on 2 October 1966, when he gave me the honour of celebrating with him an anniversary of Gandhi's birthday. Lacking Sharron's infallible sense of direction, I eventually found him at Flat No. 25, Shanker Market, Connaught Circus, New Delhi. I was mortified over my tardiness because Gandhi insisted on punctuality. Yet Pyarelal greeted me with the same jovial smile as on the cover of *Remembering Pyarelal*. In the many times I visited him thereafter, this office remained as cluttered as his writing was organized. In this crammed space, he wrote everything, including his last letter to me, soon before he died, which was hand-delivered to me later by Sushila. When his nephew, Harsh Nayar (the veteran actor and our enduring friend), cleaned up this office following his fatal heart attack in October 1982, he saw on his desk the copy of a draft on duragraha that I had sent him shortly before, asking for his comments. It was on the subject that we had discussed throughout our innumerable exchanges—the difference between satyagraha and duragraha, what we viewed as the core of nonviolent theory and practice, or, as he liked to call it, 'the key to the formula' that must be found to unlock its special power.

---

21 See Thomas Weber, *On the Salt March: The Historiography of Mahatma Gandhi's March to Dandi*, Second edition (Delhi: Rupa and Co., 2009).

We had already corresponded before this initial meeting. I easily recognized him from famous photos of Pyarelal striding alongside Gandhi on the Salt March, but although this was the first time he had seen me, the greeting was a warm embrace before I could say 'namaste'. Even with over half a century of hindsight, that instant connection we formed remains unique. It forecast a lifelong friendship of sharing intimate joys and sorrows, from the deep-felt insults over Ved Mehta's false account of him to his huge satisfaction in an experiment with Sharron, baking leavened bread without added yeast, using lemon juice in an oven tin box on top of a gas ring. Hers was a true experiment because Pyarelal had never tried it with a Registered Dietitian Nutritionist (RDN). This, unlike his unfortunate encounter with Mehta, was an astounding success. Here it should be stated that Pyarelal was not the only victim among whom Mehta called Gandhi's 'apostles'. From personal experience, I can affirm that Sushila Nayar, Mirabehn and Maurice Frydman were similarly maligned or vilified in his book.

I questioned Pyarelal closely about the Salt Satyagraha and the Calcutta fast, the cases that appealed to me most for their dramatic impact. Richard Attenborough realized the graphic quality of both and gave each prominence in his feature film, *Gandhi* (1982), as approved by Pyarelal. I felt that his depiction of this fast was the highlight of Pyarelal's opus *Mahatma Gandhi: The Last Phase* (1958), and I knew that this would be a vital resource for my book. As I've said, Nirmal Bose confirmed what various writers, from E.W.R. Lumby, the scrupulous British historian, to Manu Gandhi, would all call 'the miracle of Calcutta'. As I began firing questions at him about this historic event, he definitely didn't disappoint. In retrospect, it was miraculous that he never stopped responding to me in earnest.

Much has been written or filmed on this fast, and the most extensive description of it came from my chief informant, Pyarelal. He remained with Gandhi throughout the ordeal and recorded it at length in volume two of *Mahatma Gandhi: The Last Phase* (1958).

However, since his publications are accessible, particularly on Gandhi's fasts,[22] I have chosen to present him through passages from his letters to me, published here for the first time. They were all typed by him to me, mailed from his Delhi office address, between the 1960s and early 1980s. They cover a wide range of topics, and I haven't included discussions of certain subjects that were published, for instance, his reflections on the Calcutta fast.

Yet, although most of his correspondence has been omitted for reasons of brevity, I realize that the extent of the following quotations from his letters may seem excessive. My response to such an objection is twofold. First, only in this way can I convey the intimacy and spirit of our relationship. These letters illustrate an uncommon openness in his most personal feelings as contained in private papers, abundant interpretations of Gandhi's personality or incendiary political positions. These, written during Indira Gandhi's Emergency of 1975, are vehemently critical, enraged or agonized that publication at that time could easily have made him subject to arrest along with J.P. Narayan. His trust in my discretion was complete.

Second, they present, from a theoretical perspective, the prominence that he gave to the evident antimony that Gandhi drew between satyagraha and duragraha. As a key to Gandhi's meaning, it was critically reinforced and elaborated by Nirmal Bose in 1970. Moreover, I explained above the importance of James Tully's theory of integral nonviolence, and in the acknowledgements, how this antithetical view of nonviolent theory was still later enhanced by Thomas Weber's analysis of it in the context of his piercing article on Gene Sharp's ideological shift of view. Yet, Tully's philosophy and Weber's critique only confirmed the initial emphasis on this crucial contrast as first illuminated in Pyarelal's letters and Nirmal Bose's insights that follow. I note these multiple sources because whatever theoretical contributions

---

22 See also Pyarelal, *The Epic Fast* (Ahmedabad: Bhatt Pub., 1932).

I have made in my writings on Gandhi, they are derivative and not original. The best way to explain my own understanding of satyagraha vs. duragraha is that the former constitutes a nexus of ideas synthesized by those, like Pyarelal and Bose, who witnessed firsthand the ultimate failures of duragraha or passive resistance and then affirmed the authenticity of satyagraha with its singular power. This is the theme that Tully, himself inspired by Richard Gregg and Martin Luther King, has integrated into a stellar philosophy, unique for its inclusion of insights into the ideas of the American indigenous peoples (as further elaborated in the acknowledgements).

The significance of this distinction for the uses of nonviolence cannot be overstated. The purpose, therefore, of publishing the letters here is both personal and theoretical, and the latter remains a main feature of my writing, as evidenced in my book on Gandhi's theories of freedom and power, or the selection of his political writings (1993/2012, 1996, respectively). I firmly believe that the effectiveness of nonviolence demands focusing on the difference between satyagraha and duragraha, precisely as Pyarelal insisted. No contemporary political philosopher has enlightened me about this more than James Tully and his original analysis of Richard Gregg's thought, the extensive correspondence between us, and his other voluminous writings, as explained in this memoir and the acknowledgements.

I admit some concern that I never received permission from Pyarelal or Sushila Nayar to publish these strictly confidential letters. The fact that I've made this decision to share them is testimony to the book's inscription, 'The Force of Friendship'. I can confirm now from a vantage point of forty years since his death that his voice still speaks to me, and without fear of sounding sentimental, I never expect to have a friend nearer, even though we lived for most of our lives at a great geographical distance. This correspondence overcame any sense of separation.

Pyarelal wrote:

> I am delighted to learn of Sharron's continuing experiments with vegetarianism, in accord with Gandhiji's most popular pamphlet, 'Diet and Diet Reform'. These trials are essential because I am not a cultist but one in pursuit of truth in all of life. Therefore, my own vegetarianism is not based on any fixed dogma—nutritional, philosophical or religious—but on an urge of my inner being to see what works best to satisfy my inner and outer needs in all respects. I love all animals. How can I eat or cause pain to anything that lives, that loves life and is capable of giving affection; with which I can talk and play and from which I can even learn lessons of nonviolence, trust, self-denial, gratitude and selfless love? From this rock bottom foundation of reverence for all life, the practice of vegetarianism logically follows. At the same time, as the Buddha taught, right practice is the means to the first step in the direction of right knowledge, though at the same time, it is true that practice without a quest for knowledge is a soulless affair. Have we not discussed this many times already in distinguishing between satyagraha and duragraha? Sharron has become a satyagrahi!

In response to one of my letters about our family's vegetarian diets, he wrote:

> I confess, however, that I am a bit alarmed over your own experiment with raw foods. I was with Gandhiji as his laboratory assistant when he made this experiment with food in the late nineteen-twenties. The result was disastrous. I would like you instead to make more liberal use of cooked vegetables. Sharron is an expert at preparing them all properly. They are very appetizing, if prepared properly. I wish that I could be by her side to show you both the way. Why not try them this way?

Note how his letters continually urged us to try something one way or another. This was the core of Gandhi's pragmatic or experimental method.

Faithful to Gandhi's preoccupation with food, Pyarelal proceeded to type an entire page (8"x13" foolscap size, as always) of exact ingredients and how to prepare them: eggplant, broccoli, cabbage or cauliflower, pumpkin, spinach, green peas, turnips, radish and potatoes—cooked in their own juice without water, over a low fire, with a 'little salt', mashed with milk, 'served steaming hot and you will have a feast fit for a king'. His letters were almost always typed, but in the margin of this one, he wrote: 'Curds can be used instead of milk if the vegetables are to be taken cold.' Sharron asks to report that to this day, our family follows this practice of enjoying plain yoghurt on vegetables as well as most of Pyarelal's other nutritional advice. She also comments (as a retired professor of nutrition at New York University) that Gandhi's 'dietary reforms' are highly regarded today in this age of alarming and unprecedented obesity in America. They may be seen as a desired part of his whole constructive program, largely consonant with contemporary dietary guidelines.

His letters are characteristically laced with political or theoretical commentary, in this case ending with his views of the government or the urgent need for nonviolent action. Some are over a dozen pages long, so the signature aspect of Pyarelal's correspondence, like his conversation, was his manner of shifting from advice about diet to critiques of democratic reform that lack true satyagraha. At the core of this latter analysis is a recurrent theme, as indicated above, of the difference between satyagraha and duragraha. He could not write enough about this distinction. My edition of Gandhi's selected political writings about it are, at his specific direction, taken from Gandhi; hence there is sometimes much that is quoted from the *Collected Works* in his letters. As he repeatedly explained, this follows from his insistence on accuracy and authenticity. These are some of the quotations:

There are two methods of attaining one's goal. Satyagraha and *duragraha*. In our scriptures, they have been described respectively, as divine and devilish modes of action. In satyagraha, there is always unflinching adherence to truth. It is never to be forsaken on any account. Even for the sake of one's country, it does not permit resort to falsehood. It proceeds on the assumption of the ultimate triumph of truth. A satyagrahi does not abandon his path, even though at times it seems impenetrable and beset with difficulties and dangers, and a slight departure from that straight path may appear full of promise ... Even an inveterate enemy he conquers by the force of the soul which is love.

But *duragraha* is a force with the opposite attributes ... The wielder of this form of brute force does not scruple about the means to the end. He does not question the propriety of means, if he can somehow achieve his purpose. This is not dharma but the opposite of it. In dharma there can be no room for even a particle of untruth or cruelty, and no injury to life. The measure of dharma is love, compassion, truth. Heaven itself, if attained through sacrifice of these, is to be despised. *Swaraj is useless at the sacrifice of truth.* Such swaraj will ultimately ruin the people. The man who follows the path of *duragraha* becomes impatient and wants to kill the so-called enemy. There can be one result of this. Hatred increases. The defeated party vows vengeance and simply bides its time. The spirit of revenge thus descends from father to son. It is to be wished that India never gives predominance to the spirit of *duragraha* ... But satyagraha will triumph in the end. The duragrahi, like the oilman's ox, moves in a circle. His movement is only motion but it is not progress. The satyagrahi is ever moving forward.[23]

---

23 *CWMG* 14:63–65. Italics and ellipses as in original correspondence. Pyarelal did not have the 1958–1994 edition of the *CWMG* at his disposal but usually gave dated quotations. I cite the *CWMG* here and elsewhere for convenience. Duragraha, as Gandhi explained it in this quotation and in the Glossary, is not acknowledged or studied in literature on his thought. Gandhi used it dozens of times in his writings

or speeches, from 1917 to 1947; yet, unlike other Hindi terms such as satyagraha, ahimsa, swaraj or swadeshi, it is unmentioned in the Subject Index of the *CWMG* (vol. 98), or insufficiently in other major indexes, e.g., R.N. Iyer, *The Moral and Political Writings of Mahatma Gandhi* (Oxford: Oxford University Press, 1987, 3 vols). Joan Bondurant discussed it in 'Satyagraha Versus Duragraha: The Limits of Symbolic Violence', in *Gandhi: His Relevance for Our Times*, eds. G. Ramachandran and T.K. Mahadevan (Bombay: Bharatiya Vidya Bhavan, 1964, pp. 67–81) and again, very briefly, in her *Conquest of Violence: The Gandhian Philosophy of Conflict* (Princeton: Princeton University Press, Revised Edition, 1988, pp. 42–43, 236–37). There are very few references to Gandhi's writings on duragraha in either of these or an attempt to place the idea in its historical context. Duragraha received passing references in R.N. Iyer, *The Moral and Political Thought of Mahatma Gandhi* (New York: Oxford University Press, 1973), pp. 310–12, 315; and Ronald Terchek, *Gandhi: Struggling for Autonomy* (London: Rowman and Littlefield, 1998, pp. 184, 217). It is entirely overlooked in other studies of Gandhi's political theory, e.g., David Hardiman, *Gandhi in His Time and Ours* (New York: Columbia University Press, 2003); Bhikhu Parekh, *Gandhi's Political Philosophy: A Critical Examination* (Notre Dame, Indiana: University of Notre Dame Press, 1989); *The Cambridge Companion to Gandhi*, eds. Judith Brown and Anthony Parel (Cambridge: Cambridge University Press, 2011); and, *Debating Gandhi: A Reader*, ed. A. Raghuramaraju (New Delhi: Oxford University Press, 2006); there is a notable chapter here by A.L. Basham, 'Traditional Influences on the Thought of Mahatma Gandhi' that contrasts satyagraha with dharna, though not mentioning its related idea of duragraha, pp. 36–38). The distinguished political philosopher, James Tully, offers profound philosophical insights into the meaning of duragraha in his Introduction to Gregg, *The Power of Nonviolence* (pp. xxxviii, xlv, liii, lxi) and *James Tully: To Think and Act Differently*, ed. Alexander Livingston (London: Routledge, 2022, pp. 232–33), as also noted in 'Acknowledgements and Bibliographical

Pyarelal was at pains to point out and emphasize the vital connections here:

You will note the way that Gandhiji related Satyagraha to love in both a political and personal sense. Then in our everyday conversations, even more than in his writings, he repeatedly referred to the evils of duragraha. It is not merely 'passive resistance' because, as you can see, it's a broad way of thinking that stressed the importance of consistently using the right means to attain the end, and the means must include ridding oneself of hatred, and adopting love. Gandhiji was forever telling us about the need to purge ourselves of any feelings of vindictiveness, to the extent of taking vows against it. So Satyagraha meant adopting a state of mind as much as action. The term 'passive resistance', being an English phrase, misses all of this because it's entirely focused on the act of a person rather than speech or thought.

Furthermore, you must see that from this same speech [at the Gujarat Political Conference, 3 November 1917] how Gandhiji relates Satyagraha to swaraj. He always tried to make this connection, so he said: 'In a nation fired with the zeal for swaraj, we should observe an awakening in all departments of life. The first

---

Essay' towards the end of this book. One purpose of this book is to examine the contrast between satyagraha and duragraha as it has not been analysed previously by showing how Gandhi conceived of it in a wide range of meanings, much beyond the idea of passive resistance, its subset. He applied this paradigm to personal, social and political spheres of nonviolent action. He significantly refined and enhanced the power of satyagraha by opposing it to corrupt or counterfeit forms throughout his leadership of the nationalist movement. As this Memoir indicates, the importance of this contrast was initially suggested to the author by Pyarelal and Nirmal Kumar Bose. Dina Patel, present editor of the *CWMG* in Ahmedabad, afforded detailed references to duragraha in Gandhi's writings and also classical Hindu texts.

step to swaraj lies in the individual. The great truth 'As with the individual, so with the Universe', is applicable here as elsewhere. If we are ever torn by conflict from within, if we are ever going astray, and if instead of ruling our passions we allow them to rule us, swaraj can have no meaning for us. Government of self, then, is the first step.[24]

In a later letter, Pyarelal wrote about this dominant theme of satyagraha vs. duragraha in another context. He related a conversation with an American couple who argued that

> [N]onviolence could be efficacious only against a civilized people like the English, but not against those who did not have the basic ethical values. I told them that it was just in the cases falling under the latter category that nonviolence had the most effective use; that to 'civilize' the 'uncivilized' is also the function of nonviolence that made the British, who suppressed the 1857 Indian rising with incredible cold-blooded brutality and were happy to see two thirds of the Xhosa tribe [in South Africa] exterminated, amenable to Satyagraha during our non-violent struggle for independence. Then I had to explain to them the difference between employing true satyagraha rather than duragraha in order to achieve the desired result. This was difficult enough in itself because that latter term is, unlike 'passive resistance', unfamiliar to Western ears, so I sensed from their frown and early departure that they hadn't grasped the idea. But, after all, Gandhiji at the end, as you well know, felt despair over the country not understanding the meaning of duragraha, let alone passive resistance.

Above all, he wrote, they must understand Gandhi's conviction of the integral connection between means and ends, that we 'reap as we sow'.

---

24 *CWMG* 14:56.

In early November 1976, Pyarelal wrote to me that he had been 'invited to deliver the valedictory address at the Convocation of the Gujarat Vidyapith [the university that Gandhi had founded]. Generally, I would avoid active participation in public functions, as my hands are more than full with the work on Gandhiji.' He was then writing the fourth volume of the massive biography that Sushila would ultimately complete. Yet, he had said that his distress over the political situation then was so severe that he had resolved to present the speech that would not only be delivered by him but also be published as an article in *The Indian Express*, entitled 'The Ultimate Safeguard' (in two parts, dated 30 November and 1 December 1976). Pyarelal's acute sense of crisis (which he admitted elsewhere caused physical symptoms like hypertension) came from the fact that other close associates, like J.P. Narayan, and also the Chancellor of the Vidyapith, were being unjustly held in detention under the Emergency.

Indira Gandhi had declared this on 25 June 1975 due to what her government characterized as threats to national security and illegal, unwarranted 'internal disturbance'. The Emergency lasted until 21 March 1977. As one observer in India during the six months leading up to this declaration, I may attest to witnessing no justification whatsoever for such a serious assault on democracy.

Pyarelal concluded that civil disobedience was the sole legitimate weapon against authoritarian actions. Any belief that nonviolent resistance could not work under such rule provided only that it took the form of satyagraha, not duragraha, was belied by irrefutable historical evidence: 'The present generation,' he concluded, 'that was born and grew up under independence has no idea of the travail and agony through which India had to pass before independence was won.'

Pyarelal and I had been together in Delhi when the Emergency hit the country. In March 1975, Sushila and I had marched with JP in protest, and after he was arrested, we both made every attempt to reach him in prison. Our letters were not merely censored but prohibited.

Sushila remarked that even under the Raj, this degree of authoritarian oppression hadn't occurred. She detested Mrs Gandhi as a dictator even before the Emergency. Of course, we were not the only Gandhians alarmed by how far Mrs Gandhi would go to enforce her rule. Yet, we were disappointed by Vinoba Bhave's implicit acceptance of this blow to democracy by urging only greater 'discipline'.

In this address to the Vidyapith, Pyarelal invoked at length how Gandhi had aroused the country against the Raj, stressing especially the need to overcome the fear of the government. He recalled his firsthand recollections of the terror following the Amritsar massacre and how Gandhi's response galvanized Indian resistance. A significant aspect of this courageous call to action, however, came with how it was censored by *The Indian Express*. Because if the original draft that Pyarelal sent to me is compared with its subsequent publication, then the following was deleted: 'Gandhiji warned us that "true independence" would come not by the acquisition of authority by a few or many, <u>but by the acquisition of the capacity by all to resist authority when it is abused ... by educating the masses to a sense of their capacity to regulate and control authority</u>.'[25] Those who resist the authoritarian government must practise satyagraha, not duragraha, by scrupulously adhering to the means of nonviolence. Success depended on employing the right methods of nonviolence.

In retrospect, this letter ranks among the most meaningful that Pyarelal wrote. Because, as argued above, in many democracies, including the United States, authoritarian rule has been a corrupting force exemplified by Indira Gandhi's imposition of it. Pyarelal's insistence here is that satyagraha offers the only way to combat it nonviolently, as he emphasizes, Gandhi's 'only hope'. Yet his argument does not stop

---

25 Underlining and ellipses as in the original letter but not in the published article – another instance of press self-censorship under the Emergency.

here. It continues with a declaration about what is true satyagraha. 'Unfortunately,' Pyarelal concluded, 'what has been practiced or has passed for Satyagraha in our country since Gandhiji left us was in most cases not Satyagraha but its opposite.' The difference, as Gandhi had repeatedly emphasized, is between satyagraha and duragraha, including the confusion between the latter and passive resistance. Pyarelal then concluded this letter by quoting at length a passage from Gandhi that he declared was his favourite:

'The word "satyagraha" is often most loosely used and is made to cover veiled violence. But as the author of the word I may be allowed to say that it excludes every form of violence, direct or indirect, veiled or unveiled, and whether in thought, word or deed. It is a breach of satyagraha to wish ill to an opponent or to say a harsh word to him or of him with the intention of harming him. And often the evil thought or the evil word may, in terms of satyagraha, be more dangerous than actual violence used in the heat of the moment and perhaps repented and forgotten the next moment. Satyagraha is gentle, it never wounds. It must not be the result of anger or malice. It is never uncivil, never impatient, never vociferous. It is the direct opposite of compulsion. It was conceived as a complete substitute for violence.'[26]

Pyarelal proceeded to observe the crucial distinctions among the various forces under consideration when offering opposition to authoritarianism. The difference between overt violence and nonviolent action should be evident. Yet, the thought and speech that separate satyagraha from passive resistance are less significant than what divides satyagraha from duragraha. This passage shows the extraordinarily high standard of nonviolence set by the former and unmet by the latter. The power of satyagraha comes only when all forms of violence are

26 *CWMG* 54:416–17.

expunged, precisely as stated here. After discussing in *The Indian Express* article other distinguishing aspects of satyagraha, he concluded that 'Gandhiji shall have lived and died for us in vain if we forget to use, lose faith in the potency, or fail to develop the capacity for successful deployment, of this matchless weapon.'

Then there were the all too frequent times when he gently upbraided me for not responding promptly: 'I must confess that your relative quiescence of late has been worrying me a lot. Please write to me all you can about your present engagements and achievements, if only to relieve my worry.' (5 December 1981.) However, such requests were usually reminders at the close of most letters: 'Write to me about your current activities, pursuits, interests and all the personal news you can send.' (19 September 1977.) This was characteristic of his correspondence: he was eager to hear about *all* of my life.

As I reflect on such requests from him now, I wonder why, at that moment of receiving them, I didn't drop instantly all other obligations— for example, preparation of a class lecture, or grading exams, or sending a supposedly urgent student reference—and write to this dearest friend a long letter, responding properly to his unfailing correspondence with me. I try now, decades later, to compensate for this failure by writing at once to those emailing me now from afar, like Rajeev Kadambi, who suggested that I dedicate this book to 'The Force of Friendship'.

Yet, unlike Rajeev, whom I regard as Pyarelal's successor in this regard as the most conscientious correspondent, I simply didn't grasp the imperative of the situation, not even when Pyarelal started to confide the worsening of his 'angina and extreme fatigue' in a long letter dated 1 June 1982. He was anxious about how the pain prompted an increase in the drugs he was taking. 'Then it was suspected that my extreme exhaustion was due to the depletion of Potassium salts by daily administration of a diuretic without a countervailing dosage of Pot-Klor. So one more dosage was prescribed.' I had not the slightest idea of his actual condition or such remedies, so I consulted with Sushila again, and she replied that heart bypass surgery should be performed immediately. When I contacted Pyarelal about this, he replied, 'I have definitely and finally made up my mind. The enclosed copy of my letter to my doctor in charge will tell you the rest.' I quote Pyarelal's letter of 11 May 1982 in full because while it didn't carry the force then that it should have, it surely does now, at my own advanced age. He wrote as follows to his cardiologist who had urged surgery:

Dear Dr. Wig,

I felt very awkward the other day when Sushila was discussing with you the question of my fitness for by-pass heart surgery. After much hesitation, I have come to the conclusion that I owe it to you to lay bare the whole of my mind before you get further involved in it.

I am not a man of means. When I left home and my studies at the age of 20, I took a pledge not to have anything to do with our ancestral home assets. This pledge I have kept in all conscience ever since. I have no desire to live upon borrowed time at the cost of my survivors however dear and near, and willing to shoulder the burden and liability to be hurt by my obduracy. [Pyarelal had Sushila, his only sibling, a wife, no children but several close relatives.]

I have in my time shouldered enough burdens, and I am not so greedy of life as to wish to buy a little respite from discomfort at the cost of others without even a guarantee that this will add to any appreciable extent to my span of useful activity. Even if I had ample means of my own, I should still have scruples about my spending or allowing others to spend on me lavishly when there are so many others whose need is greater than mine and to whom even a little more or a little less can make all the difference between ruin and survival, black despair and rejoicing.

I hope that, as my physician, you would appreciate those obstinate feelings of mine difficult to still. I shall be more than ever grateful to you to help with your medical wisdom the best of what is left to me for the service of the motherland and humanity.

With kindest regards, yours sincerely, Pyarelal.

Pyarelal passed peacefully in his sleep within the year, but this is not the end of the story. After his death, Sushila came to visit us in New York to tell me herself, and she brought me his gift. It was a large box of khadi shirts because he was so pleased that I wore them while teaching all of my college classes. Since Sushila outlived him by eighteen years, we grew especially close afterwards, her staying with Sharron and me, or during meetings in New York as she lived with Harsh. Always the physician, we spoke about health and also ways to die; she had sharp criticisms of the American medical system and especially its determination to prolong life at all costs, even when a patient's condition was hopeless.

Sushila was at the hospital she founded, near Gandhi's Sevagram ashram, at her own death. The circumstances were described to me immediately after when both her niece, Nandini (herself a doctor) and Harsh broke the news. Following the example of her brother, Sushila refused all extraordinary measures, even when her doctors urged blood transfusions that would extend her life. At the very end, in the words of Nandini, Sushila seemed to will her own death. She initially managed to take a short walk around the ashram that she had first joined in 1936 to assist Gandhi, and then quietly lay down, smiled at the anxious doctors around her, shut her eyes and was gone. Nandini recalled that this was precisely as Sushila intended. Anyone who knew her well, as we did, understood that such serenity in the face of death was not beyond her, any more than against those fierce mob riots that she faced in the midst of India's civil war, at Gandhi's side in Calcutta or Delhi.

There is a singular book relevant to this story entitled *Being Mortal: Medicine and What Matters in the End* by Atul Gawande, a surgeon and professor of medicine at Harvard. It begins with an epigraph from the Mahabharata: 'I see it now—this world is swiftly passing'. This bestselling account of how the American medical system wrongly conspires to preserve life at any cost echoes exactly Sushila's own critique of her profession, as she remembered the last wishes of her brother. She practised what she had preached. Gawande relates a patient's plea as representative; when dying of terminal cancer beyond all hope, he begged: 'Don't you give up on me. You give me every chance I've got.'[27] The extraordinary power of this book gives full credence to Sushila's example. It comes from Gawande's account of his grandfather's natural demise at age 109, in his Indian village, in contrast to the excruciating death of his father, himself a physician, pleading futilely to the end for treatment in an American hospital.

The point of Gawande's eloquent and wise book is to relate, from his firsthand experience, how the American medical system is woefully mismanaging the way of dying. The hard truth is that it is fundamentally flawed, with excessive costs of end-of-life treatment and despite the best intentions of world-class expertise. As Gawande had the agonizing task of helping his father cling to life in those final moments, he realized, as he writes in the epilogue, how 'it is clear that there are times when the cost of pushing exceeds its value'.[28] This was the lesson that could be learned from Pyarelal's letter to his physician, as well as Sushila's choice to die on her own terms.

Cicero is quoted to have said, 'Gratitude is not only the greatest of virtues but the parent of all others.' The Latin phrasing is not quite this, and his own gratitude certainly wasn't returned to him by being murdered at the orders of Mark Antony. In my case, this quotation does convey my deep gratefulness towards Indian friends, and I was amply rewarded. When I first met Pyarelal and Sushila Nayar in my twenties, I couldn't possibly have imagined how much they would give me in the four decades ahead. Now I can measure and treasure how their extraordinary gifts would provide not only examples of the kindness that this world can offer, but even guidance for how to exit it.

---

27 Atul Gawande, *Being Mortal, Medicine, and What Matters in the End* (New York: Henry Holt and Company, 2014), p. 4.

28 Ibid., p. 262.

When the Gandhi Peace Foundation invited me to participate in an international conference on Gandhi in January 1970, I wrote to Nirmal Bose asking to meet him. He had already sent me drafts of his Gandhi Memorial Lecture series entitled 'Gandhism and Modern India', which he had delivered between 16 December and 11 January 1970. These constituted twelve lectures, starting with 'The Personality of Gandhi', ranging across his analyses of major campaigns, Gandhian economics, the Partition, 'Gandhism and Democracy', concluding with 'Gandhism after Gandhi'. As we began our lengthy conversations in late January, I realized that he was trying earnestly to impart a summation of his own philosophy, as well as how he believed history would judge Gandhi's overall achievement. His urgent concern was with the question of what would endure or not. It may be that the note of urgency that I detected in his voice came from the fact that he had already been diagnosed with terminal cancer, but if so, it went unmentioned.

The irony was that at the same time that I was conversing with Bose, I participated in the huge conference at the Indian International Centre. I quickly became disappointed by the latter and thoroughly entranced by the former. The contrast between American scholars unfamiliar with either Gandhi or his followers, and Bose, the most perspicacious of Gandhi's close associates, struck me as dramatic and instructive. Gene Sharp would not publish his magnum opus for another three years, but the outlines of his thought were clear as he pronounced his theory of nonviolent resistance. His confidence and sweeping, even encyclopaedic, references to episodic expressions of nonviolence, dominated the scene. As indicated elsewhere, Sharp's main theme was Gandhi as a strategist, without a moral component. Pyarelal sat next to me and passed notes as Sharp spoke, commenting that this was all about duragraha. The agreement between these two principal Gandhians, Pyarelal and Nirmal Bose, on this core issue, couldn't have been clearer. Fortunately, they were both available to exchange my views about Sharp's approach, a singular advantage that would not occur again.

While my discussions with Bose touched on Noakhali and the Calcutta fast, it was evident that he had left those historical events behind. He wanted instead to distinguish Gandhi's lasting legacy, and this could be condensed into a single word, satyagraha. Whether in the case of the Salt March or his final fasts, the key point was that they were supreme works of art, carefully honed by a skilled craftsman, and not replicated in India after Gandhi. Thus in Bose's concluding lecture entitled 'Gandhism after Gandhi', he drew the sharpest distinction between those actions that ranked as mere 'propaganda and coercion', as opposed to 'satyagraha [when] the intention is conversion not coercion of the opponent'. The difference was categorical: passive resistance as duragraha versus Gandhian nonviolence as satyagraha.[29] Neither of us could know then that in two years, Nirmal Bose would be gone. Yet, his parting words to me were memorable: 'Beware of counterfeits!' This message resonated with Pyarelal's assessment of Gene Sharp's misconstruction of nonviolence as it would later appear in the incisive writings of Thomas Weber and James Tully.[30]

I finish this memoir with a vision of a type of Socratic symposium, Indian style. This would include those mentioned above and also in the acknowledgements. Just as in Plato's *Symposium*, the dialogue would feature only a couple of main speakers, and they would be the most difficult to select. My choice would be Nirmal Bose and James Tully, both distinguished professors serving causes of nonviolent action. When I met Bose, as noted above, he was Director of the Anthropological Survey of India (1959–1964), while years later, Tully, synthesizer of 'integral nonviolence', initiated a workshop on Gandhian thought at Reed College in Portland, Oregon, near my home. In Socratic form, Bose and Tully exhibited from the start an unusual capacity for

---

29 Nirmal Bose, *Gandhism and Modern India* (Gauhati, India: Gauhati University, 1970), p. 113.

30 See especially Tully's succinct critique of satyagraha vs. duragraha in his edition of Gregg's *The Power of Nonviolence*, pp. xxxiii–xxxvi.

engaging in dialogue, with publications modelling vigorous intellectual exchange. Unlike others in Gandhi's inner circle, Bose challenged him with searching questions of critical concern that had informed my research, while Tully's *On Global Citizenship: James Tully in Dialogue* inspired our Portland seminar and my subsequent correspondence with him. Not least, Tully's long-time research into indigenous peoples matched the anthropological discipline of Bose. Above all, each wrote and spoke on the authentic qualities of satyagraha, viewing moral philosophy as being at the root of its meaning, exposing its counterfeit of duragraha. I only wish that Tully, now at the University of Victoria, might have actually met Bose so that this conversation that I envisage might exist somewhere other than in my imagination. To ensure that the philosophy of the means-ends relationship is fully expounded, Raghavan Iyer, one of my mentors at Oxford in the early 1960s, would be invited as a special guest to address his incomparable chapter on 'Means and Ends in Politics' in *The Moral and Political Thought of Mahatma Gandhi* (1973).

In such a symposium, just as most of Socrates' friends chose to listen, that would be my inclination, too, as I may enjoy the conversation along with one of Sharron's gourmet vegetarian dinners, prepared under Pyarelal's supervision, to make sure its pure contents complemented the total civility of our exchange. Sharron would prepare it scrupulously to the taste of all, including, as Gandhi had, that of Abdul Ghaffar Khan, called 'Frontier Gandhi', and the most courageous person I've ever met, when he hosted us in Kabul. I want to be seated next to him if only to apologize for American imperialism's egregious war crimes in Afghanistan. Finally, I would ask Ramachandra Guha to recount the symposium in his own inimitable style, as the best chance of preserving it for history.

Introduction

Continuity and Innovation in the Group of Seven

This book is an extended edition of the original entitled *Indian Idea of Freedom*, with a new introduction and added chapters to complement the initial text, published in 1982. The title of this enlarged edition is only slightly changed, but its extension is considerable. Now the previous selection of four Indian political thinkers has become the 'group of seven': Swami Vivekananda, Sri Aurobindo, Mahatma Gandhi, Rabindranath Tagore, M.N. Roy, B.R. Ambedkar and J.P. Narayan. These seven Indians have been chosen because they pondered deeply and published voluminously on universal concerns of political thought: human nature, pursuit of truth, how society should be constituted, democratic authority, ideas of freedom, equality and justice, and desirable methods of change. Not only this, they drew original conceptual correspondences among these key ideas. They were not systematic philosophers, yet they contributed to an intellectual tradition that invigorated an extraordinary nationalist movement and an unprecedented renaissance of political thought.

Differences among these seven thinkers are apparent to any serious reader of their extensive writings. However, their similarities are less recognized, so they will be presented here as parallel, offering a constellation of ideas. This theoretical cluster focuses on how their core ideas about freedom cohere with several other associated conceptions: the relationship of means to ends; the search for self-transformation; models of nonviolent change; and ethics in politics.

Gandhi is preeminent as India's 'drum major'[1] national leader who put his ideas into practice. In terms of the conceptual paradigm

---

1   The allusion is to Martin Luther King, Jr.'s 'The Drum Major Instinct' sermon preached on 4 February 1968. After examining the potential for destructive or constructive instincts among those who seek prominence as leaders, he concluded that he wanted to be remembered 'as a drum major for justice; a drum major for peace; a drum major for righteousness'. *A Testament of Hope: The Essential Writings and Speeches of Martin Luther King, Jr.,* ed. James Washington (San Francisco: Harper, 1986), p. 267.

King was assassinated two months after this sermon. Earlier, he frequently acknowledged the decisive influence on his thought and practice of Gandhi (Ibid., pp. 7, 16–18, 26, 32–34, 86, 103, 149, 164, 447, 485–86, 583). With the exception of Christ, these citations by King to Gandhi are far more than to any other person, anywhere in the world, an accurate testimony to Gandhi's powerful example. This impact of Gandhi applies not only to King but to other foremost African or African American national leaders, who personally sought Gandhi's counsel and always favourably.

See also Sudarshan Kapur, *Raising Up a Prophet: The African-American Encounter with Gandhi* (Boston: Beacon Press, 1992), especially 'Watch the Indian People' and 'We Need A Gandhi', pp. 24–71; D. Dalton, 'Mohandas, Malcolm and Martin', in *Mahatma Gandhi: Nonviolent Power in Action* (New York: Columbia University Press, 2012), pp. 169–87; and Rajeev Kadambi, 'Gandhi's Legacy: Beyond Black or

noted above, Jawaharlal Nehru made no significant contribution to Indian ideas of freedom however important he indisputably remains as a central figure in his nation's history. Like Franklin Delano Roosevelt, he ranks as a transformational leader, not an original thinker. Yet, he conveyed astute and eloquent analyses of Gandhi's message. 'The essence of his teaching,' Nehru wrote in *The Discovery of India*, 'was fearlessness ... not merely bodily courage but the absence of fear from the mind.' Then after naming the myriad fears fostered by the Raj, he concluded that 'It was against this all-pervading fear that Gandhi's quiet and determined voice was raised: Be not afraid.' The consequence, he claimed, was that Gandhi's leadership of the freedom struggle created 'a psychological change, almost as if some expert in psychoanalytical methods had probed deep into the patient's past, found out the origins of his complexes, exposed them to his view, and thus rid him of that burden.'[2]

An apt complement to Nehru's diagnosis comes from Ashis Nandy, who observed that 'colonialism is first of all a matter of consciousness and needs to be defeated ultimately in the minds of men ... the liberation ultimately had to begin from the colonized and end with the colonizers. As Gandhi was to so clearly formulate throughout his own life, freedom is indivisible, not only in the popular sense that the oppressed of the world are one but also in the unpopular sense that the oppressor too is caught in the culture of oppression.'[3]

White', 13 May 2021, available at: https://www.thehindubusinessline.com/blink/know/gandhis-legacy-black-or-white/article34549203.ece. Accessed on 23 May 2022.

2 Jawaharlal Nehru, *The Discovery of India* (Bombay: Asia Publishing House, 1967), p. 380.

3 Ashis Nandy, *The Intimate Enemy: Loss and Recovery of Self under Colonialism* (Oxford: Oxford University Press, 1983), p. 63.

At the same time, for all of the decisive context of colonialism, the case argued in this book is that modern Indian thinking about freedom contains a distinctive quality, moving into new theoretical territory. Gandhi conceived a nexus of ideas that defined Indian meanings of freedom. This started with his original thinking about freedom in *Hind Swaraj* (1909). He introduced here his classic distinction between 'inner' and 'outer' freedom, the relationship of swaraj as 'self-rule' to satyagraha, 'soul-force or love-force'. Gandhi brought to the fore not only the correlation of inner and outer freedom, but also the conceptual correspondences among those ideas just mentioned that bear repetition: first, freedom as both internal and external liberation; second, an imperative that means are preeminent, taking priority over ends; third, nonviolence as the right method of change; and, finally, ethics as being integral to politics. Therefore, in this short treatise, he created a remarkable synthesis, written in white heat during a sea voyage from England to South Africa, and composed by a lawyer-turned-activist, not a philosopher, at age forty. This consequent set of conceptual correspondences appears as the brightest star in a constellation of Indian political thinkers that achieved a renaissance of political theory and practice in the last century.

Gandhi's way of thinking about freedom thus appeared early in his life, and not only in his public pronouncements but in his personal correspondence as well. So, in 1910, he advised a nephew who was earnestly committed to India's independence: 'Please do not carry unnecessarily on your head the burden of emancipating India. Emancipate your own self. Even that burden is very great. Nobility of soul consists in realizing that you are yourself India. In your emancipation is the emancipation of India.'[4]

---

4   Gandhi, *Collected Works of Mahatma Gandhi* (Delhi: Publications Division, Government of India, 1964), 10:206–07; hereafter *CWMG*. An extensive analysis of *Hind Swaraj* follows in chapter 6 of this book.

This correlate of self and system became his signature theme and whatever inconsistencies or conceptual developments marked his subsequent public or private life, this idea of freedom, and the cluster of thought around it, never changed. In 1931, following the Salt Satyagraha, the highest point of his leadership, he wrote: 'The outward freedom that we shall attain will only be in exact proportion to the inward freedom to which we may have grown at a given moment ... This is the correct view of freedom.'[5]

Outward or 'external freedom' meant Indian 'independence', necessarily joined by social reforms, that is, his repeated 'three pillars of swaraj': Hindu–Muslim unity, abolition of untouchability and economic equality. The necessary correlation is an inward form of swaraj that demanded rigorous, sometimes agonizing reappraisal, as when Gandhi called it a 'painful climb' in life's arduous, endless pilgrimage, a search for truth through ceaseless experimentation, subject to the theory and practice of nonviolence.

Evidence of this intellectual renaissance comes from the striking fact that Aurobindo and Tagore both expounded this formulation of 'internal' and 'external' freedom coincident with Gandhi's formulation.[6] Moreover, there were other Indian thinkers not included in this group of seven, like B.C. Pal and B.G. Tilak, who used similar language for defining swaraj in 1907, before Gandhi's *Hind Swaraj*.[7]

See also A.J. Parel's indispensable introduction to his edition of *Hind Swaraj* (Cambridge: Cambridge University Press, 1997).

5 *CWMG*, 38:1–2, 18; 45:263–64.

6 Aurobindo Ghose, *Speeches of Aurobindo Ghose* (India: Prabartak Publishing House, 1922), pp. 93–94; and Rabindranath Tagore, *Sadhana: The Realisation of Life* (New York: The Macmillan Company, 1913), pp. 84–85.

7 *Speeches of Sri. Bipin Chandra Pal, Delivered at Madras* (Madras: Ganesh & Co., 1907), pp. 25–40, 84–86; *Bal Gangadhar Tilak: His*

The conclusion here is that by this first part of the twentieth century, a fertile intellectual groundwork had been established in Indian thinking about the meaning of freedom.

As we trace the roots of this modern Indian conceptualization of freedom, then its earliest expression occurs in Swami Vivekananda's thought, initially formed in the late nineteenth century. This had profoundly inspired others by the time of his death in July 1902. Vivekananda observed that freedom 'does not mean [only] the absence of [external] obstacles' but, correspondingly, 'spiritual freedom'; that

Writings and Speeches, Third edition (Madras: Ganesh & Co., 1922), pp. 61–67; Stanley A. Wolpert, *Tilak and Gokhale: Revolution and Reform in the Making of Modern India* (Los Angeles: University of California Press, 1961, 2020), pp. 80, 191; Rachel Fell McDermott et al. (eds.), 'Radical Politics and Cultural Criticism', in *Sources of Indian Traditions: Modern India, Pakistan and Bangladesh*, Vol. 2, Third edition (New York: Columbia University Press, 2014), pp. 250–337. This rich compendium remains an essential testament to the Indian intellectual renaissance. The relevant chapters 4, 5, and 6 cover Vivekananda, Aurobindo, Tagore, Ambedkar and Gandhi. They therefore reference all of those in the 'group of seven' and more.

As noted in chapter 4 of this book, Dadabhai Naoroji called for swaraj in a strict political sense in the 1906 convention of the Indian National Congress, as 'self-government without any necessary qualifications'. Gandhi offers him due praise in *Hind Swaraj* as the 'Grand Old Man of India'. Dinyar Patel, in a definitive biography of him entitled *Naoroji: Pioneer of Indian Nationalism* (Cambridge, Massachusetts: Harvard University Press, 2020), claims that he 'ranks among the great non-European thinkers and reformers of his era'. However, Naoroji, known especially for his 'drain theory', did not develop ideas of freedom comparable to the group of seven examined here. Dadabhai Naoroji, *Speeches and Writings of Dadabhai Naoroji* (Madras: G.A. Natesan & Co., 1910), p. 76, and Patel, *Naoroji: Pioneer of Indian Nationalism*, pp. 8–9, 222.

'one should raise the self by the self. Let each work out one's own salvation. Freedom, in all matters, is the worthiest gain of man. To advance oneself towards freedom—in its fullest sense, physical and spiritual, political and economic—and help others to do so, is the supreme prize of man. Those social rules which stand in the way of the unfoldment of this freedom are injurious, and steps should be taken to destroy them speedily. Those institutions [and moral virtues] should be encouraged by which men advance in the path of freedom.'[8]

It was Vivekananda's voice of freedom, as a process of political and spiritual evolution, personal and ethical transformation, that inspired Aurobindo in the twentieth century. He systematized it philosophically when he wrote in as early as 1916: 'Spiritual freedom is not the egoistic assertion of our separate mind and life but obedience to the Divine Truth in ourselves and our members all around us ... not only to seek one's own individual liberation or perfection, but also the political and moral freedom of others is the complete law of the spiritual being ... he who sees God in all will [give freely to everyone] the service of love; not only his own freedom, but the freedom of all.'[9]

M.N. Roy's Radical Humanism may be superficially interpreted as antithetical to Aurobindo's philosophy. In fact, they mutually evolved towards common ground in their mature thought, to write original

---

8 Swami Vivekananda, *The Complete Works of Swami Vivekananda* (Calcutta: Advaita Ashrama, 1962), Vol. 5 (1959), pp. 141–42. (Hereafter *Works*.) Not nearly enough scholarly attention has been given to Vivekananda.

9 Sri Aurobindo, *The Human Cycle* (Pondicherry: Sri Aurobindo Ashram, 1949), pp. 346, 348. Peter Heehs' *The Lives of Sri Aurobindo* (New York: Columbia University Press, 2008) is an in-depth study that examines Aurobindo's 'major works' in historical context, especially chs. 7, 8, 9, pp. 264–410. The epilogue refers to *The Human Cycle* and concludes with the central and primary role assigned to individuals (p. 415).

theories on freedom. In Roy's case, this is evidenced in his outstanding *Problem of Freedom,* published in 1945. In accord with others in this group of seven, Roy contended that 'positive' or 'internal', 'spiritual freedom' of personal morality has the advantage of being built on solid ethical foundations, thus securing a firm base of community, 'supplying the individual with the new moorings of a co-operative collective existence'.

It must be emphasized that, as philosopher James Tully, an authority on John Locke, has observed, this Indian thinking about freedom is distinctive. It should not be confused with Isaiah Berlin's famous 'two concepts of liberty' formulation that represents a binary mode of thought.[10] As Gandhi recognized in 1931, and Roy concluded later, conceiving of freedom only as independence lacked emphasis on interpersonal connectedness.[11] From self-liberation flowed collective emancipation as an evolution of ideas, not a dichotomous conceptual construction of opposites.

Therefore, for Roy, like Gandhi, India's independence was necessary but decidedly insufficient. Roy and Gandhi devoted their lifelong political careers to the attainment of 'external freedom' or what Roy called 'the absence of all obstacles to the pursuit of happiness'. Yet this must correlate with freedom in its 'positive' or internal form. This is their

---

10 James Tully, 'Two Concepts of Liberty in Context', in Bruce Baum and Robert Nichols (eds.) *Isaiah Berlin and the Politics of Freedom: 'Two Concepts of Liberty' 50 Years Later* (New York: Routledge, 2013), pp. 23–51. This is the most penetrating critique of Berlin's theory of freedom. Elsewhere, Tully engages with Gandhi's thought through the concept of 'integral nonviolence' in his uniquely incisive introduction to Richard Gregg's *The Power of Nonviolence,* pp. xxi–lxi. Further comment on Tully's contributions follows in the chapter on Gandhi in this book and in the acknowledgements.

11 M.N. Roy, Ch. VII in *Problem of Freedom* (Calcutta: Renaissance Publishers, 1945), pp. 57–65.

distinctive contribution, and it is very carefully reasoned in Roy's *Problem of Freedom*: 'Positive freedom is the condition for the self-realization of life ... Only on that philosophical and psychological foundation can the structure of collective freedom be raised by the continuous efforts and collective work of spiritually liberated individuals.' In his prolific writings on freedom after 1945, Roy explicitly identified 'positive' with 'spiritual' freedom, thus explicitly relating his conception to fellow Bengali thinkers, specifically Vivekananda and Aurobindo. As I've shown elsewhere, the explicit invocation of 'spiritual freedom' became a cornerstone of his Radical Humanism.[12]

Before turning to Ambedkar's contribution to the group of seven, this should be stressed: among the seven members of this intellectual constellation, the conceptual correspondences in thinking about freedom are striking. Evident differences exist, but not when we focus on their ideas of freedom. The point is that these leaders of the Indian national movement signify, through their ideas of freedom, aspects of a vital and enduring intellectual tradition. This was aptly termed an 'Indian renaissance' by Aurobindo and Roy.[13]

B.R. Ambedkar is a fascinating member of this ostensibly disparate group. His harsh criticisms of Hinduism and Gandhi are well known. Less studied is his interpretation and embrace of Buddhism in *The Buddha and His Dhamma*; so the following analysis of his thought here focuses entirely on it. This singular work deserves to be called his magnum opus because it marks the end of his theoretical journey as the

---

12 See D.G. Dalton, 'M.N. Roy and Radical Humanism: The Ideology of an Indian Intellectual Elite', in Edmund Leach and S.N. Mukherjee (eds.) *Elites in South Asia* (Cambridge: Cambridge University Press, 1970), pp. 152–71.

13 See also another formation by two contemporary philosophers in Nalini Bhushan and Jay Garfield, *Minds Without Fear: Philosophy in the Indian Renaissance* (Oxford: Oxford University Press, 2017).

climax of his rich reconstruction of Buddhism. As presented briefly in this introduction, and developed at length in chapter 9 on his thought, Ambedkar's idea of freedom in *Buddha and His Dhamma* ranks as his major contribution to the group of seven.[14]

In contrast to the six other Indian thinkers selected here, Ambedkar was an outstanding scholar with formidable academic credentials, as explained further in the later chapter. This is shown in his scrupulous documentation throughout *Buddha and His Dhamma* with meticulous footnotes. As only one textual example of his preoccupation with the idea of freedom, at one point in the book he repeats the word 'free' five times in a single paragraph, significantly identifying it with freedom from 'fear' (all cited from Buddha's *Dhammapada* with thirteen footnotes). In other places, he refers amply to freedom in a variety of contexts.[15] These are consistently employed to elucidate, from a Buddhist perspective, a pursuit and theory of spiritual freedom.

There is a particularly dramatic instance of this in *The Buddha and His Dhamma* that merits special attention. It occurs when Ambedkar relates what might be called the 'allegory of the dungeon' (alluding to Plato's famous allegory of the cave in *The Republic*). This passage from

---

14 The critical edition of *The Buddha and His Dhamma* (hereafter *BHD*), edited by Aakash Singh Rathore and Ajay Verma (New Delhi: Oxford University Press, 2011). Further comment on this commendable scholarly edition follows in the chapter on Ambedkar. At the same time, there can be no substitute for the complete edition of Ambedkar's works: *Dr. Babasaheb Ambedkar: Writings and Speeches*, compiled by Vasant Moon, 17 vols. (Bombay, Government of India, 1987), hereafter referred to as *BAWS*. As a standard authoritative source, this will be used throughout in comparison with other editions of his works cited.

15 Ibid., pp. 70–71, 85, 93–94,125–28, 182–86.

Buddha and His Dhamma reads as follows with the Buddha speaking
to his disciples:

> You must realize that the world is a dungeon, and man is a prisoner
> in the dungeon. This dungeon is full of darkness; so dark that
> scarcely anything at all can rightly be seen by the prisoner. The
> prisoner cannot even perceive that he is a prisoner. Indeed he has
> not only become blind by living too long in the darkness, but he
> very much doubts if any such strange thing as light can ever exist at
> all ... But the case of the prisoner is not as hopeless as it appears. For
> there is in man a thing called will. When the appropriate motives
> arise, the will can be awakened and set in motion. With the coming
> of just enough light to see in what directions to guide the motions
> of the will, man may so guide them that they shall lead to liberty.
> Thus though man is bound, yet he may be free; he may at any
> moment begin to take the first steps that will ultimately bring him
> freedom. This is because it is possible to train the mind in whatever
> directions one chooses. It is mind that makes us to be prisoners in
> the house of life, and it is mind that keeps us so. But what mind
> has done, that mind can undo. If it has brought man to thralldom,
> it can also when rightly directed, bring him to liberty ... [It only]
> requires a free mind and free thought.[16]

The similarity with Plato's allegory of the cave, in both language and
thought, is remarkable, but there are also substantial differences.
First, in Plato's cave allegory and philosophy, there is no concept of
spiritual freedom. Second, in contrast to Plato, Ambedkar asserts that
Buddha is a 'born democrat', devoted to freedom and equality for all,
while at the same time, serving as a guide to spiritual enlightenment.
This demonstrates Ambedkar's interpretation of Buddhism as a
perfect synthesis of internal and external freedom. Note that there

---

16 Ibid., pp. 70–71. The allegory has been abbreviated here because it is
given more fully in the subsequent chapter on Ambedkar.

is no binary thinking with Ambedkar, contrasted to Isaiah Berlin's theory of the irreconcilability or the essential opposition of negative to positive freedom. Instead, Ambedkar describes Buddha's allegory as a progressive cognitive journey out of the dungeon, a steadfast pilgrimage, culminating in spiritual freedom.

Now we move to another central theme that should be recognized as characteristic of this group of seven. This follows from the 'dungeon allegory', in that it shows how their ideas of freedom relate to their own personal and philosophical quests for truth and self-realization. In this respect, the group may be termed 'journey theorists'. Gandhi personified such a transformation when by 1919, he had turned into a rebel from a loyalist, with consequent change of thought. His 'experiments with truth' mentality may be contrasted with two disparate figures in the Indian independence movement: Rajani Palme Dutt and Vinayak D. Savarkar, on the extreme political left and right, respectively. These two thinkers remained fixed in their thought, unlike those in the group of seven.[17] Narratives of those in this group read like archetypal stories of those in search of truth, with Buddha's legendary example as the model. Their form of autobiographical genre starts as usual with Vivekananda. An important aspect of it focuses on the connections he makes with Buddha's archetypal journey, a signifier so crucial that it further cements common ground among the group of seven. For Vivekananda, the Buddha serves as his quintessential hero.

---

17 This insight about 'journey thinkers' was first suggested to me by Nirmal Kumar Bose, who knew well most of the men mentioned in this chapter. As explained in my memoir in this volume, Bose became a mentor from our initial meeting in 1961 until his death in 1972. See also 'Gandhi and Responses' in *Sources of Indian Traditions*, ed. McDermott et al., pp. 402–7 and 483–87 on Dutt and Savarkar, respectively. Dutt's response to Professor Leonard Gordon, quoted there, is especially revealing about this fixed frame of mind.

In all of the eight volumes of Vivekananda's *Complete Works*, dozens of references to the heroic character of the Buddha abound. This is a representative example:

> The life of Buddha has special appeal. All my life I have been very fond of Buddha ... I have more veneration for that character than any other—that boldness, that fearlessness, and that tremendous love! He was born for the good of men ... He sought truth because people were in misery. How to help them, that was his only concern ... Of all the teachers of the world, he was the one who taught us most to be self-reliant, who freed us not only from the bondages of our false selves but from dependence on the invisible being or beings called God or gods. He invited everyone to enter into that state of freedom which he called Nirvana. All must attain to it one day; and that attainment is the complete fulfillment of man.[18]

Following Vivekananda, Aurobindo forged conceptual correspondences around the idea of freedom in Hinduism and Buddhism. Like Vivekananda, he valorizes the heroic quest and gives unstinting praise of Buddha's character, referencing Vivekananda's example as well. Thus, Aurobindo wrote in his magnum opus, *The Life Divine*:

> The individual is indeed the key of the evolutionary movement ... As he develops, he moves towards spiritual freedom, but this freedom is not something separate from all existence; it has a solidarity with it because that, too, is the self, the same spirit. As he moves towards spiritual freedom, he moves also towards spiritual oneness. The spiritually realized, the liberated man is preoccupied, says the Gita, with the good of all beings; Buddha discovering the way of Nirvana must turn back to open that way to those who are still under the delusion of non-being; Vivekananda, drawn by the Absolute, feels also the call of the disguised Godhead in humanity and most the call of the fallen and the suffering. For the awakened

---

18 Vivekananda, 'Buddha's Message', in *Works*, Vol. 8 (1959), pp. 103–5.

individual the realization of this truth of being and his inner liberation and perfection must be his primary seeking.[19]

Aurobindo's theory of evolution of the individual in a journey of self-realization correlates with Ambedkar's ideas of external and internal freedoms. Both saw humanity moving towards spiritual freedom. The hope for our future lies in an ongoing forward quest as seekers. In sum, Aurobindo joined Vivekananda and Ambedkar by extolling Buddha's journey from riches to renunciation and his 'elevation of universal compassion (karuna) and sympathy for the whole earth as my family, to be the highest principle of action'.[20]

This sets the scene for Gandhi's fascination with the Buddha's archetypal quest for truth. In his autobiography, Gandhi asserts that early in life, he read Edwin Arnold's story of the life of Buddha, *The Light of Asia*, 'with even greater interest than I did the *Bhagavad Gita*.'[21] This appeal to Gandhi of Buddha's life and thought continued, so that thirty-five years later, in 1927, he delivered a series of addresses on Buddhism starting with a comparison of Buddha's message with Vivekananda that none 'dare to neglect India's starving millions'. Then he focused on the significance of Buddha's transformative journey, 'I feel even proud of being accused of being a follower of the Buddha, and I have no hesitation in declaring that I owe a great deal to the inspiration that I have derived from the life of the Enlightened One.'[22] Moving forward another twenty years, as both Indian independence and Partition neared, Gandhi's commitment to Buddha's example increased, as he urged everyone to follow in his path.[23] This personified

---

19 Sri Aurobindo, *The Life Divine* (Pondicherry: Sri Aurobindo Ashram, 1960), pp. 1248–49.

20 Ibid., p. 1052.

21 *CWMG* 39:60.

22 *CWMG* 35:232–33, 244–45 and 310–13.

23 *CWMG* 86:362 and 87:192, 399.

for him an inclusive spirit, a transcendence of communal violence, as inward and outward freedom might come together in real or purna swaraj.

Gandhi never claimed to have a profound understanding of Buddhist philosophy. However, it is relevant, in this context, to cite the authority of the eminent Buddhist scholar and monk Acharya D.D. Kosambi (1876–1947). He became closely associated with Gandhi, joined the nationalist movement, was imprisoned for six years for participating in the Salt Satyagraha, and eventually died in Gandhi's Sevagram ashram. When they first met in 1924, Gandhi remarked that he had heard that Kosambi was a 'great scholar of Buddhist literature'. Kosambi had replied: 'It is true that I have made a close study of Buddhist literature. But you are the one who understands its essence; I am only a carrier!'[24]

---

24 Meera Kosambi (ed.), *Dharmanand Kosambi: The Essential Writings* (Ranikhet: Permanent Black, 2013), p. 224. The strong bond between Gandhi and Kosambi is carefully related in the introduction that emphasizes their mutual intellectual affinities and Kosambi's 'deep reverence for Gandhiji' (p. 44). In the initial encounter, Kosambi responded to Gandhi's concern about his differences with B.G. Tilak's interpretation of the Gita: 'Let scholars find different interpretations and quarrel, if they wish. It is their profession. You have to demonstrate by your example, how politics can be conducted along the path of truth and nonviolence. Whether or not it has a basis in [sacred] books, what matters is that people should accept your experiment.'

Gandhi discouraged him from returning to his distinguished academic career as a renowned Buddhist scholar in America, where he had already spent over five years. Kosambi decided to stay to participate in the Salt Satyagraha and led a group of satyagrahis to be arrested and imprisoned. He modestly concluded that he 'was somehow able to carry on the satyagraha in accordance with Mahatma Gandhi's principles' (pp. 224–30). Kosambi's play, *Bodhisattva* (Marathi, 1949), is listed in Rathore's edition of *BHD*'s bibliography as one of the two books by Kosambi that Ambedkar consulted (p. 313). The play begins

The point here is not to claim that these seven thinkers shared a unanimous allegiance to the teachings of Buddha. It is rather to see how this group viewed life, and Buddha's example especially, as a quest for spiritual liberation and truth. They actualized this ideal within a common intellectual tradition. The archetype of Buddha's lifetime transformation and search for enlightenment served as exemplary for the evolution of their intellectual journeys.

Nonviolent means to their ends prevailed in this goal of inward joined with outward freedom. The Indian freedom struggle demanded resistance to colonialism and oppression in many forms. Yet it meant much more as it was characterized by theories and practices of nonviolence. The leaders transformed themselves as they gave their country a vision of peaceful change not found in other major political movements because of India's path of nonviolence. They infused ethics into politics. It required extraordinary courage to resist the Raj nonviolently as well as to combat caste oppression or religious fanaticism. Nonviolence meant engagement with politics joined with introspective self-examination. Some of these leaders experimented in politics more than others, but all pursued their moral quests in earnest.

These exemplary leadership qualities in twentieth-century India of integrity and honesty, civility and compassion, should not be taken for granted, as evident now from today's far lesser world leaders. India left a legacy and ethical vision that speaks eloquently to a planet locked in divisive dogmatism, political demagoguery, endemic violence, demonization of the Other, and pervasive fear of freedom. We ignore these examples of Indian leadership at our peril because the ways in which they pursued their personal or political goals personified a consistently commendable type of character. These were remarkable

---

with two epigraphs, one from the *Dhammapada* and the other by 'Gandhiji', and it concludes: 'Victory to the Buddha, victory to the Enlightened One! To him who gives knowledge and compassion to the people, and sight to those blinded by hatred!' (pp. 358–408)

leaders who demonstrated that moral visions could work in politics when applied by those who sought to know themselves, to engage in the pilgrimage to swaraj. When in doubt, they paused for self-examination or nonviolent experimentation. Today, we tend to assume that lust for power or selfish pursuit of narrow interests inevitably characterizes politics. This was emphatically not the case in twentieth-century India, where the movement was directed at a sense and spirit of common interest.

An essential theory that cements this group of seven is that of the relationship of means to ends. Vivekananda was once again the first Indian thinker to provide a crucial theoretical lynchpin of this group when he began an address in Los Angeles in 1900: 'One of the greatest lessons I have learnt in my life is to pay attention to the means of work, not to its end ... whenever failure comes, if we analyze it critically, in ninety-nine per cent of cases we shall find that it was because we did not pay attention to the means. Strengthening of the means is what we need. With the means all right, the end must come.' He concludes this speech with language that became a signature theme for this entire group of seven: 'Let us perfect the means; the end will take care of itself.'[25]

Aurobindo's inspiration for this theory came, as usual, from Vivekananda. He formulated his philosophy of means and ends in *The Life Divine* with the vision of

the need of a humanity which is missioned to evolve beyond itself ... But to realize these desirable ends, other means must be adopted instead of the violent ideas or slogans enthroned to the exclusion of all other thought, the suppression of the mind of the individual, a mechanized compression of the elements of life, a misdirected drive of the life-force through a coercion of man by the State ... It is evident that a life governed by the right means opposes

25 Vivekananda, *Works*, Vol. 2 (1963), pp. 1, 9.

enmity, brutality, destruction and violence, political strife with its perpetual conflict, frequent oppression, dishonesties, turpitudes, selfish interests, ignorance and ineptitude. In a future society of nonviolence, these vices could have no ground for existence.[26]

This theme of connecting the means-ends theory with nonviolence pervades Aurobindo's thought, evident in his *Essays on the Gita* where he denounces war, asserting that love is the only means to truth, so we must move 'towards the replacement of physical force by soul-force, of war by peace, of strife by union, of hatred by love, of egoism by universality'.[27] Aurobindo's term 'soul-force' as the path to freedom explicitly relates to Gandhi's definition of satyagraha.

Gandhi's thinking from the time of *Hind Swaraj* stressed the primacy of using moral means. It was there that he wrote in response to an imagined adversary who could have been a terrorist:

> Your belief that there is no connection between the means (sadhana) and the end (sadhya) is a great mistake. Through that mistake, even men who have been considered religious have committed grievous crimes. Your reasoning is the same as saying that we can get a rose through planting a noxious weed. ... The means may be likened to a seed, the end to a tree: and there is the same inviolable connection between the means and the end as between the seed and the tree ... We reap exactly as we sow.[28]

---

26 In Aurobindo, *The Life Divine*, pp. 1255, 1267, 1261.

27 See chapter on 'Kurukshetra', in Aurobindo, *Essays on the Gita* (Pondicherry: Sri Aurobindo Ashram, 1966), p. 41.

28 Gandhi, *Hind Swaraj*, ed. A.J. Parel, 1997, p. 81, including Parel's excellent footnotes. The 'seed' metaphor that Gandhi favours is also employed repeatedly by the Engaged Buddhists, especially Thich Nhat Hanh and in this same sense of the means-ends relationship. See Hanh's *Anger: Wisdom for Cooling the Flames* (New York: Riverhead

The first non-cooperation campaign, ending early in 1922, taught Gandhi painful lessons about a greater need for national discipline, or, as he said, a more determined search for inner freedom before the outer freedom of independence could be achieved. Gandhi's reaction to his self-described 'Himalayan blunders', was to pause and reflect on flaws in his own leadership, to 'turn the searchlight inwards', one of his favourite mantras. By 1924, he characteristically judged that the fault lay within himself and his failure to conduct how the struggle was waged. Adequate training and discipline in methods were lacking, and he took responsibility for this lapse. 'Some will say that "means are after all means". I would say that "means are after all everything". As the means so the end. Violent means will give violent swaraj. That would be a menace to the world and to India itself. There is no wall of separation between means and ends.'[29]

By early 1930, he was ready for a major test of mass political action, so he embarked on the Salt March with a select few carefully trained and committed members of his ashram. There was no violence in this unprecedented civil disobedience campaign, so he could conclude that 'If we take care of the means, [of adhering to strict nonviolence] we are

---

Books, 2001), the segment entitled 'Seeds of Anger, Seeds of Compassion', pp. 183–85, 104–6, 113, 175–76, 205, in this book alone. The Dalai Lama attests to Gandhi's influence in *Ethics for the New Millennium* (New York: Riverhead Books, 1999), pp. 28, 90 and in his autobiography, *My Land and My People* (New York: Grand Central Publishing, 1962), p. 146.

29 *CWMG*, 24:396. Compare Thich Nhat Hanh, *Interbeing: Fourteen Guidelines for Engaged Buddhism* (New York: Parallax Press, 1998): 'Means and ends cannot be separated. Means are ends in themselves.' (p. 6)

bound to reach the end sooner or later. If we resolve to do this, we shall have won the battle.'[30]

When Nehru reflected in 1953 on the distinctive trait of the Indian Independence movement in contrast to others of the twentieth century, he concluded that 'Gandhi was never tired of talking about means and ends and of laying stress on the importance of means. This is the essential difference.' It is a mode of political thinking unique to the Indian freedom struggle.[31] Moreover, M.N. Roy's split with Marxism came over the issue of ends justifying means. The crux of his break came with his assertion in 1946 that 'The truth is that immoral means necessarily corrupt the end'. This was the essence of Roy's 'new orientation' as he called it.[32]

Ambedkar is a systematic proponent of the means-ends theory by emphasizing its core in Buddhism. With the logical rigour typical of his work, he developed the idea throughout *Buddha and His Dhamma*. The following quotations from it sum up the philosophy: 'The Law of Karma was enunciated by the Buddha. He was the first to say: "Reap as you sow." He was so emphatic about the Law of Karma that he maintained that there could be no moral order unless there was a stern observance of it.'

'Since it is impossible to escape the result of our deeds, let us practice good works. "Let us inspect our thoughts so that we may do no evil, for as we sow shall we reap." What the Buddha wanted to convey was

---

30 *CWMG* 44:59.

31 Nehru, quoted in Joan V. Bondurant, *Conquest of Violence: The Gandhian Philosophy of Conflict* (Princeton, N.J.: Princeton University Press, 1958), p. xviii; and also, R.N. Iyer, 'Means and Ends in Politics', in *The Moral and Political Thought of Mahatma Gandhi*, pp. 359–71.

32 Roy, *Independent India*, 1/22/48, (Calcutta: Renaissance Press, 1948), p. 67; and Dalton, 'Gandhi and Roy', in *Gandhi, India and the World*, ed. S.N. Ray (Melbourne: The Hawthorne Press, 1970), p. 158.

that the effect of the deed was bound to follow the deed, as surely as night follows day.'

'Therefore, we argue that all things that exist are not without cause ... but our deeds produce results both good and evil. ... "let us surrender self and all selfishness; and as all things are fixed by causation, let us practice good so that good may result from our actions."'[33]

Rabindranath Tagore's political thought is included in the earlier first edition of the book that follows. This presents his dialogue with Gandhi, without mention of the means-ends philosophy. Yet, like Gandhi and Ambedkar, Rabindranath saw its crucial importance to any conception of nonviolence. He was attuned to the literature of America more than any of the others in this group of seven; as his biographers have observed, he was drawn from childhood to the Concord Transcendentalists.[34] His revealing conversation with Albert Einstein in 1930 illustrates this conceptual correspondence.[35] Moreover, a recent article by Vivekanand Rao shows essential parallels, particularly with Ralph Waldo Emerson.[36] Stephen Hay, another biographer of Tagore, placed special emphasis on Emerson's essay on 'Compensation' and this paragraph as most significant: 'Cause and effect, means and ends, seed and fruit cannot be severed; for the effect already blooms in the cause, the end preexists in the means, the fruit in the seed.'[37]

---

33 *BHD*, pp. 84, 86, 132, 179. See chapter 9 for reiteration and further development of this crucial concept of the relationship of means to end.

34 Krishna Kripalani, *Rabindranath Tagore* (New York: Grove Press, 1962), p. 27.

35 Rabindranath Tagore, *Religion of Man, The Hibbert Lectures for 1930* (London: Allen & Unwin, 1931), Appendix II, pp. 222–25.

36 Vivekananda Rao, 'Divinity in the Writings of Ralph Waldo Emerson and Rabindranath Tagore', *Research Journal of English Literature and Language and Literature* 7, no. 1 (Jan.–Mar. 2019), pp. 35–46.

37 R.W. Emerson, *Complete Essays and Other Writings*, ed. Brooks Atkinson, 'Essays: First Series' (New York: Modern Library, 1950),

Even as a poet, Tagore expounded a political theory that forged the relationships between the ideas of freedom and the means-ends theory, writing more on the idea of freedom than any other literary giant of India.[38] After asserting the 'fundamental unity' between Buddhism and Hinduism,[39] he connected this with the means-ends relationship that he found and valued in both Buddhism and Gandhi. As a special tribute to Gandhi, Tagore wrote in 1938:

> His emphasis on the truth and purity of the means, from which he evolved his creed of nonviolence, is but another aspect of his deep and insistent humanity; for it insists that men ... must only assert their rights, whether as individuals or groups, as never to violate their fundamental obligation to humanity, which is to respect all life. To say that, because existing rights ... were originally won and must be still maintained by violence ... is to create an unending circle of viciousness; for there will always be men with some grievance ... who will claim the right to gain their goal through slaughter. Somewhere the circle has to be broken, and Gandhiji wants his country to win the glory of first breaking it through the use of nonviolent means.[40]

As Tagore left the Soviet Union in 1930, after viewing its experiment with Communism, he warned, 'Violence begets violence and blind stupidity. Freedom of mind is needed for the reception of truth; terror hopelessly kills it. Therefore, for the sake of humanity, I hope that

---

p. 176; and Stephen N. Hay, *Asian Ideas of East and West: Tagore and His Critics in Japan, China and India* (Cambridge, MA: Harvard University Press, 1970), p.14.

38 See his outstanding essay 'What Then?', in *Towards Universal Man* (London: Asia Publishing House 1961), pp. 83–100.

39 Tagore, *Creative Unity* (London: Macmillan Press, 1922), p. 76.

40 'Gandhi the Man', *Gandhi Memorial Peace Number*, ed. Kshitis Roy (Santiniketan, Bolpur, Bengal: Visva Bharati, 1949), p.13.

you may never create a force of violence which will go on weaving an interminable chain of violence and cruelty.'[41]

Jayaprakash Narayan (JP) joins this group of seven as a stellar synthesizer who practised what he preached, through immense self-sacrifice, personifying a truly relentless journey of ideas. He came from a background of Marxism like M.N. Roy, but JP studied and researched it in depth in a formal university setting. When he became disillusioned over the failure of Gandhi's first non-cooperation movement in 1922, he embraced Communism as a solution. This led him to Roy's early writings. But then, like Roy, in the final phase of his journey, JP's prescriptions for revolution changed drastically as he and Roy ultimately rejected Marxism over the same issue of means and ends. Much more than Roy, though, JP not only adopted Gandhi's ideas but tried earnestly to put them into practice through Vinoba's Sarvodaya movement and then, in 1954, by founding his own ashram for constructive reform in Bihar.

In a momentous statement on the pivotal role of the means-ends theory in 1948, JP realized that the Socialist Party he led had taken a decidedly wrong turn. In his address to the party entitled 'Means and End', he began by explaining 'a problem that has deeply worried me of late; the problem of methods or means'. The speech deserves to be quoted at length, given its centrality in asserting the distinctive means-ends theory of this group of seven. JP's reasoning is as careful as any in this group, representative of his intellectual rigour:

> From time immemorial there have been politicians who have preached that there is no such thing as ethics in politics. In the old times, however, this amoralism did not spread its corrupting influence beyond a small class that played at politics and the mass

---

41 Ramachandra Guha's 'Introduction' to Tagore's *Nationalism* (Gurgaon, India: Penguin, 2017), p. xlv.

of people were left uncorrupted by what the leaders and ministers of state did. But since the rise of totalitarianism, which includes both Fascism, Nazism and Stalinism, this principle has been applied on a mass scale, and every individual in society has been affected by it. This has resulted in such an eclipse of moral values from social life that not only its political sector but every aspect of human life including even the family has been darkened.

Then, after explaining that his rejection of Communism came from this amoralism, he asserted that 'I for one have come to believe that for the achievement of socialism, a strict regard for means is of the highest importance.' He thereby declares his embrace of Gandhi's thought and appeal because of this single issue:

> There were many things that Mahatma Gandhi taught us. But the greatest thing he taught us was that means are ends, that evil means can never lead to good ends and that fair ends require fair means. Some of us may have been skeptical of this truth, but recent world events and events at home have convinced me that nothing but good means will enable us to reach the goal of a good society, which is socialism.[42]

Ten years later, after subjecting his theories to Gandhian practice, JP explained what he called the end of his 'search for an ideology'. In a speech entitled 'Back to the Mahatma', he asked,

> How can this supreme task be accomplished? The answer is: *By going back to Mahatma Gandhi.* The leaders of the country must go to the people, to live and work with them, to serve, guide and help them. They must do all this not to strengthen their parties and gather votes for themselves but in order that the people should

42 Narayan, ch. 8, *Towards Total Revolution*, Vol. 1 (1978), pp. 95–96.

rise and put their heads, hearts and hands to the tasks of national development.[43]

JP synthesized his political thought in *A Plea for Reconstruction of Indian Polity* (1959). He set forth there his concept of 'total revolution', featuring interaction between leaders and led as cooperative and interdependent agents in the quest for swaraj. This was the meaning of participatory democracy, whether in the form of the constructive programme or any aspect of satyagraha. Therefore, in the felicitous phrasing of James Tully, all participants in the movement 'actually *become free* when entering into relations of mutual service with each other'.[44]

If ever there is a categorical imperative for combating authoritarianism by waging nonviolent struggle around the world, then let this be India's enduring message, that its independence movement showed us the way to freedom in its fullest sense by practising it, as pronounced by its foremost thinkers. The appellation of 'exceptionalism' is often claimed by America, but the Indian freedom struggle is more deserving if such an assignation is ever merited. The claim should rest on the high quality of India's leaders and their intellectual tradition, the creativity and depth, unity in diversity. More than anywhere else in the twentieth century, a renaissance did occur there, 'not only a rebirth of something old, mediated by a peculiar cultural genius, but also a recovery of a national spiritual essence and way of life.'[45]

Among these seven, Aurobindo articulated the conceptual correspondences of this group systematically by connecting core themes around freedom with a call for peace and brotherhood in his exposition of 'The Religion of Humanity':

---

43 Narayan, ch. 22, in Ibid, p. 187.

44 Tully, Correspondence with author, 19 April 2021.

45 Bhushan and Garfield, 'On the Very Idea of a Renaissance', in *Minds Without Fear*, p. 68.

The union of liberty and equality can only be achieved by the power of human brotherhood, and it cannot be founded on anything else. ... When the soul claims freedom, it is the freedom of its self-development, the self-development of the divine in man in all his being. When it claims equality, what it is claiming is that freedom equally for all and the recognition of the same soul, the same godhead in all human beings ... These three things are in fact the nature of the soul; for freedom, equality, unity are the eternal attributes of the Spirit.[46]

Human society progresses really and vitally in proportion as law becomes the child of freedom ... the outward mould of his self-governed inner liberty.[47]

Aurobindo concluded these reflections with a judgement on Gandhi in 1948: 'The Power [of nonviolence] that brought us through so much struggle and suffering to freedom will achieve also the aim which occupied the thoughts of the fallen leader at the time of his tragic ending; as it brought us freedom, it will bring us unity.'[48]

Since my research started on Indian ideas of freedom in the early 1960s, rigorous scholarship of the four great mass political movements of the twentieth century has brought each into much sharper perspective. The revolutions of Russia, China, and Germany may be compared more precisely with that of India. The judgment of history should be clear. The ideas and leadership of South Asia were exceptional. The idea of freedom especially proved distinctive. This concept assumed various forms among the group of seven political thinkers discussed

---

46 Sri Aurobindo, *The Ideal of Human Unity*, in *The Human Cycle: The Ideal of Human Unity, War and Self Determination* (Pondicherry: Sri Aurobindo Ashram, 1962), p. 764.

47 Ibid., p. 566.

48 Sri Aurobindo, *Sri Aurobindo on Himself and on the Mother* (Pondicherry: Sri Aurobindo Ashram, 1959), p. 407.

here. Some, like Aurobindo and Tagore, took it to philosophical or poetic heights that have gained worldwide recognition. Gandhi insisted that the idea be tested in the crucible of ceaseless creative experiments that subsequently spread around the world to impact other societies. Scholar-activists like Ambedkar combined intense activism with high academic achievements. His pilgrimage went from the denunciation of Gandhi to composing a systematic treatise on Buddhism that advocated the very values of nonviolence that Gandhi had cherished, thus contributing mightily to India's intellectual tradition. Always these seven showed incredible freedom from fear, epitomized by J.P. Narayan.

Consider JP's example: he is the only member of this group of seven who was incarcerated by both the British, first in 1932 at age thirty, and then, finally, by his own government in 1975, where his imprisonment was unbearably brutal, breaking his health, as related in his *Prison Diaries*. While, in 1999, he was posthumously awarded the Bharat Ratna, India's highest civilian award, he deserved more recognition for his ideas in his lifetime.

In summary, this group of seven shared a quality rare among leaders of other political movements. Free from the corruption of power, they exhibited an eagerness to engage in individual quests marked by determined, unflinching insight, to search deeply within themselves and experience personal as well as political transformations. From Vivekananda's momentous encounter with Sri Ramakrishna to M.N. Roy's departure from Communism to Radical Humanism, these were journey theorists—rare in the arena of politics. As we reflect on the other major leaders of movements—Stalin, Hitler, Mussolini and Mao— we declare: 'Never again!' When history judges India's nonviolent independence movement, we ask, 'Why not again?' The answer comes from the voices of its stellar visionaries, their ideas of freedom.

Preface to the 1982 Edition

The book is concerned with the development of the idea of freedom in modern India, particularly in the political and social thought of four major Indian writers, Swami Vivekananda, Aurobindo Ghose, Gandhi and Rabindranath Tagore. Three major areas of discussion may be distinguished here.

First, there is a consideration of the common ground on which these four thinkers stand. It is argued that they comprise a 'school' of modern Indian thought, both because of the purpose that they share, and the fundamental principles on which they all agree. Chief among these principles is that concerning the nature of freedom. Two broad forms of freedom are distinguished: 'external' (political and social) and 'internal' (moral and spiritual). These two forms are seen as complementary, as corresponding qualities which must both be achieved for freedom to be wholly realized.

Second, the background of the school's thought is briefly discussed. Certain key themes in the writings of prominent nineteenth-century Indian figures are examined, to suggest the nature of the climate of opinion out of which Vivekananda's conception of freedom emerged.

Finally, the greater part of the book is devoted to an analysis of precisely what these four men thought about freedom, and how one of them, Gandhi, carried on experiments with his ideas in Indian society and politics. It is argued that while all the members of this school agree on fundamental issues, each made a distinctive contribution to the development of the idea of freedom. Vivekananda's contribution arises in the synthesis that he created of various strands of nineteenth-century Indian thought, and which he used in his formulation of a particular conception of freedom. The major aspects of this conception were developed by the other thinkers, each adding new dimensions.

If Vivekananda was the seminal influence behind the school, Aurobindo was its outstanding theoretician. He attempted to show a natural correspondence between individual freedom as self-realization and social unity as a state of universal harmony in which each had recognized his spiritual identity with all. Gandhi was the most active participant in the nationalist movement. He sought to implement his school's ideas on freedom and harmony with a programme of social and political change, a method rooted in the belief that social progress could only come through a moral transformation of the individual in society. And finally, Tagore, who is seen here as the critic or 'conscience' of the school, warning it against the cult of nationalism: the threat to individual freedom and universal harmony which the others had overlooked.

CHAPTER 1

Continuity and Innovation in the Modern Indian Idea of Freedom

'The Indian mind,' observed Louis Renou in his series of lectures on ancient Indian religions, 'is constantly seeking hidden correspondences between things which belong to entirely distinct conceptual systems.'[1]

The method of analysis used here will involve two general approaches to the study of modern Indian political and social thought. The first of these will examine the attempt of certain recent Indian thinkers to construct a social and political theory through the development of conceptual correspondences; that is, the relation of select concepts, usually derived from ancient Indian thought, to modern ideas, often imported from the West. The purpose of these particular Indian thinkers was at once to preserve continuity with their own tradition and to introduce conceptual innovations demanded by a society in the midst of rapid transition. Their thought may be considered first, then, as a specific response to the historical situation in which they found

---

1   Louis Renou, *Religions of Ancient India* (London: Athlone Press, 1953), p. 18.

83

themselves. The nature of their response was not unique: other thinkers of other civilizations, during other periods of social change, have made similar attempts at dealing with the general problem of 'continuity and innovation'. This work will confine itself exclusively to an analysis of modern Indian political and social thought, of the historical evolution of certain key concepts during the nineteenth and twentieth centuries. It will concentrate on one of these concepts in particular, the idea of freedom, as well as on its development among four major Indian thinkers, Swami Vivekananda (1863–1902), Aurobindo Ghose (1872–1950), M.K. Gandhi (1869–1948) and Rabindranath Tagore (1861–1941).

An analysis of the meaning of freedom has been selected as a central theme for two main reasons. First, during much of this century, India had been engrossed in a national movement for political and social freedom; it is natural that the minds of India's leading political thinkers should have turned increasingly to this issue. A consideration of this particular idea, which occupied a dominant place in their political thought, throws light upon their whole understanding of the nature of politics. Second, their thinking on the meaning of freedom presents a fruitful study in the theme of continuity and innovation. Through the use of this one concept, an analysis may be made of the Western impact on modern Indian political thought, with the purpose of examining the foreign ideas which that impact introduced, as well as the restatement that it induced of traditional Indian beliefs. In this sense, the idea of freedom offers a notable instance of Professor Renou's comment on the tendency of the Indian mind to seek conceptual correspondences. For, as the idea of freedom occurs in modern India, it is most often seen as a complementary principle, an idea which completes its own meaning through correspondence with other concepts, some derived from the Indian tradition, others incorporated from the West. The intention here is to analyse the idea of freedom and the manner in which it complements other themes, so that this may contribute toward a broad understanding of Indian political and social thought.

'There is always a close connection,' remarked John Plamenatz in his study of Western political philosophy, 'between a philosopher's conception of what man is, what is peculiar to him, how he is placed in the world, and his doctrines about how man should behave, what he should strive for, and how society should be constituted.'[2]

The second aspect of the method of analysis employed here will involve a consideration of some fundamental questions which have traditionally concerned Western political philosophy. These questions are suggested in the passage quoted from Plamenatz above, and they may be posed in this form: What is the nature of man? If an absolute exists, what is its form and its relevance to the sphere of politics? What is the right relation of the individual to society, and what constitutes an ideal social order? And, finally, what is the right method of social and political change? These few questions neither exhaust all the issues examined by Western political philosophers, nor are the problems they raise exclusively political in nature. They will be used, throughout this study, as a method of analysis, only because they pose questions of the Indian thinkers considered here, which reveal the fundamental assumptions of their political and social thought, as well as their essential agreement on basic issues. On the basis of this agreement, these thinkers will be referred to here as a 'school' of modern Indian political and social thought.

Vivekananda, Aurobindo, Gandhi and Tagore, all rested their political and social thought on certain religious beliefs concerning the nature of man and of the Absolute, and these beliefs were, as Plamenatz's observation would imply, closely connected with their view of 'how man should behave, what he should strive for, and how society should

---

2   John Plamenatz, *Man and Society*, 2 vols, Vol. II (London: Longmans, 1963), p. xvi.

be constituted'. For each of these Indian thinkers, a divine Absolute exists, and the individual is seen as part of that Absolute; that is, the nature of man is divine. For each, it followed from these beliefs that the highest aim of man should always remain the discovery of his own nature; the attainment of this goal they called self-realization or spiritual freedom. In order to achieve this, man's behaviour must be moral. He must follow the dictates of the Absolute, which, as Gandhi so often said, emanated from the 'still small voice' within, the individual's own conscience. Once each individual has discovered the Truth of his being, the ideal society might be achieved; a Utopia in which the highest form of freedom is coincident with a perfect state of social harmony. These are, in brief, the assumptions which underlie the thought of the Indians considered here, and this work will attempt to examine the bearing of these assumptions on the development of this school's political and social thought.

Two points need to be made here. First, in point of time, Vivekananda was the earliest of this group; the others were all figures of the twentieth century. Vivekananda was thus in a position to exert a seminal influence on modern Indian thought, and, as all of the others have testified, the influence which he did in fact exert was exceptional and profound. On the other hand, in considering the whole of modern Indian thought, one figure occupies, indisputably, the most important position, both for what he thought and did, and also for the immense influence which he had on twentieth-century Indian society. This was Mahatma Gandhi, and more attention will be devoted to him than to any other individual thinker. The least will be given to Tagore; for while his particular contribution to Indian political thought is significant, it is also very specific and limited, contained principally in his short book, *Nationalism*, and in his equally brief controversy with Gandhi. The second point concerns the scant analysis that will be given to comparisons with Western political and social theorists, and the complete omission of contemporary Muslim thinkers. Undeniably, comparative analysis of this type may offer increased insights into the Indian position. This will not, however, be the approach assumed in this study. Priority will be given here, first, to an understanding of the school's purpose, the nature of its attempt as these four thinkers conceived it; second, to an examination of the climate of thought from which the Indian idea of freedom emerged in the nineteenth century; and finally, to an analysis of precisely what these men, as Indians, thought about freedom and how they acted upon their thoughts in response to shifting cultural values and increasing pressures for social and political change.

The Western Impact and the Indian Response: 'Preservation by Reconstruction'

'The suddenness with which we stepped out of one era into another with its new meaning and values! In our own home, in our neighbourhood and community, there was still no deep awareness of human rights, human dignity, class equality.'[3] Tagore's candid characterization of late-nineteenth-century India is representative of his school. Among the attempts to revive Hinduism in the face of the Western impact, incredible claims were made for the Indian past. This school is noteworthy, both for the relative restraint it exercised towards its own past and for the vigorous attacks it made on the orthodoxy of the present. 'There are two great obstacles on our path in India,' said Vivekananda, 'the Scylla of old orthodoxy and the Charybdis of modern European civilization.'[4] And Vivekananda did see 'old orthodoxy' as an

---

3   Rabindranath Tagore, *Towards Universal Man* (London: Asia Publishing House, 1961), p. 347.

4   Swami Vivekananda, *The Complete Works of Swami Vivekananda* (8 vols.), Vol. 3 (Calcutta: Advaita Ashrama, 1960), p. 151. Hereafter *Works*.

obstacle: his vehement tirades against caste and priestcraft make those of the more Westernized reformers look pale in comparison. 'I disagree with all those,' he said, 'who are giving their superstitions back to my people. Like the Egyptologist's interest in Egypt, it is easy to feel an interest in India that is purely selfish. One may desire to see again the India of one's books, one's studies, one's dreams. My hope is to see again the strong points of that India, reinforced by the strong points of this age, only in a natural way. The new stage of things must be a growth from within.'[5]

India's growth required, in the minds of these four thinkers, an assimilation of the good aspects of the Western as well as of the Indian traditions. Negative outbursts occurred among them against the whole of Western civilization, but these were the exception.[6] The main spirit of the school is indicated in these words that Vivekananda addressed to his countrymen:

> Several dangers are in the way, and one is that of the extreme conception that we are the people in the world. With all my love for India, and with all my patriotism, and veneration for the ancients, I cannot but think that we have to learn many things from other nations. We must be always ready to sit at the feet of all, for, mark you, everyone can teach us great lessons ... The more you go out and travel among the nations of the world, the better for you and for your country. If you had done that for hundreds of years past, you would not be here today, at the feet of every nation that wants to rule India. The first manifest effect of life is expansion. You must

---

5   Vivekananda, *Works*, Vol. 8 (1959), p. 266.

6   Gandhi's *Hind Swaraj* is one of these exceptions, both to the general thinking of the school and the mainstream of Gandhi's own thought as well. A glance at his autobiography reveals a broad receptiveness to Western ideals.

expand if you want to live. The moment you have ceased to expand, death is upon you, danger is ahead.[7]

If these thinkers shared relatively few illusions about their own tradition,[8] they had even fewer about the prospects of India achieving its fruition in a Western form. They sought, above all, to create a new harmony out of what they saw as a present state of discord. Nothing troubled Vivekananda more than the 'Europeanized Indians': 'A mass of heterogeneous ideas picked up at random from every source—and these ideas are unassimilated, undigested, unharmonized.'[9] And this dissonance, they all believed, was perpetuated by problems which a foreign civilization had posed, but not solved. Tagore expressed the resultant state of mental turmoil:

For there are grave questions that the Western civilization has presented before the world but not completely answered. The conflict between the individual and the state, labour and capital, the man and the woman; the conflict between the greed of material gain and the spiritual life of man, the organized selfishness of nations and the higher ideals of humanity; the conflict between all the ugly complexities inseparable from giant organizations of commerce and state and the natural instincts of man crying for simplicity and beauty and fullness of leisure—all these have to be brought to a harmony in a manner not yet dreamt of.[10]

---

7 Vivekananda, *Works*, Vol. 3 (1960), p. 272.

8 Again, there are exceptions. Aurobindo's *Spirit and Form of Indian Polity*, following the misleading authority of K.P. Jayaswal, sees a super-abundance of democratic institutions existing in ancient India. See Sri Aurobindo, *The Foundations of Indian Culture* (Pondicherry: Sri Aurobindo Ashram, 1951), pp. 403–13.

9 Vivekananda, *Works*, Vol. 8 (1959), p. 249.

10 Rabindranath Tagore, *Nationalism* (London: Macmillan, 1950), p. 51.

Tagore, however, did not feel overwhelmed by the Western impact; rather, he regarded it as a challenging stimulus to innovation. 'The dynamism of Europe,' he said, 'made a vigorous assault on our stagnant minds—it acted like the torrents of rain that strike into the dry under-earth, give it vital stirrings and bring forth new life.'[11] The opportunity he envisioned was to use India's past as a source of inspiration, a platform for reconstruction, on which a modern framework of ideas might be built. Tagore's attitude is representative of the school, and the type of approach it induced was well-expressed by Aurobindo:

> Side by side with this movement [of Westernization in India] and more characteristic and powerful, there has been flowing an opposite current. This first started on its way by an integral reaction, a vindication and re-acceptance of everything Indian as it stood and because it was Indian ... But in reality the reaction marks the beginning of a more subtle assimilation and fusing; for in vindicating ancient things, it has been obliged to do so in a way that will at once meet and satisfy the old mentality and the new, the traditional and the critical mind. This in itself involves no mere return, but consciously or unconsciously hastens a restatement. And the riper form of the return has taken as its principle a synthetical restatement; it has sought to arrive at the spirit of the ancient culture and, while respecting its forms and often preserving them to revivify, has yet not hesitated also to remould, to reject the outworn and to admit whatever new motive seemed assimilable to the old spirituality or apt to widen the channel of its larger evolution. Of this freer dealing with past and present, this preservation by reconstruction, Vivekananda was in his lifetime the leading exemplar and the most powerful exponent.[12]

---

11 Tagore, *Towards Universal Man*, pp. 342–43.

12 Aurobindo, *The Renaissance in India* (Pondicherry: Sri Aurobindo Ashram, 1951), pp. 39–40.

No phrase describes better the overriding intent of this school than Aurobindo's term 'preservation by reconstruction': the development of 'forms not contradictory of the truths of life which the old expressed, but rather expressive of those truths restated, cured of defect, completed'.[13]

One of the main purposes behind this reconstruction was the creation of a philosophy of social and political action. The basis for this philosophy was uncovered by Vivekananda in his interpretation of the *Bhagavad Gita's* theory of Karma Yoga. Few examples illustrate better the nature of 'preservation by reconstruction' than the approach that these thinkers assumed toward the Gita.

> What, however, I have done [said Gandhi] is to put a new but natural and logical interpretation upon the whole teaching of the Gita and the spirit of Hinduism. Hinduism, not to speak of other religions, is ever-evolving. It has not one scripture like the Quran or the Bible. Its scriptures are also evolving and suffering addition. The Gita itself is an instance in point. It has given a new meaning to *karma*, *sannyasa*, *yajna*, etc. It has breathed new life into Hinduism.[14]

> The Gita is not an aphoristic work; it is a great religious poem. The deeper you dive into it, the richer the meanings you get. It being meant for the people at large, there is pleasing repetition. With every age the important words will carry new and expanding meanings. But its central teaching will never vary. The seeker is at liberty to extract from this treasure any meaning he likes so as to enable to enforce in his life the central teaching.[15]

---

13 Ibid., p. 6.

14 M.K. Gandhi, *Harijan*, 3 October 1936, in *Collected Works of Mahatma Gandhi* (hereafter *CWMG*) (Delhi: Government of India, 1994), 63:339.

15 Gandhi quoted in Mahadev Desai, *The Gita According to Gandhi* (Ahmedabad: Navajivan Publishing House, 1956), pp. 133–34 (in *CWMG* 41:100).

'The seeker is at liberty to extract from this treasure any meaning he likes'; Gandhi's words bear repetition, for they underline the nature of this school's approach. These men went to their tradition with a purpose, to uncover ideas which would meet the demands of a modern India. They were engaged in a consciously selective effort, and no one was more aware than they of the extent of this selectivity.

The broad rationale behind this eclecticism rested on a distinction between the 'essential' and 'non-essential' elements of Hinduism. Gandhi's relentless attack on untouchability as an unnatural accretion, which must be purged from the pure state of Hinduism, is the most outstanding example of this approach. But Gandhi's attempt was preceded, a generation earlier, by Vivekananda's stern indictment of 'don't-touchism' on precisely the same grounds.[16] 'In plain words,' said Vivekananda, 'we have first to learn the distinction between the essentials and the non-essentials in everything. The essentials are eternal, the non-essentials have value only for a certain time, and if after a time they are not replaced by something essential, they are positively dangerous.'[17] No member of this school, though, expressed the critical distinction between the spirit and form of Hinduism in more eloquent terms than Tagore:

The difference between the spirit and the form of religion, like that between fire and ash, should be borne in mind. When the form becomes more important than the spirit, the sand in the riverbed becomes more pronounced than the water, the current ceases to flow, and a desert is the ultimate result.

The spirit of religion says that disrespect for man confers no benefit on him who insults and on him who is insulted, but the form of religion says that failure to obey scrupulously the detailed rules for treating man with cruel contempt is apostasy. The spirit

16 Vivekananda, *Works*, Vol. 3 (1960), p. 167.
17 Ibid., p. 174.

teaches us not to destroy our own souls by inflicting unnecessary suffering on our fellow creatures, but the form warns parents that it is sin to give food and drink on specified days of the month to their widow daughter, even to relieve her of the worst suffering. The spirit tells us to atone for evil thoughts and deeds by repentance and by performance of good deeds, but the form prescribes bathing in particular rivers at the hour of solar or lunar eclipse. The spirit advises us to cross seas and mountains and develop our minds by seeing the world, but the form puts an expiatory ban on sea voyage. The spirit tells us to revere all good men irrespective of their caste, but the form enjoins respect for the Brahmin, however unworthy. In sum, the spirit of religion leads to freedom, its form to slavery.[18]

Man, God and Freedom

The God of heaven becomes the God in nature, and the God in nature becomes the God who is nature, and the God who is nature becomes the God within this temple of the body, and the God dwelling in the temple of the body at last becomes the temple itself, becomes the soul and man—and there it reaches the last words it can teach. He whom the sages have been seeking in all these places is in our own hearts; the voice that you heard was right, says the Vedanta, but the direction you gave to the voice was wrong. That ideal of freedom that you perceived was correct, but you projected it outside yourself, and that was your mistake. Bring it nearer and nearer, until you find that it was all the time within you; it was the Self of your own self.[19] ... The only God to worship is the human soul in the human body ... The moment I have realised God sitting in the temple of every human body, the moment I stand in reverence before every human being and see God in him—that moment I am free from bondage, everything that binds vanishes, and I am

18 Tagore, *Towards Universal Man*, pp. 188–89.

19 Vivekananda, *Works*, Vol. 2 (1963), p. 128.

free.[20] ... The Impersonal Being, our highest generalization, is in ourselves, and we are That. 'O Shvetaketu, thou art That'.[21]

The conceptual correspondences, evident in this passage, which are fundamental to Vivekananda's thought, were those drawn from among his ideas of human nature, the Absolute, and the meaning of freedom. Man's Self and God are seen by him as interchangeable qualities, and he considers the realization of this—of the presence of the Absolute in all humanity—to be the decisive factor in the attainment of spiritual freedom. Finally, by alluding to a well-known verse from the *Chandogya Upanishad*,[22] he links this series of correspondences with the Indian tradition. The Upanishads do, in fact, make these correspondences among the three basic concepts of man, God and freedom: Brahman, the Absolute, is seen as identical with the human soul, the Atman, the Self; and with Self-realization came mukti, spiritual freedom, release from all bondage.[23] Vivekananda adopted the essential elements of this position. Spiritual freedom meant, for him, the ultimate expansion of the human Self, which brought realization of one's identity with the Absolute, and with all mankind. However, he put this conception of spiritual freedom to an unprecedented use in the development of his social and political thought.

The ancient Indian philosophers had never championed social or political liberty in the modern Western sense. The ideal of spiritual

---

20 Ibid., p. 334.

21 Ibid., p. 334.

22 *Chandogya Upanishad* (6.10.1–6.16.1) in *The Thirteen Principal Upanishads*, trans. Robert Ernest Hume (Oxford: Oxford University Press, 1962), pp. 246–50.

23 A.L. Basham, *The Wonder That Was India* (New York: Grove Press, 1954), pp. 250–51. See also Surendranath Dasgupta, *A History of Indian Philosophy*, Vol. I (Cambridge: Cambridge University Press, 1922), p. 58.

freedom which they presented had social implications, but it did not give rise to a theory in defence of the individual's right to free thought and action vis-à-vis society, the state, or the nation. Vivekananda attempted to incorporate this modern Western view of political and social liberty into the traditional Indian theory of spiritual freedom.

The crux of his development rested with his insistence that man's expansion or growth demands enjoyment of freedom at all levels of consciousness: physical and material, as well as political and social. Man must have freedom in the lower realms to achieve the spiritual freedom of the highest. The deprivation of such freedom, at any stage of man's evolution, may retard his growth, thwart his quest for Self-realization. Thus all forms of freedom become desirable, for each may contribute to individual growth.[24] Once this innovation was introduced, though, Vivekananda turned to the task of maintaining continuity. Man may be free, he pointed out, in a physical or intellectual, social or political sense; yet, unless he directs his liberty, on these lower levels of consciousness, toward attainment of the highest goal, spiritual freedom, these lesser freedoms will prove meaningless. 'The Hindu,' he asserted, 'says that political and social independence are well and good, but the real thing is spiritual independence—Mukti. This is our national purpose.'[25] And then, in words that were often to be echoed by the later members of his school, Vivekananda said, 'One may gain political and social independence, but if one is a slave to his passions and desires, one cannot feel the pure joy of real freedom.'[26]

In one important sense, then, Vivekananda stands in agreement with the traditional view that spiritual freedom or moksha represents man's highest goal. In another sense, though, he invests the Indian tradition with a value which was quite foreign. Social and political freedom

---

24 Vivekananda, *Works*, Vol. 5 (1959), p. 216.

25 Ibid., p. 458.

26 Ibid., p. 419.

were presented not only as desirable expectations but expectations made desirable by traditional figures, often clad in a sannyasin's garb, that symbolized, above all, spiritually free souls. These figures never ceased to stress the supreme desideratum of spiritual freedom; and if this insistence on the value of spiritual freedom directed their attitude toward freedom in other forms, it pervaded, as well, their ideas on man's relation to society and the nature of the good social order.

The Individual and Society: Freedom, Harmony and Equality

Freedom and harmony [Aurobindo wrote] express the two necessary principles of variation and oneness—freedom of the individual, the group, the race, coordinated harmony of the individual's forces and of the efforts of all individuals in the group, of all groups in the race, of all races in the kind—and these are the two conditions of healthy progression and successful arrival. To realize them and to combine them has been the obscure or half-enlightened effort of mankind throughout its history—a task difficult indeed and too imperfectly seen and too clumsily and mechanically pursued by the reason and desires to be satisfactorily achieved until man grows by self-mastery to the possession of a spiritual and psychical unity with his fellow men.[27]

The ideal social order was set forth, in ancient India, in the theory of varnashrama dharma. The system of four varnas or social orders ensured, in theory, the inter-relationship of four social functions: that of the brahman (spiritual authority), kshatriya (temporal power), vaishya (wealth) and sudra (labour). The working of society depended upon

---

27 Sri Aurobindo, 'The Human Cycle', in *The Human Cycle: The Ideal of Human Unity, War and Self-Determination* (Pondicherry: Sri Aurobindo Ashram, 1962), p. 84.

the fulfilment, by each of these varnas, of its social role as prescribed by dharma, or the sacred law. The remaining element of this theory, that of ashrama, indicated the division of the individual's life into four ashramas or stages of existence: those of the student, the householder, the hermit and the wandering ascetic (sannyasin). This social order is seen in the *Brihadaranyaka Upanishad* as divinely created, and right performance of social duty, as set forth by dharma, ensured the harmony of society with the whole of the universe.[28] Only within the framework of varnashrama dharma could men attain their individual aims of artha (wealth), kama (pleasure) and dharma (righteousness).[29] The main function of the king was to protect this order and preserve social harmony, 'thereby giving the optimum chance of spiritual progress to as many individuals as possible'.[30] For the highest aim of man was moksha, spiritual freedom, and the social harmony of the four varnas remained of value only as long as it contributed to individual spiritual advancement through the four ashramas. Emphasis should be placed upon Professor A.L. Basham's observation that in ancient Indian thought,

> The ultimate aim of all valid and worthy human activity is salvation, which cannot be achieved by corporate entities such as peoples, castes and families, but only by individual human beings. Government exists to serve society, and, on final analysis, society exists to serve the individual. This latter proposition is hardly to be found in implicit form, but it is a necessary corollary

---

28 Hume, *The Thirteen Principal Upanishads*, pp. 84–85.

29 A.L. Basham, 'Some Fundamental Ideas of Ancient India', in *Politics and Society in India*, ed. C.H. Philips (London: Allen and Unwin, 1963), p. 13.

30 Ibid., p. 16.

of the fundamental presuppositions on which all Hindu thought was based.[31]

It was in this manner that the theory of varnashrama dharma sought to achieve a perfect correspondence between social harmony and spiritual freedom.

Although traditional Indian thought never viewed government as a force hostile to society, there was among ancient Indian thinkers 'general agreement that government is an unfortunate necessity in an age of universal decay.'[32] Moreover, in Professor Basham's discussion of the question of whether a theory of the State existed in ancient Indian thought, he argued:

> Many modern scholars, perhaps motivated by the idea that the concept of the state is a *sine qua non* of a civilized system of political thought, have tried to find evidence of such a concept in ancient Indian political writings. Though they have usually succeeded to their own satisfaction, it seems doubtful whether there was any clear idea of the state in pre-Muslim times. As used in the West, the term seems to imply a corporate entity controlling a definite territory, which maintains its identity and continues to exist, irrespective of changes in the governing personnel. In the writings of the more doctrinaire theorists, the state seems to take on the character of a living entity, greater than the sum of its parts. In India, such political mysticism was discouraged by the doctrine of Dharma, which concerned society and not the state, and by the fundamental individualism of all the metaphysical systems.[33]

While, then, classical Indian thought cannot be regarded as anti-political, it did see government as an 'unfortunate necessity'; and not

---

31 Ibid., pp. 21–22.

32 Ibid., p. 12.

33 Ibid., p. 21.

only did it place the social sphere above that of the political, it also insisted upon the primacy of the individual's spiritual aims.

All four of the modern Indian thinkers considered here claim to base their views of the right relation of the individual to society and of the nature of the good society on the classical Indian ideal of varnashrama dharma. Society, and never the state, serves for them as the framework within which the individual enjoys social harmony and through which he may ultimately attain spiritual freedom. Vivekananda, in describing the 'fabric of Aryan civilisation', wrote, 'Its warp is varnashramachara, and its woof, the conquest of strife and competition in nature.'[34] Tagore, moreover, extols the harmony of the four ashramas as against the discord of 'rampant individualism'.[35] And Gandhi elevates the value of social duty to a prominent position in his thought. The ideal of varnashrama dharma demanded, for him, each individual contributing to the welfare of all by responsibly fulfilling his particular role in society. The avoidance of competition and cultivation of cooperativeness and harmony through the disinterested performance of one's social duties— this is the ideal that the modern school envisioned, and they saw it embodied in traditional Indian thought.

If these thinkers drew freely on the traditional Indian theory of society, they also introduced critical innovations which had no precedent in the ancient idea of varnashrama dharma. The first of these concerns their development of a point of view which was decidedly anti-political. Traditional Indian thought had regarded government as an 'unfortunate necessity'; however undesirable as government may have appeared to the ancients, it still remained a necessity. In both the *Dharmasastra* and *Arthasastra* literature, the king is seen as an indispensable force for protection of society and maintenance of justice.

---

34 Vivekananda, *Works*, Vol. 5 (1959), p. 536.

35 Rabindranath Tagore, *The Religion of Man*, *The Hibbert Lectures for 1930* (London: Allen & Unwin, 1931), p. 202.

Spiritual freedom and social harmony were thought attainable within the framework of varnashrama dharma, and government became a necessary part of this framework. Since ancient India conceived no idea of the state comparable to that developed in the West, it could make no association of the state with government. The modern Indian thinkers, however, denied that government was a necessary element of varnashrama dharma, and this denial was based on the association which traditional Indian thought had not made: that of government with the state. On this basis, the moderns indicted both state and government as alien to society; and, although one must use extreme care in applying Western terms like 'anarchism' to the Indian situation, the fact that both Aurobindo and Gandhi saw themselves as 'philosophical anarchists' does indicate the severity of their indictment, as well as their intense distrust of political authority in general.[36] Gandhi is representative of the school, in this respect, in that he regarded 'an increase in the power of the state with the greatest fear, because ... it does the greatest harm by destroying individuality which lies at the root of all progress. The state represents violence in a concentrated and organized form. The individual has a soul, but as the state is a soulless machine, it can never be weaned from violence to which it owes its very existence.'[37] The ideal society would be one of 'enlightened anarchy', where 'everyone is his own ruler, and ... there is no political power because there is no State'.[38] This age of enlightened anarchy was not envisaged as a sudden occurrence, but rather as a product of a gradual spiritual evolution. In

---

36 See also Vivekananda's Utopian vision of an anarchist society, in *Works*, Vol. 3 (1960), pp. 196–98.

37 M.K. Gandhi, *Democracy: Real and Deceptive* (Ahmedabad: Navajivan Publishing House, 1961), pp. 28–29 and *CWMG* 59:318.

38 Gandhi, *Young India*, 2 July 1931, in *Democracy*, p. 28 and *CWMG* 47:91.

this perfect age, the moderns hoped, the essential spirit of varnashrama dharma might be realized.

The manner in which Vivekananda incorporated the Western idea of political and social liberty into his theory of the individual and society has already been mentioned. In another like attempt at innovation, the school sought to assimilate the Western concept of social equality into its theory of varnashrama dharma. Spiritual equality, in the sense that all men were thought part of the divine Absolute, was explicit throughout the traditional writings; perhaps it occurred most notably in *Advaita Vedanta* and the *Bhagavad Gita*. And it was upon this spiritual basis that the moderns tried to construct an idea of social and political equality. This attempt, once again, began with Vivekananda,[39] but its implications for a programme of social reform were most fully developed by Gandhi.

In my opinion [said Gandhi] there is no such thing as inherited or acquired superiority. I believe in the rock-bottom doctrine of *advaita*, and my interpretation of *advaita* excludes totally any idea of superiority at any stage whatsoever. I believe implicitly that all men are born equal. All—whether born in India or in England or America or in any circumstances whatsoever—have the same soul as any other. And it is because I believe in this inherent equality of all men that I fight the doctrine of superiority which many of our rulers arrogate to themselves. I have fought this doctrine of superiority in South Africa inch by inch, and it is because of that inherent belief, that I delight in calling myself a scavenger, a spinner, a weaver, a farmer and a labourer. And I have fought against the brahmanas themselves wherever they have claimed any superiority for themselves either by reason of their birth or by reason of their subsequently acquired knowledge. I consider that it is unmanly for any person to claim superiority over a fellow-

39 Vivekananda, *Works*, Vol. 1 (1962), pp. 426–29.

being. And there is the amplest warrant for the belief that I am enunciating in the *Bhagavadgita* ... But in spite of all my beliefs, that I have explained to you, I still believe in Varnashrama Dharma. Varnashrama Dharma to my mind is a law which, however much you and I may deny, cannot be abrogated.[40]

This is precisely the nature of the attempt at reconstruction which is representative of the school: first, the statement of a spiritual principle; then, its application to the Indian social order, which usually involves criticism of the old orthodoxy; and, finally, an insistence that this reinterpretation is consistent with the spirit of the traditional teachings. No single attempt in modern Indian political thought to establish social equality is more significant than Gandhi's attack on caste. The social innovation that Gandhi hoped to achieve was immense, yet he continually couched his pleas for reform in traditional language and themes.

When we have come to our own, when we have cleansed ourselves, we may have the four varnas according to the way in which we can express the best in us. But varna then will invest no one with a superior status or right; it will invest one with higher responsibility and duties. Those who will impart knowledge in a spirit of service will be called brahmanas. They will assume no superior airs but will be true servants of society. When inequality of status or rights is ended, every one of us will be equal. I do not know, however, when we shall be able to revive true Varna Dharma. Its real revival would mean true democracy.[41]

---

40 Gandhi, *Young India*, 1927–1928, 16 September 1927, Vol. III (Madras: S. Ganesan, 1935), p. 385 and *CWMG* 35:1–2 (Italics in original).

41 Gandhi, *Harijan,* 27 March, 1936, in *CWMG* 62:291.

In these few lines, Gandhi has managed to alternate the themes of continuity and innovation with values from India and the West. The discussion is of the four varnas; but with Gandhi, they become a framework for social equality. They no longer represent distinctions of social status but rather opportunities for social service, and those who fulfill the ideals embodied in these transformed varnas become not good nationalists or democrats but brahmanas. Gandhi's concluding two sentences, which equate Varna Dharma with democracy illustrate, as sharply as such few words are able, the admixture in his thought of continuity and innovation.

The Western impact reached its ideological high water mark with its introduction of the ideals of freedom and equality. The thinking behind this Indian school's response, the reasoning with which it sought to answer the challenge posed by these two great ideals are well-expressed in an early speech of Aurobindo. The assumptions underlying this key statement are directly in line with those voiced earlier by Vivekananda; they were to be further developed, not only by Aurobindo himself, in his later phase, but by Gandhi and Tagore as well. Liberty and equality, Aurobindo began, are among the great ideals which have become the 'watchwords of humanity', with 'the power of remoulding nations and governments'. Then, he continues,

These words cast forth into being from the great stir and movement of the eighteenth century continue to act on men because they point to the ultimate goal towards which human evolution ever moves. This liberty to which we progress is liberation out of a state of bondage. We move from a state of bondage to an original liberty. This is what our own religion teaches. This is what our own philosophy suggests as the goal towards which we move, mukti or moksha. We are bound in the beginning by a lapse from pre-existent freedom; we strive to shake off the bonds, we move forward and forward until we have achieved the ultimate emancipation, that utter freedom of the soul, of the body or the whole man, that utter freedom from all bondage towards which humanity is always aspiring. We in India have found a mighty freedom within ourselves; our brother-men in Europe have worked towards freedom without. We have been moving on parallel lines towards the same end. They have found out the way to external freedom. We have found out the way to internal freedom. We meet and give to each other what we have gained. We have learned from them to aspire after external as they will learn from us to aspire after internal freedom.

Equality is the second term in the triple gospel. It is a thing which mankind has never accomplished. From inequality and through inequality we move, but it is to equality. Our religion, our philosophy set equality forward as the essential condition of emancipation. All religions send us this message in a different form, but it is one message. Christianity says we are all brothers, children of one God. Mohammedanism says we are the subjects and servants of one Allah; we are all equal in the sight of God. Hinduism says there is One without a second. In the high and the low, in the Brahmin and the Sudra, in the saint and the sinner, there is one Narayana, one God, and he is the soul of all men. Not until you have realised him, known Narayana in all, and the Brahmin and the Sudra, the high and the low, the saint and the sinner are equal in your eyes, then and not until then you have knowledge, you have freedom, until then you are bound and ignorant. The equality which Europe has got is external political equality. She is now trying to achieve social equality. Nowadays their hard-earned political liberty is beginning to pall a little upon the people of Europe because they have found it does not give perfect well-being or happiness, and it is barren of the sweetness of brotherhood. There is no fraternity in this liberty. It is merely a political liberty. They have not either the liberty within or the full equality or the fraternity. So they are turning a little from what they have, and they say increasingly, 'Let us have equality, let us have the second term of the gospels towards which we strive.' Therefore socialism is growing in Europe. Europe is now trying to achieve external equality as the second term of the gospel of mankind, the universal ideal. I have said that equality is an ideal even with us, but we have not tried to achieve it without. Still we have learned from them to strive after political equality and in return for what they have given us we shall lead them to the secret of the equality within.[42]

Two observations may be made on this passage. First, Aurobindo's incorporation of the Western values of social and political freedom and equality into his theory of society is rooted in Vivekananda's earlier distinction between the 'spiritual' or 'internal' and politico-social or 'external' forms of these values.[43] The appropriation of the 'internal' forms exclusively to the Indian tradition is noteworthy and will be considered at length in the next chapter.

Second, again following Vivekananda's lead,[44] Aurobindo sees a necessary correspondence between freedom and equality: 'Not until the Brahmin and the Sudra, the high and the low, the saint and the sinner are equal in your eyes, then and not until then you have knowledge, you have freedom, until then you are bound and ignorant.' Thus, the Indian tradition is made to underwrite a theory of society which embodies not only the old goals of spiritual freedom, spiritual equality and spiritual harmony but also the necessary interrelationship of these values with social and political freedom and equality.

Method of Change

The tidal wave of Western civilisation is now rushing over the length and breadth of the country. It won't do now simply to sit

---

42 Sri Aurobindo, *Speeches* (Pondicherry: Sri Aurobindo Ashram, 1952), pp. 93–96.

43 Vivekananda distinguished between two forms of equality, as well as of freedom. See *Works*, Vol. 1 (1962), pp. 423–35.

44 Ibid., p. 426.

in meditation on mountain tops without realising in the least its
usefulness. Now is wanted—as said in the Gita by the Lord—
intense Karma Yoga, with unbounded courage and indomitable
strength in the heart. Then only will the people of the country be
roused.[45]

The final principle which unites the members of this school and
reflects their views on the themes of continuity and innovation lies in
their attempt to think out a way of right social and political action. All
of the thinkers considered here desired India's political independence
and each directed his efforts in some way toward that goal. On the
other hand, all saw their task as primarily supra-political in nature:
they insisted that though their activities might influence the political
sphere, and though their ideas may embrace political issues, their
ultimate purpose was beyond politics. This purpose was none other
than individual self-realization—the discovery, by each, of the reality
of his own nature. Only in this way, they believed, could a radical
transformation of society occur.

The inspiration for a theory of action through which this
transformation might be achieved came from Vivekananda. Much of his
thought and energy was channelled into the task of awakening a spirit
of service among the Indian people, but his plea was always based on
the belief that through service to society, the individual would further
his own quest for self-realization. 'Look upon every man, woman, and
every one as God. You cannot help anyone; you can only serve ... I
should see God in the poor, and it is for my salvation that I go and
worship them. The poor and the miserable are for our salvation.'[46] No
Indian of this age carried this aspect of Vivekananda's thought further
than Gandhi. Once, when Gandhi was asked by a Western visitor if his
work in the villages was simply 'humanitarian', he replied,

45 Vivekananda, *Works*, Vol. 7 (1958), p. 185.

46 Vivekananda, *Works*, Vol. 3 (1960), pp. 246–47.

I am here to serve no one else but myself, to find my own self-realisation through the service of these village folk. Man's ultimate aim is the realisation of God, and all his activities, political, social and religious, have to be guided by the ultimate aim of the vision of God. The immediate service of all human beings becomes a necessary part of the endeavour simply because the only way to find God is to see Him in His creation and be one with it. This can only be done by service of all. And this cannot be done except through one's country. I am a part and parcel of the whole, and I cannot find Him apart from the rest of humanity. My countrymen are my nearest neighbours. They have become so helpless, resourceless and inert that I must concentrate on serving them. If I could persuade myself that I should find Him in a Himalayan cave, I would proceed there immediately. But I know that I cannot find Him apart from humanity.[47]

It is emphatically at this point that the school's views on human nature, the Absolute, freedom and harmony support a programme of social action: the nature of man is divine; through service to mankind, the individual may realize his divinity, and with that will come spiritual freedom and a sense of his unity with all being. The effect of this idea was to promote a programme of social, and later, political reform. But at its base, the school's theory of the way of right action is motivated by an intensely individual quest for self-purification and self-realization. Only in this way might the primary aim of the spiritual transformation of the individual in society be achieved.

The end result of Vivekananda's emphasis upon social service was to reconcile an individualistic approach to self-realization with a programme of social and political reform. In making this attempt at

---

47 D.G. Tendulkar, *Mahatma: Life of Mohandas Karamchand Gandhi* (8 vols.), Vol. IV, Revised edition (Delhi: Publications Division, Ministry of Information and Broadcasting, Government of India, 1960–62), p. 88 and *CWMG* 63:240.

reconciliation, Vivekananda turned to a work which had achieved a similar reconciliation centuries before, the *Bhagavad Gita*. The problem of the Gita, however, was not Vivekananda's problem: the former sought a philosophical justification for the preservation of a particular social order; the latter desired a dynamic method of social and political change. Yet the formula that the Gita had set forth met Vivekananda's needs. This appeared in the theory of Karma Yoga (the yoga of action), which taught that one path to self-realization was disinterested action for the welfare of society. The individual should act, but in a religious spirit; that is, in a spirit of renunciation and self-sacrifice, surrendering the fruits of his action to God and to mankind. Few concepts have emerged with more meaning for modern Indian thought than that of Karma Yoga, and Vivekananda, in the concluding chapters of his book called *Karma Yoga*, indicates the meaning that this ideal had for him: 'Give up all fruits of work; do good for its own sake; then alone will come perfect non-attachment. The bonds of the heart will thus break, and we shall reap perfect freedom. This freedom is indeed the goal of Karma Yoga.'[48]

The demand for continuity and innovation in the formulation of a method of action was most fully met by Gandhi. Following the lead of Aurobindo, Gandhi stressed the need for political as well as social service in the individual's quest for freedom.

I am impatient to realize myself to attain moksha in this very existence. My national service is part of my training for freeing my soul ... For me the road to salvation lies through incessant toil in the service of my country. So my patriotism is for me a stage in my journey to the land of eternal freedom and peace. Thus it will be seen that for me there are no politics devoid of religion.[49]

---

48 Vivekananda, *Works*, Vol. 1 (1962), p. 107.

49 Gandhi, *Young India*, 3 April 1924, *CWMG* 23:349

And, in his autobiography, he insisted 'that those who say that religion has nothing to do with politics do not know what religion means.'[50] The marriage of politics and religion had been indicated by Aurobindo; it was consummated in the thought of Gandhi. He, like Aurobindo, blessed the union with sacred symbols and beliefs; unlike Aurobindo, he pointed out the path which both partners should pursue toward their common goal of swaraj. Key traditional words, themes and images—Karma Yoga, renunciation, ahimsa—all blossom forth in Gandhi's great innovation of satyagraha.

At least as early as 1896, one may see in Gandhi's pamphlet, *Grievances of British Indians in South Africa*, the formulation of ideas on the method he later called satyagraha: 'Our method in South Africa is to conquer this hatred by love ... We do not attempt to have individuals punished but, as a rule, patiently suffer wrongs at their hands.'[51] The teaching of the past, however, to which Gandhi constantly turned at this time is the 'precept of the Prophet of Nazareth, "resist not evil"';[52] and the example of the present which he repeatedly praises is that of the British suffragettes.[53] Moreover, during this early period in his weekly issues of *Indian Opinion*, Gandhi recounts and extols the lives of Mazzini, Lincoln, Washington and Lord Nelson, as supreme examples of selfless sacrifice in service of their countries.[54] And, when in September 1906, he urges the South African Indian community to adopt the first resolution on passive resistance, his charge is that the law in question is 'un-British'. Gandhi remained throughout his life a cosmopolitan figure responsive to the influences of both East and West; the striking fact, then, about his ideas in this earliest period, is

---

50 M.K. Gandhi, *An Autobiography*, CWMG 39:401.

51 *CWMG* 2:29.

52 *CWMG* 8:108.

53 *CWMG* 6:336, 385. And 7:65, 73–74, 130, 453.

54 *CWMG* 5:27, 50, 84, 111.

not merely his reliance upon Western examples and values, but rather his dependence on them to the utter exclusion of anything Indian.

A development occurs in Gandhi's thinking in a letter from July 1907, to *The Rand Daily Mail*: 'It may appear ungrateful to have to criticize your moderate and well-meant leaderette on the so-called "passive resistance" to the Asiatic Registration Act. I call the passive resistance to be offered by the Indian community "so-called" because, in my opinion, it is really not resistance but a policy of communal suffering.'[55] Already at this time, Gandhi had begun to dislike the term 'passive resistance', since it was a foreign term which implied principles that he could not wholly accept. 'When in a meeting of Europeans,' he records in his autobiography, 'I found that the term "passive resistance" was too narrowly construed, that it was supposed to be a weapon of the weak, that it could be characterized by hatred, and that it could finally manifest itself as violence, I had to demur to all these statements and explain the real nature of the Indian movement.'[56] Hatred and violence were incompatible with the method that Gandhi had developed because his theory rested squarely on the principle of ahimsa, which he variously translated as 'non-violence', 'love', and 'charity'. This idea of ahimsa he had taken from the Indian tradition, and particularly the Jain religion, where it meant a strict observance of nonviolence. Gandhi fused his own interpretation of this belief with ideas which he found in Tolstoy and the *Sermon on the Mount*; the result was a principle that evoked rich religious symbolism and contributed to a dynamic method of action unique in Indian history.

Any doubts concerning Gandhi's conscious attempt to establish continuity with the Indian tradition in his search for a method of action may be dispelled by a look at the way in which he coined the term satyagraha—a word which had not heretofore existed.

---

55 *CWMG* 7:67.

56 Gandhi, *Autobiography, CWMG* 39:318.

To respect our own language, speak it well and use in it as few foreign words as possible—this is also a part of patriotism. We have been using some English terms just as they are, since we cannot find exact Gujarati equivalents for them. Some of these terms are given below, which we place before our readers. ... The following are the terms in question: Passive Resistance; Passive Resister; Cartoon; Civil Disobedience ... It should be noted that we do not want translations of these English terms, but terms with equivalent connotations.[57]

In this manner, Gandhi announced a contest in *Indian Opinion* for the renaming of 'passive resistance'. The thinking behind this idea of a contest is further explained in his chapter 'The Advent of Satyagraha', in *Satyagraha in South Africa*:

None of us knew what name to give to our movement. I then used the term 'passive resistance' in describing it. I did not quite understand the implications of 'passive resistance', as I called it. I only knew that some new principle had come into being. As the struggle advanced, the phrase 'passive resistance' gave rise to confusion, and it appeared shameful to permit this great struggle to be known only by an English name. Again, that foreign phrase could hardly pass as current coin among the community. A small prize was therefore announced in *Indian Opinion* to be awarded to the reader who invented the best designation for our struggle.[58]

---

57 *CWMG* 7:455.

58 Gandhi, *Satyagraha in South Africa* (Ahmedabad: Navajivan Publishing House, 1961), p. 109. Gandhi relates the result of this contest in his autobiography: 'As a result, Maganlal Gandhi coined the word "Sadagraha" (Sat - truth, Agraha - firmness) and won the prize. But in order to make it clearer, I changed the word to "Satyagraha".' *CWMG* 39:255.

Gandhi's remark here, that a 'foreign phrase could hardly pass as current coin among the community', is noteworthy; but far more significant is his candid admission that 'I did not quite understand the implications of "passive resistance" as I called it. I only knew that some new principle had come into being.' This last sentence makes clear the personal need Gandhi felt for contact with his own tradition. This was a need which increased as Gandhi himself developed as a political thinker; it first found expression in South Africa.

Satyagraha may be seen as a commentary on the themes of continuity and innovation. The new interpretation of social action found in the theory of Karma Yoga and the application of traditional language and symbols to the modern Indian scene were Vivekananda's contributions to a method of social and political change. Vivekananda's approach was further developed by Aurobindo. But it was left for Gandhi to carry it to fruition through his experiments with satyagraha. The theory of satyagraha, however, was no more complete an embodiment of continuity and innovation than the satyagrahi, the Mahatma, behind it: a figure seen by some as a sannyasin, by others as a politician; a man who behaved like a karmayogin, yet spoke in these terms of his mission: 'It is the whole of Hinduism that has to be purified and purged. What I am aiming at ... is the greatest reform of the age.'[59]

---

59 Gandhi, *Harijan*, 12 August 1933, *CWMG* 55:352.

CHAPTER 2

Vivekananda and the Emergence of a Philosophy of Freedom in Modern India

Vivekananda and His Predecessors

Even now, [writes Professor A.L. Basham, in his centenary tribute to Vivekananda] a hundred years after the birth of Narendranath Datta, who later became Swami Vivekananda, it is very difficult to evaluate his importance in the scale of world history. It is certainly far greater than any Western historian, or most Indian historians would have suggested at the time of his death. The passing of the years and the many stupendous and unexpected events which have occurred since then suggest that in centuries to come he will be remembered as one of the main moulders of the modern world, especially as far as Asia is concerned, and as one of the most significant figures in the whole history of Indian religion, comparable in importance to such great teachers as Shankara and Ramanuja, and definitely more important than the saints of local or regional significance such as Kabir, Chaitanya, and the many teachers of the Nayanmars and Alwars of South India.

On the other hand, viewed in the whole sweep of the history of the Hindu religion, we cannot look upon Swami Vivekananda as blazing an entirely new trail, nor certainly, as some otherwise very able missionary writers did in the earlier parts of this century, as a reactionary ... Neither of these pictures is, of course, quite correct. We can only do the great man justice if we also do justice to his predecessors, the people before him who started the process of the revitalization of Hinduism which led up to him, and which continued through the work of such teachers as Sri Aurobindo, Mahatma Gandhi, and Vinoba Bhave.[1]

Vivekananda's considerable achievement as a political thinker rests largely upon the synthesis he created of divergent currents of nineteenth-century Indian thought, channelling them into a mainstream of influence that Aurobindo, Gandhi and Tagore all acknowledged, absorbed and developed. An appreciation of Vivekananda's accomplishment, then, involves a consideration of 'the people before him who started the process of revitalisation of Hinduism which led up to him'. Six prominent nineteenth-century Indian thinkers have been selected for analysis: Rammohun Roy, Debendranath Tagore, Keshub Chunder Sen, Dayananda Saraswati, Bankim Chandra Chatterjee and Sri Ramakrishna Paramahamsa.[2] Three main themes have been chosen, as well, for examination, each representing a focal point of each thinker's position, as well as indicating main points of contact with Vivekananda's thought. These themes include the use of Indian tradition to reinforce radical reform movements; the assertion of a

---

1   A.L. Basham, 'Swami Vivekananda: A Moulder of the Modern World', in *Vedanta for East and West* XII, no. 6 (July–August 1963): 223.

2   Professor Basham cites all of these figures in his article, except Bankim Chandra Chatterjee, as key predecessors of Vivekananda. They are listed here in rough chronological order.

distinction between the spirit and form of Hinduism to support social change; and, finally, the discrimination of two forms of knowledge, 'physical' and 'spiritual', the former being identified with the West, the latter with the Indian tradition.[3] This selection of half a dozen figures, and three major concepts, has been made to sharpen the analysis: the purpose is not to present an exhaustive treatment of nineteenth-century Indian thought; it is rather to concentrate on a few key themes and thinkers; on the roles they played in preparing the climate of ideas in which Vivekananda's thought crystallized.

More than a few studies of modern Indian political thought have begun with the ideas of Rammohun Roy. And Rammohun's reputation is well-deserved. Although he never confronted, in a profound sense, the philosophical problems which have traditionally concerned Western political thought, he did face, with prodigious energy, one of the more formidable challenges of his age: the re-interpretation of Indian tradition in light of the Western impact. His pre-eminence rests with the unprecedented intellectual equipment that he brought to bear on his task: conversant with Sanskrit, Persian and Bengali, he translated, abridged and interpreted ancient Indian texts; steeped in Christian theology, he debated with British missionaries finer points of Biblical writings in the original Greek and Latin. He wished to create a new synthesis of Indian and Western ideas, and he sought to embody this creation in his Brahmo Samaj or Society of God, a religious and ethical movement founded in 1828, which exerted a continuing influence on later Indian thought. Rammohun is known for his eloquent advocacy of Western values and institutions: freedom of the press,[4] maintenance

---

3   This last theme will be referred to here as the 'two cultures' theme, indicating its purpose: to distinguish uniquely 'Indian' and 'Western' cultural patterns and sets of values.

4   Jogendra Chunder Ghose (ed.), *The English Works of Raja Rammohun Roy*, 3 Vols., Vol. II (Calcutta: Srikanta Roy, 1901), pp. 281–86.

of an autonomous judicial system,[5] and extension of the British pattern
of education.[6] On the basis of these crucial issues, he has been rightly
regarded as a prophet of innovation.

Yet, there was another equally important aspect of Rammohun's
thought: a strong commitment to the teachings of his own tradition
as he saw them. He lavished praise on the 'government under which
they [Indians] may enjoy the liberty and privileges so dear to persons of
enlightened minds';[7] but he also insisted that this was a state of affairs
consonant with the spirit of ancient Indian tradition. In his relentless
campaign against sati, Rammohun attacked Hindu orthodoxy, and
exhorted reluctant British officials, until the practice was proscribed by
law; yet, it should be noted that his arguments do not rest on Western
evidence or examples, but rather upon his own interpretation of classical
Indian texts. His first tract on the subject, which takes the form of a
dialogue between an advocate and an opponent of sati, begins:

> *Advocate.* I am surprised that you endeavour to oppose the practice
> of Concremation and Postcremation of widows, as long observed
> in this country.

> *Opponent.* Those who have no reliance on the Shastra, and those
> who take delight in the self-destruction of women, may well
> wonder that we should oppose that suicide which is forbidden by
> all the Shastras, and by every race of men.

The subsequent argument abounds with quotations from the Vedas,
the Code of Manu and the *Bhagavad Gita*.[8] The sequel to this attack,

---

5   Ibid., pp. 11–18.

6   Ibid., pp. 324–27.

7   Ibid., p. 118.

8   Ibid., pp. 123–92.

significantly entitled 'Brief Remarks Regarding Modern Encroachments on the Ancient Right of Females, According to the Hindoo Law of Inheritance', is again replete with references to traditional Indian texts in its broad advocacy of the rights of Indian women.[9]

Rammohun's assiduous attempts to use the Indian past in support of social change were underpinned by his crucial distinction between the spirit and form of Hinduism. The social change that India needed, he insisted, should not be seen as Western reform, but rather as a re-affirmation of the spirit of the Indian tradition. In his *Defence of Hindu Theism*, he contends,

In none of my writings, nor in any verbal discussion, have I ever pretended to reform or to discover the doctrines of the unity of God, nor have I ever assumed the title of reformer or discoverer; so far from such an assumption, I have urged in every work that I have hitherto published, that the doctrines of the unity of God are real Hindooism, as that religion was practiced by our ancestors, and as it is well-known even at the present age to many learned Brahmins: I beg to repeat a few of the passages to which I allude.

In the introduction to the abridgment of the Vedant, I have said: 'In order, therefore, to vindicate my own faith and that of our forefathers, I have been endeavouring, for some time past, to convince my countrymen of the true meaning of our sacred books, and prove that my aberration deserves not the opprobrium which some unreflecting persons have been so ready to throw upon me.' In another place of the same introduction: 'The present is an endeavour to render an abridgment of the same (in Vedant) into English, by which I expect to prove to my European friends, that the superstitious practices which deform the Hindoo religion, have nothing to do with the pure spirit of its dictates.' In the introduction of the Kenopanishad: 'This work will, I trust, by explaining to my countrymen *the* real spirit of the Hindoo scriptures, which is but

---

9   Ibid., pp. 195–208.

the declaration of the unity of God, tend in a great degree to correct the erroneous conceptions which have prevailed with regard to the doctrines they inculcate.'[10]

And, in his Autobiographical Sketch, Rammohun wrote,

The ground which I took in all my controversies was, not that of opposition to Brahminism, but to a perversion of it; and I endeavoured to show that the idolatry[11] of the Brahmins was contrary to the practice of their ancestors, and the principles of the ancient books and authorities which they profess to revere and obey.[12]

The critical importance, for Vivekananda and others of his school, of this distinction between 'the true meaning of our sacred books' and 'their perversion' has been indicated in the last chapter; indeed, it provided much of the rationale for the whole attempt at 'preservation by reconstruction'.

If the distinction between the spirit and form of Hinduism was used to support domestic change within Indian society itself, then another means was employed to distinguish the superior nature of the spirit of Indian thought vis-à-vis the West. This argument sought to draw a sharp dichotomy between the spiritual nature of traditional Indian thought and the materialistic qualities of Western knowledge. Dr David Friedman has placed this argument in its proper perspective by pointing to its long history as well as to its inevitable shallowness.

---

10 Ibid., I, pp. 126–27.

11 Rammohun often asserted his opposition to 'idolatry'; but, as Debendranath Tagore repeatedly pointed out, idolatry for the Brahmos included not only worship of clay images, but all outmoded forms of Hinduism.

12 Ibid., p. 319.

For a long time it has been generally the practice on the part of both Oriental and European authors to associate the Western and Indian forms of civilisation and thought respectively with an active and affirmative philosophy of life on the one hand, and a pessimistic and 'other-worldly' one on the other. Frequently, too, Western positivism, naturalism, secularism, and materialism are confronted with the inborn spirituality, metaphysical idealism, mysticism, and intuitionalism of the East.

It is obvious that no such hard-and-fast distinctions between East and West can be made. They are a matter of emphasis rather than fact. Nowhere can the manifold expressions of human thought be imprisoned in watertight compartments. The history of human ideas evolves by contrasts. Although it is true that within the common frame of reference of a particular civilisation new philosophies grow on the basis of the old, they are mostly created in critical opposition to prevailing ideas. There is no doubt that to a large extent modern Western civilisation is dynamic, positivistic and scientific. Its deeper and essential impulses, however, are derived from a basic philosophical idealism—both Christian and humanistic—which in a perpetual struggle with rigid traditionalism has created the modes of free thought essential to human progress.[13]

The superficiality of such sweeping categorizations, however, did not preclude their widespread use by modern Indian political thinkers. Although Rammohun Roy generally maintained an unbiased position, he did succumb to the temptation of this argument, if only in response to the goading of zealous Christian missionaries.

Rammohun's position appeared in a controversy with a missionary Dr R. Tytler; the polemical nature of the exchange is suggested in this opening volley from 'A Christian', writing in defence of Dr Tytler's position:

---

13 David Friedman, 'Hinduism', in *The Year Book of Education* (London: Evans Brothers, 1951), p. 226.

Sir, It is gratifying to the lovers of science, to behold a few intelligent Hindoos emerging from the degraded ignorance and shameful superstition, in which their fathers for so many centuries have been buried ... On the other hand it is a sad contemplation, that these very individuals who are indebted to Christians for the civil liberty they enjoy, as well as for the rays of intelligence, now beginning to dawn on them, should in the most ungenerous manner insult their benefactors, by endeavouring to degrade their religion, for no other reason, but because they cannot comprehend its sublime Mysteries.[14]

Rammohun replied,

If by the 'Ray of Intelligence' for which the *Christian* says we are indebted to the English, he means the introduction of useful mechanical arts, I am ready to express my assent and also my gratitude; but with respect to *Science, Literature*, or *Religion*, I do not acknowledge that we are placed under any obligation. For by a reference to History it may be proved that the World was indebted to *our ancestors* for the first dawn of knowledge, which sprung up in the East, and thanks to the Goddess of Wisdom, we have still a philosophical and copious language of our own, which distinguishes us from other nations who cannot express scientific or abstract ideas without borrowing the language of foreigners.[15]

Rammohun does not, as later Indian thinkers were inclined to do, condemn Western technology as nothing but a crass form of materialism; rather, he expresses his 'assent and gratitude' for the 'introduction of useful and mechanical arts'. Yet, the distinction stands,[16] and it carries

---

14 *The English Works of Raja Rammohun Roy*, Vol. III, p. 145.

15 Ibid., p. 148.

16 Rammohun's differentiation between 'science' and 'useful mechanical arts' points out another prominent tendency of modern Indian

with it the claim to a kind of superiority which provided deceptive comfort to later Indian writers. One ramification of this argument was Rammohun's identification (in this same letter) of Christianity with the Indian tradition: 'almost all the ancient prophets and patriarchs venerated by Christians, nay even Jesus Christ himself, a Divine Incarnation and the *founder* of the Christian Faith, were ASIATICS, so that if a Christian thinks it degrading to be born or to reside in *Asia,* he directly reflects upon them.'[17] This contention, which seeks to explain Western moral and spiritual ideas on the basis of the Asian origin of Christianity, ignores, of course, the long and profound development of these ideas in a European context; yet, the argument became an accepted tenet of Indian thought, reiterated by Vivekananda.

These, then, were the three themes as set forth by Rammohun Roy; and his statement of them in this early period of modern Indian thought, indicates, in part, the seminal nature of his influence. Perhaps more importantly than this, however, Rammohun's thought manifests the divergent directions which Indian ideas were already following in response to the Western impact. The fact that Rammohun may be seen both as the progenitor of the more Western-orientated reform movement led by Ranade and Gokhale, as well as a proponent of themes later developed by Vivekananda, has earned him the title,

---

thinkers: the attempt to appropriate the whole field of scientific studies to ancient Indian thought. The long development of Western thinking on science is then reduced to 'technology', an inferior outgrowth of the tradition of science as begun in India. The point here is not, of course, that India lacked early scientific achievements; it is only that any attempt to draw sharp distinctions of this nature inevitably neglects, by the very logic of the argument, similar accomplishments of other civilizations.

17 *The English Works of Raja Rammohun Roy,* Vol. III, p. 149.

'The Father of Modern India'.[18] Yet, Rammohun may also be seen as a figure in whom the main intellectual currents of the period had already begun to assert their stark contradictions, and the problem that these contradictions posed became an increasingly urgent one for men in search of harmony.

The inheritor of Rammohun's mantle, as leader of a revivified Brahmo Samaj, was Debendranath Tagore. Rammohun's vigorous efforts at purifying Hinduism, that its spirit might prevail over its perversions, were continued by Debendranath; and he, like his predecessor, became concerned with the use of Indian tradition in fostering reform movements. There is, however, a noteworthy difference between them: if Rammohun represents a cosmopolitan scholar standing astride two great traditions and committed wholly to neither, a figure suggesting, to India, the choice to be made, then in Debendranath, the path has been chosen; for he went further than Rammohun, he became the Maharshi, sage of India.

> We are in and of the great Hindu community [he declared] and it devolves upon us by example and precept to hold up to us a beacon the highest truths of the Hindu shastras. In their light must we purify our heritage of customs, usages, rites, and ceremonies and adapt them to the needs of our conscience and our community. But we must beware of proceeding too fast in matters of social change, lest we be separated from the greater body whom we would guide and uplift.[19]

An insight, not found in Rammohun's writings, into the deeply personal struggle for a reconciliation of Western with Indian ideas occurs in Debendranath's *Autobiography*. If Rammohun's attempts at syncretism

---

18 William Theodore de Bary (ed.), *Sources of Indian Tradition* (Oxford: Oxford University Press, 1958), p. 572.

19 Quoted in Ibid., p. 610.

often appear as purely academic pursuits, Debendranath's narratives reveal an intense psychological commitment to the task at hand.

As on the one hand [he writes in his Autobiography] there were my Sanskrit studies in the search after truth, so on the other hand there was English. I had read numerous English works on philosophy. But with all this, the sense of emptiness of mind remained just the same; nothing could heal it; my heart was being oppressed by that gloom of sadness and feeling of unrest. Did subjection to Nature comprise the whole of man's existence? I asked. Then indeed are we undone.

The might of this monster is indomitable ...

What can we hope for, whom can we trust? Again I thought, as things are reflected on a photographic plate by the rays of the sun, so are material objects manifested to the mind by the senses; this is what is called knowledge. Is there any other way but this of obtaining knowledge? These were the suggestions that Western philosophy has brought to my mind. To an atheist this is enough, he does not want anything beyond Nature. But how could I rest fully satisfied with this? My endeavour was to obtain God, not through blind faith but by the light of knowledge. And being unsuccessful in this, my mental struggles increased from day to day. Sometimes I thought I could live no longer.

Suddenly, as I thought and thought, a flash as of lightning broke through this darkness of despondency. I saw that knowledge of the material world is born of the senses and the objects of sight, sound, smell, touch and taste. But together with this knowledge, I am also enabled to know that I am the knower. Simultaneously with the facts of seeing, touching, smelling, and thinking, I also come to know that it is I who see, touch, smell, and think. With the knowledge of objects comes the knowledge of the subject; with the knowledge of the body comes the knowledge of the spirit within. It was after a prolonged search for truth that I found this bit of light, as if a ray of sunshine had fallen on a place full of extreme darkness.

I now realised that with the knowledge of the outer world we come
to know our inner self.[20]

'I now realised that with the knowledge of the outer world we come
to know our inner self': this is the correspondence that Indian
thinkers stress throughout the nineteenth century; in this, they found
a reconciliation between their understanding of the West as 'outer
world', and of the Indian tradition as embodying the 'inner self'. It is
ironic that men who possessed such a remarkable facility for making
conceptual correspondences should have been so sorely tested by
their own needlessly stark differentiation between the philosophies
of East and West. Debendranath's narrative places their problem in
the perspective it deserves: this was not always a clever chauvinist
contrivance to assert a form of cultural superiority but was often an
honest belief, which, to a considerable extent, victimized its believers.

When, in 1859, Keshub Chunder Sen entered the Brahmo Samaj
and quickly became the chief disciple of Debendranath Tagore, it
appeared that its future leadership was ensured. Yet, in six years, the
organization was to be irrevocably split by disagreement, Keshub
withdrawing to form his own movement. One source of conflict
between Debendranath and his disciple was the former's suspicion of
Keshub as a 'semi-Europeanised young innovator', a 'denationalised
radical'.[21] In one sense, such doubts are understandable: Keshub
appears to have been a highly complex personality, who could be seen
by Debendranath as a semi-Europeanized innovator, and by a Western

---

20 Debendranath Tagore, *The Autobiography of Maharshi Debendranath
Tagore*, trans. Satyendranath Tagore and Indira Devi (London:
Macmillan, 1916), pp. 47–49.

21 P.C. Mozoomdar, *The Life and Teachings of Keshub Chunder Sen*
(Calcutta: Thacker Spink, 1891), p. 96.

academic as the prophet of 'the Indianisation of Christianity'.[22] He was, like Rammohun Roy, a representative of two traditions, but, unlike Rammohun, he pursued each with an intemperate zeal that, if anything, rendered his great aim in life, a harmony of Eastern and Western thought all the more difficult to attain. His complexity is further shown by Mozoomdar's passing observation that Keshub was visited on his deathbed by Ramakrishna, Debendranath Tagore and the Bishop of Calcutta.[23] There was a little of each of these figures in Keshub himself, and his life and thought may be seen as an attempt to harmonize his own, as well as the world's diversities.

One of the most ardent advocates of social reform of his age, Keshub established, in 1870, the 'Indian Reform Association'; patterned after its European counterparts, its aims sharply conflicted with Hindu orthodoxy. Yet Keshub did not see himself as a Europeanized reformer:

> What is the programme of reforms you think I intend to lay before you this evening? Not half-measures, like the education of this section of the community or the reformation of that particular social evil. I would most emphatically say that I do not belong to that school of secular reformers according to whom Indian reform means nothing more than strong garrisons on the frontier, irrigation, female education, intermarriage, and widow-marriage. These cannot—it is my most firm conviction—these cannot lift India as a nation from the mire of idolatry, of moral and social corruption. If you wish to regenerate this country, make religion the basis of all your reform movements.[24]

---

22 Stephen Hay in de Bary, *Sources of Indian Tradition*, p. 615.

23 Mozoomdar, *The Life and Teachings of Keshub Chunder Sen*, p. 279.

24 *Keshub Chunder Sen's Lectures in India*, Part II (Calcutta: The Brahmo Tract Society, 1900), p. 187.

This religion, he made clear, must be based not on the forms but on the spirit of Hinduism: 'Upon the surface of Hinduism floats what is popular, superstitious and erroneous. Its deeper spirituality does not often come within the range of our observation. He therefore who dives below and rescues and restores the buried pearls will have done most valuable service not only to his own country but to the whole religious world.'[25] Keshub dived and came up with a universal gospel which he called 'The New Dispensation, The Religion of Harmony'. Yet his devotion to harmony did not blind him to the highly distinctive characteristics of the two traditions which he sought to fuse.

In his essay, 'The New Dispensation—Its European and Its Asiatic Side', he wrote,

The faith that has come down to us from heaven has two aspects, the one eastern and the other western. It has a European side, and the other side is eminently Asiatic. The East loves and honours the New Dispensation as its own, and so does the West. Those traits in it which are of the European style are as follows:—

The New Dispensation is thoroughly scientific. It hates whatsoever is unscientific. It has an abhorrence of delusions and myths.

It is empirical, and relies upon observation and experiment. It has no hypothesis, and it takes nothing on trust.

It stands the severest logical tests, and is made up of demonstrable truths.

It is supported by reasoning, inductive and deductive.

It harmonizes with the latest discoveries of science and keeps pace with the progress of philosophy and exact science.

The Asiatic and oriental aspect of the New Dispensation remains to be explained. Born in the East, amid its peculiar traditions and influences, it is no wonder that it should grow as an Asiatic

25 Keshub Chunder Sen, *The New Dispensation, Or, the Religion of Harmony* (Calcutta: Bidhan Press, 1903), p. 81.

institution with marked Asiatic features. However occidental its development may have been, its root is essentially oriental. Its industry and dialectics, its intellectual and practical character tell us it is a western system of faith. But there are other features in it which show forth its eastern origin. Wherein consists this oriental character we show below ...

The New Dispensation is transcendentally spiritual. Its eyes are naturally turned inward and they see vividly the spirit-world within.

It prefers the soul-kingdom to the kingdom of the senses. It abhors materialism.

It always magnifies the spirit, and spiritualizes everything it touches.

It sees with the spirit-eye and hears with the spirit-ear. It drinks inspiration.

It builds the eternal city, the kingdom of heaven within, and dwells therein all the spare hours of the day.

The New Dispensation is the religion of poverty and asceticism ...

It is the object of the Church of the New Dispensation:—

To reconcile and harmonize the various systems of religion in the world.

To make all churches in the East and the West one undivided and universal Church of God ...

To reconcile ancient faith and modern science.

To reconcile philosophy and inspiration.

To reconcile asceticism and civilization.

To reconcile pure Hinduism and pure Christianity.

To harmonize the East and West, Asia and Europe, antiquity and modern thought.[26]

The dichotomy is drawn here in its sharpest possible outline: this devotee of harmony saw little, in Asia and the West, that was not

---

26 Sen, *The New Dispensation*, pp. 250–54.

in need of harmonizing. Indeed, the traits of the two traditions are polarized in Keshub's writings far more than in other thinkers.

The attitude, if not the doctrine, of Swami Dayananda Saraswati resembles that of Vivekananda more than any of the early Indian thinkers. For with Dayananda, the Indian response to the West becomes militant: the attempt is not merely to defend Hinduism, but to construct, on its basis, a philosophy of strength. The first source of Dayananda's influence appears in the sheer aggressiveness of his approach, which made an indelible impression upon later Indian theorists.

> Among the great company of remarkable figures [wrote Aurobindo] that will appear to the eye of posterity at the head of the Indian Renascence, one stands out by himself with peculiar and solitary distinctness, one unique in his work. It is as if one were to walk for a long time amid a range of hills rising to a greater or lesser altitude, but all with sweeping contours, green-clad, flattering the eye even in their most bold and striking elevation. But amidst them all, one hill stands apart, piled up in sheer strength, a mass of bare and puissant granite, with verdure on its summit, a solitary pine jutting out into the blue, a great cascade of pure, vigorous and fertilising water gushing out from its strength as a very fountain of life and health to the valley. Such is the impression created on my mind by Dayananda.[27]

Rammohun and Debendranath each had their skirmishes with the missionaries; at one point, in his *Autobiography*, Debendranath proudly tells of a successful confrontation with zealous Christians and concludes, 'thenceforward the tide of Christian conversion was stemmed, and the

---

27 Aurobindo, *Bankim-Tilak-Dayananda* (Pondicherry: Sri Aurobindo Ashram, 1955), p. 39.

cause of the missionary received a serious blow'.[28] But if Rammohun and Debendranath were content with stemming the Western tide, Dayananda tried to reverse it. And, for a moment in Indian history, this figure did stand, powerful and defiant, declaring that all truth, spiritual and scientific, inhered in the Vedas; India's emancipation, he insisted, depended on nothing more than devotion to her own tradition. In 1875, Dayananda founded the Arya Samaj,[29] which continued this militant tradition; but his main thrust quickly lost its momentum, rejecting as it did that element which became central to Vivekananda's whole approach: a frank assimilation of Western ideas. Although few Indian writers followed Dayananda's particular interpretations of the Vedas, Aurobindo's remark that 'Dayananda's work brings back such a principle and spirit of the past to vivify a modern mould',[30] indicates the influence which the general direction of his effort exerted.

Dayananda's attempt to underwrite social change with passages from Vedic texts was the most uncompromising of any of the early Indian reformers. In the Vedas, Dayananda discovered a striking consonance with nineteenth-century Western views on marriage and widow re-marriage; education and the rights of women; the constitutional nature of good government and the supremacy of law; the desirability of a fluid class structure; and, on the need for India to engage in international trade, commerce and social intercourse.[31]

If Dayananda did find all of this in the Vedas, he was at least aware of what to look for: if he saw no need to import ideas from a foreign

---

28 Tagore, *The Autobiography of Maharshi Debendranath Tagore*, p. 101.

29 'Society of the Aryas'.

30 Aurobindo, *Bankim-Tilak-Dayananda*, p. 45.

31 Dayananda Saraswati, *Light of Truth* or *Satyarth Prakash*, trans. Chiranjiva Bharadwaja (Lahore: K.S.V. Bharadwaja, 1927). The respective pages are 81, 23, 28, 74, 150, 152–53, 73, 87, 299.

source, he ceaselessly sought the reconciliation, in his own way, of the Indian tradition with the flood of new ideas that surrounded it. This overriding concern for harmony is expressed in the closing sentences of his major work, *Satyarth Prakash*, in terms that resemble those later to be used by Vivekananda:

> The sole aim of my life, [writes Dayananda] which I have also endeavoured to achieve, is to help to put an end to this mutual wrangling, preach universal truths, bring all men into the fold of one religion whereby they may cease to hate each other and, instead, may firmly love one another, live in peace and work for their commonweal. May this doctrine, through the grace and help of God, with the support of all truthful, honest and learned men who are devoted to the cause of humanity reach every nook and corner of this earth so that all may acquire righteousness, wealth, gratify legitimate desires and attain salvation and thereby elevate themselves and live in happiness. This alone is the chief object (of my life).[32]

Dayananda represents an extreme form of the nineteenth-century return to the Indian tradition, and Western thinkers have often sharply contrasted his position with that of Rammohun Roy—the former founder of the Arya Samaj—who usually appears as a vociferous, uncompromising reactionary; a sad but understandable casualty of the revivalist movement. Rammohun, conversely, is often portrayed as a liberal, tolerant and objective eclectic. On the basis of the analysis of the three themes considered here, however, there appears to be considerable agreement between these two reformers: each used the Hindu tradition to encourage social change, and each reinterpreted his religion in the process. Each based his interpretation on a distinction

---

32 Ibid., p. 685.

between the spirit and form of Hinduism, contending that post-Vedic accretions were perversions of ancient wisdom. On the last theme, Dayananda and Rammohun both assumed Indian supremacy in the realm of spiritual knowledge; Rammohun, however, admitted the unprecedented nature of Western technology. Yet they joined in a common quest for reconciliation of the divergent streams of thought prevalent in nineteenth-century India. It may be legitimately argued that substantial differences occur in their respective interpretations of Hinduism, but the fundamental similarities in their responses to the Western impact must also be affirmed.

The consideration, here, of Bankim Chandra Chatterjee, will concentrate on his novel *Anandamath*, which has been called 'Bankim's greatest contribution to the early growth of nationalism'.[33] In this work, he set down the words '*Bande Mataram*' (literally, 'Hail to the Mother'), which eventually became the anthem of the Indian nationalist movement. 'It was thirty-two years ago,' wrote Aurobindo in 1907, 'that Bankim wrote his great song and few listened; but in a sudden moment of awakening from long delusions, the people of Bengal looked round for the truth, and in a fated moment somebody sang *'Bande Mataram'*. The mantra had been given, and in a single day, a whole people had been converted to the religion of patriotism.'[34] In the final chapter of *Anandamath*, a remarkable passage occurs which embodies, in a condensed form, many of the ideas dominant in Bankim's period; and, in its distinction between 'spiritual' and 'physical' knowledge, it indicates clearly the two cultures theme.

33 T.W. Clark, 'The Role of Bankimcandra in the Development of Nationalism', in *Historians of India, Pakistan and Ceylon*, ed. C.H. Philips (London: Oxford University Press, 1961), p. 438.

34 Aurobindo, *Bankim-Tilak-Dayananda*, p. 13.

The historical background of *Anandamath* is the Sannyasi Rebellion in Bengal of the 1770s, which is described by Warren Hastings.[35] The novel's heroes are a band of Sannyasis led by Satyananda, an irreproachably pure but rather belligerent ascetic. At the conclusion of the story, the Sannyasis have defeated the Muslims and British in battle. Satyananda wants to pursue the rebellion, attacking the main British force in Calcutta, thus liberating the Motherland from foreign domination. At this point, however, Bankim has a supernatural character intervene, who, speaking to Satyananda with the voice of God, counsels him as follows:

He: Hindu dominion will not be established now. If you remain at your work, men will be killed to no purpose. Therefore come.

S (*greatly pained*): My lord, if Hindu dominion is not going to be established, who will rule? Will the Muslim kings return?

He: No. The English will rule.

S (*turning tearfully to the image of her who symbolized the land of his birth*): Alas, my mother! I have failed to set you free. Once again you will fall into the hands of infidels. Forgive your son. Alas, my mother! Why did I not die on the battlefield?

He: Grieve not. You have won wealth; but it was by violence and robbery, for your mind was deluded. No pure fruit can grow on a sinful tree. You will never set your country free in that way. What is going to happen now is for the best. If the English do not rule, there is no hope of a revival of our eternal Faith. I tell you what the wise know. True religion is not to be found in the worship of 33 crores of gods; that is a vulgar, debased religion, which has obscured that which is true. True Hinduism consists in knowledge not in

35 J.K. Das Gupta, *A Critical Study of the Life and Novels of Bankimcandra* (Calcutta: Calcutta University, 1937), p. 104.

action. Knowledge is of two kinds, physical and spiritual. Spiritual knowledge is the essential part of Hinduism. If however physical knowledge does not come first, spiritual knowledge can never be born. If you do not understand the physical body, you will never comprehend the subtle spirit within. Now physical knowledge has long since disappeared from our land, and so true religion has gone too. If you wish to restore true religion, you must first teach this physical knowledge. Such knowledge is unknown in this country because there is no one to teach it. So we must learn it from foreigners. The English are wise in this knowledge, and they are good teachers. Therefore we must make the English rule. Once the people of India have acquired knowledge of the physical world from the English, they will be able to comprehend the nature of the spiritual. There will then be no obstacle to the true Faith. True religion will then shine forth again of itself. Until that happens, and until Hindus are wise and virtuous and strong, the English power will remain unbroken. Under the English our people will be happy, and there will be no impediment to our teaching our faith. So, wise one, stop fighting against the English and follow me.[36]

Spiritual knowledge is regarded, here, as 'the essential part of Hinduism', and, considering the source of the counsel, is thought superior to physical knowledge. Yet, the latter, explicitly associated with the English, becomes a prerequisite for spiritual knowledge: 'If however physical knowledge does not come first spiritual knowledge will never comprehend the subtle spirit within.' And, 'Once the people of India have acquired knowledge of the physical world from the English, they will be able to comprehend the nature of the spiritual.' The closest correspondence is thus drawn here, as in Debendranath's thought, between these two forms of knowledge, and the whole of the

---

36 Translation by Clark, 'The Role of Bankimcandra', in *Historians of India, Pakistan and Ceylon*, pp. 442–43.

two cultures theme is set forth as explicitly, in this passage, as in the writings of any of Vivekananda's predecessors.

Influences upon Vivekananda Assessed

A main purpose of this chapter has been to suggest that the climate of opinion within which Vivekananda developed his political thought had a profound effect on his conclusions and that the nature of this influence was both Western and Indian in character. A closer examination may now be made of more specifics aspects of these influences. On the Western side, the main sources were British liberal thought and Christianity. T.W. Clark, in his article 'The Role of Bankimcandra in the Development of Nationalism', has pointed out Bankim's own acknowledgement of English influences on his ideas of freedom and of the evolution of society. 'By reading English,' Bankim said, 'Bengalis have learned two new words, Liberty and Independence.'[37] Moreover, Bankim specifically names Darwin and Herbert Spencer as the inspirations for his theory of social evolution.[38] Since the concepts of both freedom and social evolution are central concerns for Vivekananda, the extent of direct Western influence on these two ideas, as they occur in his thought, should be examined.

In regard to Vivekananda's idea of freedom, it was observed in the last chapter that he attributes his conception of political and social liberty to Western thought; and, since Vivekananda was acquainted with utilitarian ideas, especially those of J.S. Mill, he may easily have derived this concept from there, or from eighteenth- and nineteenth-century British liberal thought in general. Although the idea of political liberty was only one facet of Vivekananda's conception of the

---

37 As quoted in Ibid., p. 442.

38 Ibid., p. 434.

meaning of freedom, the inspiration for this one aspect, at least, was undoubtedly Western.

The extent of Darwin's and Spencer's influence on Vivekananda's theory of evolution deserves consideration, for, as a student of the natural sciences, Vivekananda had, of course, read Darwin, and he later became so attracted to Spencer's thought that he corresponded with him. A cursory comparison of Spencer's ideas with those of Vivekananda indicates some broad similarities: each made freedom a central concept in his political thought; each held government in suspect as a threat to individual liberty; and each envisioned as his utopia, 'the blessedness of final anarchy'.[39] Finally, both emphasized the evolutionary nature of man's development in society as a moral being, rising to increasingly higher levels of consciousness.[40]

A closer examination of their thought, however, reveals the fundamental differences between them, the crucial points at which Vivekananda stressed traditional Indian themes. First, Spencer respected liberty, but not in a spiritual sense, as the supreme goal of all human existence. Spencer prided himself too much on the 'scientific' nature of his philosophy to speak of freedom as did Vivekananda. 'The awakening of the soul,' said the latter, 'to its bondage and its effort to stand up and assert itself—this is called life. Success in this struggle is called evolution. The eventual triumph, when all slavery is blown away, is called salvation, Nirvana, freedom.'[41] Both men saw in the evolutionary process the grand story of human development; but with Vivekananda, the process began with 'the awakening of the soul' and ended with the attainment of spiritual liberation.

---

39 Sir Ernest Barker, *Political Thought in England, 1848 to 1914* (London: Oxford University Press, 1959), pp. 79–30.

40 Ibid., p. 83.

41 Vivekananda, *Works*, Vol. 8 (1959), p. 249.

An equally fundamental difference appears in their respective views of the dynamics of evolution. Spencer conceives the final level of human development as a stage of social integration and harmony; but when referring to the evolution towards that state, he always speaks in terms 'of struggle, selection, and survival of the fittest as the laws of society'.[42]

Vivekananda, conversely, denies that such laws exist, and sees the evolutionary process governed not by competition, but by a peaceful unfolding of man's nature. Not only did he attempt to refute the positions of Spencer and Darwin on this point but he also tried to do it, characteristically, with the use of traditional Indian sources. His most complete statement on evolution was made in a discussion on the Darwinian theory, with the Superintendent of the Zoological Garden at Alipur.

You are certainly aware [said Vivekananda] of the laws of struggle for existence, survival of the fittest, natural selection and so forth, which have been held by the Western scholars to be the causes of elevating a lower species to a higher. But none of these has been advocated as the cause of that in the system Patanjali. Patanjali holds that the transformation of one species into another is effected by the 'in-filling of nature' (प्रकृत्यापूरात्). It is not that this is done by the constant struggle against obstacles. In my opinion, struggle and competition sometimes stand in the way of a being attaining its perfection. If the evolution of an animal is effected by the destruction of a thousand others, then one must confess that this evolution is doing very little good to the world. Taking it for granted that it conduces to physical well-being, we cannot help admitting that it is a serious obstacle to spiritual development. According to the philosophers of our country, every being is a perfect Soul, and the diversity of evolution and manifestation of nature is simply due to the difference in the degree of manifestation of this Soul.

---

42 Barker, *Political Thought in England*, p. 114.

The moment the obstacles to the evolution and manifestation of nature are completely removed, the Soul manifests Itself perfectly. Whatever may happen in the lower strata of nature's evolutions, in the higher strata at any rate, it is not true that it is only by constantly struggling against obstacles that one has to go beyond them. Rather it is observed that there the obstacles give way and a greater manifestation of the Soul takes place through education and culture, through concentration and meditation, and above all through sacrifice. Therefore, to designate the obstacles not as the effects but as the causes of the Soul-manifestation, and describe them as aiding this wonderful diversity of nature, is not consonant with reason. The attempt to remove evil from the world by killing a thousand evildoers only adds to the evil in the world. But if the people can be made to desist from evil-doing by means of spiritual instruction, there is no more evil in the world. Now, see how horrible the Western struggle theory becomes![43]

Vivekananda is replying to the West, and though this in itself establishes some influence from Darwin and Spencer, a more important implication lies in the nature of his response: his emphasis is consistently upon a harmony rather than a conflict of interests, an evolution which is spiritual in nature and attains its highest level 'above all through sacrifice'—a theme later developed by Aurobindo, Gandhi and Tagore.

The necessary interrelation of conflict and progress has been a recurrent theme of modern Western political thought: it appears, throughout the nineteenth century not only in minor figures like Herbert Spencer but in the ideas of Hegel and Marx as well. And, at the close of that century, in 1896, before a Harvard seminar, Vivekananda spoke out against 'that horrible idea of competition', and continued,

The more I study history, the more I find that idea to be wrong. Some say that if man did not fight with man, he would not progress. I also used to think so; but I find now that every war has thrown

---

43 Vivekananda, *Works*, Vol. 7 (1958), pp. 152–53.

back human progress by fifty years instead of hurrying it forwards. The day will come when men will study history from a different light and find that competition is neither the cause nor the effect, simply a thing on the way, not necessary to evolution at all.[44]

Thus, while Spencer and Vivekananda both stress the evolutionary nature of man and society, substantial differences remain in their respective views on the nature of man, the Absolute, and the meaning of freedom. These fundamental differences occur not only between Vivekananda and Spencer: they are representative of this school's general position vis-à-vis modern Western political thought.

The greatest Western influence on Vivekananda, in a direct personal sense, probably came from the example and teachings of Jesus Christ. Christianity, in general, introduced many ideas, of course, which shaped the intellectual atmosphere of nineteenth-century India; and Vivekananda was well exposed to them during his education in the Scottish Church College of Calcutta.[45] But he seems to have been especially moved by the life of Christ, and he readily acknowledged it. 'Had I lived in Palestine in the days of Jesus of Nazareth,' he once said, 'I would have washed His feet, not with my tears but with my heart's blood!'[46] It is significant, too, that Vivekananda, immediately after Ramakrishna's death, gathered the disciples together, and preached to them of Jesus Christ. 'Naren began to tell the story of the Lord Jesus,' relates one of Vivekananda's disciples, 'beginning with the wondrous mystery of his birth through his death onto the resurrection. Through the eloquence of Narendra, the boys were admitted into that apostolic world wherein Paul had preached the gospel of the Arisen Christ

---

44 Vivekananda, *Works*, Vol. 5 (1959), p. 278.

45 By His Eastern and Western Disciples, *The Life of Swami Vivekananda* (Calcutta: Advaita Ashrama, 1960), p. 24.

46 Ibid., p. 449.

and spread Christianity far and wide. Naren made his plea to them to become Christs themselves, to aid in the redemption of the world, to realise God and to deny themselves as the Lord Jesus had done.'[47] Whether the original inspiration for some of Vivekananda's ideas came from Christian or Indian influences, Vivekananda makes clear that they were at least confirmed by the teaching of Christ.

Among Indian influences, the analysis may be made on the basis of the three themes which have been traced in the writings of Vivekananda's predecessors. Each of these themes represents a crucial element in Vivekananda's thought. In one sense, Vivekananda was as radical a social reformer as any that had preceded him: 'Everything,' he asserted, 'has now to be recast in new moulds.'[48] These new moulds, however, were designed after old patterns: 'It is out of this [the Indian] past that the future has to be moulded; this past will become the future.'[49] The difference between reform which drew on the Indian tradition, and that which did not, became, for Vivekananda, a most crucial distinction: the latter seemed to him destructive, while the former, at its best, furthered a natural evolutionary process, in accord with the deeper needs of Indian society. 'To the reformers,' he said with Ranade especially in mind, 'I will point out that I am a greater reformer than any one of them. They want to reform only little bits. I want root-and-branch reform. Where we differ is in the method. Theirs is the method of destruction, mine is that of construction. I do not believe in reform; I believe in growth.'[50] There were many elements in the Indian tradition which Vivekananda emphatically rejected, and his idea of growth meant that India must not merely recall her past, but

47 Ibid., p. 159.

48 Vivekananda, *Works*, Vol. 7 (1958), p. 33.

49 Vivekananda, *Works*, Vol. 4 (1955), p. 234.

50 Vivekananda, *Works*, Vol. 3 (1960), p. 213.

improve upon it.[51] His desire to resolve the tension created by this clash of two traditions becomes clear in his plea, 'Let us be as progressive as any nation that ever existed, and at the same time as faithful and conservative towards our traditions as Hindus alone know how to be.'[52]

The method he employed, as a social reformer, to underpin his arguments involved a distinction between the spirit and form of the Indian tradition.[53] This means had been used many times before him, but no Indian, prior to Vivekananda, had pressed this distinction so forcefully upon his countrymen. The strength of Vivekananda's influence lay in the fact that, like Dayananda, he was a swami who symbolized the sacred in Hindu culture, but, unlike Dayananda, Vivekananda had carried the 'spirit' of Hinduism to the West. With his addresses to the 1893 World Parliament of Religions in Chicago, he scored an extraordinary triumph: a victory which resounded throughout India. Thus, when Vivekananda returned home, he came as a conquering hero. When he spoke of the 'spirit' of Hinduism, drawing parallels with Western philosophy and science, he commanded the attention of the educated Indian elite; and, when he derided India's crumbling superstitious 'forms', the impact on the Indian people, though not as great as that later made by Gandhi, was far more powerful than that of Rammohun Roy or Keshub Chunder Sen.

If Vivekananda's Western experience strengthened, in the eyes of many Indians, his movement for social change, it also persuaded Vivekananda himself of the validity of the two cultures theme. While in England and America, in the 1890s, Vivekananda was often called 'the first Hindu missionary to the West', and, though the impact that he made on the natives, there, remains questionable, there is no doubt that the experience deeply influenced Vivekananda's own thinking.

---

51 Ibid., p. 454.

52 Ibid., p. 174.

53 See chapter 1 for a further statement on this point.

The distinction between 'spiritual India' and 'empirical West' pervades his works and has implications for every phase of his thought. He was probably familiar with this theme before he left India, but it crystallized in his mind during his years in the West.

Even the most sympathetic reader of Vivekananda must be shocked by the absurd generalizations found throughout his long essay (written in Bengali), 'The East and The West'.[54] All the old distinctions already cited in the speeches of Keshub appear, here, in their grossest form, supplemented with countless detailed differences which Keshub had somehow overlooked. The main argument of the essay is that 'every nation has a corresponding national idea'[55] and the ideas of India and of the Western nations are at sharp variance:

> With us, the prominent idea is Mukti; with the Westerners, it is Dharma. What we desire is Mukti: what they want is Dharma. Here the word 'Dharma' is used in the sense of the Mimamsakas. What is Dharma? Dharma is that which makes man seek for happiness in this world or the next. Dharma is established on work; Dharma is impelling man day and night to run after and work for happiness.[56]
>
> That inward vision of the Hindu and the outward vision of the West, are manifest in all their respective manners and customs. The Hindu always looks inside, and the Westerner outside.[57]

The implications of this facile polarization of Eastern and Western cultural values for Vivekananda's idea of freedom soon became clear. 'The Greek,' he argued, 'sought political liberty. The Hindu has always

---

54 See, for example, the criticism of a reasonably sympathetic Western commentator, Albert Schweitzer, *Indian Thought and Its Development* (London: Adam and Charles Black, 1956), p. 221.

55 Vivekananda, *Works*, Vol. 5 (1959), p. 443.

56 Ibid., p. 446.

57 Ibid., p. 478.

sought spiritual liberty.'[58] 'To care only for spiritual liberty and not for social liberty,' he continued, 'is a defect, but the opposite is a still greater defect. Liberty of both soul and body is to be striven for.'[59]

A close parallel to this conception of freedom occurs in Bankim's discrimination of two forms of knowledge. Bankim, moreover, set forth not only this distinction but also a theory of social evolution. He even implies in the conclusion to *Anandamath* that the highest stage of social evolution in India will occur when the two forms of knowledge coalesce, and spiritual truth illuminates society. 'Once the people of India have acquired knowledge of the physical world from the English, they will be able to comprehend the nature of the spiritual. There will then be no obstacle to the true Faith. True religion will then shine forth again of itself.' Vivekananda applied these correspondences drawn by Bankim to the idea of freedom: the types of spiritual and physical knowledge were not only associated with higher and lower forms of freedom; these forms were seen as corresponding stages of an evolutionary process. 'Once the people of India,' Vivekananda might well have paraphrased Bankim's *Anandamath*, 'have acquired knowledge of social and political freedom from the English, they will be able to comprehend the nature of spiritual freedom. There will then be no obstacle to their spiritual liberation.'

There is no conclusive evidence that any of Vivekananda's predecessors considered thus far exercised a direct personal influence on his thought. If writers like Debendranath, Keshub and Bankim made a significant contribution, it lies in their impact on the general climate of thought in late nineteenth-century Bengal. Vivekananda, as a student, lived in the midst of a remarkable flowering of intellectual, literary and artistic achievement, which has been well termed 'The Renascence

---

58 Vivekananda, *Works*, Vol. 6 (1963), p. 86.

59 Ibid., p. 86.

of Hinduism'.[60] While he was studying in Calcutta, and attending meetings of the Sadharan Brahmo Samaj, Bankim was publishing his influential periodical *Banga Darshan* and writing his best-known novels, notably *Anandamath* (1882). Indians were speaking with excitement of Keshub's oratory, with reverence of Debendranath's example: and Rammohun's achievement was already passing into legend. It would have been unnatural if Vivekananda, surrounded by such an atmosphere of ideas, had not absorbed many of them. The most decisive personal influence, however, upon the whole of Vivekananda's thought came neither from the philosophers of Europe, nor the Prophet of Nazareth, nor the Brahmo sages of Calcutta. It came rather from the priest of a small Hindu temple on the Ganges: Ramakrishna Paramahamsa, an uneducated mystic who often plunged into ecstatic visions as he worshipped Kali, the Mother Goddess, became Vivekananda's guru and transformed him. The next chapter will consider the nature of this transformation, its effect upon Vivekananda's thought, and the subsequent development of his idea of freedom.

---

60 Stephen Hay in de Bary, *Sources of Indian Tradition*, p. 602.

CHAPTER 3

The Development and Nature of Vivekananda's Idea of Freedom

'*Vive* Ranade and the Social Reformers!—but oh India! Anglicised India! Do not forget, child, that there are in this society problems that neither you nor your Western Guru can yet grasp the meaning of—much less solve!'[1]

—Vivekananda, *Reply to Ranade*, 1900

Ramakrishna and Vivekananda: The Special Relationship

Unlike Rammohun and Debendranath, Ramakrishna had neither learning, wealth, nor social position;[2] but like them, he attracted and

---

1   Vivekananda, *The Complete Works of Swami Vivekananda*, 8 Vols. (Calcutta: Advaita Ashrama, 1955–1963), Vol. 4, p. 307.

2   An amusing anecdote from the sayings of Ramakrishna conveys well his differences with the Maharshi. It concerns his first meeting with Debendranath: 'We talked a long time. Devendra was pleased and said to me, "You must come to our Brahmo Samaj festival." "That," I said, "depends on God's will. You can see my state of mind. There's no

144

influenced some of Bengal's leading artists and social reformers. Unlike Keshub and Dayananda, Ramakrishna abhorred both oratory and proselytism; like them, though, he sought harmony in the medley of ideas which surrounded him. Unlike Bankim, Ramakrishna enjoyed neither a government position nor literary success; yet, like him, he inspired in his admirers, a resurgent pride in the Indian tradition. And, like all five of the other reformers, Ramakrishna's teachings imply both a radical reinterpretation of orthodox Hinduism and profound social change; yet, unlike them, his ideas and efforts convey a sense of ease, innocence and harmony which their strenuous efforts at syncretism never paralleled. 'Amid the hubbub of these self-conscious efforts to check the advance of Christian influence, Hindu society suddenly discovered in its midst a genuine saint and mystic. In the end, Sri Ramakrishna's simple devotion to the traditional concepts and deities of his faith proved a more effective force than all the oratory of his predecessors.'[3]

The relationship which Vivekananda had with Ramakrishna was not of a student and teacher, as that is commonly understood in the West, but rather of a disciple and guru. Ramakrishna did influence Vivekananda's thinking on fundamental philosophical problems, but

---

knowing when God will put me into a particular state." Devendra insisted: "No, you must come. But put on your cloth and wear a shawl over your body. Someone might say something unkind about your untidiness, and that would hurt me." "No," I replied, "I cannot promise that. I cannot be a babu." Devendra and Mathur laughed. The very next day Mathur received a letter from Devendra forbidding me to go to the festival. He wrote that it would be ungentlemanly of me not to cover my body with a shawl.' *Ramakrishna: Prophet of New India*, trans. Swami Nikhilananda (New York: Rider, 1951), p. 234. Hereafter *Ramakrishna*.

3 Stephen Hay, in William Theodore de Bary (ed.), *Sources of Indian Tradition* (Oxford: Oxford University Press: 1958), p. 603.

this came after Vivekananda's intense psychological commitment to him as his guru. It is difficult to describe the nature of this relationship; and better, perhaps, to allow its meaning to appear through Vivekananda's own narrative.

The first meeting between Vivekananda and Ramakrishna occurred in November 1881, at the priest's temple in Dakshineswar, Bengal. The two men were Bengalis, spoke a common language, and had been raised in Hindu homes; beyond that, they shared few likenesses. Vivekananda, then known by his real name, Narendranath Datta, had been born, in 1863, into a wealthy, aristocratic kayastha[4] family of Calcutta lawyers. His father had insisted upon him receiving a good Western-type education, and when he first visited Ramakrishna, he was well on his way to a career in law. Ramakrishna, twenty-seven years Vivekananda's senior, was the son of a brahman, a village priest; his education consisted of memorizing devotional hymns to Kali rather than of studies in language or the natural sciences. When Vivekananda first met Ramakrishna, just five years before the latter's death, Ramakrishna was nearing the conclusion of a life of severe spiritual discipline; and he believed that he had at last achieved self-realization through ecstatic devotion to Kali. The striking differences between these two men become manifest in Vivekananda's narrative of that first encounter at Dakshineswar:

> ... [Ramakrishna] suddenly rose and taking me by the hand led me to the northern verandah, shutting the door behind him. It

---

4   Biographical accounts state that Vivekananda was a *kshatriya,* e.g., Romain Rolland, *The Life of Ramakrishna* (Calcutta: Advaita Ashrama, 1960), p. 222; and D. MacKenzie Brown, *The White Umbrella* (Berkeley and Los Angeles: University of California, 1958), p. 87. Further research, however, has indicated that Vivekananda was a kayastha, a social group which is sometimes, but not always, included within the kshatriya caste.

was locked from the outside; so we were alone. The next moment
he stood before me with folded hands and began to address me,
'Lord, I know you are that ancient sage, Nara—the Incarnation of
Narayana—born on earth to remove the miseries of mankind, and
so on!'

I was altogether taken aback by his conduct. 'Who is this man
whom I have come to see,' I thought, 'he must be stark mad!'[5]

Vivekananda understandably avoided a second meeting with
Ramakrishna for some time, but eventually his curiosity overcame him.
The second encounter had profound consequences:

I thought he might do something queer as on the previous
occasion. But in the twinkling of an eye he placed his right foot
on my body. The touch at once gave rise to a novel experience
within me. With my eyes open I saw that the walls, and everything
in the room, whirled rapidly and vanished into naught, and the
whole universe together with my individuality was about to merge
in an all-encompassing mysterious void! I was terribly frightened
and thought that I was facing death, for the loss of individuality
meant nothing short of that. Unable to control myself I cried out,
'What is it that you are doing to me! I have my parents at home!'
He laughed aloud at this and stroking my chest said, 'All right,
let it rest now. Everything will come in time!' The wonder of it
was that no sooner had he said this than that strange experience of
mine vanished. I was myself again and found everything within and
without the room as it had been before.

All this happened in less time than it takes me to narrate it,
but it revolutionised my mind. Amazed, I thought what it could
possibly be. It came and went at the mere wish of this wonderful
man![6]

5   By His Eastern and Western Disciples, *The Life of Swami Vivekananda*
     (Calcutta: Advaita Ashrama, 1960), pp. 45–46.

6   Ibid., p. 48.

During the five years preceding Ramakrishna's death, Vivekananda gradually reconciled his differences with his guru. The harmony which finally prevailed between them, however, allowed each to place varying emphasis upon different themes. 'There is no doubt about it that many of the most important of Vivekananda's doctrines, and most of his greatest inspiration, were derived from his Master, but given an individual interpretation which was Vivekananda's own.'[7]

The conceptual correspondences drawn by Ramakrishna among his fundamental beliefs are found not only in the thought of Vivekananda but in that of Aurobindo, Gandhi and Tagore as well. 'God alone has become everything,' he said, 'All things that we perceive are so many forms of God.'[8] If the Absolute is immanent in all life, it is most clearly manifest in man: 'If you seek God then seek Him in man; He manifests Himself more in man than in any other thing.'[9] This is the essential position on the ideas of the nature of man and of the Absolute, which Vivekananda ultimately adopts. His acceptance, however, came only after a prolonged period of doubt, during which he questioned, first, the existence of God, and then the belief that God exists in all being. Realization arrived in a sudden moment of contact with Ramakrishna:

The magic touch of the Master that day immediately brought a wonderful change over my mind. I was stupefied to find that really there was nothing in the universe but God! I saw it quite clearly but kept silent, to see if the idea would last. But the impression did not abate in the course of the day. I returned home, but there too, everything I saw appeared to be Brahman ... When I became normal again, I realised that I must have had a glimpse of the Advaita state. Then it struck me that the words of the scriptures

---

7   Basham, 'Swami Vivekananda: A Moulder of the Modern World', in *Vedanta for East and West* XII, no. 6 (July–August 1963) pp. 224–25.

8   *Ramakrishna*, p. 195.

9   Ibid., p. 243.

were not false. Thenceforth, I could not deny the conclusions of the Advaita philosophy.[10]

For Vivekananda, the philosophy of Advaita precluded belief in a personal God;[11] Ramakrishna, however, insisted that the two positions were not incompatible, and believed in both. The implications of this difference between them are reflected in their respective views on social service. Devotion to a God who is immanent implied, for both, devotion to the divine in man. It requires only another step to see this as a directive to active social service for the welfare of mankind. This was a position that Ramakrishna accepted, but did not adopt as the main tenet of his teaching. Not service to mankind, but an ecstatic, mystical, highly individualistic devotion to God: this was the essence of Ramakrishna's message. He leaves no doubt, in his sayings, which path he encouraged:

> Sambhu Mallick once talked about establishing hospitals, dispensaries, and schools, making roads, digging public reservoirs, and so forth. I said to him: 'Don't go out of your way to look for such works. Undertake only those works that present themselves to you and are of pressing necessity, and perform them in a spirit of detachment.' It is not good to become involved in many activities. That makes one forget God. Coming to the Kalighat temple, some, perhaps, spend their whole time in giving alms to the poor. They have no time to see the Mother in the inner shrine![12]

Yet there was a theme of service implicit in Ramakrishna's teaching, and it was this theme that Vivekananda chose to develop. Here, again,

---

10 Eastern and Western Disciples, *The Life of Swami Vivekananda*, pp. 65–66.

11 Vivekananda, *Works*, Vol. 1 (1962), p. 376.

12 *Ramakrishna*, p. 138.

as seen in the following narrative of a disciple, Vivekananda's own interpretation proved decisive:

> Hardly had he [Ramakrishna] uttered the words, 'Compassion to all creatures' when he fell into Samadhi. After a while, he came back to a semiconscious state of mind and said to himself, 'Compassion for creatures! Compassion for creatures! Thou fool! An insignificant worm crawling on earth, thou to show compassion to others! Who art thou to show compassion? No, it cannot be. It is not compassion for others, but rather service to man, recognising him to be the veritable manifestation of God!' Everyone present there, no doubt, heard those words of Shri Ramakrishna uttered from the innermost consciousness of his soul, but Naren could gauge their meaning. When Naren left the room, he said to the others, 'What a strange light have I discovered in those wonderful words of the Master! How beautifully has he reconciled the ideal of Bhakti with the knowledge of the Vedanta ... Service of man, knowing him to be the manifestation of God, purifies the heart, and in no time, such an aspirant realises himself as part and parcel of God, Existence-Knowledge-Bliss-Absolute.' Those words of Shri Ramakrishna throw an altogether new light upon the path of devotion. Real devotion is far off until the aspirant realises the immanence of God. By realising Him in and through all beings and by serving Him through humanity, the devotee acquires real devotion ... All his activities should be directed to the service of man, the manifestation of God upon earth, and this will accelerate his progress towards the goal.[13]

The last sentence of this passage suggests those correspondences which are central to Vivekananda's idea of the way of right action: he who directs his activities to the service of man, the manifestation

---

13 By His Eastern and Western Disciples, *The Life of Swami Vivekananda*, pp. 107–9.

of the Absolute, moves towards spiritual freedom. Out of this theory evolved the conception with which Vivekananda's name has become closely identified: the ideal of Karma Yoga. While Ramakrishna had explicitly discouraged Karma Yoga as a method subordinate, in this age of Kali Yuga, to bhakti,[14] Vivekananda emphasized the 'yoga of action' above all others, and developed the idea in a modern context, so that it assumed implications which Ramakrishna had not foreseen. 'Karma Yoga,' Vivekananda said, 'is the attaining through unselfish work of that freedom which is the goal of all human nature.'[15] The karmayogin symbolized the spiritually free individual, working with a sense of renunciation for the uplift of humanity. As this idea was finally developed, it held two major implications for Vivekananda's political thought: the first concerns the modern Indian idea of social and political leadership; the second involves Vivekananda's theory of the right method of social and political change.

Vivekananda's portrayal of the karmayogin as a free man, spontaneously virtuous and uniquely capable of love and compassion is not new to the Indian tradition; indeed, Ramakrishna saw the conception in this light. The development that emerges with Vivekananda lies in his emphasis upon the free individual as a national leader, a disinterested social reformer, working in a spirit of renunciation to secure values which were often foreign to the Indian tradition. 'We must prove,' said Vivekananda, 'the truth of pure Advaitism in practical life. Shankara left this Advaita philosophy in the hills and forests, while I have come to bring it out of those places and scatter it broadcast before the work-a-day world and society.'[16] This was the role of the karmayogin: a part played by Vivekananda himself, in a social, if not in a political, sense. And the correspondences which

---

14 *Ramakrishna*, p. 139.

15 Vivekananda, *Works*, Vol. 1 (1962), p. 110.

16 Vivekananda, *Works*, Vol. 7 (1958), p. 162.

he drew anticipated the emergence on the Indian political scene of a karmayogin par excellence, Mahatma Gandhi.

In writing of the 'traditional ideal of the guru or teacher, better called "spiritual advisor"', Karl Potter observes in his study of classical Indian philosophy:

> That those only are fit to guide who have gained mastery of their subject is a commonplace requirement; but the relationship of the student to his *guru*, an especially intimate one, requires the teacher not only to have mastered the variety of subject-matters included in the 'curriculum' but also, and more important, to have such insight and superior awareness—coupled with the ability to carry out the decisions that insight dictates—as to be always cognizant of his pupil's innermost needs as well as master of the exactly appropriate ways of satisfying them. It is no wonder, with this ideal in mind, that the gifted teacher remains in contemporary India a figure highly fitted in the mind of the community to take on the added burdens of political leadership. Nor is it any wonder that, in the light of the correspondence we have noted between hero, saint, and teacher, the men who appeal to Indians as leaders have been respected and revered as being at one and the same time all three. Because of their superior understanding, such men are held to be worthy of everyone's trust and allegiance, even despite apparent external inconsistencies in their behaviour. The hero, the yogi, and the guru exemplify superior mastery of themselves and their environment; they, among men, most closely approximate the ideal of complete control or freedom.[17]

The karmayogin was indeed synonymous, in Vivekananda's view, with the classical conceptions of the hero and the guru, and it was this figure, embodying these three symbols rolled into one, surrounded with an

---

17 Karl H. Potter, *Presuppositions of India's Philosophies* (N.J.: Prentice Hall, 1963), p. 5.

aura of saintliness and spiritual power, that became a dominant image in modern Indian political thought. The yogin had realized his own nature, attained freedom and was thus unquestionably fitted not only to serve mankind but to lead it in all spheres of action.

The second implication of Vivekananda's ideas on the way of right action appears in his theory of social change. Far more than Ramakrishna, Vivekananda concerned himself with social and economic reform. Yet, the main point of his teaching was the inevitable impermanency of all reform unless it emanated from a spiritual transformation of the individual in society. 'We may convert every house in the country into a charity asylum, we may fill the land with hospitals, but the misery of man must still continue to exist until man's character changes.'[18] In a political sense, this meant that Vivekananda had little faith in the ability of administrative or legislative action to secure lasting social reform:

> There is a class which still clings on to political and social changes as the only panacea for the evils in Europe, but among the great thinkers there, other ideals are growing. They have found out that no amount of political or social manipulation of human conditions can cure the evils of life. It is a change of the soul itself for the better that alone will cure the evils of life. No amount of force, or government, or legislative cruelty will change the conditions of a race, but it is spiritual culture and ethical culture alone that can change wrong racial tendencies for the better.[19]

These thoughts were often echoed later by Aurobindo and Tagore. Even Gandhi, who immersed himself in political activity, always held firm to the belief that social and political change could occur only through a moral transformation of the individual in society.

---

18 Vivekananda, *Works*, Vol. 1 (1962), p. 376.

19 Vivekananda, *Works*, Vol. 3 (1960), p. 182.

A final consequence of the different paths chosen by Ramakrishna and Vivekananda in their quest for realization emerges with the relative importance they attribute to reason and to God's grace as aids to the attainment of spiritual freedom. There was little place in Ramakrishna's thought for reason. 'One should not reason too much,' he told his disciples, 'it is enough if one loves the Lotus Feet of the Mother. Too much reasoning throws the mind into confusion. You get clear water if you drink from the surface of the pool. Put your hand deeper and stir the water, and it becomes muddy. Therefore pray to God for devotion.'[20] Neither Vivekananda nor any of the other members of his school places the power of reason above that of faith: the highest truth was knowledge of the Absolute, and Ramakrishna and Vivekananda agreed that this might be perceived only with intuition. At the same time, however, Vivekananda, as well as Aurobindo, Gandhi and Tagore, believe that reason should be developed as much as possible as a help to intuition, and that reason may be superseded only when its limits have been fully reached. 'On reason,' said Vivekananda, 'we must have to lay our foundations, we must follow reason as far as it leads, and when reason fails, reason itself will show us the way to the highest plane ... Real inspiration never contradicts reason, but fulfills it.'[21] Man, having attained the highest reasoning power of any animal, must exploit it, as he should all his faculties, in his search for knowledge.

The second implication of Ramakrishna's devotional approach to God is reflected in an emphasis upon the need of His grace for spiritual liberation. 'You may try [to see God] thousands of times,' he said, 'but nothing can be achieved without God's grace.'[22] Whereas, when a disciple asked Vivekananda, 'Can salvation (Mukti) be obtained without the grace of God?' he replied, 'Salvation has nothing to do with

20 *Ramakrishna*, p. 160.

21 Vivekananda, *Works*, Vol. 1 (1962), p. 185.

22 *Ramakrishna*, p. 158.

God. Freedom already is.'[23] This difference is reflected, above all, in the tone of their teaching. Ramakrishna, the bhakta, said, 'I never feel like saying, I am Brahman, I say, "Thou art my Lord and I am thy servant." The feeling "I am He" is not wholesome. A man who entertains such an idea, while looking on his body as the Self, causes himself great harm. He deceives himself as well as others.'[24] But with Vivekananda, the message became *tat tvam asi;* and Vivekananda's speeches pulsate with an exalted self-confidence not found in Ramakrishna: 'Truth alone triumphs, and this is true,' he said, 'I am the Infinite.'[25] There is a gentle strength, nevertheless, in Ramakrishna's simple piety that attracted many Bengali intellectuals, Vivekananda among them, and gave them a new pride in their tradition; the power of Vivekananda's teaching is of a different nature, irrepressible, aggressive and dynamic. One complemented the other, and together, they became a profound source of inspiration for Indian political thought in the twentieth century.

Freedom, Equality and Harmony: A Conceptual Trinity

In the world history, I believe that the great man whom we celebrate will always have an important place, in that he, more than any other teacher in the India of his time, taught his fellow Indians how to assimilate the old with the new.

It was Vivekananda, more than any other teacher of his generation, who taught India self-respect, inspired his fellows to accept their own traditional culture, their own traditional values, their own traditional way of life, but to mould them and alter them as seemed necessary, pruning away the dead wood, and developing the new, here and there grafting on ideas borrowed from the West

---

23 Vivekananda, *Works*, Vol. 5 (1959), p. 317.

24 *Ramakrishna*, p. 157.

25 Vivekananda, *Works*, Vol. 1 (1962), p. 376.

and from other sources, but still keeping the parent tree alive and flourishing. For that, more than to any other individual of the period, India owes a debt to Swami Vivekananda.[26]

For centuries, Western political thinkers have discussed the idea of freedom; many have analysed it in a far more systematic and profound manner than did Vivekananda. The concern, here, however, is with Vivekananda's contribution to Indian, not Western, political thought; and a large part of this contribution rests with his attempt, in his thinking about freedom, 'to assimilate the old with the new'. The remainder of this chapter, then, will concentrate on this process of assimilation as it occurred in his thought with the idea of freedom and its related concepts: equality and harmony.

When Bankim Chandra Chatterjee commented that Bengalis had learned the word 'liberty' from the British, he indicated the way many Indian intellectuals of his time saw the concept of freedom: as social and political liberty, set forth by nineteenth-century liberalism. Rammohun, Debendranath and Keshub, all understood freedom primarily in this sense. And, as Brahmo reformers, they became advocates of civil liberties: Rammohun's campaign for the abolition of sati sought a form of social liberty; his statement against restrictions on the press was a fervent plea for intellectual freedom; and he directed his reinterpretation of the Vedanta against idolatry in the name of religious freedom. One of the most memorable passages, moreover, in Debendranath's *Autobiography*, is the narrative set against the background of his father's death. His family had insisted upon the traditional performance of religious rites in spite of his view of the shraddha ceremony as involving idolatry. This was finally resolved, for Debendranath, by a dream in which his deceased mother appeared to him and approved of his own convictions. The dream did not quell the family pressure

---

26 Basham, 'Swami Vivekananda', p. 225.

or their threats of social ostracism; it only assured Debendranath that he was right in his struggle for personal freedom.[27] Painful experiences of this kind characterized the opposition of many Indian reformers to the mores of their own society, and, in their struggle with orthodoxy, they exalted the Western value of political and social liberty.

The love of freedom [wrote Keshub Chunder Sen] is the chief characteristic of the present age. This would be at once evident if we consider the boastful spirit of self-congratulation in which men talk of their living in the 'nineteenth century'. Aspirations for freedom and aversion to all manner of slavery so thoroughly pervade the spirit of the age, that they find their expression in the very name of the present century, and mark it as pre-eminently and emphatically the age of freedom. This love of freedom manifests itself in all departments of speculation and practice. In politics, men aspire to that form of government in which every section of the community may be fairly and fully represented. In education, the cry all over the civilized world is—enlighten the masses, and deliver them from the bondage of ignorance. In society, there is an earnest struggle to break through the fetters of tradition, custom, and conventionalism. In religion also we see the effects of a strong desire to enfranchise the spirit. It has unsettled men's faith in old doctrines and dogmas, and shaken their respect for authority. It has led men to believe that nothing short of the most fearless and independent investigation will enable them to obtain truth.[28]

The early Brahmo leaders' admiration and advocacy of freedom, then, was clear and unequivocal. Almost a century after Rammohun Roy's

---

27 Debendranath Tagore, *The Autobiography of Maharshi Debendranath Tagore*, trans. Satyendranath Tagore and Indira Devi (London: Macmillan, 1916), pp. 112–20.

28 K.C. Sen, *Lectures and Tracts* (London: Stratum Publishing Ltd., 1870), p. 131.

appearance on the Indian scene, B.C. Pal, assessing the contribution of the Brahmo Samaj to the struggle for independence, could write,

> ... the Raja stood out from the very beginning of his public career as the apostle of personal freedom. And it was in this message of personal freedom first delivered by Raja Rammohun Roy to modern India that our present Freedom Movement had really its birth. It is therefore impossible to separate the Movement of the Brahmo Samaj from the general Freedom Movement or what is now called the Swaraj Movement in Modern, that is, British India. We cannot appraise the real value and vitality of this Swaraj Movement unless we study it in its historical evolution from the movement of personal freedom, or the protest of individual reason and conscience of the Brahmo Samaj against all outside authority whether of scriptures or of traditions.[29]

Yet, for all this discussion of liberty, the early Brahmos never seem to have foreseen that development in the idea of freedom, which later became crucial for Pal and his contemporaries: while the Brahmos consistently sought to underwrite social change with traditional Indian values, they found no basis, in the Indian tradition, for the idea of freedom. It was left for Vivekananda to draw the correspondence, which the Nationalists later found so fruitful, between the Western idea of social and political liberty and the ultimate value of classical Indian thought, spiritual freedom.

> Now the question is: [Vivekananda asked] Is it for the good of the public at large that social rules are framed, or society is formed? Many reply to this in the affirmative; some, again, may hold that it is not so. Some men, being comparatively powerful, slowly bring

---

29 B.C. Pal, *Brahmo Samaj and the Battle of Swaraj in India* (Calcutta: Brahmo Mission Press, 1926), pp. 4–5.

all others under their control and by stratagem, force or adroitness gain their own objects. If this be true, what can be the meaning of the statement that there is danger in giving liberty to the ignorant? What, again, is the meaning of liberty?

Liberty does not certainly mean the absence of obstacles in the path of misappropriation of wealth, etc., by you and me, but it is our natural right to be allowed to use our own body, intelligence or wealth according to our will, without doing any harm to others; and all the members of a society ought to have the same opportunity for obtaining wealth, education or knowledge. The second question is: Those who say that if the ignorant and the poor be given liberty, i.e. full right to their body, wealth, etc., and if their children have the same opportunity to better their condition and acquire knowledge as those of the rich and the highly situated, they would become perverse—do they say this for the good of society, or blinded by their selfishness? In England, too, I have heard, 'Who will serve us if the lower classes get education?'

For the luxury of a handful of the rich, let millions of men and women remain submerged in the hell of want and abysmal depth of ignorance, for if they get wealth and education, society will be upset!

Who constitute society? The millions—or you, I, and a few others of the upper classes?

Again, even if the latter be true, what ground is there for our vanity that we lead others? Are we omniscient?

उद्धरेदात्मनात्मान 'One should raise the self by the self'. Let each work out one's own salvation. Freedom in all matters, i.e. advance towards Mukti, is the worthiest gain of man. To advance oneself towards freedom, physical, mental and spiritual, and help others to do so, is the supreme prize of man. Those social rules which stand in the way of the unfoldment of this freedom are injurious, and steps should be taken to destroy them speedily. Those institutions should be encouraged by which men advance in the path of freedom.[30]

---

30 Vivekananda, *Works*, Vol. 5 (1959), pp. 141–42.

This is probably the most important statement for his political thought that Vivekananda made on the idea of freedom, and it should be closely examined. The development of the argument is significant for it indicates the way in which Vivekananda's thought processes often worked. His first definition of liberty would find acceptance among both Brahmos and Western liberals of his time: 'Our natural right to be allowed to use our own body, intelligence or wealth according to our will, without doing any harm to others ...' This liberty, he says, belongs to the 'millions', and no excuse may be found for its deprivation in the interests of an 'omniscient' few. Liberty of opportunity for all becomes Vivekananda's first demand. And, on this point, he is one with Keshub; but at this point, he goes beyond into regions that the Brahmos had not explored. It is the last paragraph that contains the crux of his development, illustrating, as it does, how his mind easily assimilated a Western idea to a traditional Indian concept, yet was perfectly aware of the distinction between the two. Perhaps the most interesting aspect of this mental transition occurs with the shift in usage from 'liberty', which has more of a Western flavour, to 'freedom', which, for Vivekananda, at least, was always the broader term, inclusive of all types of liberty as well as of spiritual freedom. Until the beginning of the last paragraph, the word 'liberty' is used four times and 'freedom' not at all; in the final paragraph, 'freedom' is mentioned three times and liberty not once. This paragraph is significantly begun with a Sanskrit shlok and then moves on to the crucial correspondence between 'freedom in all matters' and 'advance towards Mukti'. This correspondence is then underwritten and spelled out with the assertion, 'To advance oneself towards freedom, physical, mental and spiritual and help others to do so is the supreme prize of man.'

At our backs we must always hear, in considering Vivekananda's thought, his words, 'To the reformers I will point out that I am a greater reformer than any one of them. They want to reform only little bits.

I want root and branch reform. Where we differ is in the method.'[31] Vivekananda was no less a champion of social, religious and intellectual liberty than the Brahmos. He asserted:

> Liberty of thought and action is the only condition of life, of growth and well-being. Where it does not exist, the man, the race, the nation must go down. Caste or no caste, creed or no creed, any man, or class, or caste, or nation, or institution which bars the power of free thought and action of an individual—even so long as that power does not injure others—is devilish and must go down.[32]

But Vivekananda's method, unlike that of, say, Ranade or Gokhale, and to a far greater extent than Rammohun or Keshub, involved a serious attempt at assimilation of traditional Indian concepts. It was with this method, believing in reform but insisting on a natural evolution, that he turned to a consideration of the idea of freedom and eventually adopted it as the dominant concept of his thought. 'There is one wonderful phenomenon,' he said, 'connected with our lives, without which "who will be able to live, who will be able to enjoy life a moment?"'—the idea of freedom. This is the idea that guides each footstep of ours, makes our movements possible, determines our relations to each other—nay, is the very warp and woof in the fabric of human life.'[33]

In a broad sense, Vivekananda has often been rightly called a great inspiration of the Indian nationalist movement, as well as of the leading political thinkers of modern India. He may also be seen, in a more particular sense, as the pivotal influence behind one theme of modern Indian political thought, the idea of freedom.

---

31 Vivekananda, *Works*, Vol. 3 (1960), p. 213.

32 Vivekananda, *Works*, Vol. 5 (1959), p. 29.

33 Vivekananda, *Works*, Vol. 4 (1955), pp. 254–55.

Equality and Harmony

The two concepts of equality and harmony are closely related in Vivekananda's thought, in several respects: they rest, first, on a common basis, Vivekananda's ideas of the nature of man and of the Absolute; they confront, second, a common problem, the reconciliation of an extreme form of individualism with a consideration for the well-being of society; and, finally, they pose a similar solution, Self-realization. At first glance, the problem of reconciling Vivekananda's radical individualism with his equal emphasis upon the value of social harmony may seem impossible. On the one hand he believes that 'Each one has a special nature peculiar to himself, which he must follow and through which he will find his way to freedom'.[34] 'I am the end, my own Self, and nothing else ... Realising my own nature is the one goal of my life.'[35] On the other hand, it is precisely Self-realization that leads to social harmony, for 'Individuality in universality is the plan of creation ... man is individual and at the same time universal. It is while realizing our individual nature that we realise even our national and universal nature.'[36]

The basis of this way of thinking about freedom and harmony has its roots in the classical Indian conception.

The route to superior control [writes Karl Potter] to the fourth and most worthwhile kind of attitude, *moksa* or complete freedom, lies in the mastery of attitude of greater and greater concern coupled with less and less attachment or possessiveness.

In fact, the fourth orientation is well understood by extrapolating from this route. In moving from *artha* to *kama*, we move from lack of concern to concern, from more attachment to less. *Moksa* or

34 Vivekananda, *Works*, Vol. 2 (1963), p. 99.

35 Vivekananda, *Works*, Vol. 5 (1959), pp. 252–53.

36 Vivekananda, *Works*, Vol. 1 (1962), pp. 422–24.

freedom is the perfection of this growth. When one attains freedom, he is both not at the mercy of what is not himself, that is to say, he is *free from* restrictions initiated by the not-self, and he is also *free to* anticipate and control anything to which he turns his efforts since the whole world is considered as himself in this orientation. The freedom-from corresponds to his lack of attachment and the freedom-to to his universal concern.[37]

The significance of this way of thinking for Vivekananda's political thought is that it served as a conceptual framework within which he considered the problems of modern India. The radically new orientation which he gave to the classical outlook is manifest in his development of the ideas of equality and harmony, or what Potter would call his use of 'freedom-to', his 'universal concern' for the social well-being.

If there is a distinction in Vivekananda's thought between these two concepts of harmony and equality, it rests with the direction he gives each of them: his ideas on equality generally concern Indian society, and his theory of harmony is most often addressed to the world at large. This is not an airtight distinction which he himself draws; it rather indicates degrees of emphasis. The method which Vivekananda employs in his approach to these two concepts is, once again, the formation of correspondences between Vedanta theories on the identity of man with the Absolute, and social and political ideas largely inspired by the West. His development of the idea of equality is a notable example of this approach. The concept of political and social equality, it has been suggested above, is foreign to the Indian tradition; by the end of the nineteenth century, however, the Western impact had induced a widespread acceptance of the value among Indian reformers. Vivekananda acknowledges the Western development of this idea but insists that his own inspiration came from Ramakrishna. Reformers, he argues, often 'talk about equality', but only one great

---

37 Potter, *Presuppositions of India's Philosophies*, p. 10.

teacher of modern India 'was able to carry theory into practice'. An incident is then related of Ramakrishna's devoted service to Pariahs, exemplifying an utter disregard for caste.[38] Yet, once again, the crucial aspect of this development occurs with Vivekananda's interpretation of his guru's example: Ramakrishna, himself, exalts not equality, but compassion, in his gospel of service; it is only with Vivekananda, who is consciously seeking a reply to the West, that 'equality' emerges as a word of common usage.

Vivekananda's fullest statement on the idea of equality appears in an essay significantly entitled 'Vedanta and Privilege'. The argument begins along familiar lines: a correspondence is first drawn among the ideas of man, the Absolute, and spiritual freedom. 'The theory of the Vedanta,' he says, 'comes to this, that you and I and everything in the universe are that Absolute, not parts, but the whole. You are the whole of that Absolute, and so are all others, because the idea of part cannot come into it. These divisions, the limitations, are only apparent, not in the thing itself ... thus the end and aim of this philosophy is to let us know that we have been free always, and shall remain free forever.'[39] Spiritual freedom, then, consists of an awareness of divinity in all men, which immediately destroys false notions of 'divisions' and 'limitations'. The argument now moves on to its main consideration, equality; its most notable aspect is the quick correspondence drawn between the spiritual oneness of mankind and the idea of social equality.[40]

---

38 Vivekananda, *Works*, Vol. 4 (1955), pp. 174–75.

39 Vivekananda, *Works*, Vol. 1 (1962), p. 419.

40 R.S. Sharma, in his article, 'Historiography of the Ancient Indian Social Order', cites numerous attempts of Indian historians to inject Western ideas on social reform into classical Indian texts, and observes that the 'specious argument of equality in spiritual rights, irrespective of sex and caste considerations is advanced to meet the demand for equality in material rights'. (In *Historians of India, Pakistan and*

Man manifests knowledge, discovers it within himself, which is pre-existing through eternity. Everyone is the embodiment of Knowledge; everyone is the embodiment of eternal Bliss and eternal Existence. The ethical effect is just the same, as we have seen elsewhere, with regard to equality.

But the idea of privilege is the bane of human life. Two forces, as it were, are constantly at work, one making caste, and the other breaking caste; in other words, the one making for privilege, the other breaking down privilege. And whenever privilege is broken down, more and more light and progress come to a race. This struggle we see all around us. Of course there is first the brutal idea of privilege, that of the strong over the weak. There is the privilege of wealth. If a man has more money than another, he wants a little privilege over those who have less. There is the still subtler and more powerful privilege of intellect; because one man knows more than others, he claims more privilege. And the last of all, and the worst, because the most tyrannical, is the privilege of spirituality. If some persons think they know more of spirituality, of God, they claim a superior privilege over everyone else. They say, 'Come down and worship us, ye common herds; we are the messengers of God, and you have to worship us.' None can be Vedantists, and at the same time admit of privilege to anyone, either mental, physical, or spiritual; absolutely no privilege for anyone. The same power is in every man, the one manifesting more, the other less; the same potentiality is in everyone. Where is the claim to privilege? All knowledge is in every soul, even in the most ignorant: he has not

Ceylon, ed. C.H. Philips [London: Oxford University Press, 1961], Vol. 3, p. 315). It would not be fair to attribute this argument to Vivekananda, for he was well aware that spiritual equality had not resulted, either in traditional or modern India, in social or political equality. Vivekananda acknowledges that the latter idea was developed in the West but argues that it is in conformity with the spirit of Indian tradition (as exemplified, for example, in the lives of some of its great saints) and thus demands acceptance among the whole of society.

manifested it, but, perhaps, he has not had the opportunity; the environments were not, perhaps, suitable to him. When he gets the opportunity, he will manifest it. The idea that one man is born superior to another has no meaning in the Vedanta; ... The work of the Advaita, therefore, is to break down all these privileges. It is the hardest work of all, and curious to say, it has been less active than anywhere else in the land of its birth. If there is any land of privilege, it is the land which gave birth to this philosophy— privilege for the spiritual man as well as for the man of birth.[41]

Vivekananda concludes the essay with a summing up of the points with which he had begun: the quest for spiritual freedom demands realization of the equality of all men; worship of the idol of inequality only ensnares men in bondage. And it is this bondage in which the orthodox brahmans, as well as the low castes of modern India, are trapped.

If I asked one of our priests in India, 'Do you believe in Vedanta?'— he says, 'That is my religion; I certainly do; that is my life.' 'Very well, do you admit the equality of all life, the sameness of everything?' 'Certainly I do.' The next moment, when a low caste man approaches this priest, he jumps to one side of the street to avoid that man. 'Why do you jump?' 'Because his very touch would have polluted me.' 'But you were just saying we are all the same, and you admit there is no difference in souls.' He says, 'Oh, that is in theory only for householders; when I go into a forest, then I look upon everyone as the same.'

Thus, [Vivekananda concludes] trampling on every privilege and everything in us that works for privilege, let us work for that knowledge which will bring the feeling of sameness towards all mankind. You think that because you talk a little more polished language, you are superior to the man on the street. Remember that

41 Vivekananda, *Works*, Vol. 1 (1962), pp. 422–24.

when you are thinking this, you are not going towards freedom, but are forging a fresh chain for your feet. ... That wonderful state of equality, that sameness. This is what is called in Vedanta attaining to freedom. The sign of approaching that freedom is more and more of this sameness and equality.[42]

When the problem of practical measures for the realization of freedom and equality was posed to Vivekananda, he stressed, like his more Westernized counterparts in reform, the matchless benefits of education. Unlike them, though, he insisted that the highest goals which education may promote are spiritual in nature, in that it helps to uncover the reality of the individual Self.

Men must have education. They speak of democracy, of the equality of all men, these days. But how will a man know he is equal with all? He must have a strong brain, a clear mind free of nonsensical ideas; he must pierce through the mass of superstitions encrusting his mind to the pure truth that is in his inmost Self. Then he will know that all perfections, all powers, are already within himself, that these have not to be given him by others. When he realises this, he becomes free that moment, he achieves equality. He also realises that everyone else is equally as perfect as he, and he does not have to exercise any power, physical, mental or moral, over his brother men. He abandons the idea that there was ever any man who was lower than himself. Then he can talk of equality; not until then.[43]

In the eyes of Vivekananda, no one confronted the idea of harmony with greater wisdom than Ramakrishna, and the latter's teaching that 'With sincerity and earnestness one can realise God through all religions',[44]

---

42 Ibid., pp. 427, 429.

43 Vivekananda, *Works*, Vol. 8 (1959), p. 94.

44 *Ramakrishna*, p. 162.

is often repeated by his disciple. It is in this spirit that Vivekananda develops, from the Vedanta, his belief in the oneness of humanity.

> The second idea [Vivekananda says] that I learned from my Master [the first being that 'religion consists in realisation'] and which is perhaps the most vital is the wonderful truth that the religions of the world are not contradictory nor antagonistic. They are but various phases of one eternal religion.
>
> To learn this central secret that the truth may be one and yet many at the same time, that we may have different visions of the same truth from different standpoints, is exactly what must be done. Then, instead of antagonism to any one, we shall have infinite sympathy with all.
>
> Just as nature is unity in variety—and infinite variation in the phenomenal, that in and through all these variations of the phenomenal runs the Infinite, the Unchangeable, the Absolute Unity—so it is with every man; the microcosm is but a miniature repetition of the macrocosm; in spite of all these variations, in and through them all runs this eternal harmony, and we have to recognise this. This idea, above all other ideas. I find to be the crying necessity of the day.[45]

Then characteristically, Vivekananda applies this traditional tenet to the ideal of international cooperation and harmony, drawing conclusions which Ramakrishna would perhaps have accepted, but never himself taught or even imagined. It is the idea of the 'solidarity of the universe,' Vivekananda says, 'which the world is waiting to receive from our Upanishads.'

> Even in politics and sociology, problems that were only national twenty years ago can no more be solved on national grounds only. They are assuming huge proportions, gigantic shapes. They can

---

45 Vivekananda, *Works*, Vol. 4 (1955), pp. 180–81.

only be solved when looked at in the broader light of international grounds, international organisation, international combinations, international laws are the cry of the day. That shows the solidarity.[46]

This argument illustrates, again, two aspects of Vivekananda's thought which he saw not as contradictory but complementary: his claim for the uniqueness of Indian wisdom, which strengthened his appeal to the Indian nationalists, is combined with a forceful advocacy of international solidarity. Once again, this may be seen in the light of his ideas on evolution: the harmony of mankind is the highest stage, and logical consequence, of an increasing Self-realization by individuals within society; only ignorance inhibits man's natural growth toward freedom and thus harmony. 'Ideas of the family brother, the caste brother, the national brother: all these are barriers to the realisation of Vedanta.'[47] The fact that Vivekananda's thought inspired forms of extreme Indian nationalism is understandable, but nationalism, for Vivekananda, is an incomplete stage of development. 'There is but one basis of well-being,' he said, 'social, political or spiritual—to know that I and my brother are *one*. This is true for all countries and all people.'[48]

The idea of freedom emerged in nineteenth-century India; it dominated the political thought of the twentieth century. In one sense, this appears only natural, for India during much of this time was engaged in a serious struggle for independence, and, for many of the Indian nationalists, freedom meant no more than termination of foreign rule. Among India's leading thinkers, however, a philosophy of freedom was developed that affirmed, on the one hand, the goal of political independence, but insisted on the other, that independence, of itself, was incomplete: that it must be fulfilled through a realization,

---

46 Vivekananda, *Works*, Vol. 3 (1960), p. 241.

47 Vivekananda, *Works*, Vol. 8 (1959), p. 139.

48 Ibid., p. 350.

by each individual, of moral and spiritual freedom. In this way, they believed, freedom would assume new meaning in the discovery of a natural correspondence with equality and harmony. Their attempt must be seen as part of a response to the Western political and social ideals of liberty and equality: these values were thought desirable but not, in themselves, sufficient. The task which Vivekananda inspired and later Indian thinkers pursued, became, above all, one of completion: the bringing to fruition of both traditional Indian and modern Western values by using one ethic to complement the other. The end result they envisioned as a harmony of political, social and spiritual ideals.

In the development of this philosophy, Vivekananda played the most significant role of any nineteenth-century Indian thinker. His search for a melody among the discordant notes of his century was representative, rather than unique. His singular achievement rests with the thematic rhythm he introduced, which resounded in the ideas of Aurobindo, Gandhi, and Tagore.

CHAPTER 4

Aurobindo Ghose: Individual Freedom and Social Harmony

Freedom and Nationalism: The Early Ideas of Aurobindo

Indian patriotism as it just now prevails in the country [wrote Bipin Chandra Pal early in the last century] is, I am afraid, a rather mixed cargo. There is great confusion in the origin and intention of this noble aspiration. The one thing that is common, if not literally universal, in the composition of this patriotism, is a deep and burning sense of wrong against the present foreign government over us. Beyond this, it is very difficult to say if there is any deep and honest unity of aim and ideal in the very large and increasing body of our political minded classes.

But though this mentality may help us to destroy the present order, it will not secure our freedom, even if we get rid of the present servitude. This is not the kind of intellectual and moral materials with which we may undertake real nation-building. This mentality may enthuse us to destroy what is, but it will not enable us to construct that which ought to be.[1]

---

1 Bipin Chandra Pal, *Swaraj: The Goal and The Way* (Madras: Upendra, 1921), pp. 45–46.

As the Indian nationalist movement gained momentum at the turn of the twentieth century, the 'burning sense of wrong against the present foreign government' to which Pal refers, increased and pervaded the political thinking of the period. The roots of this attitude lay deep in nineteenth-century Indian thought: Vivekananda may have publicly deplored any attempts to use his ideas for political purposes, but his personal correspondence shows that he was fully aware of the political implications of his teaching.[2] His emphasis upon a philosophy of action and strength, and his glorification of the Indian past and of Indian character, indicates not only the source of his appeal for later generations but also a certain tension that occurred within his own thought and personality. In general, Vivekananda felt this tension, as did B.C. Pal: as a struggle between the mentality of 'destroying what is' and 'constructing that which ought to be'. If, with Vivekananda, this tension remained latent, blurred by his dissociation from politics, then with Aurobindo, it became open and intense as a consequence of his deep involvement in the nationalist struggle. One argument of this chapter will be that this tension was only resolved, for Aurobindo, after his retirement from active politics. The first phase of his political thought, extending from 1893 to 1910, dealt with an immediate liquidation of British rule. In the second phase, which lasted until his death in 1950, he became committed to the task of constructing a political philosophy revolving around the corresponding concepts of individual freedom and social harmony. Aurobindo's later thought will be seen here as the more valuable for a study of political philosophy, not, of course, because creative political thinking necessarily demands dissociation from direct political action. The judgement rests rather on the particular experience of Aurobindo, who, unlike Gandhi, reached the summit of his capacity as a thinker only after his withdrawal from political activity.

---

2   Vivekananda, *Works*, Vol. 7 (1958), p. 281; Vol. 8 (1959), pp. 475–78.

The continuing concern of this chapter will be with the growth of Aurobindo as a political thinker. The description of this growth will focus upon the development of his thinking on the idea of freedom, a development shown in the changing relationship that the idea of freedom underwent, in his thought, with the concepts of nationalism and social harmony. The idea of nationalism dominated Aurobindo's thought during his early phase; nationalism was the weapon with which he attacked the British Raj. Yet, even in his early stage, he had begun to see that, in Pal's words, 'though this mentality may help us to destroy the present order, it will not secure our freedom, even if we get rid of the present servitude'; and this realization eventually led to a reassessment of his thinking on the nature of freedom.

Aurobindo returned to India in February 1893; he had spent over fourteen years of his youth in England and had achieved a brilliant academic record at Cambridge in European classical studies.[3] He decided to devote himself to the cause of Indian Independence while still at Cambridge, and it was this commitment, he says, that dissuaded him from joining the Indian Civil Service. Thus, he deliberately failed the riding test after satisfying all other qualifications so that he might escape the 'bondage' of government service.[4] Immediately upon his arrival in India, Aurobindo became politically involved through the publication, in the Anglo-Marathi paper *Indu Prakash*, of his series of articles entitled 'New Lamps for Old'. The title, Aurobindo says, 'was intended to imply the offering of new lights to replace the old and faint reformist lights of the Congress.'[5] This description, though, hardly captures the vituperative tone of Aurobindo's indictment:

---

3 A.B. Purani, *The Life of Sri Aurobindo* (Pondicherry: Sri Aurobindo Ashram, 1960), pp. 8, 27, 41.

4 Sri Aurobindo, *Sri Aurobindo on Himself and on the Mother* (Pondicherry: Sri Aurobindo Ashram, 1959), pp. 12–13.

5 Ibid., p. 27.

I say, of the Congress, then, this—that its aims are mistaken, that
the spirit in which it proceeds towards their accomplishment is not
a spirit of sincerity and wholeheartedness, and that the methods
it has chosen are not the right methods, and the leaders in whom
it trusts, not the right sort of men to be leaders—in brief, that we
are at present the blind led, if not by the blind, at any rate by the
one-eyed.[6]

Aurobindo's articles appear to have so shocked Ranade and other
Congress moderates that they persuaded the publisher to adopt a
subdued tone; this disappointed Aurobindo, and he soon abandoned
the series.[7]

'New Lamps for Old' and several later writings were published
anonymously since Aurobindo preferred to remain discreetly in the
background as an academic at Baroda College. In 1906, however,
following the partition of Bengal, he moved to Calcutta and immediately
seized a position of leadership among the extremist elements of the
nationalist movement. One of his first moves, in Calcutta, was to
join with B.C. Pal in the co-editorship of the English weekly *Bande
Mataram*.[8] The aim of the paper was to formulate and forcefully present
a philosophy of nationalism. The impact of *Bande Mataram* on the
movement was dramatic and effective; Aurobindo believed it 'almost
unique in journalistic history in the influence it exercised in converting

6   Aurobindo, 'New Lamps For Old', 28 August 1893, in Haridas
    Mukherjee and Uma Mukherjee, *Sri Aurobindo's Political Thought*
    (Calcutta: Firma K.L. Mukhopadhyay, 1958), p. 75.

7   Aurobindo, *On Himself and on the Mother*, p. 27.

8   Karan Singh, *Prophet of Indian Nationalism: A Study of the Political
    Thought of Sri Aurobindo Ghosh 1893–1910* (London: Allen & Unwin,
    1963), pp. 46, 62–64.

the mind of the people and preparing it for revolution.'[9] Through this publication, both Pal and Aurobindo sought to assert their roles as the philosophers of the Indian nationalist movement: to underpin the struggle with a broad rationale based mainly on the mystique of nationalism. These writings never attain the level of Aurobindo's later works, but they do represent the most accomplished political thinking of that period. It was in this role, as political thinkers, that Aurobindo and Pal each saw himself and the other, and they occasionally distinguished their contribution from that of other nationalist leaders. Aurobindo, for example, had a profound respect for Bal Gangadhar Tilak as a political leader; but Aurobindo was also quick to observe that Tilak's role was not that of a political thinker.[10] B.C. Pal, on the other hand, was, for Aurobindo, 'perhaps the best and most original political thinker in the country'.[11] The nature of Pal's and Aurobindo's contributions to the philosophy of the Indian nationalist movement was manifold, but some understanding of it may be gained through an analysis of the two themes which dominated their political thought in this early phase: the concepts of nationalism and freedom. This analysis will examine these ideas as Aurobindo and Pal set them forth, and also consider their relation to Vivekananda's thought.

Not only the central assumptions but also the basic approach of Aurobindo's and Pal's early political thought are those of nineteenth-century Indian thinkers. They are adapted, though, to meet the changing tempo of the nationalist movement. Foremost among these changes was the growth of the idea of nationalism itself. A key enterprise of nineteenth-century Indian thinkers, it has been observed, involved the use of their tradition to underwrite and assimilate Western values often

9   Aurobindo, *Sri Aurobindo on Himself and on the Mother*, p. 54.

10 Aurobindo, *Bankim-Tilak-Dayananda* (Pondicherry: Sri Aurobindo Ashram, 1955), p. 34.

11 Aurobindo, *Sri Aurobindo on Himself and on the Mother*, p. 52.

quite foreign to that tradition. At the turn of the twentieth century, the idea of nationalism began to dominate the political thinking of the Indian Independence movement. This idea was imported from the West,[12] but it quickly became absorbed into the political, social, and religious thinking of the period.

With Pal and Aurobindo, nationalism not only became Indianised: it emerged as one of India's religious faiths. 'Behind the new nationalism in India,' said Pal, 'stands the old Vedantism of the Hindus.'[13] No Indian thinker stated the relation of nationalism to religion in stronger terms than Aurobindo:

The new religion of nationalism is a creed indeed, a faith which already numbers its martyrs, which speaks through inspired voices, which looks beyond the present to a future promised by God, which seeks, converts and makes them by the thousand because a blessing is upon it, a mission before it, a mighty ideal ennobles its utterance, a mighty courage pushes it into the battlefield. If there is to be a creed, this is the only possible creed for India.[14]

On the occasion of Aurobindo's famous Uttarpara speech, his closing words were these:

12 Stephen Hay in William Theodore de Bary (ed.), *Sources of Indian Tradition* (Oxford: Oxford University Press: 1958), pp. 660–61.

13 Bipin Chandra Pal, *The Spirit of Indian Nationalism* (London: Hind Nationalist Agency, 1910), p. 38.

14 Aurobindo, 'The Creed and The People', in *Bande Mataram*, Weekly Edition, 19 April 1908, quoted in Haridas Mukherjee and Uma Mukherjee, *'Bande Mataram' and Indian Nationalism, 1906-1908: Being a Study in the Ideas of India's First Freedom Movement Based on Editorial Articles which First Appeared in the Famous Bande Mataram Daily Between 1906 and 1908* (Calcutta: Firma K.L. Mukhopadhyay, 1957), p. 183.

I spoke once before with this force in me and I said then that this movement is not a political movement and that nationalism is not politics but a religion, a creed, a faith. I say it again today, but I put it in another way. I say no longer that nationalism is a creed, a religion, a faith; I say that it is the Sanatan Dharma which for us is nationalism. This Hindu nation was born with the Sanatan Dharma, with it moves and with it grows. When the Sanatan Dharma declines, then the nation declines, and if the Sanatan Dharma were capable of perishing, with the Sanatan Dharma it would perish. The Sanatan Dharma, that is nationalism.[15]

This illustrates the remarkable position that the idea of nationalism had attained by 1909, the date of the Uttarpara speech. The rapidity with which the concept developed among the extremists is striking, but germs of this idea had appeared in late nineteenth-century India. Vivekananda had argued, at the close of that century, '... each nation has its own part to play, and naturally, each nation has its own peculiarity and individuality, with which it is born.'[16] Vivekananda's purpose in speaking of the nation in this light, was to claim for India a unique gift of spirituality. On his return from America to India, he commented with satisfaction on the reception that he, as a sannyasin, had received from his people: '... it proved the assertion which I have made again and again in the past, that as each nation has one ideal as its vitality, as each nation has one particular groove which is to become its own, so religion is the peculiarity of the growth of the Indian mind.'[17] It is in this sense that Vivekananda used freely the word nation: as a people endowed with special qualities which often distinguished them from other nations, and, in the case of India, endowed them with a peculiar

---

15 Aurobindo, *Speeches* (Pondicherry: Sri Aurobindo Ashram, 1952), p. 66. Sanatan Dharma means 'the Ethereal Religion'.

16 Vivekananda, *Works*, Vol. 3 (1960), p. 148.

17 Ibid., p. 203.

mission to fulfill. As a source of inspiration for the later development of nationalism, Vivekananda's ideas were undoubtedly of critical importance. There are, however, significant elements which appear in Pal's or Aurobindo's conception of nationalism that are foreign to Vivekananda's thought. First, the idea of nationalism as a religion, or of the nation as a spiritual entity standing apart from its individual members, is a decided innovation. 'What are nations,' Vivekananda often asked, 'but multiplied individuals?'[18] Second, Vivekananda, unlike many of his later admirers, exalted the idea of harmony among all nations, regardless of their differences. 'Each nation has a mission of its own,' Vivekananda said: but it was a mission 'to perform in this harmony of races'.[19] This idealization of harmony runs throughout the early writings of Pal and Aurobindo, but in the heat of the struggle for independence, it was always overshadowed by the deva of nationalism. It did not recover its old force until after Aurobindo's retirement from politics, when he developed it into a central concept of his mature political philosophy.[20] Finally, it is notable that the word 'nationalism' does not appear in the works of Vivekananda; and this in itself indicates that the idea, as a political concept, had not advanced far in his thought. With the widespread use of the term, especially in Pal and Aurobindo, associations rapidly grew around it; and select aspects of Vivekananda's thought were assimilated into the gospel of nationalism as easily as Vivekananda had himself absorbed, into his thought, select

---

18 Vivekananda, *Works*, Vol. 2 (1963), p. 371.

19 Ibid., p. 371.

20 It is noteworthy that B.C. Pal, too, in his later phase, placed increasing emphasis upon the goal of international harmony. This was seen by many as a betrayal of his former firm commitment to nationalism; it may also be seen, though, as a development of elements which had always been present in his thought, but had received less attention in his earlier phase.

elements of the ancient Indian tradition. By 1910, Pal could write in his *The Spirit of Indian Nationalism* of the advent of 'Neo-Vedantism'; of its close affinity with nationalism and its indebtedness to Swami Vivekananda.[21]

Nevertheless, the impetus which Pal and Aurobindo gave to a narrow form of Indian nationalism does represent a notable departure from Vivekananda's emphasis on universal harmony—a harmony of nations, as well as of races and religions. Their commitment to this form of nationalism, moreover, drove them to another equally significant departure from Vivekananda's position. Freedom became inseparably connected in their thought with the idea of the nation, and they saw freedom in terms of national liberation, rather than as an individual achievement of self-realization. Vivekananda had desired India's ultimate independence, but he did not believe that national freedom was in itself sufficient, or that by itself it could lead to a solution for India's pressing social problems. This, he insisted, would not come simply through a change in government, but rather through a transformation of moral attitudes; or, to put it in the traditional language which he preferred, through a quest, by each individual, for not mere political liberty, but moral and spiritual freedom. Once again, this was the position that Aurobindo eventually adopted, not as a result of a sudden shift of direction, but rather through a gradual evolution of his thinking on freedom. An analysis of the course of his development may begin with a consideration of the modern Indian conception of swaraj, the term that was then commonly used, especially by thinkers like Aurobindo, Pal and Tilak, to express in traditional Indian language their conception of freedom.

The meaning of swaraj is often obscure in recent Indian thinking. At least part of this ambiguity may be explained by the modern Indian attempt to trace the word to its original Sanskrit base, and

---

21 Pal, *The Spirit of Indian Nationalism*, p. 40.

then reinterpret its ancient meaning for the modern situation. As Pal, Aurobindo and Tilak often observed, the Sanskrit 'sva' does suggest 'own, one's own, my own, or self'.[22] Thus, swa-raj (स्वराज्), as used in the early Vedic texts, signified 'self-ruling', 'self-ruler', one's own rule.[23] The *Rig Veda* and *Atharvaveda* used it in this sense, of 'self-ruler' and 'king'.[24] This kingship could be either divine or terrestrial, applying to Indra, 'king' of the gods, or, occasionally, in a technical sense, to earthly kings of Western India.[25] Swaraj in the early Vedas, then, had a political meaning, signifying 'self-rule', in the sense that a king enjoys sovereignty over his own dominion. In the modern period, B.G. Tilak and others sought to use the term in this political sense. They placed swaraj, of course, in a different historical and ideological context to meet their own needs, but in calling for swaraj, they were demanding an independent rule over their own political dominion.

Sva, however, may also mean, in Sanskrit, 'self' in the purely spiritual sense of 'soul';[26] swaraj, in this sense, suggests 'soul-rule', or one who is governed only by the dictates of his own soul. The use of swaraj in this way need not exclude the political connotation, for a king might also possess 'soul-rule'; indeed, he may be thought able to maintain

---

22 Sir M. Monier-Williams, *A Sanskrit–English Dictionary*, New Edition, Enlarged and Improved (Oxford: Clarendon, 1899), p. 1275.

23 Ibid., p. 1276. 'Sva' becomes 'Swa' with most modern Indian writers. Svarajya (self-rule) is the San. Substantive.

24 A.A. Macdonell and A.B. Keith, *Vedic Index of Names and Subjects*, II (London: John Murray, 1912), p. 494.

25 *Aitareya Brahmana*, VIII.14 in Ibid., p. 494. For complete reference, see *Rigveda Brahmanas, The Aitareya and Kausitaki Brahmanas of the Rig-Veda*, trans. A.B. Keith, Harvard Oriental Series, 30 Volumes (Cambridge, Massachusetts: Harvard University Press, 1920), Vol. 25, p. 330.

26 Monier-Williams, *A Sanskrit–English Dictionary*, p. 1275.

his sovereignty precisely because he does have singular spiritual merits. Swaraj was sometimes used, however, in the classical texts, exclusively in the spiritual sense. A passage which shows this usage occurs in the *Chandogya Upanishad:*

> Now next, the instruction with regard to the Soul (atma-desa):— The Soul (Atman), indeed, is below. The Soul is above. The Soul is to the west. The Soul is to the east. The Soul is to the south. The Soul is to the north. The Soul, indeed, is this whole world.
>
> Verily, he who sees this, who thinks this, who understands this, who has pleasure in the Soul, who has delight in the Soul, who has intercourse with the Soul, who has bliss in the Soul—he is autonomous (swa-raj); he has unlimited freedom in all worlds. But they who know otherwise than this are heteronomous (anya-rajan); they have perishable worlds; in all worlds they have no freedom.[27]

The full significance of the idea of swaraj for modern Indian political thought may best be seen by tracing its historical evolution through the late nineteenth and early twentieth centuries.[28] The contemporary Indian revival of the term occurred with B.G. Tilak and other Maratha

---

27 *Chandogya Upanishad*, 7.25.2 in Robert Ernest Hume, trans. *The Thirteen Principal Upanishads* (Oxford: Oxford University Press, 1962), p. 261.

28 Some attention has been given to this problem in S.K. Ghosh, *The Influence of Western, Particularly English, Political Ideas on Indian Political Thought, with special reference to the political ideas of the Indian National Congress (1885–1919)*, PhD Thesis, SOAS, University of London, 1949, pp. 126–35. Ghosh focuses on swaraj as political independence and distinguishes between those who demanded complete autonomy (the early Tilak, Aurobindo and Pal) and those who saw swaraj as compatible with continued British Imperial rule (the Congress Moderates).

writers at the close of the nineteenth century;[29] these men associated the idea of swaraj with the political career of Shivaji (1627–1680) the Maratha leader who forged the foundation of a Confederation from the disparate sections of Maharashtra. Shivaji succeeded in his attempts both through military conquest and a fervid appeal to the common sentiment of his people as a community of Hindus.[30] Swaraj used in association with Shivaji indicated both political liberty and freedom for the spread of the Hindu religion. His goal of Swaraj involved, according to one of his biographers, 'emancipating all India from Mahomedan thraldom and ... the restoration of liberty of religion for the Hindus and a Hindu paramountcy over all India'.[31] When Tilak revived the term, along with a whole cult of Shivaji worship and festivals in the late 1890s, he used the word in the sense that it is associated with Shivaji, as political independence and the creation of a Hindu state; originally, though, he confined its application to his own region of Maharashtra.[32] Tilak eventually extended this goal to the whole of India, but although his conception of swaraj admitted of frequent redefinition, it remained a goal of political and religious liberty, or, as he called it, 'Home Rule'.[33]

---

29 Stanley A. Wolpert, *Tilak and Gokhale: Revolution and Reform in the Making of Modern India* (Los Angeles: University of California, 1961), p. 80.

30 Percival Spear, *India: A Modern History* (Ann Arbor: University of Michigan, 1961), pp. 176–79.

31 N.S. Takakhav, *The Life of Shivaji Maharaj* (adapted from original Marathi work by K.S. Keluskar) (Bombay: Manoranjan Press, 1921), p. 605.

32 Wolpert, *Tilak and Gokhale*, p. 80. It may be noted that Tilak used the term *svarajya,* which is the Marathi version of the Sanskrit swaraj. (See Ibid., p. 191).

33 Bal Gangadhar Tilak, *His Writings and Speeches* (Madras: Ganesh & Co., 1918), pp. 97–115, 152–53.

Bengali writers at first used the word swaraj strictly in the sense
that Tilak had employed it, and this may have arisen from the fact
that it was introduced to Bengal by a Maratha publicist, Sakharam
Ganesh Deuskar, in his popular life of Shivaji.[34] It is noteworthy that
after almost a century of highly productive political and social thinking
in Bengal, the word swaraj had to be imported from Maharashtra.
Vivekananda, for example, who freely incorporated into his English
writings and speeches traditional Indian terms for freedom like moksha
and mukti, never used the term swaraj. Equally significant is the fact
that once swaraj became known to Bengalis, it quickly developed into
a key concept of their thinking on freedom. This indicates not only the
fertility and absorptive powers of Bengali thinkers at that time but also
the strength of their self-conscious attempt to establish continuity with
the Indian tradition.

The meaning of swaraj became increasingly associated, in Bengal,
with the extremist elements of the nationalist movement. This
association was nourished by the frequent appearance of swaraj
in the Bengali daily newspaper *Sandhya* edited by the extremist
Brahmabandhab Upadhyay. He used swaraj in the sense of complete
freedom from British rule and, in particular, from the Firinghi
(foreigners') mentality. Swaraj thus meant a psychological liberation
from all Western influence as well as the attainment of political
independence. Emphasis upon the former aspect of swaraj brought
the idea of freedom closer to Vivekananda's conception, but with the
outstanding difference that Upadhyay consistently referred to swaraj

---

34 Singh, *Prophet of Indian Nationalism*, p. 60. And Aurobindo, *Sri
   Aurobindo on Himself and on the Mother*, p. 30. Deuskar was also the
   author of *Desher Katha*, an economic analysis of Britain's exploitation
   of India. Deuskar's family had long resided in Bengal, and his books
   were written in Bengali.

as a national goal, pursued through combat with the Firinghi.[35] It follows from Upadhyay's position that swaraj would involve practice of swadeshi, the use of products made by 'one's own country', and this identification was further developed by B.C. Pal.[36]

At this point, Dadabhai Naoroji attempted to make the term swaraj nationally respectable by giving it a restricted political definition and then setting it forth as the aim of the entire Congress, Extremists and Moderates as well. In his Presidential Speech to the faction-ridden National Congress of 1906, Dadabhai used the word swaraj for the first time from the Congress rostrum. 'We do not ask any favours,' he said, 'We want only justice. Instead of going into any further divisions or details of our rights as British citizens, the whole matter can be comprised in one word—"self-government" or *swaraj* like that of the United Kingdom or the Colonies.'[37]

Dadabhai's address was met with general acclaim, but, as Stanley Wolpert has observed, 'Each party in Congress read the patriarch's speech as a vindication of its own platform'.[38] Much of the controversy focused on the reference to 'Self-government or swaraj like that of the United Kingdom or the Colonies'. The Moderates, led by Gokhale, were content with the goal of colonial self-government under the aegis of the British Empire, and Gokhale 'firmly believed that change

---

35 See *Bengal Native Newspaper Reports*, 1906, India Office Library transcripts. *Sandhya*, 7 and 12 December 1906, pp. 1114–16; 22 November 1906, p. 1068; 12 October 1906, p. 926; 20 September 1906, p. 898. *Sandhya* is reported here as one of the largest daily newspapers in Bengal, p. 591.

36 B.C. Pal, *Swadeshi and Swaraj* (Calcutta: Yugayatri Prakashak Ltd, 1954).

37 Dadabhai Naoroji, *Speeches and Writings* (Madras: G.A. Natesan, 1910), p. 76.

38 Wolpert, *Tilak and Gokhale*, p. 194.

could best be effected through cooperation with the government'.[39] The Extremists, led by Tilak, Aurobindo and Pal, argued that neither Gokhale's conception of swaraj nor his method of attaining it was correct, and their response to Dadabhai's speech was to interpret swaraj as complete independence.

> The object of all our political movements [wrote Aurobindo in *Bande Mataram*] and therefore the sole object with which we advocate passive resistance is swaraj or national freedom. The latest and most venerable of the older politicians who have sat in the Presidential Chair of the Congress, pronounced from that seat of authority swaraj as the one object of our political endeavour, —swaraj as the only remedy for all our ills—swaraj as the one demand nothing short of which will satisfy the people of India. Complete self-government as it exists in the United Kingdom or the Colonies—such was his definition of swaraj. The Congress has contented itself with demanding self-government as it exists in the Colonies. We of the new school would not pitch our ideal one inch lower than absolute swaraj—self-government as it exists in the United Kingdom ... We believe that this newly awakened people, when it has gathered its strength together, neither can nor ought to consent to any relations with England less than that of equals in a confederacy. To be content with the relations of master and dependent or superior and subordinate, would be a mean and pitiful aspiration unworthy of manhood; to strive for anything less than a strong and glorious freedom would be to insult the greatness of our past and the magnificent possibilities of our future.[40]

Swaraj for Aurobindo and Pal, as for Tilak,[41] constituted complete independence from Britain; like Tilak, too, Aurobindo and Pal

---

39 Ibid., p. 198.

40 Aurobindo, *The Doctrine of Passive Resistance* (Pondicherry: Sri Aurobindo Ashram, 1952), pp. 69–70.

41 Wolpert, *Tilak and Gokhale*, p. 191.

surrounded their political demand with traditional words and overtones that gave it added force. Yet, unlike Tilak, they sought to go beyond a political conception of swaraj; they attempted to expand it into a philosophy of freedom which through its association with Indian traditional thought would distinguish it as theoretically different from the European idea of political liberty.[42]

References to swaraj as an individual spiritual value are scattered throughout Aurobindo's early speeches: 'Christ said to the disciples who expected a material kingdom on the spot, "the kingdom of heaven is within you." To them, too, he might say, "the kingdom of swaraj is within you."' The dominant emphasis, however, in Aurobindo's early writings falls not on an individual but on a national quest for swaraj. The passage on swaraj which has just been quoted continues, 'Let them win and keep that kingdom of swaraj, the sense of the national separateness and individuality, the faith in its greatness and future, the feeling of God within ourselves and in the nation, the determination to devote every thought and action to his service.'[43] Aurobindo insisted, like Vivekananda, and unlike Tilak, that freedom or swaraj represented much more than a change in political systems;[44] but unlike Vivekananda, Aurobindo saw in the nation an entity that possessed its own divinity and its own potential for realizing spiritual as well as political freedom. Thus, Vivekananda's distinction between two forms of freedom was applied, in a political sense, primarily to the nation rather than to the individual;[45] and Vivekananda's association of spiritual freedom with Indian civilization was used to portray the idea of *swaraj* as a unique quality of the Indian nation.

---

42 Pal, *The Spirit of Indian Nationalism*, pp. 45–48.

43 Aurobindo, *Speeches*, p. 72.

44 Ibid., pp. 85–86.

45 Ibid., p. 37.

The ideal of unqualified swaraj [wrote Aurobindo] has a charm for the national mind which is irresistible if it is put before it in the national way by minds imbued with Indian feeling and free from the gross taint of Western materialism. Swaraj as a sort of European ideal, political liberty for the sake of political self-assertion, will not awaken India. Swaraj as the fulfilment of the ancient life of India under modern conditions, the return of the *Satya yuga* of national greatness, the resumption by her of her great *role* of teacher and guide, self-liberation of the people for the final fulfilment of the Vedantic ideal in politics, this is the true swaraj for India.[46]

Perhaps the fullest statement on the meaning of swaraj and of its close relation to Indian nationalism came from B.C. Pal. His conception of spiritual freedom as realization of the Universal recalled that of Vivekananda, but the correspondence which he drew between this idea and that of nationalism was a development which he shared only with Aurobindo. In his essay 'Indian Nationalism: Hindu Standpoint', Pal defined swaraj as 'The conscious identification of the individual with the universal'. The correct meaning of swaraj, he says, derives not from Dadabhai Naoroji or Shivaji but from the Upanishads. Swaraj 'occurs in the Upanishads to indicate the highest spiritual state, wherein the individual self stands in conscious union with the Universal or the Supreme Self. When the Self sees and knows whatever is as its own self, it attains *swaraj*:—so says the *Chandogya Upanishad*.'[47]

Beginning with this definition of swaraj, Pal expounds a theory of nationalism which sets forth not only, as Aurobindo had, the value

---

46 Aurobindo, 'Ideals Face to Face', in *Bande Mataram*, 3 May 1908, as contained in Haridas Mukherjee and Uma Mukherjee, *Bande Mataram and Indian Nationalism* (1906–1908) (Calcutta: Firma K.L. Mukhopadhyay, 1957), pp. 84–85.

47 B.C. Pal, *Writings and Speeches* (Calcutta: Yugayatri Prakashak Ltd, 1958), p. 77.

of national freedom; it goes on to show that the Nation is the one suitable social unit to further the individual's personal quest for spiritual freedom. Thus, whereas Vivekananda had argued the role of society as providing a framework within which the individual achieves realization, for Pal, that function has been preempted by the nation:

> The real value of the ideal of nationality consists in the fact that it offers a much larger and broader formula of human association than the idea of either the tribe or the race ... and thus, by subordinating his individual instincts and interests, tastes and appetites, to the requirements, first of his family, then of his tribe, then of his nation, man finds even his own individual life and interests ennobled and enlarged; and through this very subjection to the authority of these larger corporations, he gradually reaches out to a much fuller and more perfect freedom than what he could ever dream of attaining, amidst the perpetual conflicts and competitions, for even the very barest necessaries of life, of mere individual existence in this world.[48]

This necessary relationship between the nation and 'a more perfect freedom', Pal argues, 'demands a fundamental reconsideration of the gospel of human freedom preached by the European Illumination of the eighteenth century. Indeed, the idea of freedom, as it has gradually developed in Europe ever since old paganism was replaced by Christianity with its essentially individualistic ethical implications and emphasis, is hardly in keeping with the new social philosophy of our age. Freedom, independence, liberty, are all essentially negative concepts. They all indicate absence of restraint, regulation and subjection.'[49] Europe would do well, then, to learn from the Indian conception of freedom, which is not negative but positive: 'It does

---

48 Ibid., pp. 73–75.
49 Ibid., p. 75.

not mean absence of restraint or regulation or dependence, but self-restraint, self-regulation, and self-dependence,' and 'the self in Hindu thought, even in the individual, is a synonym for the Universal'. In this sense, the highest freedom is 'subjection to Universal', or 'the complete identification of the individual with the Universal in every conscious relation of life'.[50] Devotion to the ideal of the nation prepares the individual for his ultimate identification with the Absolute, and Pal sees the nation as critically necessary not only for the growth of man's freedom but for the very existence of a civilized life. 'The enemy of nationalism is,' he says, 'a mortal enemy of civilisation.'[51]

The Indian philosophy of nationalism reached its apogee in the early political thought of Pal and Aurobindo. It was a philosophy that, in one sense, continued the ideas of Vivekananda by proclaiming the spiritual nature of freedom, as well as of all activity dedicated to the service of India. It departed from Vivekananda's position with the emphasis it placed upon national freedom and the sacred nature of political service for the sake of the nation. Vivekananda has exalted the individual, as a spiritual being, beyond all other considerations. He envisioned a stateless society of free individuals. And he prized, above all, the ideal of freedom with harmony, of a society of individuals where conflict and competition were supplanted by a common realization of the unity of mankind. Each of these positions Aurobindo had partially accepted before his withdrawal from politics; with each, however, he had some serious reservations, emerging mostly from his commitment to nationalism. Yet, by 1915, Aurobindo was at one with Vivekananda on all of these fundamentals and had begun their development into a political philosophy which exalted the twin ideals of not Indian Independence and nationalism but individual freedom and social harmony. An understanding of this transformation

---

50 Ibid., p. 76.

51 Ibid., pp. 81–82.

of Aurobindo's thought may begin by examining his writings in the months immediately before and after his imprisonment in the Alipore Conspiracy Case of 1908–1909; for the events surrounding this confinement had a profound effect on his thinking and appear to have precipitated his decision to withdraw from active political life.

After Aurobindo's decisive move to Calcutta in 1906, his revolutionary activities, both as a polemicist and a party organizer, mushroomed. Aurobindo relates that it was he who, in 1906, 'persuaded this [Extremist party] group in Bengal to take public position as a party, proclaim Tilak as their leader and enter into a contest with the Moderate leaders for the control of the Congress and of public opinion and action in the country'.[52] Moreover, when Pal's co-editorship of *Bande Mataram* ceased in December 1906, Aurobindo became the mind behind that operation.[53] As the year 1907 progressed, relations with the Indian government worsened, and the breach between the Moderates and the Extremists, which Dadabhai had only temporarily mollified, grew wider. Aurobindo did everything possible to exacerbate the situation. To provoke the Government, he published his series of articles in issues of *Bande Mataram* on 'Passive Resistance'. Violence on the part of the Government, he urged, must be returned with violence. The Moderates' approach was categorically rejected: 'Petitioning, which we have so long followed, we reject as impossible—the dream of a timid inexperience, the teaching of false friends who hope to keep us in perpetual subjection, foolish to reason, false to experience.'[54] As the explosive Surat Congress of December 1907 approached, Aurobindo whipped the Extremist faction into vigilance, insisting, repeatedly, that a moment of crisis was near. On 1 December 1907, he wrote in *Bande Mataram* under 'The New Faith':

52 Aurobindo, *Sri Aurobindo on Himself and on the Mother*, p. 76.

53 Ibid., p. 72.

54 Aurobindo, *The Doctrine of Passive Resistance*, p. 70.

The bureaucracy will not have to reckon this time with a few self-styled leaders who are only too eager to fall down and worship the idol of the hour but with a newly-awakened people to whom the political freedom of the country has been elevated to the height of a religious faith. The political strife has assumed a religious character, and the question now before the people is whether India—the India of the holy Rishis, the India that gave birth to a Rama, a Krishna and a Buddha, the India of Shivaji and Guru Gobinda—is destined forever to lie prostrate at the proud feet of a conqueror.[55]

Aurobindo has himself testified to the leading role he played in provoking the Surat split, and the subsequent Extremists' secession from the Congress.[56] Yet, this was not enough; he relentlessly carried on his agitation throughout the spring of 1908. In early May, Aurobindo wrote for *Bande Mataram* under the title 'The Morality of Boycott':

The sword of the warrior is as necessary to the fulfilment of justice and righteousness as the holiness of the saint. Ramdas is not complete without Shivaji. To maintain justice and prevent the strong from despoiling, and the weak from being oppressed, is the function for which the Kshatriya was created. 'Therefore,' says Sri Krishna in the *Mahabharata*, 'God created battle and armour, the sword, the bow and the dagger.'[57]

But 'The Morality of Boycott' was never published: it became instead an exhibit in the Alipore Conspiracy Case. On 4 May 1908, Aurobindo was arrested and later tried for sedition. One year later he was acquitted.

---

55 Aurobindo, *Bande Mataram*, 1 December 1907, contained in Mukherjee and Mukherjee, *Bande Mataram and Indian Nationalism*, pp. 55–56.

56 Aurobindo, *On Himself and on the Mother*, pp. 79–80.

57 Aurobindo, *Doctrine of Passive Resistance*, p. 88.

But during that year he underwent, in prison, a spiritual experience which, he says, ultimately determined his withdrawal from politics. In prison, alone in 'solitary meditation', 'hearing constantly the voice of Vivekananda' and feeling his presence,[58] Aurobindo felt that he had finally realized the deepest meaning of Hinduism.

> What happened to me during that period [he said in his Uttarpara Speech shortly after his release] I am not impelled to say, but only this that, day after day, He showed me His wonders and made me realise the utter truth of the Hindu religion. I had had many doubts before. I was brought up in England amongst foreign ideas and an atmosphere entirely foreign. About many things in Hinduism I had once been inclined to believe that they were imaginations, that there was much of dream in it, much that was delusion and Maya. But now, day after day, I realised in the mind, I realised in the heart, I realised in the body the truths of the Hindu religion. They became living experiences to me, and things were opened to me which no material science could explain.[59]

One need not believe in mystical experiences to appreciate the change in Aurobindo's outlook after his imprisonment. *Bande Mataram* had been terminated following his arrest; thus, on 19 June 1909, a month after his release, he began a new weekly journal, significantly entitled *Karmayogin*. This weekly lasted under his editorship less than eight months, but even in this short time, signs of his growing maturity as a social and political thinker began to appear. The stated policy of the journal was to deal with 'political and social problems seeking first their spiritual roots and inner causes and then proceeding to measures and remedies.'[60] This search for 'spiritual roots' had long preoccupied

---

58 Aurobindo, *Sri Aurobindo on Himself and on the Mother*, p. 115.

59 Aurobindo, *Speeches*, p. 61.

60 Aurobindo as quoted in Singh, *Prophet of Indian Nationalism*, p. 141.

Aurobindo, and its appearance, once again, represents nothing novel. What has virtually disappeared, though, is Aurobindo's occupation with political strategy, and the elevation of political success to the exclusion of ethical considerations. The determined effort in the series on 'Passive Resistance' to separate morality from politics and to construct a programme of political action purely on standards of expediency no longer concerns him. The belligerent and ruthless tone of that series has been replaced, not by a spirit of conciliation, but rather by a more abstract approach to problems of political and social change. Thus, he wrote in his article 'The Ideal of the Karmayogin', 'The task we set before ourselves is not mechanical but moral and spiritual. We aim not at the alteration of a form of government but at the building up of a nation. Of that task, politics is a part, but only a part.'[61] Moreover, for the first time in Aurobindo's writings, the gospel of Indian nationalism is questioned:

> It [nationalism] has helped itself with the intellect, rejoicing in its own lightness, clearness, accuracy, shrewd insight, but it has not been sufficiently supported by inspired wisdom. It has attached itself to imaginations and idealisms, but has not learned to discern the deeper Truth and study the will of God. It has been driven by ardent arid vehement emotions but was defective in clear will-power and the pure energy that is greater and more impetuous than any passionate feeling. Either nationalism will purify itself, learn a more sacred truth and command a diviner impulse, or it will have to abandon utterly its old body and get itself a new.[62]

The *Doctrine of Passive Resistance* had declared, 'we recognise ... no method or action as politically good or evil except as it truly helps or

---

61 Sri Aurobindo, *The Ideal of the Karmayogin* (Pondicherry: Sri Aurobindo Ashram, 1950), pp. 2–3.

62 Ibid., p. 22.

hinders our progress for its national emancipation.'[63] In *Karmayogin*, however, Aurobindo said, 'Our means must be as great as our ends,'[64] and an inner spiritual realization of swaraj became the prerequisite for political achievement. 'For it is in the spirit that strength is eternal and you must win back the kingdom of yourselves, the inner swaraj, before you can win back your outer empire ... Recover the source of all strength in yourselves and all else will be added to you: social soundness, intellectual pre-eminence, political freedom...'[65]

The most significant entry that appeared in *Karmayogin* concerned Aurobindo's thoughts on freedom. This statement, which was quoted extensively in the first chapter, set forth, it will be recalled, a distinction between 'internal' and 'external' freedom, looking to the West as a guide to the latter. 'We in India,' Aurobindo said, 'have found a mighty freedom within ourselves, our brother-men in Europe have worked towards freedom without. We have been moving on parallel lines towards the same end. They have found out the way to external freedom. We have found out the way to internal freedom. We meet and give to each other what we have gained.' This passage indicates the extent to which Aurobindo's thinking on freedom had developed before his retirement from politics; it suggests that the direction it was to take at Pondicherry—a path of harmony rather than struggle—had been established as early as 1909.

The *Karmayogin*, then, represents a first indication of Aurobindo's shift in emphasis from a glorification of the nationalist struggle to a search for 'some harmonisation' of political ideals which is 'undoubtedly the immediate future of the human race'.[66] As the paper's publication

---

63 Aurobindo, *Doctrine of Passive Resistance*, pp. 67–68.

64 Aurobindo, *The Ideal of the Karmayogin*, p. 5.

65 Ibid., p. 9.

66 Ibid., p. 49.

progressed, the theme of harmony received growing attention. In words that recall Vivekananda, Aurobindo wrote,

> There is discord in life, but mankind yearns for peace and love ... This is the essence of humanitarianism, the modern gospel of love for mankind ... It is the nature, the dharma of humanity that it should be unwilling to stand alone. Every man seeks the brotherhood of his fellows, and we can only live by fraternity with others. Through all its differences and discord, humanity is striving to become one.[67]

If Aurobindo had written nothing else after his articles in *Karmayogin*, his altered approach might be dismissed as an understandable reaction to the threat of deportation by the Government. This would seem plausible, for other victims of arrest, notably Tilak, adopted a more conciliatory tone after return from a prolonged exile. This explanation, however, takes only a partial view of Aurobindo's thought; it overlooks the considerable development which Aurobindo gave to the ideas of individual freedom and universal harmony in the later phase of his philosophy.

According to Aurobindo, the immediate cause of his retirement from politics was an adesh, or a divine command, which directed him to Pondicherry.[68] He reached the French colony on 4 April 1910; four years later, he founded *Arya*, the monthly periodical that served for the next seven years as the main vehicle of his political and social philosophy. An immediate indication of the full extent of Aurobindo's shift in outlook appears in the language of the first *Arya* publication. Old terms which he had often used and apparently still associated with the nationalist struggle virtually disappear. He continues to speak of

---

67 Sri Aurobindo, *Speeches*, p. 96, published in *Karmayogin*, July–August 1909.

68 Aurobindo, *Sri Aurobindo on Himself and on the Mother*, p. 115.

India as a culture endowed with unique spiritual qualities, but seldom does he glorify the Indian nation, and hardly ever does he refer to the ideal of nationalism. He writes constantly of freedom, but wholly abandons the word 'swaraj'. He remains occupied with problems of political and social change, but never uses the phrase 'passive resistance' or 'boycott'. Other words and phrases appear commonly, moreover, which were infrequently used in his early period: 'the religion of humanity', 'unity in diversity', 'inter-nationalism and human unity', 'the problem of uniformity and liberty': these are some of the chapter headings of his book, published serially in *Arya* from 1915 to 1918, entitled *The Ideal of Human Unity.*

The aim of *Arya,* set forth in an early issue, indicates the dominant note on which Aurobindo's thought had begun to turn:

> The problem of thought is to find out the right idea and the right way of harmony; to restate the ancient and eternal spiritual truth of the Self so that it shall re-embrace, permeate, dominate, transfigure the mental and physical life; to develop the most profound and vital methods of psychological self-discipline and self-development so that the mental and psychical life of man may express the spiritual life through the utmost possible expansion of its own richness, power and complexity; and to seek for the means and motives by which his external life, his society and his institutions may remould themselves progressively in the truth of the spirit and develop towards the utmost possible harmony of individual freedom and social unity.[69]

This, then, is the cardinal problem which Aurobindo confronted in his later thought and the theme that pervades his later writing: 'the utmost possible harmony of individual freedom and social unity'. It

---

69 Aurobindo, *Ideals and Progress* (Pondicherry: Sri Aurobindo Ashram, 1951), p. 68 and Purani, *The Life of Sri Aurobindo,* pp. 181–82.

was a problem that had been considered by Vivekananda. Aurobindo, like Vivekananda, examined the ideas of individual freedom and social harmony against the background of fundamental problems of political philosophy, problems which concern the nature of man, of the Absolute, of the good society, and of the right relation between the individual and society. On each of these problems the position of Aurobindo, in his later phase, is essentially that which was set forth a generation earlier by Vivekananda; and here, one appreciates Romain Rolland's judgement that 'Aurobindo was the real intellectual heir of Vivekananda.'[70] This inheritance had been received by Aurobindo in Bengal, but it was fully realized only at Pondicherry.

---

70 Romain Rolland, *Prophets of the New India,* trans. E.F. Malcolm-Smith (London: Cassell and Co., 1930), p. 499.

CHAPTER 5

Aurobindo on the Nature of Freedom

The most substantial theoretical development of the modern Indian idea of freedom occurs in the political philosophy of Aurobindo. Yet substantial as his statement may be within the context of recent Indian thought, it may appear quite incomplete when measured against modern European theories of social and political liberty. For Aurobindo is notably unconcerned with certain features of Western thinking on freedom, some of which have been often regarded as essential components of the idea. Aurobindo says little, for example, of the need for the rule of law as a safeguard of civil liberties. He says still less about the desirability of an independent judiciary or legislature, or even of a free opposition to government. And he mentions not at all that freedom concerning the right to possess private property.

The paucity of consideration given to these aspects of freedom, not only by Aurobindo but also by the other members of his school, itself suggests the nature of the interpretation which they placed upon their political and social experience—the experience from which the modern Indian idea of freedom emerged. The elements of which this idea was not constituted are no less significant perhaps than those of which it was, and although this study will confine itself to an analysis of the latter, a recognition of what the Indian idea of freedom was not, as well as what it was, offers insight into the response which the school made to its particular historical experience. One aim of this chapter will be to examine how Aurobindo, in his response, sought to fulfill the common goal shared by his school: the free expression and growth of the individual in society.

The suspicion rightly exists of any political philosophy rooted in the idea of an Absolute, whether in the form of a nation, Natural Law, or a Divine Truth, that individual freedom may not only be sacrificed before the altar of political unity but that this sacrifice may be justified on the basis of some supra-rational standard. Belief in an Absolute constitutes a main pillar of Aurobindo's philosophy. The political implications of this belief in an authoritarian ideology are readily discernible in his early thought: in his identification of the Indian nation with the Absolute. Not only did love of nation signify, for him as well as for Pal, devotion to God; it indicated possession of the highest freedom as well. These early ideas of Aurobindo, however, are neither representative of his school, nor are they consistent with his own later development. The ideas which do characterize the school—ideas not absent from Aurobindo's earlier period, but decidedly undeveloped at that time—are those which elevate the individual to a pre-eminent position; the individual exceeding, as Aurobindo later said, 'the limits of the family, the clan, the class, the nation.'[1] They are ideas which insist that political and social liberties are personal values necessary to human development, to the individual's quest for self-realization.

---

1   Sri Aurobindo, *The Ideal of Human Unity*, in *The Human Cycle: The Ideal of Human Unity, War and Self Determination* (Pondicherry: Sri Aurobindo Ashram, 1962), p. 380. All quotes from *The Human Cycle, The Ideal of Human Unity* and *War and Self Determination* are from the 1962 edition, unless mentioned otherwise.

'Man needs freedom of thought and life and action,' wrote Aurobindo in *Arya* on the theme that was to dominate his later philosophy, 'in order that he may grow, otherwise he will remain fixed where he was, a stunted and static being.'[2]

Aurobindo saw as a main purpose of his later political thought the support of the widest possible enjoyment of freedom, at every stage of individual and social development. This broad conception of freedom made even more difficult the central problem which he faced: the task of achieving 'the utmost possible harmony of individual freedom and social unity'. His approach rests upon his view of the nature of man and of the Absolute; a view, he says, rooted in 'the old Indian discovery that our real "I" is a Supreme Being which is our true self and which it is our business to discover and consciously become and, secondly, that that Being is one in all, expressed in the individual and the collectivity and only by admitting and realising our unity with others can we entirely fulfill our true self-being.'[3] Like Vivekananda, Aurobindo constructed his entire philosophy on this fundamental conception; but more than Vivekananda, he explored its implications for the idea of political and social freedom. This appears most clearly with the attention that Aurobindo gave to the question of the right relation of the individual to society and, in particular, to the problem of reconciling individual freedom with social and political order. The essence of his approach emerges in the following passage:

> By liberty we mean the freedom to obey the law of our being, to grow to our natural self-fulfilment, to find out naturally and freely our harmony with our environment. The dangers and

---

2   Ibid., p. 284.

3   Ibid., p. 59. *The Human Cycle, The Ideal of Human Unity* and *War and Self-determination*, first appeared, serially, in *Arya*, 1915–20. Revised editions appeared later; of *The Human Cycle* in 1949 and *The Ideal of Human Unity* in 1950.

disadvantages of liberty, the disorder, strife, waste and confusion to which its wrong use leads are indeed obvious. But they arise from the absence or defect of the sense of unity between individual and individual, between community and community, which pushes them to assert themselves at the expense of each other instead of growing by mutual help and interchange and to assert freedom for themselves in the very act of encroaching on the free development of their fellows. If a real, a spiritual and psychological unity were effectuated, liberty would have no perils and disadvantages; for free individuals enamoured of unity would be compelled by themselves, by their own need, to accommodate perfectly their own growth with the growth of their fellows and would not feel themselves complete except in the free growth of others. Because of our present imperfection and the ignorance of our mind and will, law and regimentation have to be called in to restrain and to compel from outside. The facile advantages of a strong law and compulsion are obvious, but equally great are the disadvantages. Such perfection as it succeeds in creating tends to be mechanical, and even the order it imposes turns out to be artificial and liable to break down if the yoke is loosened or the restraining grasp withdrawn. Carried too far, an imposed order discourages the principles of natural growth which is the true method of life and may even slay the capacity for real growth. We repress and overstandardise life at our peril; by over-regimentation we crush Nature's initiative and habit of intuitive self-adaptation. Dwarfed or robbed of elasticity, the devitalised individuality, even while it seems outwardly fair and symmetrical, perishes from within. Better anarchy than the long continuance of a law which is not our own or which our real nature cannot assimilate. And all repressive or preventive law is only a makeshift, a substitute for the true law which must develop from within and be not a check on liberty, but its outward image and visible expression. Human society progresses really and vitally in proportion as law becomes the child of freedom; it will reach its perfection when, man having learned to know and become spiritually one with his fellow-man, the spontaneous law of his society exists only as the outward mould of his self-governed inner liberty.[4]

What emerges from this passage is Aurobindo's conception of freedom as both the means and the object of human fulfilment. As a means, liberty allows men to grow; and ultimately, because of their nature, to 'find out naturally and freely our harmony with our environment'. A society that appreciates this truth 'will give the same freedom to man seeking for political and social perfection and to all his other powers and aspirations'.[5] As an object of fulfilment, or as a culmination of individual growth, freedom is seen as the highest state of spiritual realization: 'This great indefinable thing, liberty, is in its highest and ultimate sense a state of being'.[6] Once this 'state of being' is realized, law and order become an outward expression of an inward realization of freedom and harmony; for the individual has then discovered the truth of his own Self, and thus his spiritual oneness with mankind.

Social Evolution and the Growth of Freedom

Aurobindo sees a growth of spiritual consciousness as manifest in the historical evolution of society, from its earliest stages to its future form of perfection. Individual and social progress amounts to an increasing fulfillment of the values of freedom and harmony, and Aurobindo's judgement of any society and of the political regime that it has raised is based on the degree of freedom and harmony that has been achieved. An analysis of Aurobindo's theory of evolution is important for his political philosophy since it contains both his criticism of existing

---

4   Aurobindo, *The Ideal of Human Unity*, pp. 564–66.

5   Aurobindo, *The Human Cycle*, pp. 242–43.

6   Aurobindo, *War and Self-Determination*, p. 835.

political systems and his conception of the direction in which society should move if the individual is to achieve the highest level of freedom.

The pattern of social and political evolution set forth is divided into three broad cyclic periods of time: the infrarational (or irrational), the rational, and the spiritual, developing progressively in that order. The first of these covers, historically, all of the pre-modern period; it is characterized by a primitive consciousness, dominated by instinct and innocent of rational judgement.[7] This early phase is traced to the beginning of ancient Greek civilization, as well as to the prehistoric period of India; and, as Aurobindo traces the gradual movement of India and the West towards the rational age, he makes several notable observations. First, certain periods of Indian history, like the age of the Upanishads, are seen as marked by 'immense spiritual development'. Yet Aurobindo regards this advance as abortive, for it rested on faulty foundations: spiritual insight was achieved without a corresponding advance in rational judgement, and without the support of reason, a civilization cannot survive.[8] A second attempt at balancing traditional Indian beliefs with more modern assumptions appears in Aurobindo's strong criticism of 'the world-shunning monk, the near ascetic', who cannot be 'the true guide of mankind and its lawgiver'. For 'the monastic attitude implies a fear, and aversion, a distrust of life and its aspirations.'[9] Finally, Aurobindo says that a movement from the infrarational to the rational age can only be achieved 'when not a class or a few, but the multitude has learned to think, to exercise its intelligence actively—it matters not at first how imperfectly—upon their life, their needs, their rights, their duties, their aspirations as human beings'.[10]

---

7   Aurobindo, *The Human Cycle*, pp. 246–47.

8   Ibid., pp. 252–53.

9   Ibid., p. 241.

10   Ibid., p. 254.

The rational or modern age, which man has now entered, has, in itself, three successive stages of development. The first is individualist and democratic, an age of liberty; the second is socialistic and communistic, an age of equality and of the state; the third is anarchic 'in the highest sense of that much abused word, either a loose voluntary co-operation or a free communalism with brotherhood or comradeship and not government for its principle'.[11] In his consideration of the rational age, Aurobindo offers his criticism of contemporary democracy and socialism. After associating the emergence of democracy with an increase in freedom and individualism as well as in reason, Aurobindo argues that as an idea and a political movement, democracy has, nevertheless, failed; and he blames its foibles on man's obdurate irrationality. The average man 'does not use his freedom to arrive at a rational adjustment of his life with the life of others; his natural tendency is to enforce the aims of his life even at the expense of or, as it is euphemistically put, in competition with the life of others.'[12] It is this characteristic of competition or irrational strife that Aurobindo abhors most in a democracy, as is evident from the following passage:

> The individualistic democratic ideal brings us at first in actual practice to the more and more precarious rule of a dominant class in the name of democracy over the ignorant, numerous and less fortunate mass. Secondly, since the ideal of freedom and equality is abroad and cannot any longer be stifled, it must lead to the increasing effort of the exploited masses to assert their down-trodden right and to turn, if they can, this pseudo-democratic falsehood into the real democratic truth; therefore, to a war of classes. Thirdly, it develops inevitably as part of its process a perpetual strife of parties, at first few and simple in composition, but afterwards as at the present time an impotent and sterilising chaos of names, labels,

11 Ibid., p. 259.
12 Ibid., p. 264.

programmes, war-cries. All lift the banner of conflicting ideas or ideals, but all are really fighting out under that flag a battle of conflicting interests. Finally, individualistic democratic freedom results fatally in an increasing stress of competition which replaces the ordered tyrannies of the infrarational periods of humanity by a sort of ordered conflict. And this conflict ends in the survival not of the spiritually, rationally or physically fittest, but of the most fortunate and vitally successful. It is evident enough that whatever else it may be, this is not a rational order of society; it is not at all the perfection which the individualistic reason of man had contemplated as its ideal or set out to accomplish.[13]

Aurobindo's critique of democracy does recognize its advances in education, social and political freedom and equality of opportunity. But, after all this, he returns to his main criticism that 'instead of a harmoniously ordered society there has been developed a huge organized competitive system ...'[14] The natural reaction to this excessive competition occurred with the rise of socialism.

[Socialism's] true nature, its real justification is the attempt of the human reason to carry on the rational ordering of society to its fulfillment, its will to get rid of this great parasitical excrescence of unbridled competition, this giant obstacle to any decent ideal or practice of human living. Socialism sets out to replace a system of organised economic battle by an organised order and peace.[15]

The way in which socialism attacks the unsolved problems of democracy, however, is to supplant individual liberty with political and social equality; not only equality of opportunity but of status. This involves

---

13 Ibid., pp. 264–65.

14 Ibid., p. 267.

15 Ibid., p. 268.

an unwarranted deprivation of freedom and a denial of the dignity of the individual.[16] Aurobindo deplores the excessive competition which democracy permits, but he is not willing to sacrifice individual liberty for social harmony, and he sees socialism as wrong in making this sacrifice. As the collective tendency toward socialism increases, the old democratic values of liberty, equality and fraternity disappear, stifled along with the suppression of the individual.

> The only liberty left at the end would be the freedom to serve the community under the rigorous direction of the State authority; the only equality would be an association of all alike in a Spartan or Roman spirit of civic service with perhaps a like status, theoretically equal at least for all functions; the only brotherhood would be the sense of comradeship in devoted dedication to the organised social Self, the State. In fact the democratic trinity stripped of its godhead would fade out of existence; the collectivist ideal can very well do without them, for none of them belongs to its grain and very substance.[17]

Aurobindo expands his attack on socialism into a vigorous indictment of totalitarianism, which includes, for him, both Soviet Communism and Italian and German Fascism. In the Soviet Union, there has emerged 'a rigorous totalitarianism on the basis of the dictatorship of the proletariat, which amounts in fact to the dictatorship of the Communist party in the name or on behalf of the proletariate.'[18] He applies this criticism of Communism to Fascism as well:

> The essential features are the same in Russia and in Fascist countries. There is the seizure of the life of the community by a dominant

---

16 Ibid., pp. 269–70.

17 Ibid., p. 274.

18 Ibid., p. 275.

individual leader, Fuhrer, Dux, dictator, head of a small active
minority, the Nazi, Fascist or Communist party, and supported by a
militarised partisan force: there is a rapid crystallisation of the social,
economic, political life of the people into a new rigid organisation
effectively controlled at every point; there is the compulsory casting
of thought, education, expression, action into a set iron mould, a
fixed system of ideas and life-motives, with a fierce and ruthless,
often a sanguinary repression of all that denies and differs; there is a
total unprecedented compression of the whole communal existence
so as to compel a maximum efficiency and a complete unanimity of
mind, speech, feeling, life.[19]

The great danger in the rise of Communism and Fascism lies in their
sweeping annihilation of individual freedom, and thus of the rational
development and further expansion of man. 'Reason cannot do its
work, act or rule if the mind of man is denied freedom to think or
freedom to realise its thought by action in life.'[20] Aurobindo's attack
on socialism as a political theory concludes with his indictment of
the whole conception of the state. 'As State government develops,'
he says, 'we have a real suppression or oppression of the minority by
the majority or the majority by the minority, of the individual by the
collectivity, finally, of all by the relentless mechanism of the State.'[21]
Even if the socialistic state somehow transformed itself and became
democratic, its change would be a 'chimera', for the very essence of the
state is the imposition of a forced unity, and the subsequent suppression
of creative thought. Thus, 'Whatever the perfection of the organised
State, the suppression or oppression of individual freedom by the will
of the majority or of a minority would still be there as a cardinal defect

---

19 Ibid., p. 276.

20 Ibid., p. 277.

21 Ibid., p. 283.

vitiating its very principle.'[22] For Aurobindo, then, the state is an evil because it inevitably suppresses liberty, and liberty is a spiritual as well as a political value. Socialism as a theory, 'ignores the complexity of man's being and all that that complexity means. And especially it ignores the soul of man and its supreme need of freedom ...'[23]

The final phase of the rational era is that of anarchism. Aurobindo explicitly rejects the 'violent anarchism which seeks forcibly to react against the social principle or claims the right of man to "live his own life" in the egoistic or crudely vitalistic sense'.[24] Anarchism demands an internal change of the individual in society, for 'the more the outer law is replaced by an inner law, the nearer man will draw to his true and natural perfection'.[25] This further evolution demands the growth of a higher form of freedom. 'The solution lies in ... a spiritual, an inner freedom that can alone create a perfect human order.'[26]

The social and political framework within which this further evolution may occur cannot be that of the nation-state system. The nation, Aurobindo now believes, is wholly inadequate for providing the structure within which a continued growth of freedom and harmony may occur. A political order is needed 'in which respect for individual liberty and free growth of the personal being to his perfection is harmonised with respect for the needs, efficiency, solidarity, natural growth and organic perfection of the corporate being'.[27] On a world level, this order must take the form, not of an inter-related system of

---

22 Ibid., p. 286.

23 Ibid., p. 281.

24 Ibid., p. 290.

25 Ibid., p. 292.

26 Ibid., pp. 295–96.

27 Aurobindo, *The Ideal of Human Unity*, p. 523.

nation-states, or even of a 'world state', but of a 'world union'. The implication is of a movement beyond the idea of a nation to that of a cosmopolitan community, which would maintain the diversity that now exists, and yet elicit a new spirit of cooperation. Aurobindo's concern is essentially with the preservation of a maximum degree of diversity among not only individuals within a particular society but also of individual cultural groups within a world community. He calls his ideal that of 'unity in diversity' and explains it in these terms:

> Uniformity is not the law of life. Life exists by diversity; it insists that every group, every being shall be, even while one with all the rest in its universality, yet by some principle or ordered detail of variation, unique. The over-centralisation, which is the condition of a working uniformity, is not the healthy method of life. Order is indeed the law of life, but not an artificial regulation. The sound order is that which comes from within, as the result of a nature that has discovered itself and found its own law and the law of its relations with others. Therefore the truest order is that which is founded on the greatest possible liberty; for liberty is at once the condition of vigorous variation and the condition of self-finding.[28]

Only with the development of a new spirit of 'unity in diversity' within the new political structure of a world union, where each individual or each group is dedicated to the fulfillment of all, 'could there come the psychological modification of life and feeling and outlook which would accustom both individual and group to live in their common humanity first and most, subduing their individual and group-egoism, yet losing nothing of their individual or group-power to develop and express in its own way the divinity in man which, once the race was

28 Ibid., pp. 684–85.

assured of its material existence, would emerge as the true object of human existence.'[29]

The climax of this evolution occurs with a movement from the rational to the spiritual age. 'It is this kingdom of God within, the result of the finding of God not in a distant heaven but within ourselves, of which the state of society in an age of the Truth, spiritual age, would be the result and the external figure.'[30]

The relation of this millennial vision of a spiritual age to Aurobindo's political thought is most fully developed in the concluding chapters of his magnum opus, *The Life Divine*, a work which purports to set forth the whole of his philosophy.[31] It is here that Aurobindo attempts to answer that which he had posed as the 'central problem of thought', the task of achieving 'the utmost possible harmony of individual freedom and social unity'. The solution that he sees is emphatically a spiritual one, which regards all exclusively political approaches as nothing but palliatives. He flatly dismisses 'the political, social, or other mechanical remedies which the mind is constantly attempting and which have always failed and will continue to fail to solve anything.'[32]

> The most drastic changes made by these means change nothing; for the old ills exist in a new form: the aspect of the outward environment is altered, but man remains what he was ... Only a spiritual change, an evolution of his being from the superficial

---

29 Ibid., p. 732. The question of what form the political organization of this world union should assume is left untouched by Aurobindo.

30 Aurobindo, *The Human Cycle*, p. 343.

31 The first volume of *The Life Divine* was written in 1914–1916; much of volume two was finished later. The complete two-volume edition was first published in 1939–1940.

32 Aurobindo, *The Life Divine* (Pondicherry: Sri Aurobindo Ashram, 1960), p. 1053.

mental towards the deeper spiritual consciousness, can make a real and effective difference. To discover the spiritual being in himself is the main business of the spiritual man and to help others towards the same evolution is his real service to the race; till that is done, an outward help can succour and alleviate, but nothing or very little more is possible.[33]

Once the evolution to a higher form of spiritual consciousness is achieved, the problem of harmonising individual freedom and social unity will be solved. The kernel of Aurobindo's reasoning on this problem is set forth in the final chapter of *The Life Divine,* in a passage that offers the most complete statement of his mature political philosophy.

The individual as spirit or being is not confined within his humanity; he has been less than human, he can become more than human. The universe finds itself through him even as he finds himself in the universe, but he is capable of becoming more than the universe, since he can surpass it and enter into something in himself and in it and beyond it that is absolute. He is not confined within the community; although his mind and life are, in a way, part of the communal mind and life, there is something in him that can go beyond them. The community exists by the individual, for its mind and life and body are constituted by the mind and life and body of its composing individuals; if that were abolished or disaggregated, its own existence would be abolished or disaggregated, though some spirit or power of it might form again in other individuals; but the individual is not a mere cell of the collective existence; he would not cease to exist if separated or expelled from the collective mass. For the collectivity, the community is not even the whole of humanity and it is not the world: the individual can exist and find himself elsewhere in humanity or by himself in the world.

---

33 Ibid., pp. 1053–54.

If the community has a life dominating that of the individuals which constitute it, still it does not constitute their whole life. If it has its being which it seeks to affirm by the life of the individuals, the individual also has a being of his own which he seeks to affirm in the life of the community. But he is not tied to that; he can affirm himself in another communal life, or, if he is strong enough, in a nomad existence or in an eremite solitude where, if he cannot pursue or achieve a complete material living, he can spiritually exist and find his own reality and indwelling self of being.

The individual is indeed the key of the evolutionary movement; for it is the individual who finds himself, who becomes conscious of the Reality. The movement of the collectivity is a largely subconscious mass movement; it has to formulate and express itself through the individuals to become conscious: its general mass consciousness is always less evolved than the consciousness of its most developed individuals, and it progresses in so far as it accepts their impress or develops what they develop. The individual does not owe his ultimate allegiance either to the State which is a machine or to the community which is a part of life and not the whole of life: his allegiance must be to the Truth, the Self, the Spirit, the Divine which is in him and in all; not to subordinate or lose himself in the mass, but to find and express that truth of being in himself and help the community and humanity in its seeking for its own truth and fullness of being must be his real object of existence. But the extent to which the power of the individual life or the spiritual reality within it becomes operative depends on his own development: so long as he is undeveloped, he has to subordinate in many ways his undeveloped self to whatever is greater than it. As he develops, he moves towards a spiritual freedom, but this freedom is not something entirely separate from all-existence; it has a solidarity with it because that too is the self, the same spirit. As he moves towards spiritual freedom, he moves also towards spiritual oneness. The spiritually realised, the liberated man is preoccupied, says the Gita, with the good of all beings; Buddha discovering the way of Nirvana must turn back to open that way to those who are still under the delusion of their constructive instead of their real being—or non-being; Vivekananda, drawn by the Absolute, feels also the call of the disguised Godhead in humanity and most the call of the fallen and the suffering, the call of the self to the self in the obscure body of the universe. For the awakened individual, the realisation of his truth of being and his inner liberation and perfection must be his primary seeking—first, because that is the call of the Spirit within him, but also because it is only by liberation and perfection and realisation of the truth of being that man can arrive at truth of living. A perfected community also can exist only by the perfection of its individuals, and perfection can come only by the discovery and affirmation in life by each of his own spiritual being and the discovery by all of their spiritual unity and a resultant life unity.[34]

This passage, which begins with an extreme statement of individualism, attempts to set forth the basis of the Indian reasoning on the reconciliation of individual freedom with social unity. The individual's allegiance, first, must not be to the state, which is at once rejected as 'a machine' or even to the community, but to the Absolute, and thus to himself, as part of the Absolute. Yet once the individual attains realization, to 'help the community and humanity in its seeking for its own truth and fullness of being must be his real object of existence'. This because 'as he moves towards spiritual freedom, he moves also towards spiritual oneness'; he comes to know that truth which the Indian classical texts, the Upanishads, set forth, the identity of all being. And the path, a path of service to man, has already been indicated: by the Buddha, the *Bhagavad Gita* and Vivekananda. Aurobindo emphasizes that the road he has indicated is the sole way to spiritual, and thus social, harmony. 'A perfected community can exist only by the perfection of

---

34 Ibid., pp. 1247–49.

its individuals, and perfection can come only by ... the discovery by all of their spiritual unity and resultant life unity.'

Aurobindo's writing illuminates, as much as any of the other thinkers considered here, the fundamental assumptions of his school. His effectiveness as an exponent of modern Indian political thought may be largely attributed to the way in which he regarded the enterprise he had undertaken; the purpose of his philosophy as he understood it. Few modern Indian writers have been more eminently equipped than Aurobindo, in academic training and intellectual capacity, to absorb and adapt ideas from the Western tradition. Rammohun Roy may appear as a comparable figure; for he, like Aurobindo, was versed in several European languages and influenced by wide reading and travel abroad. Aurobindo, like Rammohun, was a Bengali brahman bent on reinterpreting his own tradition in the light of Western ideas; and no less than Rammohun, he was familiar with these ideas. Aurobindo's prolonged residence and education in England brought him into close contact with Christian teachings as well as with British liberal, social and political thought; his thinking was certainly influenced, to some extent, by this climate of opinion. More than Rammohun, Aurobindo seems to have been attracted to French thought and culture. As a Cambridge undergraduate, he expressed enthusiasm for Paris as 'the modern Athens' of the world,[35] and his continuing admiration for French civilization is reflected in a variety of ways throughout his life. His writings often extol the French revolutionary ideals of liberty, equality and fraternity; even the language he uses is peppered with French expressions, for he seems to have maintained a fluency in it until his death. The colony where he chose to spend most of his life was French, and the closest personal and spiritual relationship that he ever established arose with a French woman disciple, 'The Mother',

---

35 A.B. Purani, *The Life of Sri Aurobindo* (Pondicherry: Sri Aurobindo Ashram, 1960), p. 49.

who succeeded him as head of the Pondicherry ashram. The important place that Europe occupied in Aurobindo's life and thought, then, should be appreciated.

At the same time, the extent of Western influence on Aurobindo's philosophy must not be exaggerated, for such an exaggeration would obscure the dominant purpose of his thought as he himself saw it. This purpose was the reconstruction of traditional Indian thought into a modern body of political, social, ethical and spiritual ideas. It was a purpose that had guided the writings of the major nineteenth-century Indian thinkers: Rammohun Roy, Debendranath Tagore, Keshub Chunder Sen, Bankim Chandra Chatterjee and Vivekananda. The major assumptions underlying their thought were shared by Aurobindo, and the development which he gave to some of them comprised the main body of his political philosophy. This development occurred within a growing tradition of modern Indian ideas, and it may best be understood, and itself best become an instrument for understanding, by considering it as a part of this emergent tradition.

Of all the thinkers, Western or Indian, that Aurobindo mentions, no higher tribute is reserved than for Ramakrishna and Vivekananda.[36] Infatuated, as Aurobindo always was, throughout his life, with a pride of Indian civilization, he wrote in exuberant tones of 'the Indian Renaissance' which had begun with Vivekananda:

It was in religion first that the soul of India awoke and triumphed. There were always indications, always great forerunners, but it was when the flower of the educated youth of Calcutta bowed down at the feet of an illiterate Hindu ascetic, a self-illuminated ecstatic and 'mystic' without a single trace or touch of the alien thought or education upon him that the battle was won. The going forth of

---

36 For Aurobindo's judgement of Ramakrishna, see Aurobindo, *Sri Aurobindo on Himself and on the Mother* (Pondicherry: Sri Aurobindo Ashram, 1959), p. 206.

Vivekananda, marked out by the Master as the heroic soul destined to take the world between his two hands and change it, was the first visible sign to the world that India was awake not only to survive but to conquer.[37]

Aurobindo wholly identified himself with the spirit of this great adventure. 'The work that was begun at Dakshineshwar,' he declared, 'is far from finished; it is not even understood. That which Vivekananda received and strove to develop, has not yet materialised.'[38] Aurobindo saw himself as carrying this work to its completion. The task undertaken at Pondicherry was dominated, if not intoxicated, but a desire to fulfill the ideas and aims suggested, for Aurobindo, by the spirit of Indian civilization and personified in figures like Ramakrishna and Vivekananda. It is in this light that Aurobindo may be approached and, hopefully, understood; and with this in mind, his writings should be used to gain insight into the ideas of his contemporaries. He was a thinker who sought both to 'preserve by reconstruction' his ancient tradition and to continue, to bring to fruition, the tradition of nineteenth-century Indian thought. The problems with which Aurobindo struggled, and the premises directing his responses, had been suggested by Vivekananda. Equally important, they were to be shared, developed, and given still other directions and dimensions by Mahatma Gandhi.

---

37 Sri Aurobindo, *The Ideal of the Karmayogin* (Pondicherry: Sri Aurobindo Ashram, 1950), pp. 26–27.

38 Ibid., p. 23.

CHAPTER 6

Gandhi: Individual Freedom and Social Action

'In my opinion, we have used the term "swaraj" without understanding its real significance. I have endeavoured to explain it as I understand it, and my conscience testifies that my life henceforth is dedicated to its attainment.'[1]

—Gandhi, 1909

The Early Development of Gandhi's Ideas on Freedom

'If you want to speak of politics in India,' Vivekananda told a California audience in 1900, 'you must speak through the language of religion.'[2] Already at that time, in India, the truth of this remark had become clear: in Bengal, Aurobindo and Pal had begun to formulate

---

1 M.K. Gandhi, *Hind Swaraj or Indian Home Rule* (Ahmedabad: Navajivan Publishing, 1938) p. 104; *CWMG* 10:64 and *Hind Swaraj and Other Writings*, ed. A.J. Parel (Cambridge: Cambridge University Press, 1997), p. 119.

2 Vivekananda, *Works*, Vol. 8 (1959), p. 77.

a theology of nationalism; in Maharashtra, Tilak had found in Shivaji the symbol of a regenerated Hindu *Raj*, and, there too, G.K. Gokhale, soon to establish The Servants of India Society, looked ahead to 'the spiritualisation of Indian politics'. The future political leadership of India, however, was not, in 1900, being decided in either Bengal or Maharashtra. Experiments in the application of religious language and belief to the sphere of politics were being conducted elsewhere, outside India, in South Africa. All the major nationalist leaders at the turn of the century were aware of these experiments, but few, if any, foresaw their ultimate significance. Nor could they have perceived what was ahead for the man behind them, Mohandas Karamchand Gandhi.

'He is a man,' said Gokhale of Gandhi, 'who may be well described as a man among men, a hero among heroes, a patriot amongst patriots, and we may well say that in him, Indian humanity at the present time has really reached its high watermark.'[3] But this was in 1909: Gandhi had already spent sixteen years working with the Indian community in South Africa. And even Gokhale's appraisal came far ahead of its time; for he, almost alone among nationalist leaders, had taken a close interest in problems concerning the South African Government's discrimination against Indian immigrants. Gokhale had visited Gandhi on the 'Tolstoy Farm' outside Pretoria; he had witnessed the early flowering of satyagraha, and he had acquired insight into Gandhi's emerging philosophy of life. Other Indian Congressmen did not know Gandhi this intimately. Thus, when he finally left South Africa and arrived in Bombay on 9 January 1915, several political notables effused over his accomplishments, but there is no sign that any, outside Gokhale, even remotely anticipated that in less than six years, Gandhi would have gained leadership of the Indian National Congress.

---

3   D.G. Tendulkar, *Mahatma: Life of Mohandas Karamchand Gandhi* (8 vols.), Vol. I (Delhi: Publications Division, Ministry of Information and Broadcasting, Government of India, 1960–62), p. 112.

Nor does the British anticipation of Gandhi's ascent appear to have been any sharper. Lord Willingdon, then Governor of Bombay, may have presaged something, for he asked Gokhale to arrange a meeting with Gandhi immediately upon his arrival. 'I ask one thing of you,' he said to Gandhi. 'I would like you to come and see me whenever you propose to take any steps concerning government.'[4] The general reaction, though, of the Government to Gandhi at this time seems to have been sympathetic rather than suspicious. Edwin S. Montagu, after his first interview with Gandhi in November 1917, recorded in his diary,

> He is a social reformer; he has a real desire to find grievances and to cure them, not for any reasons of self-advertisement, but to improve the conditions of his fellowmen. He is the real hero of the settlement of the Indian question in South Africa where he suffered imprisonment. He has just been helping the government to find a solution for the grievances of the indigo labour in Bihar. He dresses like a coolie, forswears all personal advancement, lives practically on the air, and is a pure visionary. He does not understand details of schemes; all he wants is that we should get India on our side. He wants the millions of India to leap to the assistance of the British throne.[5]

Montagu's impression should not be regarded as misguided, for it reflects the actual state of Gandhi's mind at this time. Until 1920, Gandhi not only remained loyal to the Empire, he actively supported it throughout the First World War. His friends upbraided him for inconsistency with his early ideas. However, Gandhi defended his

---

4   Ibid., p. 158.

5   Edwin S. Montagu, *An Indian Diary*, ed. Venetia Montagu (London: Heinemann, 1930), p. 58.

position by explaining the unique virtues of the British government, which allowed him freedom to pursue his ideals.

> During my three months' tour in India as also in South Africa [Gandhi told a Madras Law Dinner in April 1915] I have been so often questioned how I, a determined opponent of modern civilization and an avowed patriot, could reconcile myself to loyalty of the British Empire ... It gives me the greatest pleasure ... to re-declare my loyalty to this British Empire and my loyalty is based upon very selfish grounds ... I discovered that the British Empire had certain ideals with which I have fallen in love and one of those ideals is that every subject of the British Empire has the freest scope possible for his energies and honour and whatever he thinks is due to his conscience. I think that this is true of the British Empire as it is not true of any other government. I feel, as you here perhaps know, that I am no lover of any government, and I have more than once said that government is best which governs least. And I have found that it is possible for me to be governed least under the British Empire.[6]

It may be argued that, in the period of 1915 to 1920, not only did Gandhi believe that the political ideas which he had developed in South Africa were compatible with British rule, but also that during this time he did, in fact, pursue these earlier ideas. At least two points would seem to substantiate this argument. First, Gandhi's theories of swaraj and satyagraha freely developed in this five-year span; a fuller expression of these two concepts in particular was achieved. Second, Gandhi actually undertook satyagraha in several instances, most notably in Champaran in 1917. The local government administration there attempted to suppress his efforts, but he eventually overcame

---

6   M.K. Gandhi, *Speeches and Writings*, Fourth Edition (Madras: G.A. Natesan, 1938), p. 310.

their opposition. He then carried the struggle to a successful climax without unduly alienating the government.[7] From this, it may appear that during this time, Gandhi, enjoying full freedom under British rule, consistently maintained the ideas he had developed in South Africa.

One striking incident, however, belies this whole argument. In 1918, the government called for increased Indian support of the war effort. Lord Chelmsford invited Gandhi to attend a Delhi War Conference in April and asked for Gandhi's support of the resolution on recruitment. Tilak and Jinnah had not been invited, for they had raised the question of the terms on which Indian cooperation might be extended to the government. Their qualms indicated a strong hesitation among many Indian leaders who wanted convincing evidence of government concessions to nationalist demands. Gandhi at first hesitated, but then was persuaded to attend, and he supported the resolution.[8] He set forth his reasoning in a letter to Lord Chelmsford written immediately after the Conference.

> I recognise that in the hour of its danger, we must give, as we have decided to give, ungrudging and unequivocal support to the Empire of which we aspire in the near future to be partners in the same sense as the Dominions Overseas. But it is the simple truth that our response is due to the expectation that our goal will be reached all the more speedily. On that account, even as performance of duty automatically confers a corresponding right, people are entitled to believe that the imminent reforms alluded to in your speech will embody the main general principles of the Congress-League Scheme, and I am sure that it is this faith which has enabled many

7   See, for example, the sentence already quoted from Montagu's *Diary*: 'He has just been helping the government to find a solution ... in Bihar.'

8   B.R. Nanda, *Mahatma Gandhi: A Biography* (London: Allen and Unwin, 1958), p. 168.

members of the Conference to tender to the government their full hearted co-operation.[9]

After the Conference, Gandhi turned himself into a 'recruitment officer' and toured the country giving speeches. The arguments that he set forth in this campaign for mass enlistment can only be regarded as a complete contradiction of the beliefs which he had advanced earlier in South Africa.[10] Gandhi not only argued from the standpoint of political expediency, but he also glorified participation in the war as a good in itself:

> There can be no friendship between the brave and the effeminate. We are regarded as a cowardly people. If we want to become free from that reproach, we should learn the use of arms.[11] ... The foregoing argument will show that by enlisting in the army we help the Empire, we qualify ourselves for *Swarajya*, we learn to defend India and to a certain extent regain our lost manhood.[12]

The nature of this argument is reminiscent of the early Aurobindo; it sets forth a belief in the relation of violence to manliness, not unlike the Indian terrorists, though quite unlike anything Gandhi had said before 1918, or was to say after that time. He had not forgotten his earlier ideas, but he had neatly compartmentalized them, in 1918, from the mainstream of his activity.[13] Two events quickly brought these early

---

9   Gandhi, *Speeches and Writings*, p. 437

10   Thomas Weber and Dennis Dalton, 'Gandhi and the Pandemic', *Economic and Political Weekly* 55, no. 25 (June 2020): 34–39.

11   Ibid., p. 443.

12   Ibid., p. 445.

13   Ibid., p. 420. 'Military training,' Gandhi said at the time, in defence of his action, 'is intended for those who do not believe in satyagraha.' But this did not explain why he, as a satyagrahi, urged military training.

ideas back into permanent focus: the Amritsar tragedy of 1919 and the British settlement of the Khilafat question early the following year.

On 13 April 1919, a crowd of Indian demonstrators assembled in Jallianwala Bagh, a small, enclosed square in the city of Amritsar. Mob violence had occurred throughout the Punjab in connection with similar demonstrations, and General Dyer, who was in command of the contingent at Amritsar, felt that drastic action had become necessary. He entered the square with fifty riflemen, fired suddenly and steadily into the crowd, and killed about 400 Indians in ten minutes.[14] When Gandhi heard the reports he was considerably shaken. One of his closest friends, Charles Andrews, remarks,

> No one can understand Mahatma Gandhi's attitude towards Great Britain and the British Empire unless he has come to realize that 'Amritsar' was the critical event which changed Mahatma Gandhi from a wholehearted supporter into a pronounced opponent.[15]

General Dyer's icy defence of his action reeked to Gandhi of unspeakable brutality, and the subsequent Hunter Commission Report seemed only to whitewash the event. Perhaps nothing shocked Gandhi more, though, than the reaction of the British public: he had expected unanimous repentance, in accord with his belief in the English sense of justice, but he found instead ambivalence, and even efforts to exonerate Dyer completely.[16]

The Khilafat issue was seen by Gandhi and the Indian Muslims as representing a British breach of promise. Lloyd George, they contended, had promised the preservation of the Turkish Sultan's

14 Tendulkar, *Mahatma*, Vol. I, p. 258.

15 C.F. Andrews, *Mahatma Gandhi's Ideas* (London: Allen & Unwin, 1930), p. 230.

16 Nanda, *Mahatma Gandhi*, pp. 176–80.

temporal powers; but the treaty with Turkey, concluded in 1920, had betrayed this assurance. The Khilafat incident contributed to Gandhi's growing disillusionment with British rule, but it did not affect him in the same way as Amritsar. The latter filled him with a sense of moral repulsion and perhaps convinced him that Britain would not give up India gracefully. The former issue, however, gave Gandhi a stand on which he could champion the Muslims' cause and thus rally all-Indian support; it presented an exceptional opportunity for gaining Hindu–Muslim unity, a chance, Gandhi remarked, which would probably not recur for a hundred years.[17] The Non-cooperation movement emerged from the grievances surrounding the Amritsar and Khilafat issues; together, they prompted Gandhi's unequivocal opposition to the British Raj. 'The knowledge of the Punjab and Khilafat betrayal,' he wrote in late 1920, 'has revolutionised my view of the existing system of government.'[18]

However, the shock of Amritsar and the 'Khilafat betrayal' were only the immediate and not the fundamental causes of Gandhi's volte-face. These two events merely revealed to him the implications of political attitudes that he had developed much earlier; they made him fully aware, for the first time, of the logical consequences of all that he had learned and taught in South Africa. This would explain why, in the years immediately before the crystallization process of 1919–1920 occurred, his thoughts and actions on the war effort should have been so muddled and sharply contradictory to earlier held beliefs. Once the war was over, Gandhi quickly returned to these beliefs; and they now remained at the fore for the rest of his life. To understand them, and especially his idea of freedom, one must turn to the genesis of Gandhi's thought, his South African experience.

---

17 Ibid., p. 185.

18 M.K. Gandhi, *Young India*, 1919–1922, 29 September 1920, I (1922), p. 375.

South Africa and Hind Swaraj

'What Gandhi did to South Africa,' observes one of his biographers, 'was less important than what South Africa did to him.'[19] South Africa, as it has often and accurately been said, provided the laboratory for Gandhi's experiments; it proved an excellent testing ground since many of the problems which he later found in India occurred there in miniature. Moreover, no Indian had confronted these problems in South Africa before: Gandhi was writing on a clean slate, he was able to try out almost any methods he chose.

Gandhi had formed beliefs before he arrived in South Africa. His *Autobiography* testifies to the lasting impression of childhood experiences, impressions and lessons which were to effect the later development of the two ideas that dominated his thought: truth and nonviolence.[20] Then almost three years were spent as a law student in London. During this time Gandhi discovered the *Sermon on the Mount*, and came to understand the *Bhagavad Gita* through Sir Edwin Arnold's English translation.[21] Gandhi later recalled that at this time, 'My young mind tried to unify the teaching of the Gita, *The Light of Asia* and the *Sermon on the Mount*. That renunciation was the highest form of religion appealed to me greatly.'[22] Religious and moral attitudes had thus begun to form in London. But they took definite shape only in South Africa. Moreover, he does not appear to have given any thought at all to political questions before his direct involvement with the problems of the Indian community in Natal.

---

19 Nanda, *Mahatma Gandhi*, p. 121.

20 Gandhi, *Autobiography*, *CWMG* 39:4, pp. 190–91, 401–2.

21 Ibid., p. 60.

22 Ibid., p. 61.

Gandhi remarked tersely in *Young India* in 1927, 'South Africa gave the start to my life's mission.'[23] The ideas which inspired that mission merged there into a coherent body of thought. This mission was one of self-realization, but before Gandhi left South Africa, he knew that that must involve a struggle for India's freedom as well. He had left Bombay for Durban in 1893 as a legal counsel for Dada Abdulla and Company; he returned to India twenty-one years later with a sense of mission, a reservoir of practical experience in social and political reform, and with the ideas which form the basis of his political thought. That is what South Africa did for Gandhi.[24]

The main ideas which emerged from Gandhi's South African experience are contained in his short work, *Hind Swaraj*, easily one of the key writings of his entire career. The original text was written in Gandhi's native language of Gujarati in 1909 during a return voyage from London to South Africa. This was first published serially in Gandhi's newspaper, *Indian Opinion*. Later, it went through numerous reprints, became a text for the Indian nationalist movement, and was occasionally banned by the government. In a significant comment on *Hind Swaraj* written in 1921, Gandhi stated the purpose behind the book.

---

23 *Young India*, 17 March 1927, Ibid., 33:165.

24 The chief influences on Gandhi's thought during his South African experience, aside from the *Sermon on the Mount* and the Gita, came from Tolstoy's *The Kingdom of God is Within You*, Ruskin's *Unto This Last*, and Thoreau's essay *On Civil Disobedience*. The two main personal influences were both Indian: Raychandbhai, a Jain religious teacher and G.K. Gokhale. Gandhi also read Vivekananda and was sufficiently impressed to have tried (unsuccessfully) to see him while in Calcutta. The actual extent of any of these influences on Gandhi's thought is difficult to determine, for he gave to each a personal twist, using it as he saw fit.

It was written ... in answer to the Indian school of violence, and its prototype in South Africa. I came in contact with every known Indian anarchist in London. Their bravery impressed me, but I feel that their zeal was misguided. I felt that violence was no remedy for India's ills, and that her civilization required the use of a different and higher weapon for self-protection. The Satyagraha of South Africa was still an infant hardly two years old. But it had developed sufficiently to permit me to write of it with some degree of confidence ... It [*Hind Swaraj*] teaches the gospel of love in the place of that of hate. It replaces violence with self-sacrifice. It pits soul-force against brute force.[25]

The aim of *Hind Swaraj* was to answer the anarchists with an alternative to violence, derived from Gandhi's earliest experiments with satyagraha. Equally important is the book's concern with the concept from which it takes its title: this is Gandhi's first extensive statement on swaraj, and the ideas on it that he sets forth here provide the basis for much of his future thinking on the meaning of freedom. *Hind Swaraj*, then, is a statement on both the method and the goal of Gandhi's thought: satyagraha and swaraj. The correspondence which is drawn here between these two concepts is one of the crucial messages of the book.

Gandhi had written of swaraj before 1909, but his reference to the term is seldom, and it indicates only a limited awareness of the concept as it was then developing in India. The first explicit use of swaraj in Gandhi's *Collected Works* occurs with a brief reference to Dadabhai Naoroji's Congress Presidential Address in 1906. Gandhi wrote in *Indian Opinion:*

The address by the Grand Old Man of India is very forceful and effective. His words deserve to be enshrined in our hearts. The substance of the address is that India will not prosper until we wake

25 *Young India*, 26 January 1921, Ibid., 19:277.

up and become united. To put it differently, it means that it lies in
our hands to achieve swaraj, to prosper and to preserve the rights
we value ... For our part we are to use only the strength that comes
from unity and truth. That is to say, our bondage in India can cease
this day, if all the people unite in their demands and are ready to
suffer any hardships that may befall them.[26]

These few sentences contain the germs of the concept of freedom that
Gandhi was soon to develop, and thirty-four years later, he was still
admonishing the Congress, and the Indian people, that swaraj 'will not
drop from heaven, all of a sudden, one fine morning. But it has to be
built up brick by brick by corporate self-effort.'[27]

In the months following Naoroji's address, and before the writing
of *Hind Swaraj*, Gandhi rarely uses the term swaraj; he does write
occasionally, though, on his idea of freedom. It is noteworthy that
immediately before his departure for London in June 1909, Gandhi
had spent three months in a Pretoria prison for civil disobedience.
There he read the Gita, Upanishads, and the Bible, as well as Ruskin,
Tolstoy, Emerson and Thoreau. Of these writers, he seems to have
been most impressed, at this time, by Thoreau, and particularly by this
passage from *On Civil Disobedience*:

I saw that, if there was a wall of stone between me and my townsmen,
there was a still more difficult one to climb or break through before
they could get to be as free as I was.[28]

Gandhi remarks on these lines that the individual who pursues truth
through civil disobedience may be imprisoned, but 'his soul is thus

26 Gandhi, *Indian Opinion*, 5 January 1907 in *CWMG* 6:269.

27 Tendulkar, *Mahatma*, Vol. VI, p. 34.

28 Thoreau, quoted by Gandhi in Tendulkar, *Mahatma*, Vol. I, p. 100.

free', and 'taking this view of jail life, he feels himself quite a free being'. He concludes that a right understanding and enjoyment of freedom 'solely rests with individuals and their mental attitude ...'[29] Several years later, Gandhi was to write:

> Whilst the views expressed in *Hind Swaraj* are held by me, I have but endeavoured humbly to follow Tolstoy, Ruskin, Thoreau, Emerson and other writers, besides the masters of Indian philosophy.[30]

When Gandhi left Cape Town for London, then the strands of his ideas on freedom, gleaned from both Indian and Western sources, as well as from his own experience, were in his mind; the stimulus for weaving them together into a coherent pattern, and fusing them with a programme of social action, came during his four months' stay in London.

Gandhi arrived on 10 July; nine days earlier, London had been shaken by the murder of Sir Curzon Wyllie. The assassin was the young Indian terrorist Madanlal Dhingra, who delivered, at his trial, a stirring speech on patriotism. The city was afire with discussions among anarchists, nationalists and terrorists; Gandhi became intensely involved. He argued the views on satyagraha, which were soon to become an integral part of his political and personal creed: India could only gain her freedom through nonviolence; terrorism would only cause disruption and decay. From these conversations emerged the ideas set forth in *Hind Swaraj*.[31]

Hind Swaraj takes the form of a dialogue between 'Reader' and 'Editor'. The former argues, with haste and rashness, terrorist ideas;

---

29 Ibid., p. 100.

30 *CWMG* 10:189.

31 Gandhi describes *Hind Swaraj* as 'a faithful record of conversations I had with workers, one of whom was an avowed anarchist.' *CWMG* 67:170.

the latter presents Gandhi's own case. At the outset, the Editor appears on the defensive; gradually and patiently, he subdues the anarchist's storm, and the Reader yields, not only to superior reasoning, but to the force and novelty of an alternative which seems more revolutionary than his own position. As a statement of political thought, *Hind Swaraj* has considerable limitations: it is a brief polemical tract more than a logical development of a serious and measured argument; written hastily, in less than ten days, it suffers from occasional disjointedness and egregious overstatement. Yet the essence of Gandhi's political and social philosophy is here, and he could write in 1998, 'after the stormy thirty years through which I have since passed, I have seen nothing to make me alter the view expounded in it'.[32]

The book opens with the Reader's attack upon the Indian Congress as 'an instrument for perpetuating British rule'; Moderates like Naoroji and Gokhale are indicted as unworthy 'friends of the English'. Gandhi rises to their defence: he insists that they, along with Englishmen like Hume and Wedderburn, deserve India's respect for their selflessness and for preparing the foundations of Indian Home Rule. The nature of Gandhi's argument, however, is crucial. He neither identifies himself with the Moderates nor does he consider their position adequate; he only argues that their contribution was necessary to make further advance possible. 'If, after many years of study,' the Editor contends, 'a teacher were to teach me something, and if I were to build a little more on the foundation laid by that teacher, I would not, on that account, be considered wiser than the teacher. He would always command my respect. Such is the case with the Grand Old Man of India.'[33] The Reader reluctantly agrees, but then turns his ire against Gokhale, and elicits this reply: 'Professor Gokhale occupies the place of a parent. What does it matter if he cannot run with us? A nation that is desirous

---

32 Ibid., p.18.

33 Ibid., p. 8. (The reference is to Dadabhai Naoroji, 1825–1917.)

of securing Home Rule cannot afford to despise its ancestors. We shall become useless, if we lack respect for our elders.' 'Are we, then, to follow him in every respect?' 'I never said any such thing. If we conscientiously differed from him, the learned Professor himself would advise us to follow the dictates of our conscience rather than him.'[34] Thus, the Moderates are defended in a proper, almost reverential, spirit; yet, in fact, they are set aside as 'ancestors' who have played out their roles. The Congress appears in much the same manner, worthy of respect but no longer a dynamic organ of progress. 'All I have to show,' the Editor concludes, 'is that the Congress gave us a foretaste of Home Rule.'[35] And this indeed is all that he does show.

Gandhi's attitude toward the Congress, and the Moderates who in 1909 controlled the Congress, is clear; but he has not yet mentioned the Extremists. Aurobindo, Pal, Tilak and Lajpat Rai were all Extremist leaders of considerable renown at this time, yet their names do not appear in *Hind Swaraj*. A passing, but revealing, reference is made to the Extremist group at the end of the second chapter. 'Our leaders,' the Editor observes, 'are divided into two parties: the Moderates and the Extremists. These may be considered as the slow party and impatient party.'[36] 'Slow' and 'impatient': this is how Gandhi characterizes the two main sections of Indian political leadership. India cannot move ahead with slow leaders, yet hasty and rash action may only result in ultimate retrogression. The Moderates have been left behind, but the Extremists are found to be irresponsible. It is no coincidence that the Editor often criticizes the Reader for his 'impatience': *Hind Swaraj* is a direct reply to the Extremists as well as to the lunatic fringe of Indian anarchists and terrorists. Early in the book, then, Gandhi dismisses the leadership of both national parties in India as unviable. The moment has arrived

---

34 Ibid., p. 10.

35 Ibid., p. 11.

36 Ibid., p. 13.

for a statement of his own position: a philosophy and programme of
action which appear to gain the best of both sides, not through steering
a mean course, but rather by moving forward to a new alternative and
a fresh conception of freedom.

What is Swaraj?

The Reader now poses a central question, 'What is swaraj?' and the
remainder of the book is occupied with a consideration of that question.
The Reader gives his version of swaraj first:

> As is Japan, so must India be. We must have our own navy, our
> own army, and we must have our own splendour, and then will
> India's voice ring through the world. If the education we have
> received be of any use, if the works of Spencer, Mill and others be
> of any importance, and if the English Parliament be the Mother
> of Parliaments, I certainly think that we should copy the English
> people ... It is, therefore, proper for us to import their institutions.[37]

The Editor disagrees:

> You have drawn the picture well. In effect it means this: that we
> want English rule without the Englishman. You want the tiger's
> nature, but not the tiger; that is to say, you would make India
> English. And when it becomes English, it will be called not
> Hindustan but Englishtan. This is not the swaraj that I want ...
> It is as difficult for me to understand the true nature of swaraj as
> it seems to you to be easy. I shall therefore, for the time being,
> content myself with endeavouring to show that what you call
> swaraj is not truly swaraj.[38]

---

37 Ibid., pp. 15–16.
38 Ibid., p. 16.

The subsequent discussion, which occupies the middle section of the book, comprises Gandhi's notorious blanket condemnation of Western civilization. The argument is grossly overstated, often misguided, and, in some instances, as with the criticism of doctors and hospitals, lapses into pure fantasy.[39] The main point of this section is that all Western civilization should be shunned, for it 'takes note neither of morality nor of religion.'[40] All its trappings, from its parliamentary system of government to the whole of its industrial complex, are foreign to real civilization. If Indians are to attain swaraj, they must not imitate the Western example but construct a civilization on the simple ethical and religious truths found in their own tradition.[41] 'The tendency of the Indian civilisation is to elevate the moral being, that of the Western civilisation is to propagate immorality. The latter is godless; the former is based on a belief in God.'[42] This sweeping categorization of Eastern and Western civilizations as 'moral' and 'immoral' was, by the time Gandhi wrote, commonplace in modern Indian thought; no indictment of the West, however, appeared that was more severe than that of *Hind Swaraj,* for everything modern was here placed on the chopping block. Gokhale thought this outburst so crude that he predicted the whole book's early destruction by Gandhi himself.

Although Gandhi always maintained concurrence with these early views set forth in *Hind Swaraj,* he sought later to modify his judgement of Western civilization. In 1921 he accepted as an immediate, though not ultimate, goal, 'Parliamentary swaraj'. 'The least that swaraj means,' he said, 'is a settlement with the government in accordance with the wishes of the chosen representatives of the people.'[43] Similarly with his

---

39 Ibid., pp. 35–36.

40 Ibid., p. 20.

41 Ibid., pp. 36–38.

42 Ibid., p. 38.

43 *Young India,* 15 December 1921, *CWMG* 22:18.

views on machinery, he modified his stand, contending in 1924, 'What I object to is the craze for machinery, not machinery as such ... I am aiming not at eradication of all machinery, but limitation.'[44] Yet the substance of the view of civilization advanced in *Hind Swaraj* remained intact throughout Gandhi's life and deeply affected his conception of the nature of the good society. At its worst, this view manifests itself in a negative suspicion of the West, and a highly provincial world outlook. At its best, it moulded a theory of the good society suited to the Indian situation; a social order of small communities, each seeking attainment of individual freedom and social equality through mutual cooperation and respect. This was his vision of Sarvodaya, the 'Welfare of All': the pattern of an Indian society that had indeed achieved swaraj:

> In this structure composed of innumerable villages, there will be ever widening, never ascending circles. Life will not be a pyramid with the apex sustained by the bottom. But it will be an oceanic circle whose centre will be the individual always ready to perish for the village, the latter ready to perish for the circle of villages, till at last the whole becomes one life composed of individuals, never aggressive in their arrogance but ever humble, sharing the majesty of the oceanic circle of which they are integral units.
>
> Therefore, the outermost circumference will not wield power to crush the inner circle but will give strength to all within and derive its own strength from it.[45]

A right form of civilization, Gandhi concludes in *Hind Swaraj*, 'is that mode of conduct which points out to man the path of duty. Performance of duty and observance of morality are convertible terms. To observe morality is to attain mastery over our minds and

---

44 Gandhi, *Young India*, 1924–1926, 13 November 1924, II, p. 1029 and *CWMG* 24:548.

45 Gandhi, *Harijan*, 21 July 1946 in *CWMG* 85:33.

our passions. So doing, we know ourselves. The Gujarati equivalent for civilization means "good conduct".'[46] In striving to build this civilization, Indians will not only construct a free nation, they will also come to realize swaraj within themselves. For just as a free civilization demands 'mastery over our mind and our passions', so freedom for the individual consists of each person establishing rule over himself, mastery of his mind and passions. 'If we become free, India is free. And in this thought you have a definition of swaraj. It is swaraj when we learn to rule ourselves. It is, therefore, in the palm of our hands … but such swaraj has to be experienced, by each one for himself.'[47] This is the core of Gandhi's idea of freedom. He reiterates it at the end of *Hind Swaraj*: 'Real home-rule is self-rule or self-control.'[48] As a concept, this idea is at one with Vivekananda's understanding of the meaning of freedom. And Aurobindo said, 'By liberty we mean the freedom to obey the law of our being'. Like Vivekananda and Aurobindo, Gandhi was above all concerned with right obedience to one's self. Several years after writing *Hind Swaraj*, he declared, 'The only tyrant I accept in this world is the "still small voice" within.'[49] For Gandhi, as well as for other members of this school, such tyranny was a necessary element of swaraj.

Three main aspects of Gandhi's idea of swaraj may be noted, at this point, to indicate the form which it came to assume after his initial statement of it in 1909. First, Gandhi always saw freedom as primarily an individual and not a collective quality; in this respect, he was at one with Vivekananda and Aurobindo. 'Swaraj of a people,' Gandhi affirmed, 'means the sum total of the swaraj (self-rule) of individuals.'[50]

---

46 Gandhi, *Hind Swaraj*, in *CWMG* 10:37.

47 Ibid., p. 64.

48 Ibid., p. 64.

49 Tendulkar, *Mahatma*, Vol. II, p. 91.

50 Gandhi, *Harijan*, 25 March 1939, in *Socialism of My Conception* (Bombay: Bharatiya Vidya Bhavan, 1957), p. 143.

Just as Aurobindo emphasized that the realization of spiritual freedom demanded an enjoyment of civil liberties, so Gandhi stressed the necessity of individual political and social freedom.

> If the individual ceases to count what is left of society? Individual freedom alone can make a man voluntarily surrender himself completely to the service of society. If it is wrested from him, he becomes an automaton and society is ruined. No society can possibly be built on a denial of individual freedom. It is contrary to the very nature of man.[51]

As Gandhi's thought matured, he placed increasing emphasis upon nonviolence, and saw its observance as closely linked with the preservation of liberty. He argued that 'Civil Liberty consistent with the observance of non-violence is the first step towards swaraj. It is the foundation of freedom.'[52] Yet Gandhi would not allow even this commitment to nonviolence to jeopardize the individual's enjoyment of political and social freedom. 'If I had my way as the president of a non-violent Indian republic, I should not hesitate to give those who are violently inclined, the liberty of violent speech.'[53] He summed up his belief in the elementary importance of individual liberty, near the end of his life, when he said:

> [T]o make mistakes as a free man ... is better than being in bondage in order to avoid them [for] the mind of a man who remains good under compulsion cannot improve, in fact it worsens. And when

---

51 Gandhi, *Harijan*, 1 February 1942, in *Democracy: Real and Deceptive* (Ahmedabad: Navajivan Publishing House, 1961), p. 31.

52 Tendulkar, *Mahatma*, Vol. V, p 129.

53 Ibid., p. 328.

compulsion is removed, all the defects well up to the surface with even greater force.[54]

Second, although Gandhi carefully specified the conventional civil liberties of the press, speech, association and religion as fundamental to swaraj,[55] he held that the essence of freedom must constitute more than social, political or economic liberty. Swaraj 'is infinitely greater than and includes independence'.[56]

Let there be no mistake about my conception of swaraj. It is complete independence of alien control and complete economic independence. So, at one end you have political independence; at the other, economic. It has two other ends. One of them is moral and social; the corresponding end is Dharma, i.e. religion in the highest sense of the term. It includes Hinduism, Islam, Christianity, etc., but is superior to them all. You may recognize it by the name of Truth, not the honesty of experience, but the living Truth that pervades everything and will survive all destruction and all transformation. Moral and social uplift may be recognized by the term we are used to, i.e. Non-violence. Let us call this the square of swaraj, which will be out of shape if any of its angles is untrue. We cannot achieve this political and economic freedom without Truth and Non-violence in concrete terms, without a living faith in God, and hence moral and social elevation.[57]

---

54 *Harijan*, 29 September 1946 in Pyarelal, *Mahatma Gandhi: The Last Phase* (Ahmedabad: Navajivan Publishing House, 1958), 2 vols., Vol. II, p. 671.

55 Tendulkar, *Mahatma*, Vol. II, p. 78 and Vol. V, pp. 326–27.

56 *Young India*, 12 January 1928, III, p. 547.

57 Gandhi, *Harijan*, 2 January 1937 in *Socialism of My Conception*, p. 120. It should be noted that Gandhi's conception of 'economic independence', though considered by him to be an aspect of swaraj, as

These were the four points on Gandhi's compass of swaraj: Truth, Nonviolence, political and economic independence; swaraj remained incomplete without the realization of each, since each, for Gandhi, was interwoven with all.

Finally, Gandhi's conception of swaraj made the same distinction between 'inner' and 'outer' forms of freedom conceived of earlier by Vivekananda and Aurobindo. In Vivekananda's thought, this distinction involved a relegation of political freedom and national independence to a subsidiary position. But as the struggle for political independence quickened, it became increasingly difficult for India's leaders to appreciate the advantages of 'inner' freedom. Aurobindo attempted to identify national with spiritual freedom, but this resulted in an extreme form of religious nationalism which threatened individual liberty. This approach was eventually abandoned by Aurobindo, and it was never attempted by Gandhi. Gandhi consistently emphasized the supreme value of a supra-political form of freedom, but few other Indian political leaders shared his views on this issue. His difficulties are well expressed in this 'Message to the Ceylon National Congress', delivered in Ceylon in 1927:

It is, I know, a pleasurable pastime (and I have indulged in it sufficiently as you know) to strive against the powers that be, and to wrestle with the government of the day, especially when that government happens to be a foreign government and a government under which we rightly feel we have not that scope which we should have, and which we desire, for expansion and fullest self-expression. But I have also come to the conclusion that self-expression and self-government are not things which may be either taken from us by anybody or which can be given us by anybody. It is quite true that if those who happen to hold our destinies, or seem to

well as a vital component of his Constructive Programme, will not be examined here, in this analysis of his political thought.

hold our destinies in their hands, are favourably disposed, are sympathetic, understand our aspirations, no doubt it is then easier for us to expand. But after all, self-government depends entirely upon our own internal strength, upon our ability to fight against the heaviest odds. Indeed, self-government which does not require that continuous striving to attain it and to sustain it is not worth the name. I have therefore endeavoured to show both in word and in deed, that political self-government—that is self-government for a large number of men and women—is no better than individual self-government, and therefore it is to be attained by precisely the same means that are required for individual self-government or self-rule, and so as you know also, I have striven in India to place this ideal before the people in season and out of season, very often much to the disgust of those who are politically minded merely.[58]

Gandhi argued, until the end of his life—not only before Indian independence but also in the months after—that swaraj must remain hollow and meaningless without the acquisition of 'inward freedom', and for this, a course of action should be followed through which Indians might gain sovereignty over themselves as well as over their nation.

The outward freedom, therefore, that we shall attain will only be in exact proportion to the inward freedom to which we may have grown at a given moment. And if this is the correct view of freedom, our chief energy must be concentrated upon achieving reform from within. In this much needed work, all who will can take an equal share. We need neither to be lawyers nor legislators to be able to take part in the great effort. When this reform takes place on a national scale, no outside power can stop our onward march.[59]

---

58 *Young India*, 1 December 1927, III, p. 487.
59 *Young India*, 1 November 1928, III, pp. 901–2.

Satyagraha

The origins of satyagraha in Gandhi's South African experience were
traced in the first chapter. A closer consideration may now be made
of the relationship between satyagraha and swaraj. This involves,
primarily, an examination of the various forms which satyagraha
assumes in its development from an elementary method of civil
disobedience to an all-embracing approach to problems of moral,
social, and political reform. Since Gandhi believed in the inseparable
relationship of swaraj to satyagraha, a development in one was always
paralleled, in his thought, by a similar development in the other: as a
reformer, engrossed in problems of change, Gandhi sought to keep his
goal of swaraj firmly tied to his method of satyagraha.

The basic premise underlying the relationship between these two
concepts is set forth in *Hind Swaraj*; there, swaraj is defined as self-rule,
and satyagraha represents the way in which the individual, through
voluntary self-sacrifice, may gain control over himself. The special
function of satyagraha, when extended to the political realm, is to
strengthen the individual's 'soul-force' as he offers civil disobedience
against the government.

> Passive resistance [remarks the Editor in *Hind Swaraj*] is a method
> of securing rights by personal suffering; it is the reverse of resistance
> by arms. When I refuse to do a thing that is repugnant to my
> conscience, I use soul-force. For instance, the government of the
> day has passed a law which is applicable to me. I do not like it. If
> by using violence I force the government to repeal the law, I am
> employing what may be termed body-force. If I do not obey the law
> and accept the penalty for its breach, I use soul-force. It involves
> sacrifice of self.[60]

---

60 Gandhi, *Hind Swaraj*, p. 48.

When the individual's spiritual power, or soul-force, becomes fully
developed through self-sacrifice, he has mastered the technique and
has attained swaraj. 'Control over the mind is alone necessary [for
the passive resister] and when that is attained, man is free ...'[61] The
belief in achieving self-realization through voluntary self-sacrifice and
suffering is embedded in the Indian tradition; Gandhi's innovation
emerged with his relation of this ancient belief to the modern Indian
call for social and political change. The government came to serve as the
object on which the satyagrahi sharpened his horns of self-discipline.
The aim of self-realization or swaraj became inseparably linked with
the political demand of Home Rule. And finally satyagraha or passive
resistance was seen as the only way to achieve swaraj for 'there is just
the same inviolable connection between the means and the end as
there is between the seed and the tree,' and the lofty goal of swaraj
may thus only be attained with the purest of means.[62] 'Real Home-
Rule,' the Editor concludes, 'is self-rule or self-control. The way to it is
passive resistance: that is soul-force or love-force.'[63] The fundamental
correspondences were thus drawn before Gandhi left South Africa; the
further developments which occurred in these two key concepts of
swaraj and satyagraha were considerable, but they all rested upon the
premises set forth in *Hind Swaraj*.

The development in Gandhi's thinking on the concepts of satyagraha
and swaraj after his arrival in Bombay on 1 January 1915, may be
indicated through a comparison of two of his writings. One of these
was written in 1914, immediately before his departure from South
Africa; the other was delivered as a Presidential Address before the First
Gujarat Political Conference in November 1917. The earlier writing
was published in Gandhi's South African paper, *Indian Opinion*, under

---

61 Ibid., p. 82.

62 Ibid., pp. 43–46.

63 Ibid., p. 64.

the title 'Theory and Practice of Passive Resistance'. The discussion of satyagraha in this article remains substantially unchanged from that presented five years earlier in *Hind Swaraj.*

Gandhi still objects to the phrase 'passive resistance' as inexpressive of the positive forces that satyagraha represents, but he has not yet abandoned the phrase for satyagraha, even though he had coined the latter term seven years earlier. This suggests that at this point, he continued to conceive of satyagraha in the limited sense of civil disobedience. He speaks of the method, in this writing, as 'based upon the immutable maxim that government of the people is possible only so long as they consent either consciously or unconsciously to be governed'.[64] A series of examples follow of the technique's efficacy in South Africa: all are instances of civil disobedience against the government.[65]

A strikingly different note appears in the Gujarat Address, and this difference may only be attributed to the problems which confronted Gandhi after his return to India. He had known of these problems in South Africa, but he does not seem to have worked out a method of approach there or fully anti-coated their seriousness in India. Gokhale had asked Gandhi to abstain for one year, after his arrival, from the expression of political views and from all political activity; he was to learn of India's major political and social problems and consider potential avenues of approach. Gandhi followed this advice, and when the period of abstinence ended, he seems to have formed conclusions which guided his immediate efforts. The great single goal remained the achievement of swaraj and, as before, it was seen in the Gujarat Address as a task which must begin with the acquisition of self-rule by the individual.

---

64 Gandhi, *Speeches and Writings*, p. 190.

65 Ibid., pp. 189–91.

The first step to swaraj lies in the individual. The great truth: 'As
with the individual so with the universe,' is applicable here as
elsewhere. If we are ever torn by conflict from within, if we are ever
going astray, and if instead of ruling our passions we allow them
to rule us, swaraj can have no meaning for us. Government of self,
then, is primary education in the school of swaraj.[66]

From this point, however, the meaning of swaraj expands: it embraces
the moral and social aims which eventually form the basis of Gandhi's
Constructive Programme. These are the aims which, after 1915, Gandhi
decided swaraj must encompass, and toward which he directed his
method of satyagraha: the abolition of untouchability, improved health
and hygiene in the cities and villages, temperance reform, Hindu–
Muslim unity, Swadeshi, advancement of women, and establishment
of closer contact between the educated elite and the villagers.[67] Many of
these issues had been championed before by social reformers; Gandhi's
contribution was, as a national political leader, to insist that these
reforms were integral components of swaraj itself. No argument was
to become more central than this to Gandhi's idea of freedom, and he
now set it forth in the Gujarat Address:

We may petition the government, we may agitate in the Imperial
Council for our rights, but for a real awakening of the people,
internal activity is more important ... One sometimes hears it
said: 'Let us get the government of India in our own hands and
everything will be all right.' There could be no greater superstition
than this. No nation has thus gained its independence. The
splendour of the spring is reflected in every tree, the whole earth is
then filled with the freshness of youth. Similarly, when the swaraj
spirit has really permeated society, a stranger suddenly come upon

66 Ibid., p. 409.
67 Ibid., pp. 410–17, 421.

us will observe energy in every walk of life, he will find national servants engaged, each according to his own abilities, in a variety of public activities.[68]

One instance of the 'internal activity' to which Gandhi refers had occurred throughout the very year of the Gujarat Conference in Champaran. Gandhi had gone there, to the northwestern corner of Bihar, in April 1917, at the request of indigo sharecroppers to investigate their grievances with the planters. He began his inquiry, but the local government intervened and ordered him to leave Champaran immediately. He elected to offer civil disobedience; the Lieutenant-Governor of the province responded by dismissing the case. Gandhi proceeded with his investigation and compiled a long indictment of the planters. A commission was eventually formed of planters and government officials; Gandhi represented the peasants. The result was a settlement for repayment of funds which the planters had extorted.[69] From the time of Gandhi's arrival in Champaran, however, he concerned himself with more than the legal aspects of the problem. The poverty in the area was immense, and he soon launched his Constructive Programme. Swaraj itself, he remarked on his arrival, depended upon the uplift of these villagers.[70] A series of schools were constructed, village industries established, sanitation and personal hygiene programmes begun, medical relief offered, and volunteers organized for the construction of wells and roads. Later he wrote with some regret of his efforts in Champaran, 'It was my desire to continue the constructive work for some years, to establish more schools and to penetrate the villages more effectively.'[71] This hope was not to be

---

68 Ibid., p. 416.

69 Louis Fischer, *The Life of Mahatma Gandhi* (London: Jonathan Cape, 1951), pp. 167–73 and Tendulkar, *Mahatma*, Vol. I, pp. 198–213.

70 Tendulkar, *Mahatma*, Vol. I, p. 201.

71 Gandhi, *Autobiography*, CWMG 39:338.

fulfilled. But Champaran had taught Gandhi some valuable lessons: here, he discovered the full potential of the Constructive Programme; the manifold nature of satyagraha opened to him, and he came to know the essential connection between social reform and the political aims of the nation. These lessons were later recorded in his *Autobiography*: 'The Champaran struggle was a proof of the fact that disinterested service of the people in any sphere ultimately helps the country politically.'[72]

Gandhi came to the Gujarat Conference, then, fresh from his Champaran success, and it is not surprising that his Presidential Address concludes with a development of his concept of satyagraha, as well as an expression of confidence in its abundant potentialities. He advocates satyagraha for the resolution of India's major social and religious problems, as well as for political reform. 'Upon reflection we find that we can employ Satyagraha even for social reform. We can rid ourselves of many defects in our social institutions. We can settle the Hindu–Mohammedan problem, and we can deal with political questions. It is well that, for the sake of facilitating progress, we divide our activities according to the subjects handled. But it should never be forgotten that all are interrelated.'[73]

> This Satyagraha [he concluded] is India's special weapon. It has had others, but Satyagraha has commanded greater attention. It is omnipresent and is capable of being used at all times and under all circumstances. It does not require a Congress license. He who knows its power cannot help using it. Even as the eye-lashes automatically protect the eyes, so does Satyagraha, when kindled automatically, protect the freedom of the soul.[74]

The significance of the 1917 Gujarat Address lies in the development which it signals of Gandhi's earlier ideas: a series of advances made in

72 Ibid., p. 330.

73 Gandhi, *Speeches and Writings*, p. 421.

74 Ibid., pp. 418–19.

response to the political and social problems which he encountered after his arrival in India. With this Address, constructive work has found a permanent place alongside non-cooperation; for the fulfilment of swaraj is seen to rely upon 'internal activity' or social reform. Satyagraha has become the method for pursuing this activity, the sovereign corrective of India's social, as well as political, ills. Henceforth the term 'passive resistance', with its non-Indian and non-religious associations, disappears: satyagraha has outgrown civil disobedience. The theme of 'swaraj through satyagraha' now dominates Gandhi's political thought, growing in theory as well as in religious symbolism; above all, these ideas merge together into an inseparable relationship.

In *Hind Swaraj*, Gandhi had stressed the essential relationship of the means to the end; twenty years later, asked to define his national goal, he placed even greater emphasis upon attention to a way of right action:

> After all, the real definition [of swaraj] will be determined by our action, the means we adopt to achieve the goal. If we would but concentrate upon the means, swaraj will take care of itself. Our explorations should, therefore, take place in the direction of determining not the definition of an indefinable term like swaraj but in discovering the ways and means.[75]

By the time these thoughts were recorded, in 1927, Gandhi had learned some hard lessons through his experiments with ways and means. The next twenty years were to prove no easier, but only to test, with increasing rigour, this satyagrahi in search of swaraj.

---

75 *Young India*, 13 January 1927, III, p. 26.

CHAPTER 7

Swaraj through Satyagraha

'The highest form of freedom carries with it the greatest measure of discipline ...'[1]

—Gandhi, 1926

Changing Emphases in Satyagraha: The Growth of the Constructive Programme

The heady optimism evident in Gandhi's writings of 1918 regarding the British Government's intentions toward the granting of Indian Independence was shattered soon after the War's ending. His faith in satyagraha, however, as a supreme method of political and social change strengthened with each obstacle it faced; this faith was not to be checked until early 1922, when the tragedy of Chauri Chaura forced a rigorous reassessment.

In 1920, Gandhi's confidence in his method and mission had reached a high peak; and on 4 September, at a Special Session of the Indian Congress in Calcutta, he presented for adoption his method

---

1   *Young India*, 3 June 1926, II, p. 791.

of political action against the Government. This method, set forth in the 'Resolution on Non-co-operation', signified far more than just another Congress attempt at redress of grievances. It meant, at least for Gandhi, open rebellion;[2] and, thus, as he said in moving the resolution, the step marked 'a definite change in the policy which the country has hitherto adopted for the vindication of the rights that belong to it, and its honour.'[3] The resolution was approved, and with it, not only was a radical shift in national policy sanctioned, but a new leadership was created. Gandhi became the mind behind the method, which embodied, he told the Congress, 'the result of my many years of practical experience in non-co-operation.'[4]

Significant as this move by the Congress may have been, it only reflected the growth of a larger body of Indian public opinion. 'I do not rely merely on the lawyer class,' Gandhi said, 'or highly educated men to carry out all the stages of non-co-operation. My hope is more with the masses...'[5]

And Gandhi knew that this expectation was well-founded. The one man who, before Gandhi, had combined mass appeal with power within the Congress had suddenly slipped from the scene: one month before the Special Calcutta Session, B.G. Tilak, the 'Lokamanya', had died, leaving the field open to Gandhi. The latter quickly gained a

---

2   Gandhi wrote in *Young India* in 1921, 'Lord Reading must understand that non-co-operators are at war with the Government. They have declared rebellion against it.' In B.R. Nanda, *Mahatma Gandhi: A Biography* (London: Allen and Unwin, 1958), p. 187.

3   D.G. Tendulkar, *Mahatma: Life of Mohandas Karamchand Gandhi* (8 vols.), Vol. II (Delhi: Publications Division, Ministry of Information and Broadcasting, Government of India, 1960–62), p. 11.

4   Ibid., p. 11.

5   Ibid., p. 15.

hold on both the Congress and the masses which Tilak had never approached.

Gandhi's immense appeal must be explained largely in those terms suggested by Vivekananda at the opening of the last chapter: The Mahatma learned to 'speak of politics in India ... through the language of religion'. Gandhi was neither a Moderate nor an Extremist; he was rather a towering figure who, with uncanny dexterity, fused the divergent traditions which he faced, and then formulated a language of his own through which he could communicate his ideas to the Indian people. Like a poet, he used his past with affection, drawing from the Indian classics old words—ahimsa, Karma Yoga, Ram Raj, Sarvodaya—and charging them with fresh meaning, until they became symbols of both the past and future. None of Gandhi's terms, however, were infused with richer traditional Indian symbolism than the two key concepts of his thought, swaraj and satyagraha.

No one remained more sensitive than Gandhi to the crucial role of traditional Indian language and symbols in the national movement. When the members of Congress proposed, for purposes of greater clarity, to substitute the word 'independence' for 'swaraj' in future resolutions, Gandhi countered:

I defy anyone to give for independence a common Indian word intelligible to the masses. Our goal at any rate may be known by an indigenous word understood by the three hundred millions. And we have such a word in swaraj, first used in the name of the nation by Dadabhai Naoroji. It is infinitely greater than and includes independence. It is a vital word. It has been sanctified by the noble sacrifices of thousands of Indians. It is a word which, if it has not penetrated the remotest corner of India, has at least got the largest currency of any similar word. It is a sacrilege to displace that word by a foreign importation of doubtful value.[6]

---

6   *Young India*, 12 January 1928, III, p. 547.

Gandhi liked the word swaraj because it had traditional Indian roots, and he argued that because of this, it possessed a unique meaning quite different from that of 'independence'. 'The word swaraj is a sacred word, a Vedic word, meaning self-rule and self-restraint, and not freedom from all restraint which "independence" often means.'[7] Gandhi seldom missed an opportunity to evoke the religious symbolism explicit in the ideas of swaraj and satyagraha. 'To the orthodox Hindus I need not point out the sovereign efficacy of *tapasya*. And satyagraha is nothing but *tapasya* for Truth.'[8] And of swaraj, he remarked, 'Government over self is the truest swaraj, it is synonymous with *moksha* or salvation ...'[9]

It seems paradoxical that while none of Gandhi's ideas was more liberally endowed with traditional symbolism than swaraj and satyagraha, none were more thoroughly misunderstood, both by his party and his people. The Congress followed him, on the whole, for his political experience and insights; the masses revered him as a Mahatma. Gandhi wanted understanding and appreciation of his thought, and not reverence, either of a saint or a politician. Yet, he must bear some of the responsibility for losing his countrymen along the way. The sheer vagueness and contradiction recurrent throughout his writing made it easier to accept him as a saint than to fathom the challenge posed by his demanding beliefs. Gandhi saw no harm in self-contradiction: life was a series of experiments, and any principle might change if Truth so dictated. Truth, moreover, had a habit of positing extraordinarily high moral standards, and for those who had neither conducted the experiments nor acquired an unshakeable faith in the premises behind them, Gandhi's ideas posed formidable demands. One might worship him from afar as a Mahatma; or, as the alternative

---

7   Gandhi, *Young India*, 19 March 1931, in *India of My Dreams* (Ahmedabad: Navajivan Publishing House, 1959), p. 7.

8   *Young India*, 14 August 1924, II, p. 838.

9   *Young India*, 8 December 1920, I, p. 886.

which most Congressmen took, accept his judgements as 'policy' but not as a 'creed'. Neither path was that of the satyagrahi, nor could either lead to what Gandhi called swaraj. Instead, each undermined Gandhi's thought and message, for neither could give him support when the going became rough. At the very end, when it was indeed the roughest, Gandhi stood, tragically, alone; he now fully realized his failure to persuade both the Congress leadership and the Indian people of the central meaning of his philosophy. 'Intoxicated by my success in South Africa,' he admitted in 1947, 'I came to India. Here too the struggle bore fruit. But I have now realized that it was not based on non-violence of the brave. If I had known so then, I would not have launched the struggle.'[10] It is remarkable that an individual of Gandhi's insight did not appreciate this sooner. For indications of critical differences between his beliefs and those of the Congress leaders appear very early during his public career in India. Chief among these differences was that which concerned method; early evidence of this occurs in Gandhi's controversy with Tilak a few months before the latter's death.

In 1920, when Gandhi outlined his programme of total non-cooperation with the Government, several key Congress leaders, Tilak and C.R. Das among them, objected strongly to a boycott of the government councils. They argued that Indian nationalists should seek entry to these councils, and then 'wreck them from within'. Gandhi, however, contended that it would be untruthful and therefore morally wrong to enter the councils under false pretences; such a deceptive move, even if politically advantageous, could only have undesirable consequences from an ethical point of view. This particular dispute reflected a broader area of disagreement on the question of the relation

---

10 Gandhi, *Harijan*, 27 July 1947, in Pyarelal, *Mahatma Gandhi: The Last Phase* (Ahmedabad: Navajivan Publishing House, 1958), 2 vols., Vol. II, p. 315.

of means to ends, and of morality to politics. The crux of this difference came to light in the columns of *Young India*, in a revealing exchange of views between Gandhi and Tilak.

Gandhi began the discussion with a brief criticism of Tilak's view of politics: 'L. Tilak represents a definite school of thought of which he makes no secret. He considers that everything is fair in politics. We have joined issue with him in that conception of political life … We believe that nothing but the strictest adherence to honesty, fair play and charity can advance the true interests of the country.'[11] Tilak immediately took issue with the remark and, in a letter to *Young India*, replied:

> I am sorry to see that in your article on 'Reform Resolution' in the last issue, you have represented me as holding that I considered 'everything fair in politics'. I write this to you to say that my view is not correctly represented herein. Politics is a game of worldly people, and not of Sadhus, and instead of the maxim 'akkhodhenajine kkhodham'[12] as preached by Buddha, I prefer to rely on the maxim of Shri Krishna 'ye gatthaa maam prapadyamthe thaamthatthaiva bhajaamyaham.'[13] That explains the whole difference and also the meaning of my phrase 'responsive co-operation'. Both methods are equally honest and righteous, but the one is more suited to this world than the other.[14]

---

11 *Young India*, 14 January 1920, in *CWMG* 16:284.

12 *akkadhena jine kodham*: 'Overcome anger by loving kindness, evil by good' in the *Dhammapada*, trans. Narada Maha Tera (Calcutta: Maha Bodhi Society of India, 1952), p. 165.

13 *yeyatha mam prapadyamte tams tathawa bhajamyaham:* 'In whatsoever way any come to Me, In that same way I grant them favour.' In the *Bhagavad Gita*, IV, 11, trans. F. Edgerton (New York: Harper, 1964), p. 24.

14 *Young India*, 28 January 1920, *CWMG* 16:490–91, with Tilak's letter of 18 January 1920, quoted in footnote #2. See also Dennis Dalton, *Mahatma Gandhi: Nonviolent Power in Action*

Gandhi answered:

I naturally feel the greatest diffidence about joining issue with the
Lokamanya in matters involving questions of interpretation of
religious works. But there are things in or about which instinct
transcends even interpretation. For me there is no conflict between
the two texts quoted by the Lokamanya. The Buddhist text lays
down an eternal principle. The text from the Bhagavad Gita shows
to me how the principle of conquering hate by love, untruth by
truth, can and must be applied. If it be true that God metes out the
same measure to us that we mete out to others, it follows that if we
would escape condign punishment, we may out-return anger for
anger but gentleness even against anger. And this is the law not for
the unworldly but essentially for the worldly. With deference to the
Lokamanya, I venture to say that it betrays mental laziness to think
that the world is not for Sadhus. The epitome of all religions is to
promote Purushartha, and Purushartha is nothing but a desperate
attempt to become Sadhu, i.e., to become gentleman in every sense
of the term.

Finally, when I wrote the sentence about 'everything being fair
in politics' according to the Lokamanya's creed, I had in mind his
oft-repeated quotation 'shaddham prathi shaddhyam'.[15] To me it
enunciates bad law ... In any case, I pit the experience of a third
of a century against the doctrine underlying 'shaddham prati
shaddhyam'. The true law is 'shaddham pratyapi satyam'.[16]

Tilak and Gandhi shared several aims and attributes in common, and
no one was quicker to observe these similarities than Gandhi himself.[17]

(New York: Columbia University Press, 2012), pp. 35–36 and
240–41, notes 18 and 19.

15 'Tit for Tat', in Ibid.

16 'Do only that which is truthful.' In Ibid., I, pp. 784–85.

17 *Young India*, 13 July 1921, I, pp. 783–85.

Nor was Gandhi sparing in his praise of Tilak's contribution to the independence movement.[18] Yet the difference between them remained fundamental, and Gandhi concluded their controversy with the laconic remark: 'I am conscious that my method is not Mr. Tilak's method.'[19]

This contrast in method, arising from a different way of looking at the relation of morality to politics, corresponded with a different understanding of the meaning of swaraj. Tilak defined swaraj as political independence and demanded, as a minimum, Home Rule for India similar to that of other colonies within the Empire. He used the term swaraj to exploit its traditional overtones, but as a concept it remained, for him, synonymous with the Western idea of political independence. To many Congressmen, this view of swaraj seemed clear, direct, and attainable. When Gandhi assumed leadership, however, swaraj could no longer be understood in these simple terms. Nehru observed that in 1920, when Gandhi spoke of swaraj, he was 'delightfully vague on the subject'.[20] Other Congressmen, though, were not delighted with Gandhi's vagueness, and they continued to regard swaraj as nothing more than the replacement of British Raj by Congress Raj. Gandhi contributed to this misunderstanding of his position. In 1920, when he assumed leadership of the Congress, he promised 'swaraj in one year'; this proclamation was understandably met with a wild burst of enthusiasm among those thirsting for national independence. Early the following year, Gandhi carefully set down his 'conditions of swaraj', which made it clear that a considerable social transformation would have to occur before Indians could expect to win swaraj.[21] Gandhi should have foreseen the confusion that would

---

18 *Young India*, 4 August 1920, I, pp. 788–91.

19 *Young India*, 13 July 1921, I, p. 784.

20 B.R. Nanda, quoting Nehru, in *Mahatma Gandhi*, p. 205.

21 *Young India*, 23 February 1921, I, pp. 871–72.

arise from presenting such a complex and formidable goal in the form of a simple, deceptive slogan.

As Gandhi's thought and experience mature, however, all mention of 'swaraj in one year' vanishes. Instead, an increasing emphasis falls upon the indissoluble relationship between swaraj and the Constructive Programme. Three main aspects of that programme were singled out as particularly vital: Hindu–Muslim unity, the abolition of untouchability, and the use of khaddar (homespun cloth) as well as the charkha (spinning wheel). The achievement, through non-violent means, of this 'three point programme' constituted the essence of swaraj. Gandhi wrote in November 1921:

> Swaraj does consist in the change of government and its real control by the people, but that would be merely the form. The substance that I am hankering after is a definite acceptance of the means and, therefore, a real change of heart on the part of the people. I am certain that it does not require ages for Hindus to discard the error of untouchability, for Hindus and Musalmans to shed enmity and accept heart friendship as an eternal factor of national life, for all to adopt the charkha as the only universal means of attaining India's economic salvation and finally for all to believe that India's freedom lies only through non-violence, and no other method. Definite, intelligent and free adoption by the nation of this programme, I hold, as the attainment of the substance. The symbol, the transfer of power, is sure to follow, even as the seed truly laid must develop into a tree.[22]

This emphasis upon the Constructive Programme did not mean an abandonment of civil disobedience as an integral form of satyagraha. Gandhi's faith in mass civil disobedience, however, was considerably shaken in 1922 by several acts of violence; no incident distressed him

---

22 *Young India*, 17 November 1921, I, pp. 793–94.

more and forced a harder re-examination of satyagraha than that of
Chauri Chaura.

In December 1921 and January 1922, government action
against the campaign of non-cooperation intensified; 30,000 non-
cooperators were imprisoned, volunteer organizations became illegal,
and public meetings were dispersed. The National Congress convened
at Ahmedabad in December 1921; Gandhi was appointed its sole
executive authority, and he was pressed by various members to launch
mass civil disobedience.[23] He realized that no weapon of satyagraha was
more dangerous than this; yet he also believed it to be the duty of an
individual to resist unjust rule. 'I wish I could persuade everybody,' he
wrote on 5 January 1922, 'that Civil disobedience is the inherent right
of the citizen ... At the same time that the right of Civil Disobedience
is insisted upon, its use must be guarded by all conceivable restrictions.
Every possible provision should be made against an outbreak of
violence or general lawlessness.'[24] On 1 February, he made the decision
to begin mass civil disobedience in the single district of Bardoli; if it
succeeded there, he would extend it throughout India. He immediately
communicated this to Lord Reading, the Viceroy, and warned him that
unless the government freed the non-cooperators and lifted restrictions
on the Press, the action would be taken.[25] Gandhi's demands were
rejected, and Bardoli prepared for mass civil disobedience.

On 5 February, a procession of nationalists formed in Chauri
Chaura, a village in Uttar Pradesh, a number of constables attempted to
intervene, and when the demonstrators turned on them, they opened
fire. Their ammunition soon became exhausted, and they withdrew to
a thana; the crowd set fire to the building, and twenty-two officers were
subsequently burnt alive and hacked to death in the midst of the mob's

---

23 Nanda, *Mahatma Gandhi*, p. 229.

24 *Young India*, 5 January 1922, I, pp. 943–44.

25 Nanda, *Mahatma Gandhi*, p. 230.

fury.[26] Gandhi received the news on 8 February, and his reaction was immediate. He called a meeting of the Congress Working Committee and advised cancellation of civil disobedience; they disagreed with him, but his will prevailed. He then imposed upon himself a five days' fast as a penance for the violence. When nationalists throughout the country rebuked him for his decision to call off the campaign, he replied, 'God spoke clearly through Chauri Chaura.'

> No provocation can possibly justify the brutal murder of men who had been rendered defenceless and had virtually thrown themselves on the mercy of the mob. And when India claims to be non-violent and hopes to mount the throne of Liberty through non-violent means, mob-violence, even in answer to grave provocation, is a bad augury.
>
> The tragedy of Chauri Chaura is really the index finger. It shows the way India may easily go, if drastic precautions be not taken. If we are not to evolve violence out of non-violence, it is quite clear that we must hastily retrace our steps and re-establish an atmosphere of peace, re-arrange our programme and not think of starting mass Civil Disobedience until we are sure of peace being retained in spite of mass Civil Disobedience being started and in spite of government provocation.[27]

'We dare not enter the kingdom of Liberty,' Gandhi concluded in this article entitled 'The Crime of Chauri Chaura', 'with mere lip homage to Truth and Non-Violence.'[28]

February 1922 was not the last time that Gandhi brandished the weapon of civil disobedience; but his use of it, after this time, became severely restricted, and generally inclined toward the exercise of

---

26 Tendulkar, *Mahatma*, Vol. II, p. 82.

27 *Young India*, 16 February 1922, I, pp. 994, 997.

28 Ibid., p. 998.

individual, rather than mass, action. Henceforth, Gandhi began fully
to realize the difficult and manifold nature of the task which he had
undertaken; he turned increasingly to other aspects of satyagraha in his
quest for swaraj. 'The pilgrimage to swaraj,' he concluded in 1925, 'is
a painful climb.'[29]

'The Three Pillars of Swaraj'

'The sooner it is recognized,' Gandhi wrote in 1928, 'that many of
our social evils impede our march towards swaraj, the greater will be
our progress towards our cherished goal. To postpone social reform till
after the attainment of swaraj is not to know the meaning of swaraj.'[30]
Foremost among the aims of social reform were those which Gandhi
called 'the three pillars of swaraj': Hindu–Muslim unity, the abolition
of untouchability and the uplift of India's villages.[31] The Constructive
Programme, launched to fulfill these three aims, represented to
Gandhi the way in which swaraj may best be attained through
satyagraha. As a method of social reform, the Constructive Programme
illustrates the conceptual relationship in Gandhi's thought between
freedom and social harmony. This relationship recalls the ideas of
Vivekananda and Aurobindo, but it differs from them in its persistent
attempt to resolve particular social issues, to heal divisions which had
historically torn Indian society. A right approach to the three main
aims of the Constructive Programme would bring, Gandhi believed,
not only a free but a harmonious social order. His campaign against
untouchability was, above all, a movement to create a common feeling
among castes and untouchables; his struggle for Hindu–Muslim unity
sought a harmony of religious sympathies; and his attempt to advance

---

29 *Young India*, 21 May 1925, II, pp. 928–29.

30 *Young India*, 28 June 1928, III, p. 772.

31 Gandhi, *Young India*, 24 November 1927 in *Hindu Dharma*, p. 331.

the use of khaddar and the spinning wheel was an effort at bridging the gulf between groups of educated Indians and the majority in the villages. Gandhi forever remained an apostle of harmony, a devotee of compromise and co-operation. From a lesson learned early in his South African experience, he concluded, 'All my life through, the very insistence on truth has taught me to appreciate the beauty of compromise. I saw in later life that this spirit was an essential part of satyagraha.'[32] It is difficult to pinpoint any major phase of Gandhi's public life that was not involved with the reconciliation of parties, the integration of apparently divergent interests. The supreme example of this single-minded effort to restore harmony to a country torn by schism is found in that endeavour which consumed most of his life, the Constructive Programme.

Gandhi's personal objection to untouchability dated back to a childhood experience;[33] and, in South Africa, he often expressed his abhorrence of the institution.[34] Not until his arrival in India, though, in 1915, does he emphasize it as a major obstacle to the country's growth. In a speech of early 1916, he condemned untouchability in the strongest possible terms as 'an ineffaceable blot that Hinduism today carries with it ... This miserable, wretched, enslaving spirit of untouchableness'. 'It is, to my mind, a curse that has come to us, and as long as that curse remains with us, so long I think we are bound to consider that every affliction that we labour under in this sacred land is a fit and proper punishment for this great and indelible crime that we are committing.'[35] Gandhi soon came to see the fight against untouchability as an integral part of satyagraha and its resolution as a prerequisite for swaraj. This necessary relationship of swaraj to the

---

32 Gandhi, *Autobiography*, p. 122.

33 Tendulkar, *Mahatma*, Vol. I, p. 27.

34 Gandhi, *CWMG* 4:230 and 6:470.

35 Gandhi, *Speeches and Writings*, p. 387.

abolition of untouchability which Gandhi saw, was seldom, however, seen by others. Thus one correspondent wrote to *Young India*:

> I am unable to understand the relation between the existence of this evil and the establishment of swaraj. After all, 'unapproachability' is only one of the many evils of the Hindu society—perhaps a greater evil—and as long as society exists similar evils do exist, as no society is free from evils. How is this an impediment to the obtaining of swaraj and why do you make its removal a condition precedent to our fitness for swaraj? Is it not possible for this to be set right when swaraj is obtained, if not voluntarily, at least by legislation?[36]

Gandhi replied:

> Swaraj for me means freedom for the meanest of our countrymen. If the lot of the Panchama is not improved when we are all suffering, it is not likely to be better under the intoxication of swaraj. If it is necessary for us to buy peace with the Mussalmans as a condition of swaraj, it is equally necessary for us to give peace to the Panchama before we can with any show of justice or self-respect talk of swaraj. I am not interested in freeing India merely from the English yoke. I am bent upon freeing India from any yoke whatsoever. I have no desire to exchange 'king log for king stork.' Hence for me, the movement of swaraj is a movement of self-purification.[37]

These last few sentences contain a vital element of Gandhi's conception of freedom: the conviction that tyranny over another inevitably corrupts the character of the tyrant, and so enslaves the tyrant himself. 'We have become "pariahs of the Empire" because we have created "pariahs" in our midst. The slaveowner is always more hurt than the slave. We shall

36 *Young India*, 12 June 1924, II, p. 601.
37 Ibid., pp. 601–2.

be unfit to gain swaraj so long as we would keep in bondage a fifth of the population of Hindustan.'[38] Again, speaking in 1928 on the reform of untouchability, he asked, 'Shall we not have the vision to see that in suppressing a sixth (or whatever the number) of ourselves, we have depressed ourselves? No man takes another down a pit without descending into it himself and sinning in the bargain. It is not the suppressed that sin. It is the suppressor who has to answer for his crime against those whom he suppresses.'[39]

Despite these arguments, many Congressmen remained unconvinced of the connection between swaraj and the abolition of untouchability. At the Forty-First Congress of 1926, Mr S. Srinivasa Iyengar delivered the Presidential Address; after paying high tribute to Gandhi's thought, he turned to the gospel of swaraj:

> Our foremost duty is to keep constantly before our eyes the vision of swaraj, what it is, what it requires of us, and what it will not permit us. It means nothing less than that the Congress should have the fullest control over the people and should have a steadily increasing number of workers knit together in bonds of unshakeable loyalty and perfect understanding. It is only in proportion as the control of the Congress over the people increases in area and in intensity we can obtain or establish swaraj.[40]

This view of swaraj lay outside the main stream of Gandhi's thought, though he might have accepted it within a larger context. Iyengar, however, then moved on to ideas decidedly at variance with Gandhi's position. He described the use of khaddar and the abolition of

---

38 *Young India*, 24 November 1920, I, p. 643.

39 *Young India*, 29 March 1928, III, p. 673.

40 *Congress Presidential Addresses*, 1911–1934, Second series (Madras: G.A. Natesan, 1937), pp. 800–1.

untouchability as 'vital aspects of our national movement'.[41] But, he contended, 'Neither foreign nor domestic critics are right when they assert that untouchability is a formidable obstacle for swaraj, or that its removal will automatically bring about swaraj. We cannot wait for swaraj till it is removed any more than we can wait till caste is abolished ... I would deprecate the iterated rhetorical stress on untouchability as a serious impediment to swaraj.'[42] Gandhi was quick to note this comment on untouchability in Iyengar's address, and he soon answered it in *Young India*:

> There is, too, confusion regarding swaraj. The term swaraj has many meanings. When Sjt. Iyengar says that removal of untouchability has nothing to do with swaraj, I presume he means that its existence can be no hindrance to constitutional advance. It can surely have nothing to do with dyarchy or greater and effective powers being given to the legislatures ... Real organic swaraj is a different question. That freedom which is associated with the term swaraj in the popular mind is no doubt unattainable without not only the removal of untouchability and the promotion of heart unity between the different sections but also without removing many other social evils that can be easily named. That inward growth which must never stop, we have come to understand by the comprehensive term swaraj. And that swaraj cannot be had so long as walls of prejudice, passion and superstition continue to stifle the growth of that stately oak.[43]

This was the aspect of untouchability that Gandhi disliked most: the 'walls of prejudice, passion and superstition' that it created, prohibiting 'promotion of heart unity between the different sections'. Gandhi uses,

---

41 Ibid., p. 804.

42 Ibid., pp. 806–7.

43 *Young India*, 10 March 1927, III, pp. 107–8.

for the first time in this passage, the term 'organic swaraj', and this holds a special significance: it suggests a freedom which seeks to include a sense of social harmony. 'Organic' as opposed to 'constitutional' or 'parliamentary' swaraj included individual civil liberty and national independence, but it also sought to go beyond these to a realization of 'heart unity'.

Gandhi wanted, then, to establish an organic swaraj, a solid spirit of social unity, in three major areas of Indian society: among the untouchables and the various castes, between Hindus and Muslims; and, finally, he wished to overcome the considerable gap that had grown between the rural, traditional, largely illiterate villagers, on the one hand, and the urban, Westernized, educated classes on the other. Gandhi interpreted this last aspect of social separateness as another form of untouchability. 'To me, the campaign against untouchability has begun to imply ever so much more than the eradication of the ceremonial untouchability of those who are labelled untouchables. For the city dweller, the villages have become untouchables.'[44]

Gandhi continually emphasized the necessity for identification with the villagers, who represented the masses of India, that their attitudes might be understood and their needs met.

> We must first come in living touch with them [the masses] by working for them and in their midst. We must share their sorrows, understand their difficulties and anticipate their wants. With the pariahs we must be pariahs and see how we feel to clean the closets of the upper classes and have the remains of their table thrown at us. We must see how we like being in the boxes, mis-called houses, of the labourers of Bombay. We must identify ourselves with the villagers who toil under the hot sun beating on their bent backs and see how we would like to drink water from the pool in which the villagers bathe, wash their cloths and pots and in which their

---

44 Tendulkar, *Mahatma*, Vol. IV, p. 2.

cattle drink and roll. Then and not till then shall we truly represent the masses and they will, as surely as I am writing this, respond to every call. We cannot all do this, and if we are to do this, good-bye to swaraj for a thousand years and more, some will say. I shall sympathise with the objection. But I do claim that some of us at least will have to go through the agony and out of it only will a nation full, vigorous and free be born.[45]

This call for service did not begin in modern India with Gandhi. He had said that he wished to serve India's villagers 'because I recognize no God except the God that is to be found in the hearts of the dumb millions ... and I worship the God that is Truth or Truth which is God through the service of these millions'.[46] Vivekananda, though, had set forth precisely the same idea a generation earlier; even the word which Gandhi used, 'Daridranarayan', to mean the divinity of the masses, had been used by Vivekananda; Gandhi had taken the word from C.R. Das.[47] But Gandhi did not derive this gospel of service exclusively from Das or Vivekananda; he had found it in numerous sources; the *Sermon on the Mount*, Tolstoy, texts and saints of the Indian tradition, and in the recollection of simple childhood experiences. Gandhi imbibed these influences and directed the lessons he learned toward problems of the Indian villager.

Gandhi, moreover, was not the only major political leader of his time to call attention to the crucial importance of the Indian villages. C.R. Das, in his Congress Presidential Address of 1922, had urged, as a requisite of swaraj, the 'organization of village life and the practical

---

45 *Young India*, 11 September 1924, II, pp. 378–79.

46 Tendulkar, *Mahatma*, Vol. V, p. 58.

47 Gandhi, *Young India*, 4 April 1929, cited in V.P. Verma, *The Political Philosophy of Mahatma Gandhi and Sarvodaya* (Agra: Lakshmi Narain Agarwal, 1959), p. 59.

autonomy of small local centres'. Village communities must not exist as 'disconnected units' but rather be 'held together by a system of co-operation and integration'. 'I maintain that real swaraj,' Das declared, 'can only be attained by vesting the power of government in these small local centres'; and he suggested that the Congress 'draw up a scheme of government' based on this principle.[48] As a result of this recommendation, an *Outline Scheme of Swaraj* was drafted by C.R. Das and Bhagavan Das,[49] and presented to the Congress in early 1923. This plan urged the creation, after independence was granted, of a highly decentralized form of government, 'a maximum of local autonomy', and 'a minimum of control by higher centres'.[50] The organ of administration would be the panchayat, organized into village, town, district, provincial, and all-India units of government.[51] The purpose behind this scheme was the uplift of India's villages, and 'the idea underlying this condition is that which has been discussed and emphasized before, the idea of spiritualizing politics by changing the whole culture and civilization of society from its present mercenary to a missionary basis'.[52] Gandhi, then, was not unique among Congress leaders in his approach to the villages. His contribution lies first, in the sustained emphasis which he gave to this aspect of his Constructive Programme, and second, in his use of traditional symbols and concepts to further understanding of a problem that had psychological as well as political and economic roots.

---

48 C.R. Das, *Freedom Through Disobedience*, Presidential Address at 37th Indian National Congress (Madras: Arka, 1922), p. 40.

49 Bhagavan Das, *Ancient versus Modern Scientific Socialism* (Madras: Theosophical Publishing House, 1934), p. 135.

50 C.R. Das, *Outline Scheme of Swaraj*, National Convention Memoranda, No. 2 (Madras: Besant Press, 1923), p. 3.

51 Ibid., p. 4.

52 Ibid., p. 27.

Vivekananda had perceived that which most early Congress
Moderates had ignored: not only that traditional Indian language and
symbols were needed to involve the people in the national movement,
but also that the educated had to overcome a substantial psychological
barrier to achieve rapport with the masses. Gandhi directed his efforts
toward both aspects of this problem. He approached the villagers
through the use of Indian tradition; the endless plea for village
sanitation, personal hygiene, and basic education came to them this
time, not from just another Westernized social reformer, but from a
Mahatma. Gandhi remained equally concerned, however, with his
other adversary, the educated Westernized Indians. No single major
proposal that Gandhi made during his period of Congress leadership
induced greater ridicule than that concerning the use of the spinning
wheel and the wearing of khaddar. Gandhi asked Congressmen to
wear the homespun cloth and to devote a certain amount of time each
day to the spinning of yarn. The proposal was set forth in Congress
resolutions, and many members paid lip service to it; few seemed to
appreciate Gandhi's purposes in advocating it.

'I can only think of spinning,' Gandhi wrote, 'as the fittest and most
acceptable sacrificial body labour. I cannot imagine anything nobler or
more national than that, for we should all do the labour that the poor
must do and thus identify ourselves with them and through them with
all mankind.'[53] The wearing of khaddar by each Indian Gandhi felt
to be a privilege which should 'make him proud of his identity with
every drop of the ocean of Indian humanity'.[54] The spinning wheel
was seen as 'the cement to bind the masses to us national servants',[55]
the instrument for 'creating an indissoluble bond between the rich and

53 *Young India*, 20 October 1921, I, p. 501.
54 Tendulkar, *Mahatma*, Vol. VI, p. 25.
55 *Young India*, 23 April 1925, II, p. 275.

poor',[56] and 'the symbol of social service of the highest order'.[57] Few examples illustrate better than the spinning wheel Gandhi's reliance upon the force of a symbol.

'Satyagraha,' Gandhi wrote in 1919, 'is like a banyan tree with innumerable branches ... Satya and ahimsa together make the parent trunk from which all innumerable branches shoot out'.[58] Nonviolence remained an essential element of satyagraha, and the Constructive Programme, one of its 'innumerable branches', relied solely upon the use of nonviolent means for the creation of a social and political revolution in India. The right means could only be non-violent; only these would produce Gandhi's ideal of a nonviolent social order. 'They say "means are after all means". I would say "means are after all everything". As the means so the end. Violent means will give violent swaraj.'[59] Gandhi's belief in ahimsa which he variously translated as 'love' and 'charity' as well as 'non-violence', was for him a religious persuasion, and a necessary element in his quest for self-realization. He concludes in this *Autobiography*:

> My uniform experience has convinced me that there is no other God than Truth. And if every page of these chapters does not proclaim to the reader that the only means for the realisation of Truth is Ahimsa, I shall deem all my labour in writing these chapters to have been in vain ... this much I can say with assurance, as a result of all my experiments, that a perfect vision of Truth can only follow a complete realisation of Ahimsa.[60]

---

56 *Young India*, 17 September 1925, II, p. 1109.

57 *Young India*, 23 April 1925, II, p. 275.

58 Tendulkar, *Mahatma*, Vol. I, pp. 261–62.

59 *Young India*, 17 July 1924, II, p. 364.

60 Gandhi, *Autobiography*, p. 401.

Gandhi believed that non-violent means were not only truthful but efficacious. 'You need not be afraid,' he once replied to an Indian terrorist who had challenged the workability of his method, 'that the method of non-violence is a slow, long-drawn-out process. It is the swiftest the world has seen, for it is the surest. You will see that it will overtake the revolutionaries whom you imagine I have misjudged.'[61]

The most severe test of Gandhi's ahimsa, indeed of satyagraha itself, came at the end of his life with the complete rupture of Hindu–Muslim relations. The problem of Hindu–Muslim friction had always been, for him, one more manifestation of the evil of untouchability. 'When we learn to regard these five to six crores of outcastes as our own,' he wrote in 1926, 'we shall learn the rudiments of what it is to be one people. That one act of cleansing will probably solve the Hindu–Muslim question. For in it too, the corrosive poison of untouchability is consciously or unconsciously working its way.'[62] 'The corrosive poison' of this form of untouchability, however, was not checked by the effect of Gandhi's Constructive Programme; it ultimately created a state of violent social discord which he had not anticipated. Another weapon in the satyagraha arsenal was needed, and the concluding section of this chapter will consider how Gandhi used that weapon in his struggle for communal harmony. The analysis will be of a single instance of satyagraha: Gandhi's Calcutta Fast for Hindu–Muslim Unity of September 1947.

The Nature of Satyagraha: A Test Case

I had realized early enough in South Africa that there was no genuine friendship between the Hindus and the Musalmans. I never missed a single opportunity to remove obstacles in the way

---

61 *Young India*, 30 April 1925, II, p. 916.
62 *Young India*, 25 March 1926, II, p. 750.

of unity. It was not in my nature to placate anyone by adulation, or at the cost of self-respect. But my South African experiences had convinced me that it would be on the question of Hindu–Muslim unity that my Ahimsa would be put to its severest test, and that the question presented the widest field for my experiments in Ahimsa. The conviction is still there.[63]

This is Gandhi, writing in 1927, in his *Autobiography*, under the title, 'Passion for Unity'. In South Africa, Gandhi had written forcefully both in *Indian Opinion* and in *Hind Swaraj* on behalf of Hindu–Muslim unity;[64] when he returned to India in 1915, he recognized the problem as a major national issue and made its resolution a prerequisite for swaraj. His Gujarat Address urges full use of satyagraha to 'settle the Hindu–Mohammedan problem'.[65] In 1919, he decided to make a total commitment to Muslim interests through the Khilafat issue. This decision, which involved the Congress in a futile cause, is explicable only in terms of Gandhi's single-minded desire to forge the interests of the two religious communities together. 'What then does the Hindu–Mohammedan Unity consist in, and how can it be best promoted?' he asked in 1920.

The answer is simple. It consists in our having a common purpose, a common goal and common sorrows. It is best promoted by co-operating to reach the common goal, by sharing one another's sorrows and by mutual toleration ... Today, seeing that the Mahomedans are deeply touched on the question of Khilafat, and their case is just, nothing can be so powerful for winning

---

63 Gandhi, *Autobiography*, CWMG 39:350.

64 Gandhi, *Hind Swaraj*, pp. 28–32.

65 Gandhi, *Speeches and Writings*, p. 421.

Mahomedan friendship for the Hindu as to give his wholehearted support to the Mahomedan claim.[66]

During this time of the Khilafat question, the columns of *Young India* abound with comments on the Hindu–Muslim problem, insisting that swaraj cannot come without religious unity. 'The union that we want is not a patched up thing but a union of hearts based upon a definite recognition of the indubitable proposition that swaraj for India must be an impossible dream without an indissoluble union between the Hindus and the Muslims of India.'[67] After the abortive collapse of the Khilafat agitation, Gandhi continued to stress the urgency of a reconciliation between the two communities. Often he devoted issues of *Young India* to the publication of letters from Hindu and Muslim correspondents which were filled with mutual recrimination: forced conversion of Hindu women; desecration of Muslim mosques; wanton slaughter of cows by Muslims; deliberate disruption of Muslim religious services by Hindus; fanaticism followed by fanatical retaliation. Gandhi replied to each charge, urging patience, understanding, conciliation and forgiveness.

In early September 1924, a sudden increase in communal violence occurred. Gandhi warned that 'The question of Hindu–Muslim Unity is getting more serious every day',[68] and he pleaded for sanity. But the only reply to his plea was a major riot at Kohat; thirty-six people were killed, and 145 were wounded. Gandhi said, 'The news from Kohat set the smouldering mass aflame. Something has got to be done.'[69] He soon decided on a remedy; on 18 September he issued a statement from the house of a Muslim friend in Delhi: 'The recent events have

---

66 *Young India*, 25 February 1920, pp. 399–400.

67 *Young India*, 6 October 1920, I, p. 404.

68 Gandhi, *Speeches and Writings*, p. 993.

69 Tendulkar, *Mahatma*, Vol. II, p. 148.

proved unbearable for me. My helplessness is still more unbearable. My religion teaches me that whenever there is distress which one cannot remove, one must fast and pray ... I am therefore imposing upon myself a fast of twenty-one days commencing from today.'[70]

One immediate consequence of Gandhi's decision was a Unity Conference in Delhi, presided over by Motilal Nehru and attended by 300 delegates representing 'almost every school of thought in the country'.[71] The Conference passed resolutions, communal violence subsided, and Gandhi, after three weeks, broke his fast. The results of this fast, however, are less important than the motives behind it; and an understanding of these involves some acquaintance with Gandhi's personal belief in the merit of fasting, as well as with his use of fasting as an instrument of social reform. During his Delhi fast of 1924, Gandhi said, 'This fast is but to purify myself, to strengthen myself.'[72] This conviction, that self-suffering imposed by fasting might increase one's self-discipline and spiritual insight, is a dominant aspect of Indian traditional belief. The Vaishya community of Kathiawar, into which Gandhi was born, is closely associated with the Jain religion; and one leading British historian has recently stressed Gandhi's indebtedness to the Jains, for whom nonviolence is a cardinal religious tenet.[73] Jain ascetics are noted, also, for their rigorous pursuit of salvation through penance and prolonged fasting.[74] Gandhi himself acknowledges the early and profound influence which Raychandbhai, a Jain religious

---

70 *Gandhi*, Speeches and Writings, p. 999.

71 Tendulkar, *Mahatma*, Vol. II, p. 153.

72 Ibid., p. 153.

73 Percival Spear, *India: A Modern History* (Ann Arbor: University of Michigan, 1961), pp. 61, 357.

74 A.L. Basham, *The Wonder That Was India* (New York: Grove, 1954), p. 292 and William Theodore de Bary (ed.), *Sources of Indian Tradition* (Oxford: Oxford University Press, 1958), p. 50.

mystic, exerted upon him; it was he who persuaded Gandhi of the merits of brahmacharya and thus prompted Gandhi's life-long commitment to a severe form of self-restraint and denial.[75] Early in his life, Gandhi relates in his *Autobiography*, he came to believe that fasting, both 'physical' and 'mental', were essential for an individual's self-realization.[76]

This deep religious belief in fasting corresponded with a full awareness of the force that a fast might exert as an instrument of social reform. Gandhi referred to the technique of fasting as a 'fiery weapon';[77] he regarded it as 'an integral part of the satyagraha programme, and it is the greatest and most effective weapon in its armoury ...'[78] The efficacy of fasting emerged largely from its reliance on the greater power of nonviolence.

> Non-violence in its positive aspect as benevolence ... is the greatest force because of the limitless scope it affords for self-suffering without causing or intending any physical or material injury to the wrong-doer. The object always is to evoke the best in him. Self-suffering is an appeal to his better nature, as retaliation is to his baser. Fasting under proper circumstances is such an appeal par excellence.[79]

The fast worked in Gandhi's view because it could, through the non-violent self-sacrifice of one individual, 'evoke the best' in an adversary. If, though, the fast possessed this considerable power, it also had

---

75 Gandhi, *Autobiography*, CWMG 39:165–171.

76 Ibid., p. 266.

77 Gandhi, *Harijan*, 13 October 1940 in N.K. Bose, *Studies in Gandhism* (Calcutta: Indian Ass. Pub. Co., 1947), p. 157.

78 Gandhi, *Harijan*, 26 July 1942, in Bose, *Studies in Gandhism*, pp. 156–57.

79 Ibid., p. 157.

definite limitations. First, Gandhi emphasized that it should only be used as a last resort when all other branches of satyagraha had failed.[80] A fast indicated a desperate attempt at sudden conversion; it could never replace the Constructive Programme as the foundation of satyagraha, but only complement that Programme when an extreme situation prevailed. Second, fasts should only be attempted by a genuine satyagrahi, an individual free from selfishness, anger or impatience, and firmly committed to nonviolence.[81] As an instrument of reform, the fast is morally neutral; thus the motive of the person using it becomes all-important.[82] Apart from the aim of self-purification, a satyagrahi fasts to gain the repentance of others for wrongs they have committed, to awaken their consciences and to induce them to re-examine their own positions.[83] Thus, the fast must always be undertaken for the reform of the adversary and not for extorting advantages from him. Gandhi attaches an important condition to the fast; he says that the satyagrahi should always fast against a 'lover', that is, one who shares an underlying sympathy with his aim.[84] This condition is significant for at least two reasons. On the one hand, it indicates Gandhi's awareness of the fast's inherent limitations. He concedes that 'You cannot fast against a tyrant ... I will not fast to reform, say, General Dyer who not only does not love me but who regards himself as my enemy.'[85] On the other hand, the condition reflects Gandhi's insight into the real source of the fast's power: in his case, the sympathy of the Indian people. Gandhi's fasts worked most effectively when waged against his own countrymen: some responded to the call of 'Gandhiji' a leader whom

---

80 Gandhi, *Harijan,* 21 April 1946, in *India of My Dreams,* p. 87.

81 Ibid., pp. 86–87.

82 Ibid., p. 87.

83 Pyarelal, *Mahatma Gandhi,* Vol. II, p. 738.

84 *Young India,* 1 May 1924, II, pp. 825–26.

85 Ibid., p. 825.

they adored; others revered him, and followed him, as the Mahatma, a holy ascetic who symbolized the highest attainments of their religious traditions. Gandhi was fully aware of this source of his power. As a Hindu, he knew intuitively through which symbols, imagery, language and behaviour he could communicate with that community; but he was also cognizant of those religious associations which held meaning for the Muslims.[86] The fast had the value of appealing to both Hindus and Muslims, and, in the hands of Gandhi, both because of his own strong personal convictions, and also because of the traditional religious beliefs of his fellow Indians, it became a weapon of considerable power. With the Partition of India, the extreme situation for which the fast was designed suddenly emerged; Gandhi summoned its powers to meet a challenge which, forty years earlier, he had foreseen as posing the ultimate test of satyagraha.

'If we could transform Calcutta,' Gandhi mused to a fellow Constructive Worker in 1928, 'we should transform the whole of India.'[87] Almost twenty years later, Gandhi arrived in Calcutta with precisely this purpose: the transformation of the whole of India by bringing peace to its great strife-torn city. Calcutta was not the only area of turmoil in 1947: the Punjab had unparalleled communal rioting, and Gandhi himself had already spent several months quieting Noakhali and Bihar. Calcutta, though, had experienced more than

---

86 During Gandhi's 1924 fast, a Muslim friend, Maulana Shaukat Ali tried to persuade Gandhi to terminate it. Gandhi replied, 'Fasting and prayer are common injunctions in my religion. But I know of this sort of penance even in Islam. In the life of the Prophet, I have read that the Prophet often fasted and prayed ... Even at this moment I see before me the picture of the Prophet thus fasting and praying ... I am speaking to you as though I was a Mussalman, because I have cultivated that respect for Islam which you have for it.' In *Young India*, II, pp. 106–7.

87 *Young India*, 13 December 1928, III, p. 998.

its gruesome share of communal violence; for it was here that the cauldron had first boiled over. In July 1946, Jinnah's growing suspicion of both the British Cabinet Mission and the Indian Congress erupted; he accused the British of bad faith and of 'playing into the hands of the Congress'. The only alternative open to the Muslim League was to seize a fresh initiative: a 'Direct Action Day' was set for 16 August, to demonstrate en masse for the creation of Pakistan.[88] That day – 16 August – became the day of the 'Great Calcutta Killing'. Communal riots raged for four days, and official estimates placed casualties at 4,000 killed and 10,000 injured.[89] 'No communal riot in British–Indian history had ever reached such dimensions. It was in fact the beginning of civil war in an odious and horrible form.'[90] The Calcutta slaughter set off a grim chain reaction: in late August, the Muslim majority of Noakhali retaliated against the Hindus for the Calcutta killings; in late October, the Hindus then wreaked their vengeance in Bihar; the worst reaction of all, though, occurred in the Punjab.

> By the end of 1946, India was drifting rapidly to chaos. The real power had passed from British hands; senior officials, anxious about their own future, were conscious that they were caretakers under notice and were disheartened. Ministers, paralysed by the communal situation, seemed unable to come to grips with the problems of administration; and the unparalleled communal riots in Calcutta, together with serious disorder in many parts of India, made it clear that nobody was in effective control.[91]

---

88 Spear, *India*, pp. 414–16, 466 and V.P. Menon, *The Transfer of Power in India* (London: Longmans, 1957), pp. 282–84.

89 Spear, *India*, p. 466.

90 Ibid., p. 415.

91 Percival Griffiths, *Modern India* (London: Ernest Benn, 1957), p. 85.

'Never did he show himself to greater advantage than during those fateful days when like a Titan he rushed from one danger spot to another to prop up the crumbling heavens.'[92] From early November 1946 to late May 1947, Gandhi moved throughout Northern India, chiefly in Bengal and Bihar, often on foot, occasionally staying for months in a single village in the midst of an infested area; his purpose was to reassure the people, to instill trust and courage after the shattering experiences of communal bloodshed. June and July of 1947 were spent in Delhi, in consultations with the government and the Congress high command; after this, he turned to Calcutta. Lord Mountbatten, anticipating increased carnage in the Punjab, established in late July a Boundary Force in the Punjab Partition Areas, under the military command of Major General 'Pete' Rees, whom Mountbatten later described as 'perhaps his ablest divisional commander in the Burma Campaign'.[93] The force itself consisted of approximately 55,000 men with a high proportion of British officers; one of Mountbatten's associates called it 'probably the largest military force ever collected in any one area of a country for the maintenance of law and order in peacetime'.[94] Gandhi arrived in Calcutta on 9 August; Lord Mountbatten wired him there just seventeen days later:

My dear Gandhiji,

In the Punjab we have 55 thousand soldiers and large scale rioting on our hands. In Bengal our forces consist of one man, and there is no rioting.

---

92 Pyarelal, *Mahatma Gandhi*, Vol. II, p. 428.

93 Alan Campbell-Johnson, *Mission with Mountbatten* (London: Robert Hale, 1951), p. 175.

94 Ibid., p. 139.

As a serving officer, as well as an administrator, may I be allowed
to pay my tribute to the One Man Boundary Force, not forgetting
his Second in Command, Mr. Suhrawardy.[95]

Gandhi's destination, early in that August of 1947, was not Calcutta,
but Noakhali. He intended to stop over in Calcutta for a day, and then
move on to Noakhali, where he anticipated serious disturbances on and
after 15 August, the day of independence. Immediately upon his arrival
in Calcutta, though, Gandhi was met by several Muslim delegations
which pleaded with him to stay; sporadic communal riots were
occurring at that time, and the Muslim minority feared what might
lie ahead. Gandhi agreed to postpone his departure, and this move
proved decisive. For on 11 August, Shaheed Suhrawardy, then (until
independence) de jure Chief Minister of Bengal, arrived in Calcutta
and persuaded Gandhi to remain there indefinitely. Gandhi's consent
rested on one condition: that Suhrawardy would live with him, under
the same roof in a disturbed Muslim quarter of the city, without armed
protection. Suhrawardy accepted the condition, and Gandhi wrote to
Sardar Patel: 'I have got stuck here and am now going to undertake
a grave risk. Suhrawardy and I are going from today to stay together
in a Muslim quarter. The future will reveal itself. Keep close watch.'[96]
Sardar replied, 'So you have got detained in Calcutta and that too in a
quarter which is a veritable shambles and a notorious den of gangsters
and hooligans. And in what choice company too.'[97]

Suhrawardy was a Muslim leader who did not enjoy much Hindu
confidence. He had been Chief Minister of Bengal during the Great
Calcutta Killing, and the carnage had been blamed partly on his

---

95 Gandhi, *Correspondence with the Government, 1944–47* (Ahmedabad:
     Navajivan Publishing House, 1959), p. 277.

96 Pyarelal, *Mahatma Gandhi*, Vol. II, p. 364.

97 Ibid., p. 365.

unwillingness to quell Muslim demonstrations.[98] Gandhi, however, knew that Suhrawardy exercised substantial influence over Bengali Muslims, and he wanted to set an outstanding example of Hindu–Muslim comradeship. On 13 August, just two days before independence, they moved together into 'Hydari Mansion', 'an old abandoned Muslim house in an indescribably filthy locality' of the city.[99] This immediately sparked a violent reaction: Hindu demonstrators besieged the house, smashed windows, demanded their departure. Gandhi met their attack with cool, firm reasoning. 'I put it to you, young men,' he argued, 'how can I, who am a Hindu by birth, a Hindu by creed and a Hindu of Hindus in my way of living, be an "enemy" of Hindus? Does this not show narrow intolerance on your part?'[100] The words worked, the Hindus withdrew, and the next forty-eight hours remained calm. Independence Day provoked demonstrations: but of friendship, not strife. Hindu–Muslim fraternization reached a new peak, and Gandhi's efforts were acclaimed as 'the Calcutta Miracle'. Gandhi himself, while touring the city with Suhrawardy, was struck by the transformation and wrote to a friend on a rare note of optimism, 'It reminds me of old days in South Africa and the Khilafat days here. For the moment I am no enemy. Who knows how long this will last? Hindus and Muslims have become friends practically in a day.'[101] Gandhi's prayer meetings were now being attended by hundreds of thousands; even the Muslim League passed a resolution on 24 August expressing 'its deep sense of appreciation of the services rendered by Mahatma Gandhi to the

---

98 Ramachandra Guha, *Gandhi: The Years That Changed the World, 1914–1948* (N.Y.: Alfred Knopf, 2018), pp. 763–64.

99 Ibid., p. 365.

100 Ibid., p. 367.

101 Gandhi, *Letters to Rajkumari Amrit Kaur* (Ahmedabad: Navajivan Publishing House, 1961), p. 245.

cause of restoration of peace and good will between the communities in Calcutta.'[102]

But the test was yet to come. Continuous reports streamed into Calcutta of Punjab atrocities. Gandhi wired Nehru for advice on where he was most needed; Nehru hesitated, but as the Punjab situation became more desperate, he cabled Gandhi on 31 August to leave for there.[103] On that same evening, however, violence began once more in Calcutta. At 10 p.m., a large Hindu procession converged on Hydari Mansion with an injured Hindu in its midst; the crowd alleged that he had been attacked by Muslims and demanded that Gandhi take action against the outrage. The crowd surged for hours around the building, and finally became uncontrollable and stormed in. Gandhi attempted to calm its leaders, but this time without success; he was attacked and only escaped through police intervention. The violence quickly gained momentum, and riots raged throughout the city. The *London Times* reported thirteen persons killed and seventy-five injured;[104] Gandhi wrote to Sardar Patel, 'What was regarded as the "Calcutta Miracle" has proved to be a nine days' wonder. I am pondering what my duty is in the circumstances.'[105] When Rajagopalachari, then Provincial Governor of West Bengal, came to visit him on the evening of 1 September, Gandhi had already made his decision. He proposed a fast. 'Can one fast against the goondas?' Rajaji asked. 'I want to touch the hearts of those who are behind the goondas,' Gandhi replied. 'The hearts of the goondas may or may not be touched. It would be enough for my purpose if they realise that society at large has no sympathy with their aims or methods and that the peace-loving element is determined

102 Pyarelal, *Mahatma Gandhi*, Vol. II, 381.

103 Ibid., p. 3944.

104 *London Times*, 3 September 1947 (Dateline: Calcutta, 2 September 1947), p. 4.

105 Pyarelal, *Mahatma Gandhi: The Last Phase*, Part 2, Vol. X, p. 406.

to assert itself or perish in the attempt.' Rajaji urged him to 'wait and watch a little', but Gandhi was adamant. 'The fast has to be now or never. It will be too late afterwards. The minority community cannot be left in a parlous condition. My fast has to be preventive if it is to be of any good. I know I shall be able to tackle the Punjab too if I can control Calcutta. But if I falter now, the conflagration may spread…'[106]

'What my word in person cannot do,' Gandhi said in his public statement that evening on the fast, 'my fast may. It may touch the hearts of all the warring elements in the Punjab if it does in Calcutta. I, therefore, begin fasting from 8.15 tonight to end only if and when sanity returns to Calcutta.'[107] Looting, rioting, widespread demonstrations and military action against the mobs marked the first day of the fast. The impact of Gandhi's move had not yet been felt, but he remained confident. 'My fast is an appeal to everybody to search his heart. It should result in all-round self-purification. When the initial cleansing of the hearts has been effected, parties of Hindus and Muslims should go out together to patrol the troubled areas and relieve the police of its arduous duties.'[108] On 3 September, the second day of the fast, quiet came to Calcutta. A mixed procession of Hindus and Muslims saw Gandhi and promised to reconcile their differences. Then the entire police force of North Calcutta, European and Indian, commenced a twenty-four-hour fast in sympathy while remaining on duty. 'The leaven has begun to work,' Gandhi remarked.[109] On 4 September, the effect of the fast on Gandhi had begun to tell: he became weak, giddy, with a rapid faint pulse. He was a man seventy-eight years old.

---

106 Ibid., p. 407.

107 Ibid., p. 409

108 Ibid., p. 412.

109 Ibid., p. 418.

Then the miracle happened. As the leaden hours crept by and slowly life ebbed out of the frail little man on the fasting bed, it caused a deep heart churning in all concerned, bringing the hidden lie to the surface. People came and confessed to him what they would have confided to no mortal ear. Hindus and Muslims combined in an all-out effort to save the precious life that was being offered as ransom for disrupted peace between brother and brother. Mixed processions, consisting of all communities, paraded through the affected parts of the city to restore communal harmony.[110]

Scores of members of Hindu 'resistance groups', formed since Direct Action Day, admitted before Gandhi their role as instigators and pledged maintenance of order. This was the kind of assurance that he had wanted, but it was not enough. 'The function of my fast is to purify our hearts and intellects and to release our energies by overcoming our mental sluggishness, inertia, not to paralyse us or render us inactive.'[111] A large gang of hooligans came to him; their ringleader made a full confession and offered, 'I and the whole party under me will gladly submit to whatever penalty you may impose, only you should now end your fast.' Gandhi replied, 'My penalty for you is that you should go immediately among the Muslims and assure them full protection. The minute I am convinced that real change of heart has taken place, I will give up the fast.'[112]

Now, Calcutta was not only free from violence: it was mobbed with processions to Hydari Mansion clamouring for an end to the fast. At 6 p.m. on this third day of the fast, a decisive breakthrough occurred: a deputation of leading citizens of Calcutta, representing all communities, came and pleaded with Gandhi. Gandhi demanded two promises from them: first, that communal violence would not recur in Calcutta, and

---

110 Ibid., p. 419.

111 Ibid., p. 420.

112 Ibid., p. 421.

second, that if it did recur, they would 'not live to report failure' but lay down their lives to maintain order. If these pledges were given and broken, then Gandhi vowed he would fast until death. 'If you deceive me, if you say one thing and mean another in your heart, my death will be upon your head. I want a clear and straight answer. Your assurance must be in writing.'[113] The deputation withdrew to another room, deliberated, argued and agreed; Rajaji dictated the draft of the pledge: 'We the undersigned promise to Gandhiji that now that peace and quiet have been restored in Calcutta once again, we shall never allow communal strife in the city and shall strive unto death to prevent it.'[114] Gandhi immediately broke the fast: it had lasted seventy-three hours. Calcutta remained true to its word; communal violence ceased, not to return. 'Gandhiji has achieved many things,' said Rajagopalachari, 'but there has been nothing, not even independence, which is so truly wonderful, as his victory over evil in Calcutta.'[115]

This has been the verdict of most historians: Gandhi rose to his greatest heights in the closing months of his life, and the purest success story in satyagraha is that of his 1947 Calcutta fast. V.P. Menon writes in his *Transfer of Power in India*:

> It is gratifying to note that while the north was in the throes of a communal holocaust, the rest of India remained comparatively peaceful. In Bengal, particularly in Calcutta, the situation might have become serious but for one man, and that man was Gandhiji … No word of government could have given so much confidence and assurance as this one man alone had inspired in the minorities on either side.[116]

---

113 Ibid., p. 422.

114 Ibid., p. 423.

115 Tendulkar, *Mahatma*, Vol. VIII, p. 133.

116 Menon, *The Transfer of Power in India*, p. 434.

Western historians of this period have been equally unstinting in their tributes. 'His triumph was complete,' wrote E.W.R. Lumby in his description of the fast, 'and the peace he brought was destined to endure. A League newspaper, acknowledging the debt Calcutta Muslims owed him, said, "he was ready to die so that they might live peacefully". He had in fact worked a miracle, perhaps the greatest of modern times.'[117]

Yet few commentators on Gandhi's last days have chosen to point out the supreme irony of the situation: the fact that Gandhi, renowned as India's great 'freedom fighter', should have achieved most in the few short months after independence had been attained. Behind this apparent irony lies the simple truth that Gandhi's goal was not merely national independence. Over twenty years before, he had said, 'The fight for swaraj means not mere political awakening but an all around awakening—social, educational, moral, economic and political.'[118] Now that the political goal had been attained, Gandhi could only remind the nation how much more was required.

> The Congress has won political freedom, but it has yet to win economic freedom, social and moral freedom. These freedoms are harder than the political, if only because they are constructive, less exciting and not spectacular. All-embracing constructive work evokes the energy of all the units of the millions. The Congress has got the preliminary and necessary part of her freedom. The hardest has yet to come.[119]

---

117 E.W.R. Lumby, *The Transfer of Power in India, 1945–1947* (London: Allen and Unwin, 1954), p. 193. See also Penderel Moon, *Divide and Quit* (London: Chatto and Windus, 1961), pp. 248–49, 290, and Spear, *India*, p. 424.

118 *Young India*, 26 August 1926, II, p. 1231.

119 Pyarelal, *Mahatma Gandhi*, Vol. X, pp. 677–78.

With this larger goal of swaraj in mind, and with a firm belief in the Constructive Programme as the means for its achievement, Gandhi drafted, on the day before his death, a Congress Resolution which sought 'to disband the existing Congress organization and flower into a Lok Sevak Sangh'.[120] The Congress, transformed into a people's service association, would direct the organization of the country into a system of panchayats, extending from the village to the national level. The Congress members, whose function Gandhi now saw exclusively in terms of social service, would then be brought into intimate contact with the needs of the villagers. This approach, Gandhi believed, would bring India closer to the goal of 'social, moral and economic' freedom for its 'seven hundred thousand villages'.[121] Only eleven days before drafting this resolution, which has since become known as Gandhi's 'Last Will and Testament', he had ended, in Delhi, his last fast for Hindu–Muslim unity. Thus, Gandhi's activity during the last month of his life was directed entirely towards the problem of communal violence. Yet, as the Draft Resolution shows, he maintained until the end his belief in the Constructive Programme for meeting the long-term needs of India's development.

Gandhi has been called a politician or a saint, and both of these, and neither. One of his acquaintances in government said 'amongst saints he is a statesman, and amongst statesmen, a saint'.[122] But Gandhi has seldom been called a political theorist; indeed, on occasion, he has been dismissed as anything but that.[123] Gandhi was a political activist

---

120 Ibid., Appendix B, p. 819.

121 Ibid., p. 819.

122 R.G. Casey, *An Australian in India* (London: Hollis and Carter, 1947), p. 60.

123 Joan Bondurant, *Conquest of Violence: The Gandhian Philosophy of Conflict* (Princeton, N.J.: Princeton University Press, 1958), p. 7 and

who confronted practical problems and immediate social issues; he remained intensely involved, throughout most of his life, in the Indian Nationalist Movement, and he derived continuing strength and inspiration from the historical situation in which he found himself. He thought always in terms of 'experiments with Truth' rather than of constructing philosophical systems. But all this does not necessarily mean that Gandhi was not a political theorist.

One day during the Partition riots, Gandhi, in search of sustenance, reaffirmed his own faith in the power of the idea. 'One active thought,' he said, 'proceeding from the depths, in its nascent purity and endowed with all the undivided intensity of one's being, can become dynamic and make history.'[124] The thought which emerged from the depths of Gandhi's experience, and became 'endowed with all the individual intensity of his being' was the conception that he shared with Vivekananda and Aurobindo of the divine nature of man and of Truth, the Absolute, as the ground of all being. Gandhi's aim, swaraj, and his method, satyagraha, could not have been more deeply rooted in this view of human nature and the Absolute. The highest form of freedom was moral and spiritual in quality because man was essentially moral and spiritual; man became free when he realized this reality of his own self. Satyagraha, 'holding fast to Truth', was the way in which the individual might best make this discovery, and then reveal it to others.

Gandhi, then, was an activist whose course of political and social action was directed by a particular theory of man and the Absolute; this theory was constantly used as a basis for self-examination, for experimentation with himself and his environment, and for analysis of social and political events and behaviour. It is quite easy to find instances where Gandhi, in his thought and action, seems to have

Nanda, *Mahatma Gandhi*, pp. 8, 381.

124 Gandhi, quoted in Pyarelal, *Mahatma Gandhi*, Vol. IX, p. 353.

been inconsistent, but it is always necessary to consider these instances in terms of a certain context of belief that he constructed. From his experiences in childhood, in London, and in South Africa, emerged a conceptual frame of reference within which Gandhi, as a political and social actor, moved about in a continuing search for areas of experimentation. The boundaries of this context of belief or frame of reference become readily identifiable if one attempts to imagine Gandhi acting within the modern Indian historical situation, but wholly outside the philosophy which he developed: for example, as a violent revolutionary on the one hand, or an otherworldly recluse on the other. Gandhi once said, 'I must respond to varying conditions, and yet remain changeless within'. [125] If there was a changeless aspect of Gandhi's life and thought, it rested with those values which he formed, early in life, concerning man, Truth, and freedom; and his adherence to these values compelled, as one writer on Gandhi has observed, 'a consistency impossible of achievement, even for the Mahatma himself'. [126]

---

125 Gandhi, *Young India*, 20 August 1925, II, p. 553.

126 Hugh Tinker, *Magnificent Failure?—The Gandhian Ideal in India After Sixteen Years* (London: Royal Institute of International Affairs, 1964), p. 271.

CHAPTER 8

Tagore: Freedom and Nationalism

'I regard the Poet as a sentinel warning us against the approach of enemies called Bigotry, Lethargy, Intolerance, Ignorance, Inertia and other members of that brood.'[1]

—Gandhi, 1921

The Early Development of Tagore's Ideas on Nationalism

... [T]ruth is in unity, and therefore freedom is in its realization. The texts of our daily worship and meditation are for training our mind to overcome the barrier of separateness from the rest of existence and to realize advaitam, the Supreme Unity ... Also in the social or political field, the lack of freedom is based upon the spirit of alienation, on the imperfect realization of the One. There our bondage is in the tortured link of union. One may imagine that an individual who succeeds in dissociating himself from his fellows attains real freedom, inasmuch as all ties of relationship imply obligation to others. But we know that, though it may sound paradoxical, it is true that in the human world, only a

---

1   Gandhi, *Young India*, 13 October 1921, I, p. 669.

perfect arrangement of interdependence gives rise to freedom. The most individualistic of human beings who own no responsibility are the savages who fail to attain their fullness of manifestation. They live immersed in obscurity, like an ill-lighted fire that cannot liberate itself from its envelope of smoke. Only those may attain their freedom from the segregation of an eclipsed life who have the power to cultivate mutual understanding and co-operation. The history of the growth of freedom is the history of the perfection of human relationship.[2]

This view of individual freedom and social harmony had been suggested by Vivekananda; it had then been developed by Aurobindo, and Gandhi had applied it to the resolution of India's social strife. Tagore welcomed all these efforts; but he insisted on developing the idea in still another direction, until it challenged the dominant political belief of his age and of modern Indian politics: the gospel of nationalism. Aurobindo had extolled the ideal of universal harmony, but he had not singled out Indian nationalism as a threat to that ideal; his criticism was rather reserved for the Western nation-state system. Tagore asserted that in principle there was no distinction: 'Nationalism is a great menace,' he declared; and with this generalization, Aurobindo may have agreed. But Tagore added: 'It is the particular thing which for years has been at the bottom of India's troubles.'[3] None of the three other thinkers considered here would have gone this far; and Tagore not only declared his position in unequivocal terms, but he also made the theme of individual freedom versus the nation-state a central feature of his social and political thought. This chapter will briefly consider his criticism of nationalism and of its various manifestations in modern India.

---

2   Rabindranath Tagore, *The Religion of Man, The Hibbert Lectures for 1930* (London: Allen & Unwin, 1931), pp. 186–88.

3   Rabindranath Tagore, *Nationalism* (London: Macmillan, 1950), p. 111.

Tagore's case against nationalism was originally made against the Western nation-state system, and at its base was his disillusionment over the events of the Boer War. Appalled with the brutality and futility of that struggle, and sensing the deeper implication of the attitudes which it represented, Tagore expressed his feelings in a sonnet composed on the last day of the nineteenth century.

> The last sun of the century sets amidst the bloodred
>   clouds of the West and the whirlwind of hatred.
>
> The naked passion of self-love of Nations, in its drunken
>   delirium of greed, is dancing to the clash of steel and
>   the howling verses of vengeance.
>
> The hungry self of the Nation shall burst in a violence of fury
>   from its own shameless feeding.
>
> For it has made the world its food...[4]

The poem concludes with a warning to India to 'keep watch', and,

> Be not ashamed, my brothers, to stand before the
> proud and the powerful
> With your white robe of simpleness.
>
> Let your crown be of humility, your freedom, the
>   freedom of the soul.
>
> Build God's throne daily upon the ample bareness
>   of your poverty
>
> And know that what is huge is not great and pride
>   is not everlasting.[5]

---

4   Tagore, 'The Sunset of the Century', in *Nationalism*, p. 133.

5   Ibid., p. 135.

The events of the early twentieth century only increased Tagore's fear of nationalism, and his desire for international harmony. In his famous collection of poems *Gitanjali* of 1912, he yearned for an age of freedom,

> Where the mind is without fear and the head is
> held high;

> Where knowledge is free;

> Where the world has not been broken
> up into fragments by narrow domestic walls...[6]

With the outbreak of the First World War, all of Tagore's fears seemed to him confirmed; his cry of protest came in three lectures on nationalism, delivered in 1916. These comprised a frontal attack on an idea which had then reached its apogee, and Tagore directed this attack against nationalism throughout the world: he called his lectures 'Nationalism in the West', 'Nationalism in Japan', and 'Nationalism in India'.

The primary concern that dominates these lectures is that of the suppression of individual freedom by the cult of nationalism. 'This nationalism,' he begins, 'is a cruel epidemic of evil that is sweeping over the human world of the present age, and eating into its moral vitality.'[7] In Japan, 'the voluntary submission of the whole people to the trimming of their minds and clipping of their freedom by their government, which through various educational agencies regulates their thoughts, manufactures their feelings' has led to an acceptance of an 'all-pervading mental slavery with cheerfulness and pride because of their nervous desire to turn themselves into a machine of power called

---

6   Rabindranath Tagore, *Gitanjali (Song Offerings)* (London: Macmillan, 1920), p. 27.

7   Tagore, *Nationalism*, p. 16.

the nation…'[8] In the West, nationalism has corrupted the colonizers no less than the colonies. 'Not merely the subject races,' Tagore told America, 'but you who live under the delusion that you are free, are every day sacrificing your freedom and humanity to this fetish of nationalism, living in the dense poisonous atmosphere of world-wide suspicion and greed and panic.'[9]

Tagore was most distressed, not with the prevalence of nationalism in the West, but with its infection of India. The idea was a Western importation, but Tagore realized that his own countrymen, and especially his Bengali contemporaries, had developed it into a peculiar Indian type. Bankimchandra, Vivekananda, Pal and Aurobindo were the main philosophers of early Indian nationalism; and, ironically, as Tagore was in America, preaching against nationalism, C.R. Das, another Bengali, was telling his Indian audiences, 'I find in the conception of my country the expression also of divinity. With me, nationality is no mere political conception, borrowed from the philosophy of the West … I value this principle of nationality as I value the principle of morality and religion.'[10]

The greatest disservice which nationalism had rendered India, Tagore argued, was to have directed the country's attention away from its primary needs. 'Our real problem in India,' Tagore contended, 'is not political. It is social.'[11] The nationalist urge leads to a pursuit of political goals to the neglect of pressing social problems. Neither the Congress Moderates nor the Extremists realized this critical need. The former had 'no constructive idea', no sense that 'what India most needed was constructive work coming from within herself'.[12] They

---

8   Ibid., pp. 26–27.

9   Ibid., p. 26.

10 C.R. Das, *India for Indians* (Madras: Ganesh & Co., 1918), p. 9.

11 Tagore, *Nationalism*, p. 97.

12 Ibid., p. 12.

lost power 'because the people soon came to realize how futile was the half policy adopted by them'.[13] The Extremists pretended to root their programme in traditional Indian truths but, in reality, they were nothing but advocates of Western nationalism. 'Their ideals were based on Western history. They had no sympathy with the special problems of India. They did not recognize the patent fact that there were causes in our social organization which made the Indian incapable of coping with the alien ... the domination in India of the caste system, and the blind and lazy habit of relying upon the authority of traditions that are incongruous anachronisms in the present age.'[14] Nationalism cannot prompt a social and moral reform of the nature that is needed; rather, it will only whet the popular appetite for increased political warfare. The real task before India is that of building a good society, and 'society is the expression of those moral and spiritual aspirations of man which belong to his higher nature'.[15] If India pursues political independence to the exclusion of all else, she may attain a sovereign state; it will be one, however, in which the old social and moral maladies are not purged but magnified. Above all, a narrow quest for political liberty will only obscure India's real goal, which must always remain that of moral and spiritual freedom for the individual in society.

> Our social ideals create the human world, but when our mind is diverted from them to greed of power then in that state of intoxication we live in a world of abnormality where our strength is not health and our liberty is not freedom. Therefore political freedom does not give us freedom when our mind is not free. An automobile does not create freedom of movement, because it is a mere machine. When I myself am free, I can use the automobile for the purpose of my freedom.

13 Ibid., p. 113.

14 Ibid., pp. 113–14.

15 Ibid., p. 12.

We must never forget in the present day that those people who have got their political freedom are not necessarily free; they are merely powerful. The passions which are unbridled in them are creating huge organizations of slavery in the disguise of freedom. Those who have made the gain of money their highest end are unconsciously selling their life and soul to rich persons or to the combinations that represent money. Those who are enamoured of their political power and gloat over their extension of dominion over foreign races gradually surrender their own freedom and humanity to the organizations necessary for holding other peoples in slavery. In the so-called free countries, the majority of the people are not free; they are driven by the minority to a goal which is not even known to them. This becomes possible only because people do not acknowledge moral and spiritual freedom as their object. They create huge eddies with their passions, and they feel dizzily inebriated with the mere velocity of their whirling movement, taking that to be freedom. But the doom which is waiting to overtake them is as certain as death—for man's truth is moral truth and his emancipation is in the spiritual life.

The general opinion of the majority of the present-day nationalists in India is that we have come to a final completeness in our social and spiritual ideals, the task of the constructive work of society having been done several thousand years before we were born, and that now we are free to employ all our activities in the political direction. We never dream of blaming our social inadequacy as the origin of our present helplessness, for we have accepted as the creed of our nationalism that this social system has been perfected for all time to come by our ancestors ... This is the reason why we think that our one task is to build a political miracle of freedom upon the quicksand of social slavery ... Those of us in India who have come under the delusion that mere political freedom will make us free have accepted their lessons from the West as the gospel truth and lost their faith in humanity. We must remember whatever weakness we cherish in our society will become the source of danger in politics. The same inertia which leads us to our idolatry of dead forms in social institutions will create in our politics prison-houses with immovable walls. The narrowness of sympathy which makes it possible for us to impose upon a considerable portion of humanity the galling yoke of inferiority will assert itself in our politics in creating the tyranny of injustice.[16]

The Tagore–Gandhi Controversy

Many of the ideas which Tagore voices in the above passage are in profound agreement with those of Gandhi, as well as with Vivekananda and Aurobindo. All agree, ultimately, on the primary need for social reform in India, as well as on the supremacy of moral or spiritual freedom. Tagore's unique contribution rests with his early and emphatic assertion that though India's adoption of nationalism might further the struggle for Independence, it could only thwart the essential quest for moral and spiritual freedom. This point of view inevitably sparked off a controversy with India's arch-nationalist, Mahatma Gandhi.

'Indian nationalism is not exclusive, nor aggressive, nor destructive. It is health-giving, religious and therefore humanitarian.'[17] This is Gandhi, replying to Tagore's criticisms, and the view he expresses here accurately represents his general position on Indian nationalism. It may rightly be argued that Gandhi did not advocate many of the forms of nationalism which had sprung up around 1900 in Bengal. Gandhi did not see the nation as a transcendent entity, possessed of a soul and a form of freedom of its own, apart from its individual human components. He thought of swaraj in terms first of the individual and then of society. 'Swaraj of the people,' he said, 'means the sum total of the swaraj (self-rule) of individuals.' Yet, although Gandhi was not an exponent of nationalism after the fashion of Pal or C.R. Das, his ideas

---

16 Ibid., pp. 120–23.

17 Gandhi, *Young India*, 13 October 1921, I, p. 673.

did support other forms of nationalism, which he frankly endorsed, and which, as Tagore soon discovered, posed threats to individual freedom.

In March 1919, Gandhi called upon the people of India to observe 6 April as a mass hartal: a day of fasting, public meetings and suspension of labour. The intent was to mobilize popular opposition to the government's enactment of the Rowlatt Bills; the effect of the hartal was to demonstrate the considerable power potential of the non-cooperation programme. On 12 April, Tagore wrote to Gandhi from Shantiniketan urging him to exercise caution in the use of non-cooperation; the letter represents the first written evidence of Tagore's qualms over Gandhi's emerging political leadership. 'Power in all its forms is irrational,' Tagore began, 'it is like the horse that drags the carriage blind-folded.' He expressed his concern over recent acts of government repression and questioned the good that could result from pressing the campaign further. 'I have always felt,' he continued, 'and said accordingly, that the great gift of freedom can never come to a people through charity. We must win it before we can own it. And India's opportunities for winning it will come to her when she can prove that she is morally superior to the people who rule her by their right of conquest.' The present non-cooperation movement, he implied, did not seem to him representative of India's moral superiority, and he concluded this letter with these telling lines: 'I pray most fervently that nothing that tends to weaken our spiritual freedom may intrude into your marching line, that martyrdom for the cause of truth may never degenerate into fanaticism for mere verbal forms, descending into the self-defence that hides itself behind a moral name.'[18]

Tagore sailed for England and America early the next year. While abroad, he seems to have made up his mind as to whether Gandhi's

---

18 R.K. Prabhu and Ravindra Kelekar (eds.), *Truth Called Them Differently (Tagore–Gandhi Controversy)* (Ahmedabad: Navajivan Publishing House, 1961), pp. 14–17.

movement had in fact 'degenerated into fanaticism for mere verbal forms', hiding itself 'behind a moral name'. 'I wish I were the little creature Jack,' he wrote from Chicago in reference to the non-co-operation campaign, 'whose one mission is to kill the Giant Abstraction, which is claiming the sacrifice of individuals all over the world under highly tainted masks of delusion.'[19] In July 1921, he returned to India, after fourteen months abroad, to confront the campaign at its peak. His battle against the Giant Abstraction soon began in earnest.

On 29 August, Tagore delivered at a Calcutta public meeting an address entitled 'The Call of Truth'. This is a remarkable commentary, for it offered, at once, both a trenchant criticism of Gandhi's leadership and an eloquent defence of individual freedom with which Gandhi, above all Indian leaders of this time, had identified himself. Tagore begins his remarks with a proposition common to Vivekananda, Aurobindo and Gandhi: 'it is in the nature of man to struggle for self-realization or spiritual freedom; this must remain the individual's highest aim, and success may only be gained through conquest of his own self.'[20] Reiterating a maxim that both he and Gandhi had stressed for the last decade, Tagore said, 'They who have failed to attain swaraj within themselves must lose it in the outside world too.'[21] Political independence was a great desideratum. But it was not swaraj, nor could it even ensure swaraj if not accompanied by a moral or spiritual transformation of the individual in society. Tagore often expressed his ideas through metaphor; in the 'Call of Truth', he drew on this medium to set forth his conception of the relation of social and moral to political reform. The metaphor is his own, but the idea was shared by Gandhi:

---

19 Rabindranath Tagore, *Letters to A Friend*, ed. C.F. Andrews (London: Allen & Unwin, 1928), p. 132.

20 Rabindranath Tagore, *Towards Universal Man* (London: Asia Publishing House, 1961), p. 233.

21 Ibid., p. 254.

When we turn our gaze upon the progress of other nations, the political cart-horse comes prominently into view—on it seems to depend wholly the speed of the vehicle. We forget that the cart behind the horse must also be in a fit state to move; its wheels must have the right alignment, its parts must have been properly assembled. The cart is the product not simply of materials on which saw and hammer had worked; thought, energy and application have gone into its making. We have seen countries that are outwardly free, but as they are drawn by the horse of politics the rattle rouses all the neighbourhood from sleep and the jolting makes the limbs of the passengers ache; the vehicles break down repeatedly on their way and to put them in running order is a terrific business. Yet they are vehicles of a sort, after all. The fragments that pass for our country not only lack cohesion but are comprised of parts at odds with one another. To hitch it to anger or avarice or some other passion, drag it along painfully with much din and bustle, and call this political progress! How long could the driving force last? Is it not wiser, then, to keep the horse in the stable for the time and take up the task, first, of putting the vehicle in good shape?[22]

From this passage may be anticipated the nature of the criticism that follows: it consists, in effect, of Tagore turning Gandhi's own arguments against him. While abroad, Tagore says, he had heard nothing but high praise of the non-cooperation movement; he had come to believe, from this, that India was at last on the path to 'real liberation'.[23] Then, in a chilling paragraph, he tells of what he found on his return to India:

So, in the excited expectation of breathing the air of a new-found freedom, I hurried back to my homeland. But what I have seen and felt troubles me. Something seems to be weighing on the people's

22 Ibid., pp. 259–60.
23 Ibid., p. 262.

spirit; a stern pressure is at work; it makes everyone talk in the same voice and make the same gestures.[24]

This climate of opinion, Tagore believed, was a manifestation of nationalism at its worst. 'Slave mentality' of this nature, rather than alien rule, is, he said, 'our real enemy and through its defeat alone can swaraj within and without come to us.'[25] Gandhi's directives, which urged, among other things, the manual spinning of yarn, and burning of foreign cloth, were not being weighed by critical minds; rather, they had been accepted as dogma. And, 'As dogma takes the place of reason, freedom will give way to some kind of despotism.'[26] Tagore himself remained highly critical of Gandhi's directives; he found Gandhi's dicta on spinning and cloth-burning negative and destructive. 'Swaraj is not a matter of mere self-sufficiency in the production of cloth. Its real place is within us—the mind with its diverse power goes on building swaraj for itself.'[27] These particular tenets of Gandhi struck Tagore as medieval in their compulsive desire for simplicity; they closed doors to economic advance. In their rabid advocacy of a narrow form of swadeshi, they cramped Indian attitudes into a restrictive provincial mould, inhibiting the mind's 'diverse power' to go on 'building swaraj for itself'. 'As everywhere else, swaraj in this country has to find its basis in the mind's unfoldment, in knowledge, in scientific thinking, and not in shallow gestures.'[28] Gandhi's approach to social reform, Tagore contended, would not stimulate the 'mind's unfoldment', but rather

---

24 Ibid., pp. 262–63.

25 Ibid., p. 270.

26 Ibid., p. 268.

27 Ibid., p. 268.

28 Ibid., p. 268.

restrict its development and lead to its atrophy. On a national level, this approach would result in a deplorable attitude of isolationism and hostility toward the rest of the world. 'The Call of Truth' ends with a characteristic appeal to answer the 'urgent call' of 'universal humanity' by shedding the limitations of narrow nationalism, and recognizing 'the vast dimensions of India in its world context'.[29] 'Henceforth, any nation which seeks isolation for itself must come into conflict with the time-spirit and find no peace. From now onward, the plane of thinking of every nation will have to be international. It is the striving of the new age to develop in the mind this faculty of universality.'[30]

The Tagore–Gandhi controversy thus focused on two aspects of the meaning of freedom. Tagore argued, first, that on a domestic level, Indians had placed themselves in bondage through their unthinking acceptance of arbitrary dicta; they idolized a leader who, however saintly, had harnessed their blind allegiance to a gospel of retardation rather than growth. A second and related feature of Gandhi's teaching was its implications on an international level. Gandhi's ideas, Tagore argued, had fostered, for the most part, an unhealthy sense of separateness which foolishly spurned the knowledge and advances of the Western world. Each of these attitudes inhibited India's growth and thus restricted her freedom.

Gandhi replied to the first of Tagore's charges that he did not wish to produce a 'deathlike sameness in the nation', but rather to use the spinning wheel to 'realize the essential and living oneness of interest among India's myriads'.[31] Spinning was not intended to replace all other forms of activity, but rather to symbolize 'sacrifice for the whole

---

29 Ibid., p. 272.

30 Ibid., p. 271.

31 Gandhi, *Young India*, 5 November 1925, II, p. 712.

nation'. 'If the Poet span half an hour daily his poetry would gain in richness. For it would then represent the poor man's wants and woes in a more forcible manner than now.'[32] Spinning for Gandhi, then, was a symbolic form of self-sacrifice for the masses; Tagore, however, remained suspicious of any such abstract appeal and tended to identify this symbolism with aspects of Indian nationalism. Moreover, when Tagore accused Gandhi of narrow provincialism, the latter replied, 'I hope I am as great a believer in free air as the great Poet. I do not want my house to be walled in on all sides and my windows to be stuffed. I want the cultures of all the lands to be blown about my house as freely as possible. But I refuse to be blown off my feet by any.'[33] And, when Tagore warned him of the inevitable danger inherent in his nationalism, Gandhi argued, 'My patriotism is not exclusive; it is calculated not only not to hurt any other nation but to benefit all in the true sense of the word. India's freedom as conceived by me can never be a menace to the world.'[34] Yet, despite these assurances, Gandhi did espouse an extreme form of Indian nationalism. 'The interests of my country,' he once wrote, 'are identical with those of my religion';[35] and, on another occasion, 'The attainment of national independence is to me a search after truth'.[36] Considering the fact that Gandhi held nothing more sacred than his religion and the quest for truth, it is clear how highly he placed the interests of his country and the struggle

---

32 Ibid., p. 712.

33 Gandhi, *Young India*, 1 June 1921, I, p. 460.

34 Gandhi, *Young India*, 3 April 1924, II, p. 2.

35 Gandhi, *Young India*, 23 February 1922, I, p. 681.

36 D.G. Tendulkar, *Mahatma: Life of Mohandas Karamchand Gandhi* (8 vols.), Vol. III, Revised edition (Delhi: Publications Division, Ministry of Information and Broadcasting, Government of India, 1960–62), p. 273.

for Indian Independence. Tagore detected in such feelings a threat to individual freedom. That he himself was reviled by his countrymen for his heretical criticism of the non-cooperation movement, and accused of everything from high treason to an inveterate jealousy of Gandhi, suggests that his fear of the Giant Abstraction was not altogether unjustified.

Gandhi did contribute, as a political leader and thinker, to the growth of Indian nationalism as much as any figure of this century, and nowhere does he seem to recognize the implicit danger in nationalism to individual freedom, as well as to India's own free development vis-à-vis the rest of the world. On the contrary, he dismissed all attacks on Indian nationalism, not only from Tagore but also from his Western friends, as totally without foundation. Charles Andrews, perhaps his closest British friend, wrote to Gandhi with shock and dismay, in September 1921, concerning the burning of foreign cloth. 'The picture of your lighting that great pile,' Andrews said, 'including beautiful fabrics, shocked me intensely. We seem to be losing sight of the great beautiful world to which we belong and concentrating selfishly on India, and this must (I fear) lead back to the old bad selfish nationalism. If so, we get into the vicious circle from which Europe is now trying so desperately to escape.'[37] Gandhi replied, 'In all I do or advise, the infallible test I apply is, whether the particular action will hold good in regard to the dearest and the nearest.'[38] He then concludes, 'Experience shows that the richest gifts must be destroyed without compensation and hesitation if they hinder one's moral progress.'[39] On this point of view, Tagore made a telling observation: 'Experience ... has led me to

---

37 Charles Andrews quoted in *Young India,* 1 September 1921, I, p. 557.
38 Ibid., p. 559.
39 Ibid.

dread, not so much evil itself, as tyrannical attempts to create goodness. Of punitive police, political or moral, I have a wholesome horror. The state of slavery which is thus brought on is the worst form of cancer to which humanity is subject.'[40] Tagore, almost alone in his time, insisted not only that there may be more than one path to 'moral progress', but also that the greatest obstacle to be found on each of them was the 'slave mentality' that characterized nationalism. This was his contribution to the Indian idea of freedom.

---

40 Rabindranath Tagore, *Reminiscences* (London: Macmillan, 1920), p. 128.

Conclusion to the 1982 Edition

Vivekananda, Aurobindo, Gandhi and Tagore contributed more to the development of modern Indian social and political thought than any other thinkers of their time. The general nature of their contribution was twofold. Their first task, as they saw it, was to respond to the Western impact through the formulation of a social and political philosophy which would meet the demands of a modern India. Their approach sought to draw conceptual correspondences between Western ideas and traditional Indian beliefs. The necessity of accepting Western ideas on political freedom and social equality had become apparent to Vivekananda before the close of the nineteenth century. It was equally evident to these four thinkers that the method of this acceptance must be through assimilation: the development of a social and political philosophy which would draw upon the resources of the Indian tradition. The subsequent attempt at 'preservation by reconstruction', then, involved the reinterpretation and use of ancient Indian language and symbols, as well as philosophical themes, in a manner that might at once admit the most radical innovations, and still maintain continuity with the past.

The other contribution of this school of thought rests in its response to fundamental questions of political philosophy: problems concerning the nature of man and of an Absolute, the right relation of the individual to society and the nature of the good society, and a method of social and political change. The essential agreement among the members of this school on each of these questions is significant; equally important, however, are the various ways in which each thinker developed certain aspects of these questions. One main purpose of this study has been to illustrate how all four thinkers began with similar assumptions on the nature of man, the Absolute, and the meaning of freedom; and then how each contributed, in a distinctive way, through his individual treatment of particular political and social problems, to the construction of a modern Indian philosophy of freedom.

If emphasis were to be placed upon any one aspect of the idea of freedom as it has been examined in this book, it should be on that of its essential quality: it is, above all, Indian. The consideration that this school gave to problems of political thought becomes significant when seen within the Indian context. The contribution made by each member of the school revolves around the use which each made of the Indian tradition: the insistence by all that the Indian experience must provide the reference point for the conception, development and implementation of each idea.

Vivekananda, in the words of Professor A L. Basham, 'more than any other teacher in the India of his time, taught his fellow Indians how to assimilate the old with the new'.[1] The accuracy of this assessment may be tested through an examination of the themes which came to dominate Indian political and social thought in this century. The ideas of freedom, social harmony, and a way of right action, as set forth by

---

1   A.L. Basham, 'Swami Vivekananda: A Moulder of the Modern World', in *Vedanta for East and West* XII, no. 6 (July–August 1963), pp. 224–25.

Vivekananda, directed not only the premises of later Indian thinkers but also the way in which they used their tradition to shape these premises.

No member of Vivekananda's school used his tradition more skillfully than Gandhi. His achievement may be appreciated by focusing on the two main pillars of his thought, swaraj and satyagraha. Together, these two ideas represent the most significant conceptual relationship in modern Indian thought; they epitomize his school's response to basic problems of political philosophy. And they do this in a manner which is emphatically Indian. Gandhi conceived swaraj and satyagraha in such a way as to embody a vast wealth of traditional associations, symbols, images and beliefs. His use of the Indian tradition charged these concepts with their abundant meaning; the Indian social and political experience directed the purpose and the presuppositions that determined their nature. Together, they comprise the essence of the Indian idea of freedom.

DIMENSIONS OF THE IDEA OF FREEDOM IN THE GROUP OF SEVEN

CHAPTER 9

B.R. Ambedkar's Idea of Freedom

One of the most brilliant and original thinkers, statesmen and reformers of twentieth-century India, Dr Bhimrao Ramji Ambedkar (1891–1956), was born into the Untouchable Mahar (village servants) caste of Maharashtra. The key to his rise was education. At a time when less than 1 per cent of his caste was literate, Ambedkar secured a BA in Bombay, an MA and PhD from Columbia University in New York and a DSc from London University; he was also called to the bar from Gray's Inn, London. This extraordinary education, added to his conviction in democracy and his lifelong commitment to improving the lives of Untouchables, culminated in his conversion to Buddhism. This enabled him to improve the status of all of India's lowest castes and set a singular example for this group of twentieth-century leaders and theorists.

Ambedkar's father had left the traditional low-status work of the Mahars to join the British Army. The birth of Bhimrao, his fourteenth child, coincided with a time when a number of Mahars had freed themselves from the village structure and begun to protest the limitations of their status. Ambedkar, pushed by his family and aided by Hindu caste reformers, secured the education that enabled him to organize and dominate this burgeoning movement. The direction was set in the early 1920s: organization for social and political activity, attempts to secure civil and religious rights, and the building of pride and self-respect. In his thirty-five years as a leader of the movement, Ambedkar's activities paralleled those of African American leaders in the United States: the scholarship and literary interests of W.E.B. Du Bois, and the charisma and innovative methods of Martin Luther King.

His earliest efforts included a newspaper, an organization of all 'Depressed Classes' in Bombay to present grievances to the government, the opening of a hostel to facilitate the education of Untouchables, testimony to government commissions investigating political conditions and education, and the holding of conferences for Depressed Classes all over the Marathi-speaking area. Not until the 1930s did Ambedkar become an all-India personage. He was selected by the British as a delegate to the London Round Table Conferences (1930–1933), and there, confronted with demands for separate electorates by all the minorities of India, he stated his case for the Untouchables as a minority entitled to its own electorate.

The granting of special electorates for the Untouchables was unacceptable to Gandhi, who began a fast in 1932 against their separation from the Hindu body politic. Faced with the possibility of causing Gandhi's death, Ambedkar very reluctantly capitulated, accepting Gandhi's offer of separate electorates during primary elections, an increased number of reserved seats for Untouchables and joint electorates for assembly seats. This involved drawing up a schedule of those castes needing special representation, and 'Scheduled Castes' became thereafter the governmental name for Untouchables.

From this time on, Gandhi and Ambedkar pursued separate yet complementary political paths to Indian Independence—Gandhi, as leader of the Indian Congress, giving the name 'harijan' (people of God) to Untouchables and pleading with caste Hindus to abolish untouchability, and Ambedkar planning a political party and then embarking on an intellectual journey, remarkable for its creativity and courage. Ambedkar first joined others in attempting to secure temple entry and religious rights for Untouchables. When that failed, he rejected Hinduism and continued the drive towards education and ultimate conversion to Buddhism. Ambedkar's Independent Labour Party won fourteen seats in the Bombay Legislative Assembly in 1937; those elected under its banner included eleven Scheduled Caste members. The party attempted to abolish hereditary discrimination in village economic structures, to ban the use of the term 'harijan', and to secure family-planning measures. Because it was a small minority party, it was unsuccessful, so like M.N. Roy (as we will see below), he never found the key to political power through the party system. In 1936, he wrote a landmark address entitled *Annihilation of Caste*. An undelivered speech that has appeared in annotated form, edited by S. Anand, with a lengthy introduction by Arundhati Roy.[1]

Throughout the 1930s, he led many conferences, including one to discuss conversion to another religion and broadening the movement, but Ambedkar also concerned himself with other issues. As Member for Labour in the viceroy's Executive Council, he worked on labour laws and dam projects. He taught at the Government Law College in Bombay. He wrote on the need to reform and liberalize the university system while affirming Buddhist virtues. In 1945, he founded the People's Education Society; a year later, he opened Siddharth College in Bombay. But as India drew near to independence, he again stressed separatism from other Hindu groups as the way to empower the Scheduled Castes in the battle for equality and integration. He was now known all over India as Babasaheb ('respected sir'), the champion

---

1   B.R. Ambedkar, *Annihilation of Caste: The Annotated Critical Edition*, ed. S. Anand (New Delhi: Navayana Publishing, 2014). See also *BAWS*, Vol.1, Part I, 1987, Chapter 2, pp. 21–96.

of the Untouchables. On India's independence in 1947, he was appointed as Law Minister and Chairman of the Constitution Drafting Committee, a task that he subsequently performed with distinction, as author of that distinguished document. He did not formally convert to Buddhism until the last year of his life, but it was the journey to this culmination that brought him into the group of seven thinkers examined in this book.

The introduction to this book stated briefly Ambedkar's mature theory, noting especially his theory of the means-ends relationship. The writings by him examined here will focus on three key sources finished during the last year of his life. In 1956, in declining health, he struggled to complete the following: first, an essay entitled 'Buddha or Karl Marx' (1956); second, an address delivered on 20 November in Kathmandu on 'Buddhism and Communism'; and third, the indisputable culmination of his thought, his magnum opus entitled *Buddha and His Dhamma* (published posthumously). He died on 6 December, so this single year ranks as his most prolific period as a thinker. Naturally, these ideas had been forming in Ambedkar's thought during the 1950s, so there's no implication that they all sprang forth suddenly without prior contemplation. At the same time, his determination to get them finished reveals an intense development of his thought and expression of his mature philosophy.

Ambedkar on Marx, Communism, Buddhism

The title of the first writing examined here, 'Buddha or Karl Marx',[2] is significant because the 'or' indicates the antinomy that Ambedkar now sees between Buddhism and Communism, evident throughout

---

2 All quotes in this section are from 'Buddha or Karl Marx' in *The Essential Writings of B.R. Ambedkar*, ed. Valerian Rodrigues (New Delhi: Oxford University Press, 2002), pp. 172–89, or *BAWS* as indicated.

the essay.[3] It opens with his declaration that he has studied them both, and the purpose is now to evaluate which is the better path. He turns immediately to outline 'The Creed of the Buddha', before contrasting it with 'The Original Creed of Karl Marx'. He succinctly lists twenty-five tenets of the former as against ten of the latter, suggesting the relative worth he attaches to each. Then he pronounces what is right and wrong for any religion or belief system: 'Religion is necessary for a free Society, [but] not every Religion is worth having.' Therefore, Marxism or Communism, as non-religious theories, already fail to meet the first requirement. A religion must 'relate to facts of life and not theories and speculations about God, or Soul, or Heaven or earth'. Belief in God or salvation of the soul should not be at the centre of religion. Rather, 'Real religion lives in the heart of man and not in the Shastras'. 'Man and morality must be the centre of Religion' as the 'law of life'. Its function 'is to reconstruct the world and to make it happy'. Causes of unhappiness are 'conflict of interest' and possession of private property that 'brings power to one class and sorrow to another'. He affirms the equality of all human beings according to their worth with importance placed especially on 'high ideals and not noble birth'.

Here, he introduces the essential virtue of '*maitri* or fellowship towards all ... even to one's enemy'. Again, the antinomy of the title is shown because maitri is alien to Marxist, especially Communist, theory. As examined below, it is at the core of his mature philosophy, notably distinguished from Western leftist thought, and terms like 'fraternity', 'brotherhood' or 'love of mankind' to an inclusive extension

---

3   I am indebted to the eminent Ambedkar scholar, Aakash Singh Rathore, for stressing a crucial distinction in Ambedkar's thought between the ideas of Marx and Stalinist Communism, with his critique directed principally at the latter. In fact, Ambedkar conflates the two subjects at times, which can produce confusion if the full context of his writing is not studied carefully.

of love and compassion for all living beings. This is a key point that demands emphasis at the outset because it brings Ambedkar away from Communism into the group of seven and the Indian intellectual tradition. Maitri is not only unmentioned in relatively early tracts like *Annihilation of Caste*, but it is irrelevant to his purpose then, at that stage of his philosophical quest.

Therefore, the centrality of maitri will be expanded in *Buddha and His Dhamma* and emphasized there. He also introduces the Buddhist doctrine that 'Everything is subject to the law of causation', which becomes a key component of his theory of means-ends, as noted in the introduction. After declaring against war (though not affirming here an absolute commitment to ahimsa), he concludes about this creed: 'How ancient but how fresh! How wide and how deep are his teachings!' Such enthusiasm is notably not expressed about either Marx or Communism.

There is nothing original or even vaguely inspired about his summation of Marxism as he restates in formulaic terms the principles clearly set forth in the *Communist Manifesto*: class division, conflict, exploitation of the workers and the primacy of economic forces. Then he concludes that 'much of the ideological structure raised by Marx has broken to pieces. There is hardly any doubt that Marxist (sic) claim that his socialism was inevitable has been completely disproved' and many of the other propositions of the doctrine 'have also been demolished both by logic as well as by experience'. He admits, however, that the 'residue' that remains valid includes that 'the function of philosophy is to reconstruct the world', along with the existence of class conflict, injustice of private ownership of property through exploitation and the necessity of abolishing it. While parallels between them are very briefly drawn on these goals, he significantly proceeds to devote the largest segment of the essay to the crucial importance of means. Here, he dwells on the superiority of Buddhist methods as embodying 'virtues one must practice to his utmost capacity', the Buddhist 'gospel' which was 'enunciated as a result of his enlightenment to end the sorrow and misery in the world'.

Ambedkar's Theory of the Relationship of Means to End

This begins one of his central statements on the means-ends theory that marks his break with Communism, so it should be quoted at some length:

> It is clear that the means adopted by the Buddha were to convert a man by changing his moral disposition to follow the path voluntarily. The means adopted by the Communists are equally clear, short and swift. They are (1) Violence and (2) Dictatorship of the Proletariat. The Communists say that there are only two means of establishing Communism. The first is violence. Nothing short of it will suffice to break up the existing system. The other is the dictatorship of the proletariat. Nothing short of it will suffice to continue the new system. It is now clear what the similarities and differences between Buddha and Karl Marx are. The differences are about the means. The end is common to both.[4]

Then Ambedkar closes the argument by asking,

> Whose means are superior and lasting in the long run? Can the Communists say that in achieving their valuable end they have not destroyed other valuable ends? They have destroyed private property. Assuming that this is a valuable end, can the Communists say that they have not destroyed other valuable ends in the process of achieving it? How many people have they killed for achieving their end? Has human life no value? Could they not have taken property without taking the life of the owner? ... We must not

---

4   Ambedkar, 'Buddha or Karl Marx', in Rodrigues (ed.), *The Essential Writings*, p. 183.

consider whose means are more lasting. One has to choose between government by force and government by moral disposition ... What the Buddha wanted was that each man should be morally so trained that he may himself become a sentinel for the kingdom of righteousness.[5]

Then after a further scathing indictment of Communism, he concludes the last paragraph by emphasizing that the contrast between these two systems of belief rests on which has valid means. The choice and value of the right method must be the determining factor when contrasting these two philosophies: 'The Buddha's method was different. His method was to change the mind of man: to alter his disposition so that whatever man does, he does it voluntarily without the use of force or compulsion. His main means to alter the disposition of men was his Dhamma and the constant preaching of Dhamma ... It cannot be emphasized that in producing equality, society cannot afford to sacrifice fraternity or liberty. Equality will be of no value without fraternity or liberty. It seems that the three can exist only if one follows the way of the Buddha. Communism can give one but not all.'[6]

We turn now to the second of the two writings under consideration. This is a revealing address that Ambedkar delivered only two weeks before his death when he made the difficult journey to Kathmandu while suffering from severe hypertension, diabetes and failing eyesight. Yet, he was determined to deliver a keynote speech at a conference of a World Fellowship of Buddhists on the subject of Buddhism versus

---

5   Ibid., pp. 185–86.

6   *Dr. Babasaheb Ambedkar: Writings and Speeches*, compiled by Vasant Moon, Vol. 3, Part IV (Bombay: Hari Narake, 1987), pp. 441–62; and also 'Buddha or Karl Marx' in *The Essential Writings of B.R. Ambedkar*, ed. Rodrigues, pp. 183, 185–86, 189. See also *BAWS*, Vol.3, Part IV, pp. 441–62.

Marxism. This was a relatively short speech, but it presents his most forceful and unequivocal critique of Communism. He has now come to a crucial juncture with a climax that fits his extraordinary intellectual exploration. The opening begins with a now-familiar indictment of Marxism over means-ends and then concludes with a ringing call for the proselytization of the faith. He had officially and formally converted to Buddhism less than two months earlier. Here in Nepal, birthplace of the Buddha, he spoke with the passion of a true convert, having prepared his followers earlier that year by declaring that 'I am going to give this religion a new lease of life. All our problems will end only on our going over to the Buddhist faith … It is unnecessary for the Buddhist people to go to Karl Marx to get the foundation. The foundation is already there, well-laid.'

The Kathmandu address ranks as among Ambedkar's final thoughts, so they should be quoted at length and from the beginning.

The topic of his speech is argued consistently throughout, and he significantly starts with the means-ends theory that joins him to others in this school of seven, as well as marking the crux of his rejection of Communism. Just as Gandhi, when he staunchly refuted 'Bolshevism' (Gandhi does not mention Marx in his writings but Communism instead), specifically warned against 'short-violent-cuts to success',[7] so Ambedkar at this point condemned Communism because of its 'devious path … to rush up and to take what we call short cuts. Short cuts in life are always dangerous, very dangerous'. The similarities between Ambedkar and Gandhi, in terms of language and meaning, are significant not only for these two leading thinkers but for others in the school of seven as well. This is emphatically shown in the following passage on the right method of change:

---

7 *The Collected Works of Mahatma Gandhi* (Delhi: Government of India, 1994), Vol. 25, pp. 423–24. Hereafter *CWMG*.

What are the ways and means which Karl Marx or the Communists wish to adopt in order to bring about Communism? That is the important question. The means that the Communists wish to adopt in order to bring about Communism (by which I mean the recognition of Dukkha, the abolition of property) is violence and killing of the oppressed. Therein lies the fundamental difference between the Buddha and Karl Marx. The Buddha's means of persuading people to adopt the principles are by persuasion, by moral teaching and by love. He wants to conquer the opponent by inculcating in him the doctrine that love and powers can conquer anything. That is where the fundamental difference lies, that the Buddha would not allow violence, and the Communists do. No doubt the Communists get quick results because when you adopt the means of annihilating men, they do not remain to oppose you. You go on with your ideology, you go on with your way of doing things. The Buddha's way, as I said, is a long way, perhaps some people may say a tedious way, but I have no doubt about it, that it is the surest way.

We go back to the Buddha and ask this question in relation to the Dhamma. What does he say? The greatest thing that the Buddha has done is to tell the world that the world cannot be reformed except by the transformation of the mind of the man, and the mind of the world. ... The Buddha has energized you, and your conscience itself is acting as a sentinel in order to keep you on the right path. There is no trouble when the mind is converted and the thing is permanent. The Communist system is based on force. Supposing tomorrow the dictatorship in Russia fails, and we see signs of its failure, what would happen? I really like to know what would happen to the Communist system. As I see it, there would be bloody warfare among the Russian people for appropriating the property of the state. That would be the consequence of it. Why? Because they have not accepted the Communist system voluntarily. They are obeying it because they are afraid of being hanged. Such a system can take no roots, and therefore in my judgment, unless the Communists are able to answer these questions, what would happen to their system? When force disappears, there is no use pursuing it. Because, if the mind is not converted, force will always be necessary, and this is what I want to say in conclusion, that one of the greatest things I find in Buddhism is that its system is a democratic system.

Therefore, I have been a student of politics, I was a Professor of Economics, and I have spent a great deal of time in studying Karl Marx, Communism, and all that, and I have also spent a good deal of time in studying the Buddha's Dhamma. After comparing the two, I came to the conclusion that Buddha's advice with regard to the great problem of the world, namely, that there is Dukkha [suffering], and that Dukkha must be removed, and the Buddha's method was the safest and the soundest.

Then Ambedkar closed with a striking peroration urging his youthful audience to spread Buddhism as a religion:

If I may say so in conclusion, if any peril arises to the Dhamma in a Buddhist country, the blame shall have to be cast upon the Bhikkus [disciples] because I personally think that they are not wholly discharging the duty which devolves on them. Where is preaching? The Bhikku is living in his cloister ... That is not the way of propagating religion ... but religion, if it is to be a moral force for the regeneration of society, you must constantly din it into the ears of people ... The time has turned, and we must now copy some of the ways of the Christians in order to propagate our religion among the Buddhist people. They must be made aware, every day and all the time, that the Buddha's Dhamma is there, standing by them like a policeman to guard lest they should go the wrong way. Without that this religion will remain probably in a very decadent state. Do not be allured by Communist successes. I am quite confident that if we all become one-tenth as enlightened as the Buddha was, we can bring about the same result by the methods of love, of justice and good will.[8]

Appeals to religious transformation, the power of love or worldwide spiritual liberation of the world were dramatically preached by Vivekananda and practised by Gandhi. The point here is that by 1956 or earlier, Ambedkar had changed his mind, and the focal point of his conversion directly involved his theory of means related to end. This core concept is now firmly placed into a Buddhist philosophical framework.

Ambedkar's (and M.N. Roy's) critique of Marx and Communism over the logic and ethics of the means-ends relationship has been supported by Steven Lukes in *Marxism and Morality*, who concludes that 'Marxism has never come properly to grips with the means-ends issue, and the problem of dirty hands. For it is resistant to the perception that moral conflict is at issue here: that in pursuing the course of action with the best overall consequence, we may do what is wrong.'[9]

The strongest philosophical argument on this theory in the western intellectual tradition was made by John Dewey, throughout his works and specifically in his debate with Leon Trotsky. Dewey asserted with convincing theoretical analysis that there must be a 'genuine interdependence of means and ends'.[10] While there are conceptual

---

8 Ambedkar, 'Speech delivered at Kathmandu (Nepal) on November, 1956', in Nanak Chand Rattu, *Last Few Years of Dr. Ambedkar* (New Delhi: Amrit Publishing House, 1997), Appendix IV, pp. 242–48.

9 Lukes, *Marxism and Morality* (London: Oxford University Press, 1985), p. 147.

10 Dewey's direct confrontation with Trotsky, who produced the most thoughtful discourse of any Marxist on this concept, is reproduced in *Their Morals and Ours*, ed. George Novack (N.Y.: Pathfinder Press, 1986), pp. 67–71. As acknowledged elsewhere, I am indebted to Scott Stroud for his correspondence with the author and his publications

similarities with Western thinkers on this point, and especially between Ambedkar and Dewey, the attempt here is to establish the close parallels in thought among the Indian group of seven.

The Buddha and His Dhamma: Preliminary Bibliographical Commentary

The Buddha and His Dhamma is by far the most important text for this examination of Ambedkar's thought. It merits a preliminary bibliographical essay rather than the conventional footnote to preface the analysis. The book (referred to as *BHD* in the references below) has been reprinted and rendered in several editions. The one selected for examination here is introduced and annotated by Aakash Singh Rathore and Ajay Verma.[11] This is an outstanding 'critical edition' of the text, exemplifying stellar standards of scholarship, commendable for its ample and exacting commentary.

This edition may be compared with Eleanor Zelliot's excellent translation of the same text on the Columbia University website dedicated to Ambedkar's life and selected works, assembled by Frances Pritchett.[12] The latter edition, by two distinguished Ambedkar scholars, declares in Pritchett's introduction that 'It [*BHD*] remains a testament

---

on the influence of John Dewey on Ambedkar. His article, 'What Did Bhimrao Ambedkar Learn from John Dewey' (in *The Pluralist* 12, no. 3 [Summer 2017]: 78–103) offers a uniquely in-depth analysis of their mutual theories of the means-ends relationship.

11 B.R. Ambedkar, *The Buddha and His Dhamma: A Critical Edition*, edited, introduced and annotated by A.S. Rathore and Ajay Verma, (New Delhi: Oxford University Press, 2011). Hereafter *BHD*.

12 See complete text of *BHD* in *BAWS*, Vol. 11, 1992, pp.1–599 and 'Supplement to BHD', Vol. 11, 1995, 'Sources and Index' by Vasant Moon. Also see Frances Pritchett's indispensable website at: http://www.columbia.edu/itc/mealac/pritchett/00ambedkar/ambedkar._buddha/00_pref_unpub.html.

322 INDIAN IDEAS OF FREEDOM

to its author's love not only for the figure of the Buddha, but for social justice, humane values, and a clear-eyed honesty in looking at life'. Zelliot, faithful to the original text, helpfully enumerates Ambedkar's various points for clarity as well as accuracy.

However, while both editions have been consulted for this essay, the former by Rathore and Verma is preferred because it includes invaluable footnotes by the respective editors and other scholars; e.g., 'To Live in Nibbana is Dhamma', the third chapter, provides not only references to verses from original related Buddhist texts but also comments by Christopher S. Queen, a leading Ambedkar scholar,[13] and several others.

In any reputable edition, *The Buddha and His Dhamma* stands indisputably as Ambedkar's masterpiece, the culmination of his philosophy, over which he laboured during his final reflective years, completing it, as noted above, only in the closing months of his life.[14] The previous two writings by Ambedkar showed how he abandoned Communism for Buddhism as a critical summation of his journey.

Of course, one may always infer allusions to Communist doctrine in this text, yet the method of examination here does not attempt such inferences. Rather the purpose is to offer a close textual analysis that follows or adheres strictly to the author's stated construction. This mode of enquiry neither affirms nor denies alternative approaches to understanding a classic. As observed above, when footnotes with commentary are provided, they are appreciated and judged in terms of how far they illuminate the meanings or intentions of the author. Therefore, the Rathore/Verma edition has been selected in large part, as explained above.

---

13 *BHD*, pp. 127–28.

14 Dhananjay Keer, *Dr. Babasaheb Ambedkar*, Fourth edition (Bombay: Popular Prakashan, 2009), p. 491.

Furthermore, as indicated by references to Rathore above, I am not only indebted to him for his critical assessment of this essay on Ambedkar, but in awe of his prolific scholarship. In 2020 alone, he published not only an original study of Ambedkar entitled *Ambedkar's Preamble: A Secret History of the Constitution of India*, but also his edition of a massive three-year project of editing five volumes of interpretative writings from Ambedkar scholars around the world. Rajeev Kadambi, whose article on Ambedkar is referenced below, introduced me to Rathore, his colleague at the Jindal School of Liberal Arts and Humanities, and while the present essay cannot do justice to Rathore's scrupulous commentary, his extraordinary depth and breadth of writings about Ambedkar and other aspects of Indian political thought, present a challenging example for all those engaged in a study of this subject. I have also noted his contribution to this work in the Acknowledgements with his superlative comparison of Ambedkar and Gandhi in *Indian Political Theory: Laying the Groundwork for Svaraj* (2017).

The Buddha and His Dhamma has received less analysis than his earlier *Annihilation of Caste*, a comparatively brief address. This seems unfortunate because the former has justly been acclaimed by Ambedkar scholars as his major work. Thus, in *The Essential Writings of B.R. Ambedkar*, editor Valerian Rodrigues comments, 'His magnum opus, *The Buddha and His Dhamma* highlights the central issues that concerned him throughout his life.'[15] K.N. Kadam[16] concurs with Rodrigues in similar language. Narendra Jadhav[17], in a chapter entitled 'Buddha and his Dhamma', acknowledges that '*The Buddha and His*

---

15 Rodrigues (ed.), *The Essential Writings of B.R. Ambedkar*, p. 25.

16 *The Meaning of the Ambedkarite Conversion to Buddhism and Other Essays* (Mumbai: Popular Prakashan, 1997), p. 99.

17 *Ambedkar: Awakening India's Social Conscience* (New Delhi: Konark Pub., 2014), p. 581.

Dhamma is Dr. Ambedkar's mnemonic opus. Professor Christopher Queen of Harvard University calls it "a daring interpretation of traditional teachings" which "tells the story of Buddha and summarizes his teachings".'[18] A.K. Narain and D.C. Ahir, in *Dr Ambedkar, Buddhism and Social Change*,[19] write, 'That Dr Ambedkar was greatly influenced by the social gospel of the Buddha is more than evident from his monumental work, *The Buddha and His Dhamma*.' They then quote from Ambedkar to support this judgement.[20]

Eleanor Zelliot, in only one of her many longstanding distinguished contributions to Ambedkar scholarship, *From Untouchable to Dalit: Essays on the Ambedkar Movement*,[21] refers to *The Buddha and His Dhamma* as 'Dr. Ambedkar's Bible', and incisively explains its importance to the Buddhist movement in India.[22] In an endnote and also the Acknowledgements at the close of this volume, I express my sincere gratitude to Scott Stroud for his extensive articles on Ambedkar,

---

18 Christopher Queen ranks among the most prominent scholars of both Buddhism and Ambedkar and his trenchant exposition of Ambedkar's 'redefinition of Buddhist liberation' is analysed in his essay 'Dr. Ambedkar and the Hermeneutics of Buddhist Liberation', in *Engaged Buddhism: Buddhist Liberation Movements in Asia*, ed. Christopher S. Queen and Sallie B. King (Albany: State University of New York Press, 1996), pp. 45–71. His critique of the differences between Ambedkar and Gandhi here is noteworthy, presenting a challenging viewpoint that runs counter to the theme of the present book that stresses the similarities between them.

19 A.K. Narain and D.C. Ahir, *Dr. Ambedkar, Buddhism and Social Change* (Delhi: Buddhist World Press, 2010), p. 6.

20 Ibid., p. 6, 41–42.

21 Eleanor Zelliot, *From Untouchable to Dalit: Essays on the Ambedkar Movement*, Third edition (New Delhi: Manohar, 2011).

22 Ibid., p. 250.

as well as his critical comments on this section. His scholarship on John Dewey's influence on Ambedkar is singular and superlative.

A final example of outstanding and established writing on Ambedkar is by Gail Omvedt. Her prolific publications on Dalit history and politics, accompanied by activism in anti-caste movements, have earned her high academic recognition in Indian universities directly associated with Ambedkar. Just as Stroud argues forcefully for the continuing influence on Ambedkar of Dewey, so Omvedt contends for the enduring presence of Marxism in his thought.[23] Therefore, while the various positions of the above scholars may not be in agreement with my interpretation of Ambedkar's thought, notably the theme of his inclusion in this group of seven, I greatly respect and value their estimable contributions. The responsibility for the analyses of all the thinkers discussed in this book is solely mine.

The Buddha and His Dhamma: Textual Analysis

The Buddha and His Dhamma deserves close textual analysis from several angles. This may start with a philosophy of the means-ends relationship familiar to modern Indian thinkers. The concept has already been examined in the introduction to this volume and above, but it bears further explication here, not only because of its intrinsic centrality within this group of seven but also to emphasize it as the crux of his repudiation of Marxism or Communism.

Ambedkar writes in *The Buddha and His Dhamma*: 'He [Buddha] was the first to say, "Reap as you sow."' This core concept, using the same phrase, is repeated elsewhere in the text: '"Since it is impossible to escape the result of our deeds, let us practice good works."... "Let us inspect our thoughts so that we do no evil, for as we sow so we

---

23 See, for instance, Gail Omvedt, *Ambedkar: Towards an Enlightened India* (New Delhi: Penguin Books, 2004), pp. 60–61.

shall reap.".…'What the Buddha wanted to convey,' Ambedkar
concludes, 'was that the effect of the deed was bound to follow the
deed, as surely as night follows day … Thus the Buddha's answer to the
question of how the moral order of the universe is sustained is so simple
and irrefutable.'[24]

As argued in the introduction, Ambedkar, more than any of the
figures studied in this book, elaborates on the means-ends relationship
in philosophical depth, grounding it in the Buddhist theory of causation
and kamma. In his careful exposition of the doctrine's rational basis,
he explains that Buddha 'maintained that not only every event has
a cause, but the cause is the result of some human action or natural
law.' Therefore, 'If man is free, then every event must be the result of
man's action, or of an act of Nature. There cannot be any event which
is supernatural in its origin.' The implications of this for his idea of
freedom are evident from the 'law of Kamma or Causation … to free
man to go in search of truth … This doctrine of Kamma and Causation
is the most central doctrine in Buddhism. It preaches Rationalism, and
Buddhism is nothing if not rationalism.'[25]

---

24 *BHD*, pp. 84, 86, 132 and 179.

25 *BHD*, p. 133. In *The Buddha and His Dhamma*, Ambedkar makes
three explicit references to Marx. These occur in the Rathore edition
on pp. 122 and 265, with only the first of these being consequential.
This presents Ambedkar's own thinking about 'What the Buddha
Taught'. He wrote: 'The question that arises is—"Did the Buddha
have no Social Message?" When pressed for an answer, students of
Buddhism refer to the two points [regarding the "origin and growth
of religion"]. They say—"The Buddha taught Ahimsa." "The Buddha
taught peace!" Asked, "Did the Buddha give any other Social Message?"
"Did the Buddha teach justice?" "Did the Buddha teach love?" "Did
the Buddha teach liberty?" "Did the Buddha teach equality?" "Did
the Buddha teach fraternity?" "Could the Buddha answer Karl Marx?"
These questions are hardly ever raised in discussing the Buddha's

Ambedkar expounds his interpretation of Buddhist philosophy starting with the twenty-two vows that he composed for his famous mass conversion at Nagpur in October 1956. Twice he repeats the vow to 'have compassion and loving kindness for all living beings and protect them', and again, to 'practice compassion and loving kindness in everyday life'.[26] The centrality of this concept of 'loving kindness' is featured throughout *The Buddha and His Dhamma*. In the hierarchy of ten virtues that Ambedkar presents as 'The Buddha's First Sermon', there is a distinction between the last two: 'Karuna is loving kindness to human beings. Maitri is extending fellow feelings to all beings, not only to one who is a friend, but also to one who is a foe; not only to man, but to all living beings.'[27] Maitri is therefore privileged over karuna.

Dhamma. My answer [Ambedkar concludes] is that the Buddha has a Social Message. He answers all these questions. But they have been buried by modern authors.' (p. 122). In an explanatory footnote (#4), Rathore comments that 'This passage has led to numerous commentary, and there are dozens of articles and essays on the topic of Ambedkar's treatment of the Buddha and Karl Marx,' as cited in this edition's Bibliography. This includes an 'interpretative essay on the topic wherein he [Rathore] examines Ambedkar's Buddhist critique of Marx while attempting, at the same time, to uncover the subtle influence that Marx had on Ambedkar's own understanding of Buddhism.' (Ibid.) With all due respect to Ambedkar scholars like Rathore, it is not within the scope of this present essay to make a similar attempt at discovering such subtleties when limited to this reference to Marx in *The Buddha and His Dhamma*. There are perhaps enough existing controversies for the present author to enter into any more. The main purpose here is to examine how *The Buddha and His Dhamma* may relate to similar ideas among the six other thinkers analysed in this book.

26 *BHD*, p. xxi.

27 *BHD*, p. 72.

This requires emphasis to appreciate how this virtue lies at the core of Ambedkar's thought now as never before, distinguishing it from earlier stages of development. Ambedkar's repetition of the exact words in these two pages commending the superiority of maitri are noteworthy:

> It means fellowship not merely with human beings but with all living beings. It is not confined to human beings. Is not such maitri necessary? What else can give to all living beings the same happiness which one seeks for one's own self, to keep the mind impartial, open to all, with affection for every one and hatred for none? ... 'Love is not enough; what is required is maitri. It is wider than love.' ... Maitri alone means 'hatred for none'. It categorically rejects evil in all its forms, as 'the qualities of the good man are: do no evil, think nothing that is evil, get his livelihood in no evil way, and say nothing that is evil or is likely to hurt anyone'.[28]

Ambedkar qualified the Jain absolutist application of ahimsa, asserting that 'Ahimsa Permo Dharma is an extreme doctrine', arguing that while in its general sense it is 'a perfectly sound moral doctrine which everyone must respect', certain exceptions must be admitted.[29] Yet there is no such qualification placed on maitri. To the contrary, its connection to non-injury is explicit and notably extended to harmful speech: 'Cause no hurt; cherish no ill will. This is the Buddhist Way of Life ... To speak no ill, to do no harm, to practice restraint in conformity with the discipline, this is the counsel of the Buddha. Kill not, nor cause slaughter. He who is seeking his own happiness, does not punish or kill beings who also long for happiness, will find happiness. He who inflicts pain on an innocent and harmless person will soon come to grief.'[30]

---

28 *BHD*, pp. 72–73.

29 *BHD*, pp. 182–83.

30 *BHD*, pp.188–89.

Therefore, maitri, in all of its challenging spirit, ranks as the prominent virtue featured in *The Buddha and His Dhamma*. In his ardent advocacy of maitri, Ambedkar quotes at length Buddha's demanding counsel to his Bhikkus:

> Just as the earth does not feel hurt and does not resent, just as the air does not lend itself to any action against it, just as the Ganges water goes on flowing without being disturbed by the fire, so also you Bhikkus must bear all insults and injustices inflicted on you, and continue to bear maitri towards your offenders. So, almsmen, maitri must flow and flow forever. Let it be your sacred obligation to keep your mind as firm as the earth, as clean as the air, and as deep as the Ganges. If you do so, your maitri will not be easily disturbed by an act, however unpleasant. For all who do injury will soon be tired out. Let the ambit of your maitri be as boundless as the world, and let your thought be vast and beyond measure, in which no hatred is thought of ... None of the means employed to acquire religious merit, O Monks, has a sixteenth part of the value of loving kindness [maitri]. Loving kindness, which is freedom of the heart, absorbs them all; it glows, it shines, it blazes forth.[31]

A distinction between karuna and maitri in *BHD* may be compared with that of maitri and 'fraternity'. The latter is featured as a prominent value in Ambedkar's *Preamble to the Constitution of India* while the former is preferred, and markedly different, in *BHD*. The expansive inclusiveness of maitri represents a significant indication of the spiritual transformation with his conversion to Buddhism.

---

31 *BHD*, pp. 159–61. Ambedkar's analysis of maitri as a more expansive Buddhist virtue than karuna may be further distinguished from his earlier conceptualization of 'fraternity'. The identification of fraternity with maitri is presented by Aakash Rathore in *Ambedkar's Preamble: A Secret History of the Constitution of India* (Delhi: Random House India, 2020), p. 118.

An incisive examination of Ambedkar's 'ethical practices' appears in Rajeev Kadambi, 'Ambedkar's Framing of the "Political" within Ethical Practice'.[32] Kadambi's close analysis of *The Buddha and His Dhamma* not only connects a series of ten core Buddhist concepts concluding with maitri as 'extending fellow feeling to all beings', but relates these to Ambedkar's ethic of freedom. Kadambi quotes *The Buddha and His Dhamma* extensively, as in Ambedkar's conclusion that 'Let the ambit of your maitri be as boundless as the world, and let your thoughts be vast and beyond measure, in which no hatred is thought of'. Then Kadambi observes that 'If Karuna was anthropocentric, maitri was the fullest ecological expression of all living phenomena'. Again quoting from this source, that maitri 'means fellowship not merely with human beings but with all living things. Is not such maitri necessary? What else can give to all living beings the same happiness which one seeks for one's self, to keep the mind impartial, open to all, with affection for everyone and hatred for none?'[33] Ambedkar's ecology should underline his relevance for issues of climate change. Therefore, at this vital point, ecological and ethical spheres meet.

Ambedkar's Idea of Freedom

The thesis of this book is that among the group of seven thinkers examined, ideas of freedom remained in essential terms consistent, 'The outward freedom that we shall attain will only be in exact proportion to the inward freedom in which we may have grown at a given moment. And if this is the correct view of freedom, our chief energy must be concentrated upon achieving reform from within.'

---

32 In *Studies in Indian Politics* 4, no. 2 (2016): 143–58. Lokniti, Center for the Study of Developing Societies, SAGE Publications.

33 *BHD*, p. 73; and Kadambi, 'Ambedkar's Framing of the "Political" within Ethical Practice', pp. 153–54.

Indian Independence or 'outward freedom' remained secondary to those striving to achieve 'true freedom', through 'improvement of in the self'.[34] This is Gandhi writing in 1928, and while the idea is implicit in *Hind Swaraj*, the clear distinction between 'moral' or 'spiritual freedom' and 'political' freedom had been made before Gandhi by Vivekananda and Aurobindo.

Ancient Hindu and Buddhist texts distinguished freedom in these terms.[35] However, as observed before, there is no attempt or pretence to argue the consistency of ancient Hindu or Buddhist philosophy with any of the thinkers in this school of seven. This must be emphasized because it avoids issues of whether Ambedkar's interpretation of Buddhism accords with its classical foundations, much less the validity of Vivekananda's or Gandhi's reinterpretations of ancient Hindu texts. Aurobindo announced the purpose of the 'Indian Renaissance' as 'preservation by reconstruction',[36] and the meanings or implications of this purpose comprise a central theme of this comparative analysis, now including Ambedkar. Other scholars may legitimately undertake explorations of this group's concordance with ancient sources. This is not a task undertaken here.

Once Ambedkar left Marxism or Communism behind, his philosophy of freedom followed in *The Buddha and His Dhamma* to develop parallels with other Indian thinkers because of its climactic formulation. Rajeev Kadambi (as cited above) articulates the conceptual correspondences with maitri by observing that 'It was not possible to be free if we deny another's freedom. Freedom was not grounded in legality, but in something prior. Taking care of oneself mandated taking care of others since, very literally, practices on the self were ways to

---

34 *CWMG* 38:1–2; 18.

35 See also my *Indian Idea of Freedom*, Ch. 1, republished here.

36 Sri Aurobindo, *The Renaissance in India* (Pondicherry: Sri Aurobindo Ashram, 1953), pp. 39–40 and my *Indian Idea of Freedom*, chapter 1.

acquire additional insight. Freedom in this relational way meant that to be free we must exercise friendship towards all.'[37]

The sharp contrast between Ambedkar's *Annihilation of Caste* (1936) and *The Buddha and His Dhamma* becomes especially evident with the development of his idea of freedom. In the former treatise, he proclaimed his allegiance to democracy in classic Western liberal terms:

My ideal would be a society based on liberty, equality and fraternity. And why not? ... Few object to liberty in the sense of a right to free movement, in the sense of a right to life and limb. There is no objection to liberty in the sense of a right to property ... it [also] involves liberty to choose one's profession. But to object to this kind of liberty is to perpetuate slavery.

Ambedkar demands that Hindus not only 'kill Brahmanism and caste' in order to save itself, but, more than this, it 'must give a new doctrinal basis to your religion—a basis that will be in consonance with liberty, equality and fraternity; in short, with democracy.'[38]

The evolution in his thinking about freedom was signalled in 1954 when in an All-India Radio broadcast, he spoke on 'My Personal Philosophy':

Positively, my social philosophy may be said to be enshrined in three words: liberty, equality and fraternity. Let no one, however, say that I have borrowed my philosophy from the French Revolution. I have not. My philosophy has roots in religion and not in political science. I have derived them from the teachings of my master, the Buddha. In his philosophy, liberty and equality had a place: but he added that unlimited liberty destroyed equality, and absolute equality left no room

37 Kadambi, 'Ambedkar's Framing of the "Political" within Ethical Practice', pp. 153–54.

38 *Annihilation of Caste*, pp. 260–61, 310–11.

*for liberty. In his philosophy, law had a place only as a safeguard against
the breaches of liberty and equality; but he did not believe that law can
be a guarantee for breaches of liberty or equality.*[39]

Then he concludes that '*My philosophy has a mission. I have to do the
work of conversion.*'[40] It had taken Ambedkar eighteen years to reach this
proclamation of his national mission, and another two years before, as
noted above, he would lead the mass conversion in 1956.

The conceptual change by this time is significant in terms of his
philosophy of freedom. No longer is it attributed to Western thought
but rather to a homegrown religion of India. In *The Buddha and
His Dhamma*, as in his Kathmandu address, Marxist or Communist
theory becomes irrelevant to his self-proclaimed mission of widespread
Buddhist conversion. The fervency in his appeal is striking, with a full-
blown advocacy of Buddhist Dhamma.

As emphasized throughout this study of the group of seven thinkers,
the purpose of this comparative analysis is both to observe common
ground among them on a set of concepts and, in the course of this
examination, to explain their interpretations of respective religious

---

39 Quoted in K.N. Kadam (ed.), *Dr. B.R. Ambedkar: The Emancipator
of the Oppressed*, A Centenary Commemoration Volume (Bombay:
Popular Prakashan, 1993), p.1. Italics added. See *BAWS*, Vol. 17, Part
III, p. 503. This passage from Ambedkar's speech has been italicized
because of its crucial evidence of Ambedkar's evolution of thought.
This quotation accordingly appears as the epigraph of volume 17,
recognizing its singular significance. Therefore, the main point of the
argument presented in this discussion of Ambedkar in the Introduction
and chapter 9 is that he largely departed from both Communism
and American liberalism in his embrace and unqualified advocacy of
Buddhism by the 1950s.

40 Also quoted in Ibid.

or moral traditions, whether in the form of Hinduism, Buddhism or humanism.

It cannot be overstated that basic and irreconcilable differences do exist among a wide range of modern Indian thinkers. As only one example of this recognition, these are examined in such studies as *Sources of Indian Traditions*,[41] where contrasts are fairly set forth at length. A multitude of Indian thinkers are represented there, including all of the seven for selection here and many more (notably excluding references to Western philosophers). However, in the present book, the analysis is aimed at another type of endeavour, to discern conceptual correspondences or parallels, a purpose clearly proposed at the outset of the first edition and expanded in the present revised text.

Therefore, in the context of Ambedkar, with this exegesis of his *The Buddha and His Dhamma*, the aim is neither to delineate differences with other modern Indian thinkers nor to ask whether his interpretation of Buddhism is consonant with its literal ancient texts or the teachings of its prophet. In this respect, Ambedkar aims at 'preservation by reconstruction'[42] because he is reaffirming certain values of the Indian intellectual tradition. Whatever the manifest differences in this group of seven, most specifically, there is manifest commonality regarding their ideas of freedom, anchored in their theories of the intrinsic connection between means and ends.

Ambedkar conveys the story of freedom in compelling and vivid language. He draws from a dramatic metaphor in the Buddha's First Sermon, striking perhaps to a Western mind because it bears a resemblance to Plato's allegory of the cave in *The Republic*, though without any reference to the latter. Unlike either the modern Western thinkers whom Ambedkar had referenced earlier, much less Plato,

---

41 *Sources of Indian Traditions*, ed. Rachel Fell McDermott et al., Third edition, Vol. 2 (New York: Columbia University Press, 2014).

42 See fn 37 above.

Buddha tells the tale of freedom in spiritual, not political, terms. Buddha's parable illuminates his theory of Samma Ditti or 'Right Views, the first and foremost element in the Ashtanga Marga, or the Path of Righteousness'. The aim is to attain a virtue that 'requires a free mind and free thought'.

The Buddha preached:

You must realize that the world is a dungeon, and man is a prisoner in the dungeon. This dungeon is full of darkness. So dark is it that scarce anything at all can rightly be seen by the prisoner. The prisoner cannot see that he is a prisoner. Indeed, man has not only become blind by living too long in the darkness, but he very much doubts if any such strange thing as light is said to be, can ever exist at all. Mind is the only instrument through which light can come to man. But the mind of these dungeon-dwellers is by no means a perfect instrument for the purpose. It lets through only a little light, just enough to show to those with sight that there is such a thing as darkness. Thus defective in its nature, such understanding as this is. But the case of the prisoner is not as hopeless as it appears. For there is in man a thing called will. When the appropriate motives arise, the will can be awakened and set in motion. With the coming of just enough light to see in what directions to guide the motions of the will, man may so guide them that they shall lead to liberty. Thus though man is bound, yet he may be free; he may at any moment begin to take the first steps that will bring him to freedom. This is because it is possible to train the mind in whatever directions one chooses. It is mind that makes us to be prisoners in the house of life, and it is mind that keeps us so. But what mind has done, that mind can undo. If it has brought man to thralldom, it can also, when rightly directed, bring him to liberty. This is what *Samma Ditti* can do.[43]

---

43 *BHD*, p. 70.

Flowing from this dramatic proclamation of spiritual freedom is another principal idea that directs Ambedkar's Buddhist philosophy. This is Nibbana, meaning a path to happiness through 'exercise of the control over the flames of the passions which are always on fire'. The Buddhist task here is to develop an aversion to the fires of greed (*lobha*), anger (*dosa*) and delusion (*moha*); and, in conceiving this aversion, 'he becomes divested of passions, and becomes free, and when he is free, he becomes aware that he is free'.

Risking redundancy for stark clarity, Buddha repeatedly connects his basic doctrines to the concept of freedom from the all-pervasive forms of mental bondage:

> Excited by greed, brothers, furious with anger, blinded by delusion, with mind overwhelmed, with mind enslaved, men reflect on their own misfortune, men reflect on the misfortune of others, men experience mental suffering and anguish. If, however, greed, anger and delusion are done away with, men reflect neither upon their own misfortune nor on mental suffering and anguish ... What makes man unhappy is his falling a prey to his passions. These passions are called fetters which prevent a man from reaching the state of Nibbana. The moment he is free from the sway of his passions, that is, he learns to achieve Nibbana—man's way to happiness is open to him.[44]

Ambedkar is careful to explain, through attention to the text, how Buddha's idea of freedom must apply to the mind as well as to behaviour:

> Expunge all bad thoughts. Here is the way to expunge them. You are to expunge them by resolving that, though others may be harmful, you will be harmless. That, though others may kill, you will never kill ... That, though others may be possessed by sloth

---

44 *BHD*, pp. 126–27.

and torpor, you will free yourself therefrom. That though others may be puffed up, you will be humble minded. That, though others may be perplexed by doubts, you will be free from them. That though others may harbor wrath, malevolence, envy, jealousy, niggardliness, avarice, hypocrisy, deceit, imperviousness, arrogance, forwardness, unscrupulousness, lack of instruction, inertness, bewilderment, and unwisdom, you will be the reverse of all these things.[45]

From this point, Ambedkar reiterates the conception of freedom in connection with a series of concepts. The supreme value of maitri, or 'loving kindness', as noted above, is explicitly called 'freedom of heart' three times in thirteen lines of text.[46] In a key section entitled 'The Buddhist Way of Life' on the subject of 'Good, Evil and Sin', freedom from lust, fear and sorrow are paramount. All are connected with 'craving': 'To him who is wholly free from craving, there is neither sorrow nor fear.' The repetition of the word 'free'[47] moves in this section to an emphasis on freedom from anger, especially in a manner in accord with other Indian thinkers:

Cherish no anger. Forget your enemies. Win your enemies by love. This is the Buddhist Way of Life. The fire of anger should be stilled … Let a man overcome anger by love; let him overcome evil by good; let him overcome the greedy by liberality, the liar by truth. Speak the truth, do not yield to anger … For hatred does not cease by hatred at any time: hatred ceases by love. This is an old rule.[48]

---

45 *BHD*, pp. 211–12.

46 *BHD*, p. 161.

47 *BHD*, pp. 187–88; six times in a page of text.

48 *BHD*, p. 189. The point about repetition of the word 'freedom' in *BHD* carries a special significance. Aakash Rathore compares the various usages by Ambedkar of swaraj, freedom and liberty, asserting

that 'choosing his words with utmost care', Ambedkar preferred 'liberty' to the others in order to avoid 'the mystification of the term "freedom" in relation to swaraj', while 'the concept of "freedom" was contaminated by a Brahmanically imbued "swaraj"'. Therefore, 'Liberty, then, was far more preferable than freedom'. (See *Ambedkar's Preamble*, pp. 55–56.) This thesis is scrupulously argued by Rathore in the chapter titled 'Liberty: Swaraj Is Whose Birthright?' that contends, 'This spiritualization of freedom grounded its ineluctable association with Swaraj and imbued the idea with a taint of exclusivist Hindu nationalism within the overall discourse of modern India, noting its meaning by Tilak, Aurobindo and Vivekananda, and, of course, Gandhi.' (p. 36) Rathore might have extended this lineage to include M.N. Roy, the secular humanist, with his emphatic focus on 'freedom' as will be seen in the following segment.

Rathore's main premise pertaining to Ambedkar's preference for 'liberty' in both his *Preamble* as well as in his *Annihilation of Caste* is transparently valid. However, this preferred usage does not continue in *BHD*, where Ambedkar's language shifts to 'free' or 'freedom', as the above quotations from the latter demonstrate. Compare the abundant use of 'liberty', for example, in *Preamble* and *Annihilation of Caste* (ed. S. Anand), with how in *BHD*, Ambedkar either uses 'liberty' interchangeably with 'free'/'freedom' (pp. 70–71) or the latter exclusively (pp. 161, 187–88). Therefore, this difference in word usage among the three texts offers a revealing index of the significant transformation of Ambedkar's thought consequent with language. That is, *BHD*'s consistent preference for 'freedom' signifies, in Rathore's terms, a 'spiritualization of freedom'. Moreover, if this same criterion of word usage is applied to M.N. Roy's later writings, then the introduction of his phrase 'spiritual freedom' and decided preference for it rather than 'liberty' as indicated in the essay on Roy that follows. This allies him with Ambedkar, thus showing how both joined the group of seven. Once again, the present author is indebted to Rathore for prompting this interpretation, following from *Ambedkar's*

This is surely an ancient truth in Indian spiritual traditions. Its distinctive and deliberate assertion of Buddhist ethics is evident from a core section of the text entitled 'Religion and Dhamma'. At the centre of this is the connection between freedom of self with that of society, as vital to Ambedkar's philosophy of freedom as it is familiar to his Indian intellectual tradition. This section is entitled 'On Self and Self-Conquest' and begins with the idea that closely resembles that of swaraj: 'If one has self, let him practice self-conquest. This is the Buddhist Way of Life. Self is the lord of self—who else could be the lord? ... By oneself the evil is done, by oneself one suffers, by oneself evil is left undone, by oneself one is purified ... First establish thyself in the right; then thou mayest counsel others.'[49] Or as Gandhi advised a nephew worried over the Indian freedom struggle, 'Please do not carry unnecessarily on your head the burden of emancipating India. Emancipate your own self. Even that burden is very great. Apply everything to yourself. In your emancipation is the emancipation of India.'[50]

The Buddha and His Dhamma repeatedly counsels advice about control of one's emotions. In a footnote dealing with Buddha's quest for truths, Christopher Queen perceptively observes: 'But here again the emphasis is redirected to ethical life in society; cessation of passions is seen as a precondition for righteousness.'[51] This properly illustrates the importance of ethics. Yet such stress on discipline, whether for the Bhikkhu or not, contrasts Ambedkar's theory here with that of

---

Preamble. In the spirit of honest and generous scholarship, Rathore not only read an early draft of this Ambedkar essay at my request but also pointed me to the part of his *Ambedkar's Preamble* that would likely cause a difference of interpretation between us. The resulting responsibility for this interpretation is solely mine.

49 *BHD*, p. 191.

50 *CWMG* 10:206–7.

51 *BHD*, note #11, pp. 127–28.

Communism. For example, the preoccupation with 'lust' is remarkable, to the point of insisting on abstinence in all its forms does not represent a 'middle way'.[52] This includes warnings like 'The tide of lust is a danger common to all; it carries away the world' and 'This truth (to loathe lust and seek to promote their spiritual existence) ... is not for the hermit alone; it concerns every human being, priest and layman alike.'[53] However this is interpreted, whether greed for property or from sexual craving, it follows logically from Ambedkar's Buddhist idea of freedom.

Furthermore, Ambedkar declares that Buddha's 'first object was to lead man to the path of rationalism', away from 'superstition'. Therefore, he 'preaches Rationalism, and Buddhism is nothing if not rationalism. That is why worship of the supernatural is not Dhamma.'[54] Apart from the question of how reasonable is the demand for abstinence and restraint of lustful passions, there is the evident problem of Buddha's reliance on miraculous powers in his conversion of thieves. The tale of the conversion of Angulimala, the robber, admirably extols the Buddha's noble goal of making this robber a 'righteous man', but the means are miraculous, by employing superhuman speed or persuading other criminals to repent and become disciples as Buddha transforms himself magically into awe-inspiring supernatural guises.[55]

It does not support an insistence on Buddhist rationalism in a footnote that certain passages from the original text have been eliminated to 'omit the miraculous voice' invoked for another conversion.[56] Or, for example, the dubious interpretation of the conversion of Angulimala offered by Aishwary Kumar in *Radical*

---

52 Ibid., pp. 11–15, 67–69, 79, 86, 127, 144, 171, 175, 187–88.

53 Ibid., p. 86.

54 Ibid., p. 133.

55 Ibid., pp. 112–15 and also p. 78.

56 Ibid., pp. 82–83.

Equality. Viewing this episode as a 'key moment in *The Buddha and the Dhamma*', the power of conversion is here attributed by Kumar to the Buddha's 'forever renouncing violence against all creatures'.[57] Thus, the transformation of this notorious criminal represents the supreme virtue of maitri. Interpreted in this manner, it brings Ambedkar closer to the school of seven than to Communism. This ethos of expansive nonviolence is commendable but not principally because it is grounded in reason.

The point here is that a full reading of *The Buddha and His Dhamma* reveals that Ambedkar's insistence on the rationalism of Buddhism is problematic. An evident example of the irrational nature of the religion occurs first with the Angulimala story. The authoritative account of 'Who was Angulimala' by Richard Gombrich,[58] illustrates the fantastical quality of the so-called 'conversion campaign' that covers a substantial amount of Ambedkar's book.[59] This narrative does not concur with Kumar's claim that 'There is no metaphysical expectation, no invocation of spirit here. Instead, Angulimala's evil is converted to renunciation by the empirical truth, the finite body and knowledge manifest in the mortal figure of the Buddha himself.'[60] To the contrary, such an ethos comes metaphorically from the realm of mythology, allegory and fable, not unlike various uses of stories shared by other members of this group, e.g., Gandhi's allegorical interpretation of the

---

57 Aishwary Kumar, *Radical Equality: Ambedkar, Gandhi, and the Risk of Democracy* (Stanford: Stanford University Press, 2015), p. 335.

58 Richard F. Gombrich, 'Who was Angulimala?', in *How Buddhism Began: The Conditioned Genesis of the Early Teachings* (New Delhi: Munshiram Manoharlal Publishers, 1997), pp. 135–64, as cited by Kumar.

59 *BHD*, pp. 76–111.

60 Kumar, *Radical Equality*, p. 335.

Bhagavad Gita, or the archetypal legend of the Buddha's stages of moral development.

Tales of a horse weeping 'hot tears' at his master's departing the palace;[61] or 'a savage Naga king', himself 'possessed of dreadful powers' brought to worship Lord Buddha because he was 'struck by a miracle', in awe of him as 'only a miracle maker and nothing more';[62] or Buddha's single-handed spiritual conquest of five hundred robbers and murderers, at the overwhelming sight of him, 'falling to the ground [as] they exclaimed "What God is this?"'[63]—this is the stuff of parables that carry a certain moral appeal beyond the realm of reason. They are entirely consistent with Ambedkar's idea of freedom, even enhancing it, as numerous allegories have been used by philosophers to convey major concepts.

The Virtue of Courage in Ambedkar's Buddhism

A final virtue featured in *The Buddha and His Dhamma* is the quality of courage. Ambedkar returns to this theme repeatedly, often interpreting it with extraordinary eloquence, invoking individual integrity and righteousness. The Buddha, he writes, 'gave great importance to courage to stand by what is right, even if one is alone.' Do this

> [B]y resolving that, though others may be harmful, you will be harmless. That though others may kill, you will never kill. That though others may steal, you will not. That though others may not lead the higher life, you will. That though others may lie, traduce, denounce or prattle, you will not. That though others may be covetous, you will covet not. That though others may be malignant, you will not. That though others may be given over to

---

61 *BHD*, pp. 27–28.

62 Ibid., pp. 78–79.

63 Ibid., pp. 114–15.

wrong views, wrong aims, wrong speech, wrong actions, and wrong concentration, you will not. That though others will be wrong about the truth ... you will free yourselves therefrom.[64]

Buddha identifies all these virtues and more with the Noble Eightfold Path.

The virtue of courage has been identified with Gandhi in several appraisals of his thought and leadership. One political theorist claims that Gandhi introduced an unprecedented concept of a 'new courage' to the nationalist movement.[65] This strong association of Gandhi with courage also occurs in R.N. Iyer, *The Moral and Political Thought of Mahatma Gandhi*.[66] 'The courage which he advocated for himself and others and as an essential requirement in politics and society was the courage of the soul.'[67]

Ambedkar broadens this conceptualization of courage significantly by relating it to Buddhism as central to the Noble Eightfold Path and thereby removing it from the context of anti-colonialism where it was mainly identified with Gandhi. For Ambedkar, the virtue becomes one of an entire religion allied to the specific population of Dalits, who must resist not a foreign power that will eventually leave the country

---

64 Ibid., p. 153.

65 Susanne Rudolph and Lloyd Rudolph, *Gandhi: The Traditional Roots of Charisma* (Chicago: University of Chicago Press, 1967, 1983), pp. 29–38.

66 R.N. Iyer, *The Moral and Political Thought of Mahatma Gandhi* (New York: Oxford University Press, 1973).

67 Ibid., pp. 136–38 and *passim*. Bhikhu Parekh writes in *Gandhi's Political Philosophy: A Critical Examination* (London: Macmillan Press, 1989): 'For Gandhi, courage was one of the highest human values...' (p. 46 and *passim*).

but rather overcome an institution and psychology embedded in Hinduism for millennia.

According to Gandhi's biographers, the aim of his leadership was 'repairing wounds of self-esteem inflicted by generations of imperial subjection, restoring courage' to fight the Raj.[68] Or, as Jawaharlal Nehru put it in his praise of Gandhi's power, 'The essence of his teaching was fearlessness ... not merely bodily courage but the absence of fear from the mind ... But the dominant impulse in India under British rule was that of fear—pervasive, oppressing, strangling fear.'[69]

Ambedkar shifted the scene and language to champion courageous struggle against the vast majority of his own caste-ridden country, to bravely resist and overcome the enemy within. Yet, he rooted this appeal in a religion born of Hinduism, as Dhananjay Keer emphasizes at the end of his biography of Ambedkar.[70] Therefore, the quest he undertook became an arduous internal struggle for freedom that could not cease when the British departed and independence was achieved. The fear among Dalits, as he knew better than anyone in this group of seven, was omnipresent, not easily identified by skin colour and inherent in the age-old practice of varna. Many Indian freedom fighters could follow Gandhi to conceive of swaraj as rule over self and the colonial system. Ambedkar could comprehend it as more than this, as a freedom struggle against one's neighbour, especially Hindus, who ruthlessly dominated Dalits as a matter of routine oppression at local water wells or temple worship. The 'pilgrimage' for Ambedkar became a courageous journey of mind and body comparable to that of the Lord Buddha's compelling life story.

Rudolph and Rudolph, *Gandhi*, p. 3.

Jawaharlal Nehru, *The Discovery of India* (Bombay: Asia Publishing House, 1967), pp. 379–80.

Keer, *Dr. Babasaheb Ambedkar*, p. 522.

Conclusion: The Journey of Discovery and Rediscovery

Broad parallels with Ambedkar's Indian contemporaries firmly remain within their ideas of freedom. Freedom is a quest for self-knowledge, and such a realization becomes the primary task of a Buddhist, Hindu or humanist. Thus Ambedkar's intense quest for personal and philosophical liberation, the transformation of deep, lifelong convictions into a new world of theory and practice, may take us now to M.N. Roy. Because his remarkable internal and external journey across continents and philosophies, with a consequent share of self-sacrifice and suffering, may be compared to his exact contemporary, Babasaheb Ambedkar.

These two creative theorists definitely had their stark differences, but both contributed powerfully to the modern Indian intellectual tradition. In the case of Ambedkar, Ananya Vajpeyi incisively concludes that he 'was both attracted and repelled by it', but 'At least he realized this much: no individual, no caste or community, no religious group could flourish in India without constructing some kind of relationship to tradition, some narrative of selfhood compatible with India's quest for its proper self, some foothold in the past to stabilize its presence in the future.'[71]

M.N. Roy might be viewed, even more than Ambedkar, as making every effort to burn his bridges with this tradition. In fact, the essay on him that follows shows that his Radical Humanism ultimately revealed a way of thought that remained integral to it. The centrality of his ideas of freedom and of the means-ends relationship demonstrates his inclusion in the school of seven.

---

71 Ananya Vajpeyi, *Righteous Republic: The Political Foundations of Modern India* (Cambridge, Massachusetts: Harvard University Press, 2012), p. 242.

T.S. Eliot was inspired to incorporate vital elements of Indian religions. Not only in famous lines from *The Waste Land*, but in other poems, too, there is implied the depth and breadth of Indian tradition. Among the group of seven, Narendranath Datta, following his encounter with Sri Ramakrishna, became the legendary Swami Vivekananda; Aurobindo, a Bengali extremist, changed into the sage of Pondicherry; Gandhi from an anglicized lawyer to satyagrahi. Then, moving to the transformations of Ambedkar, M.N. Roy and J.P. Narayan, each committed to the philosophy of Marxism or Communism in their varied iterations, then renouncing those doctrines for Indian ideas of freedom.

Eliot's tortured conversion to Catholicism was totally different from any of these seven Indian thinkers, and it's unlikely that they knew much about him or vice versa. Yet, perhaps his verse may carry certain implications to their quests for freedom: 'We shall not cease from exploration / And the end of all our exploring / Will be to arrive where we started / And know the place for the first time.'[72]

---

72 T.S. Eliot, 'Little Gidding', *Four Quartets* in *The Complete Poems and Plays. 1909–1950* (New York: Harcourt, Brace and Co., 1951), p. 145.

CHAPTER 10

M.N. Roy on Freedom*

The aim of this chapter is to examine the thought of M.N. Roy as it evolved from his Marxist to Radical Humanist phases, with a focus on his idea of freedom. The analysis will be concerned with the relationship of these ideas to those of the other thinkers in this group

---

* The genesis of this study of M.N. Roy began, like most of my ideas on the subject of this book, when I conversed with Nirmal Kumar Bose in 1961. He spoke highly of Roy, whom he had studied thoroughly, commenting that among the Indian thinkers he met, two giant intellectuals were foremost, B.R. Ambedkar and M.N. Roy. He meant by this not that they stood out for originality but rather for their immense breadth of knowledge. This gives one pause to wonder how professors Nalini Bhushan and Jay Garfield, noted below in the text for their *Minds with Fear: Philosophy in the Indian Renaissance* (Oxford: Oxford University Press, 2017), might consider Bose's judgement, because they omit both Ambedkar and Roy from their study and also comment that 'Vivekananda and Aurobindo were religious leaders and public intellectuals, not academic philosophers. Nonetheless, their philosophical ideas set the stage for the scholarly

INDIAN IDEAS OF FREEDOM

of seven and following from conceptual parallels suggested in the previous chapter on B.R. Ambedkar. It is hoped that this analysis will

articulation of Vedanta as a philosophical system ... that is at once traditional and modern' (pp. 232–33). There will be no attempt here to make fine distinctions of this sort but only to observe that the broad terms of 'Indian intellectual tradition' and 'Indian renaissance' are meant to embrace the group of seven included in this book. There is no implication of them being 'academic philosophers', and one presumes that Bhushan and Garfield would associate Gandhi and Tagore (whom they do include) with Vivekananda and Aurobindo in their categorization. Of course, the association of Vedanta would not apply to Ambedkar or Roy.

Returning to Nirmal Bose, as explained in my 'Memoir', after he enabled my admission to the University of Chicago, Bose strongly urged me to focus on Roy because he rightly believed that his mature thought had been overlooked; therefore, after corresponding with Bose for guidance, I submitted my MA thesis to the Committee on Southern Asian Studies and the Political Science Department at Chicago on 'M.N. Roy and Radical Humanism' (1962). Bose's prior tenure there in the Anthropology Department further facilitated my work through his friendship with Professor Milton Singer, who led the committee that included esteemed anthropologists. Those who supervised my graduate work on Roy there were W.H. Morris-Jones (a visiting professor of Political Science) and Professor Stephen Hay.

After leaving Chicago for SOAS, professors Hugh Tinker and Morris-Jones became my supervisors; both were acquainted with Roy during their mutual experiences in India before its independence (See W.H. Morris-Jones, 'A Biographical Note', in *The States of South Asia: Problems of National Integration [Essays in Honor of W.H. Morris-Jones]*, edited by A.J. Wilson and Dennis Dalton [Honolulu: University of Hawaii Press, 1982], pp. vii–xiii). Morris-Jones had attended Roy's 'retreats' in Dehradun while Hugh Tinker introduced me to Professor Richard Park, a former intimate friend of Roy's and present at his death in January 1954. Park connected me to the Royists described in

illustrate the significance of Roy's thought for a general study of the idea of freedom in modern India. As will be indicated in the chapter, Radical Humanism featured this concept, becoming synonymous with the mature political thought of Roy.

Roy's political theory, like the intellectual tradition of modern India itself, is characterized by elements of continuity and innovation. The evolution of his ideas demonstrates this movement. At least four major phases of Roy's thought may be distinguished. The first of these begins at the turn of this century, with Roy as a young terrorist in Bengal under the personal leadership of Jatin Mukherjee and the intellectual

---

my Memoir. These included Sibnarayan Ray, editor of *Selected Works of M.N. Roy*, Vols.1–4 (Delhi: Oxford University Press, 1990). See also Dennis Dalton, 'Gandhi and Roy: The Interaction of Ideologies in India', in *Gandhi India and the World: An International Symposium*, ed. S.N. Ray (Melbourne: The Hawthorne Press, 1970), pp. 156–70.

Ray, J.P. Narayan, Hugh Tinker, Stephen Hay and Agehananda Bharati have contributed chapters to this 'International Symposium' edited by Ray; my discussions of Roy with each of them also provide sources for the present chapter. An early version of it was previously published as D. Dalton, 'M.N. Roy and Radical Humanism', in *Elites in South Asia*, edited by Edmund Leach and S.N. Mukherjee (Cambridge: Cambridge University Press, 1970), pp. 152–71. Discussions and correspondence with John Haithcox and the influence of his important work, *Communism and Nationalism in India: M.N. Roy and Comintern Policy, 1920–1939* (Princeton, New Jersey: Princeton University Press, 1971) are acknowledged here. Although Haithcox's book does not examine Roy's Radical Humanism, the scrupulous examination of Roy's earlier writings provided background for this chapter.

Finally, see recent and revealing Roy scholarship by Kris Manjapra, *M.N. Roy: Marxism and Colonial Cosmopolitanism* (NY: Routledge, 2010) and his article 'The Impossible Intimacies of M.N. Roy' in *Postcolonial Studies* 16, no. 2 (2013): 169–84. The concluding chapter of his book entitled *Radical Humanism* pertains here.

influence of Vivekananda. It ends with his conversion to Marxism in 1919. The second stage of his thought covers Roy's active career as a devout Communist; this begins in Mexico and ends in India with his imprisonment in 1931. The third phase can be seen as a period of transition. It includes Roy's six critical years in prison, his brief flirtation with the Indian National Congress, and his subsequent formation of the Radical Democratic Party (RDP), in opposition to the Congress. The final phase of his thought provides the main source of the present study. It extends from Roy's transformation of the RDP into the Radical Humanist Movement in 1948 until his death in January 1954.

Roy remained, throughout much of his life, and particularly during his Marxist phase, alienated from the Indian nationalist tradition.[1] As in the case of Ambedkar, this alienation was not concealed – it was outspoken and vehement; and, as with Ambedkar, a radical transformation became explicit in the final decade.

Roy's Marxist writings, beginning in the early 1920s, are crammed with diatribes against India's 'much vaunted spiritualist tradition', its 'reactionary ideology' of Gandhism, and most of the political leaders.[2]

---

1   The term 'Indian nationalist tradition', like the related terms of 'intellectual tradition' and 'Indian renaissance', refers to the stream of thought that coursed through nineteenth- and twentieth-century India; that is, to that common stock of myths and symbols, attitudes and ideas that developed in India since Rammohun Roy and eventually included the 'group of seven'. For clarification of my own conception of the Indian broad stream of thought since Rammohun Roy, see D.G. Dalton, 'The Idea of Freedom in the Political Thought of Vivekananda, Aurobindo, Gandhi and Tagore', PhD thesis (unpublished), University of London, 1965; and Rachel Fell McDermott et al. (eds), *Sources of Indian Traditions: Modern India, Pakistan and Bangladesh*, Vol. 2, Third edition (New York: Columbia University Press, 2014).

2   M.N. Roy, *India's Message*, Vol. I of *Fragments of Prisoner's Diary*, Second revised edition (Calcutta: Renaissance Publication, 1950), p. 149.

His opposition especially to Gandhi was as emphatic as Ambedkar's and his attacks started even earlier and were more philosophically developed. That was because Roy's direct involvement with Bolshevism and scrupulous study of Marxism were unparalleled in this group of seven.

On the basis of this deep engagement with communism at the highest levels as early as the 1920s, the conventional interpretation of Roy's life and thought has seen him as a thoroughly denationalized émigré, significant chiefly for his contribution as a revolutionary Marxist. One Indian analyst regards Roy as 'the Indian Edward Bernstein' and believes that the 'tragedy of M.N. Roy was that ... he failed to strike roots in Indian society'.[3] This interpretation either ignores Roy's Radical Humanism altogether or treats it as the discursive ramblings of a Marxist who has at last gone off the rails. The final phase of his political theory is thus underrated.

The argument of this chapter will not be in accord with this interpretation. It will be suggested here that, while Roy was without roots in Indian nationalist politics, he nevertheless remained profoundly grounded in the Indian intellectual tradition as a whole. Indeed, it was the very depth of these roots that led Roy, after his excursions into Marxism, back to a way of thinking that has much in common with ideas reaching back to Vivekananda.

The thought and culture of this Indian tradition and the type of intellectual experience it nurtured was a complex blend of structure and change, challenge, response and counter-response. From this cultural complex more than from anything else, Roy, as a youth in nationalist Bengal, received his early and decisive orientation. In this respect, certain aspects of the aforementioned poetic insight from T.S. Eliot applies to Roy as well as to Ambedkar. Their focus on the idea

---

3   V.P. Varma, *Modern Indian Political Thought* (Agra: Lakshmi Narain Agarwal, 1961), pp. 659–61.

of freedom, in particular, flows strongly in the stream of the country's dominant discourse.

Roy and Nationalism in Bengal

Towards the end of his life, Roy reflected on the early sources of his attitudes and those values that had guided his thought:

> When as a boy of fourteen I began my political life, which may end in nothing, I wanted to be free ... in those days, we had not read Marx. We did not know about the existence of the proletariat. Still, many spent their lives in jail and went to the gallows. There was no proletariat to propel them. They were not conscious of class struggle. They did not have the dream of Communism. But they had the human urge to revolt against the intolerable conditions of life ... I began my political life with that spirit, and I still draw my inspiration rather from that spirit than from the three volumes of Capital or three-hundred volumes by the Marxists.[4]

Roy was born into an orthodox Brahmin family in a village near Calcutta in 1886. Bengal had already established itself as the centre of that flowering of thought and literature, which later historians and philosophers would call 'The Indian Renaissance'. Indeed, as the explication of Aurobindo above indicates, he was using this term as early as 1918, and academic philosophers like professors Nalini Bhushan and Jay Garfield, in *Minds Without Fear: Philosophy in the Indian Renaissance*, apply it to thinkers like Vivekananda and Aurobindo, writing in 2017. In ancient Athens, magnificent literature preceded monumental philosophy, so in late nineteenth-century India, Bankim Chandra Chatterjee was publishing his influential periodical, *Bengal*

---

4   M.N. Roy, *New Orientation* (Calcutta: Renaissance Publication, 1946), p. 183.

Darsan, and writing his renowned novels, notably *Anandamath* in 1882. This was soon followed by a young university student, Narendranath Datta, soon to become Vivekananda, frequenting a Kali temple on the Ganges to sit at the feet of an illiterate bhakta, Ramakrishna Paramahamsa. Educated Indians were speaking in enraptured tones of Keshub Chunder Sen's oratory, with reverence to Debendranath Tagore's saintly example, and Rammohun Roy's achievements were already passing into legend. Late nineteenth-century Bengal fostered a climate of opinion, an intense atmosphere of ideas and sentiments, that pervaded India in the first half of the twentieth century, intermingling with Gandhian ideas. The influence which it had upon those young revolutionary intellectuals growing up in its midst was immense. It was this early influence that set the pattern of Roy's political and social thought, in terms of explaining its underlying presuppositions, the way in which it developed, and to some extent, its final form.

Roy begins his *Memoirs* abruptly with the year 1914, and biographical accounts are scarcely more informative about his first, and undoubtedly formative, twenty-eight years. This untold story, however, pieced together from various sources,[5] appears to be as follows. His

---

5   For Roy's early period, biographical sources include the following:

(a) *Interviews with numerous figures in India both inside and out of the Radical Humanist Movement:* The most helpful for this early period were with Aloke Nath Chakravarty (tape-recorded interview in Calcutta in May 1967) and K.K. Sinha (interview and response to questionnaire in Calcutta in May 1967). The former source was one of Roy's younger associates in the terrorist movement under Jatin Mukherjee. He stressed the influence on Roy of Jatin and Vivekananda, and outlined Roy's religious affiliations at that time. The latter, Mr Sinha, was kind enough to make a lengthy written reply to my questionnaire, and to discuss points raised about Roy's early period in some detail. Interviews on Roy's entire life with Justice V.M. Tarkunde, Philip Spratt, G.D. Parikh and S.N. Ray.

father was a priest and a schoolteacher, who, as Roy himself remarked, 'spent his life in teaching Sanskrit to would-be clerks or prospective lawyers'.[6] Roy received his primary education in his village school, and then joined the National University founded by Aurobindo Ghose; he soon withdrew, however, to become committed, while still in his teens,

---

(b) *Government of India Records:* Statement (confession) of Fanindra Kumar Chakravarty in Simla Records 2. Government of India, Home Department Political-A. Proceedings January 1917, Nos. 299–301 and Mr K. W. Chakravarty reports that in 1911, after release from the 'Howrah Gang Case', 'Noren' (Roy) 'decided to become a sannyasi', and visited Banares. It appears that Roy did this more to escape the police than out of religious conviction.

(c) *Political Report:* James Campbell Ker, I.C.S. (from 1907 to 1913, Personal Assistant to the Director of Criminal Intelligence), *Political Trouble in India* (Calcutta: Superintendent of Government Printing India, 1917), p. 4. See especially report on Norenda Nath Bhattacharji alias C.A. Martin.

(d) *Periodicals and Books:* Various issues of *The Radical Humanist*, especially 7 February 1954 and 25 January 1956; biographical sketches in *Memoirs* (Introduction and Epilogue) by G.D. Parikh and V.B. Karnik; M.N. Roy, *Letters from Jail*, Vol. 3 of *Fragments of a Prisoner's Diary* (Calcutta: Renaissance Publication, 1943); Niranjan Dhar, *The Political Thought of M.N. Roy* (Calcutta: Eureka Publishers, 1966) Introduction; Ramyansu S. Das, *M.N. Roy, The Humanist Philosopher* (Calcutta: Tower Publishers, 1956); A.K. Hindi, *M. N. Roy, The Man Who Looked Ahead* (Ahmedabad: Modern Publishing House, 1938); Gene D. Overstreet and Marshall Windmiller, *Communism in India* (Berkeley and Los Angeles: University of California Press, 1959); Sibnarayan Ray (ed.), *M.N. Roy, Philosopher–Revolutionary* (Calcutta: Renaissance Publication, 1959) and *Selected Works of M.N. Roy*, Vols. I–IV (Delhi: Oxford University Press, 1987–1990).

6   M.N. Roy, *Memoirs* (London: Allen and Unwin, 1964), p. 567.

to the Bengali Extremist movement. From 1906 to 1914, Roy was implicated in a series of revolutionary offences, the major one being the Howrah Conspiracy Case of 1910, which led to an imprisonment of twenty months before acquittal for lack of evidence. During this time, moreover, he seems to have held strong religious beliefs, particularly in Vaishnavism, and while in prison, he became engrossed in religious texts. Upon release, he rejoined the terrorist movement and rose quickly to become one of its bright young lights. Two influences were critical at this time. First, there was the intellectual impact of Vivekananda, whose speeches on *Karma Yoga, The Mission of the Vedanta* and *The Work Before Us* were avidly studied by Roy's circle. These were a key source of his ideological inspiration.

The other influence was a personal one. Soon after Roy joined the movement in 1906, Aurobindo Ghose became a power in it, but Aurobindo retired from politics to Pondicherry in 1909 and Roy never developed a personal relationship with him. Roy did become intimate with one of Aurobindo's successors, Jatin Mukherjee, who became the 'Commander and Chief of Staff' of the Bengali Revolutionaries. 'Jatinda' was a devout Hindu and a daring terrorist whose use of violence against the Raj led to his untimely execution in 1915. The personal influence which Jatin exercised on Roy lasted throughout his life. In his *Memoirs,* Roy recalls that Jatin was 'the only man I ever obeyed almost blindly ... I admired Jatinda because he personified the best of mankind'.[7] Following Jatin's orders, Roy left India on a revolutionary mission in early 1915; he was not to return until 1930.

In sum, one may discriminate at least three important elements in Roy's youthful experience in Bengal. First, there was his apparently happy childhood in a Brahmin family, his father a Sanskrit pandit. The Brahmanical outlook on life, which is so congenial to an elitist view of society, remained with Roy until the end, influencing, in particular,

---

7   Ibid., pp. 35–36.

his theory of leadership. The second element appears in his marked receptiveness to the general ideological and religious climate of Bengal; that is, his acceptance of Vaishnavism, his attraction to Vivekananda, and his strong commitment to nationalism and terrorism. Finally, there was his active involvement in the revolutionary movement under the lasting personal influence of Jatin Mukherjee.

Roy and Marxism

When Michael Borodin baptized Roy into Marxism in 1919, Roy came from Indian nationalism to the new faith with the zeal commonly found amongst fresh converts. 'Marxism is a wonderful philosophy, is it not?' he exclaimed to a fellow comrade in 1923. 'It has made of history such an exact science.'[8] Roy's first major work, *India in Transition* (1922), attempted to apply this 'exact science' in orthodox Marxist fashion to an analysis of British imperialism and Indian nationalism. For Roy, it was evident that 'It is only the philosophy of Historic Materialism and the programme of Marxism, Socialism, that can show the way out'.[9] When an Indian comrade expressed mild qualms over 'Bolshevism', Roy snapped back, 'Let me be brutally frank and tell you openly that the salvation of India lies through Bolshevism.'[10] Nowhere in Roy's early Marxist polemics does one find a hint of his later heresies. The Communist doctrines which he eventually repudiates are here vigorously employed in his analysis of Indian politics. In a tract of 1926, for example, Roy applies the Marxist theories of class struggle, dialectical materialism, economic determinism, and the proletarian revolution to establish the inevitability of a Communist conquest of

---

8   Roy, *Political Letters* (Zurich: Vanguard Bookshop, 1924) p. 14.

9   Ibid., p. 7.

10 Ibid., p. 48.

India. The need of the masses is for revolutionary leadership and 'The Communist Party of India is called upon by history to play this role'.[11] This theoretical orthodoxy was matched in practice by a position of high status in the Communist International (Comintern), where Roy attained the height of his influence in 1926. Whether his subsequent decline and expulsion from the Comintern are attributed to Roy's own tactical blunders or Stalin's need for a scapegoat, it was certainly not as a result of any theoretical departure from Marxism. At least until 1931 when he entered his 'quiet country-town jail' in Cawnpore, Roy remained an orthodox Marxist.[12]

Roy was imprisoned for almost six consecutive years. Those who were closest to Roy have said that no experience had a more profound effect upon his thought than this. Pandit Nehru wrote of his own imprisonment that 'A person who was at all sensitive was in a continuous state of tension'.[13] Roy had plenty of sensitivity, but few of the special privileges accorded to prominent figures like Nehru. His *Letters from Jail* suggest the acute mental tension and the intolerable physical strain he suffered. An interesting sidelight on this experience and its impact on Roy's personality might perhaps be gleaned from Philip Spratt's 'notes on jail psychology'.[14] Spratt, a British Communist in India, had a prison experience similar to Roy's. After his release, Spratt became one of Roy's close associates in the Radical Democratic

---

11 Roy, *The Aftermath of Non-Co-operation* (London: The Communist Party of Great Britain, 1926), pp. 13, 47.

12 Roy, *Letters from Jail, Fragments of a Prisoner's Diary*, Vol. 3 (Calcutta: Renaissance Publication, 1943), p. 1.

13 Jawaharlal Nehru, *Toward Freedom: The Autobiography of Jawaharlal Nehru* (Boston: Beacon Hill, 1961), p. 4.

14 P. Spratt, 'Some Notes on Jail Psychology', *Modern Review* LXI, no. 6 (June 1937): 649–54, and LXII, no.1 (July 1937): 31–36.

Party (RDP). Spratt writes in these articles on jail psychology that a prolonged prison experience produces the effect of a 'psychological hothouse' where there is an overwhelming 'concentration of emotion upon the self'. This encourages latent elements of thought and feeling to rise and flourish through the stimulus of intense introspection. The element that flourishes best is man's 'urge towards religion'. Spratt regards jail as 'a forcing house for religion'; he relates that in his own case, 'I had myself no religious belief, and had been very critical of religion, but I felt the force of its appeal'.[15]

Roy did not experience in prison a mystical revelation like that claimed by his erstwhile Bengali leader, Aurobindo Ghose. Indeed, the scorn that Roy pours on such 'revelations' in his essay 'Psychology of the Seer' (written in prison) would seem to make nonsense of any 'religious conversion' at this time. Yet, it remains true that a marked change in Roy's thought and personality did occur, and it may not be entirely wrong to see this change as a response to the sort of religious appeal that Spratt describes. One thing at least is certain: Roy's movement away from orthodox Marxism towards the foundations of Radical Humanism began in prison. The first clear sign of this shift appeared shortly after his release in the article, 'Marxism is Not a Dogma'. First, this writing stresses the limitations of Marxism. New discoveries in science combined with those 'practical problems' and historical developments unforeseen by Marx establish the need to 'revise certain fundamental conceptions of classical Materialism'. 'The modern Marxist,' Roy says, 'cannot follow literally the line predicted by Marx ... we cannot say that developments here in India must necessarily follow the same line as Marx predicted for European developments.'[16]

At this point, however, he insists that he remains nevertheless a Marxist and asserts the enduring positive value of Marxism. He does

---

15 Ibid.

16 In M.N. Roy and K.K. Sinha, *Royism Explained* (Calcutta: Saraswaty Press, 1938), pp. 22–23.

this in a manner reminiscent of Bengali reformers like Vivekananda, who sought to reconstitute Hinduism by distinguishing between its 'spirit' and 'form'. Marxism, Roy argues, is not a dogma; it is a 'philosophy of life'. As such, it is 'greater than Communism', which is merely a particular 'phase of human development'. Roy's aim now is to reinterpret Marxism as a liberal, humanist philosophy. He discovers 'the essence of Marxism' in the idea that Man is God, and therefore 'the master of history'. The old emphasis upon economic determinism and historical inevitability has disappeared; in their place is the view that 'the foundation of Marxism is Rationalism' and the Marxist philosophy must be appreciated together with its great heritage, the European Renaissance.

The message of Marxism for India is that the country needs a 'Renaissance movement', a 'philosophical revolution'.[17] This is the theme that is to develop during the next decade, eventually providing one of the bases for Radical Humanism. In 1947, Roy reflected back upon this critical juncture in his thought and wrote: 'I still spoke as an orthodox Marxist criticising deviations from or faulty understanding of the pure creed. Nevertheless, the tendency to look beyond Communism was already there in a germinal form.'[18] The nature and significance of this metamorphosis from Marxism to Radical Humanism will now be analysed in the context of two major aspects of Roy's political thought, his conception of freedom as related to the ideas of power, leadership and revolution.

Roy's Conception of Freedom

The analysis of Roy's idea of freedom is intended not only to illustrate the evolution of his thought, but also to argue the close parallels which

---

17 Ibid., pp. 23–25.

18 Roy, 'Preface', in *Scientific Politics*, Second Edition (Calcutta: Renaissance Publication, 1947), p. vii.

this concept ultimately developed with the ideas of others in this group of seven. The implication of this argument is not that these conceptual parallels necessarily emerged as a direct result of the influences among thinkers, e.g. of Gandhi on Roy. The point is rather that the evolution of Roy's thought may be seen in terms of his continuing response to the Indian intellectual tradition. Moreover, the broad inference that may be drawn is that the presuppositions of this tradition can be explained in the context of the similar way that Roy and the others formulated their parallel theories.

With Indian Marxists as well as other thinkers examined here, Roy always asserted that freedom meant more than political independence. India might gain her independence from Britain, they all asserted, but freedom for the Indian people would not necessarily follow. However, there were two ways of interpreting this proposition. The Marxists contended that political independence did not equal freedom since the latter involved economic rights and opportunities for the masses far beyond what mere political liberation from England implied.

Others in this group claimed to recognize the importance of economic reform, but they emphasized the 'moral' aspect of freedom. Gandhi thus preferred to use the term swaraj, which for him had two meanings: not only political independence but also (as he wrote as early as 1909) 'self-rule or self-control'.[19] This view of freedom in fact dominated the Indian intellectual tradition, and it was explicitly pronounced before Gandhi's treatise among Bengali thinkers. Aurobindo often distinguished between 'internal' (moral) and 'external' (political and economic) freedom. Perhaps Vivekananda summed up the idea earliest and best when he wrote at the close of the last century, 'One may gain political and social independence, but if

---

19 M.K. Gandhi, *Hind Swaraj and Other Writings*, edited A.J. Parel (Cambridge: Cambridge University Press, 1997), p. 118.

one is a slave to his passions and desires, one cannot feel the pure joy of real freedom.'[20]

In 1937, Roy was much closer to the Marxist than the Gandhian view of freedom. In the very first issue of his weekly *Independent India*, Roy wrote, under the heading 'National Freedom', that 'Political independence is not the end; it is the means to an end which is radical transformation of the Indian society ... The required change in the social structure of our country will be brought about primarily through the transfer of the ownership of land to the cultivator'; and, once this is attained, the transformation will be completed by 'a rapid growth of modern mechanized industry', the 'guarantee to the cultivator of ... the entire product of his labour', the 'abolition of all privileges' and a wide and fair 'distribution of newly created wealth'.[21] This was the revolutionary programme, Roy believed, that would usher in 'real freedom'. At this point, then, Roy as a Marxist, conceived of freedom and also social change in terms of sweeping economic reforms.

A fascinating aspect of Roy's thought may be seen in the way his conception of 'spiritual freedom' first appears, then co-exists for a decade with the 'materialist' view of freedom, and ultimately gains ascendancy to dominate the value-theory of the Radical Humanist period. As early as in his *Fragments of a Prisoner's Diary*, we find Roy writing of the need for a new philosophy to 'indicate the way to real spiritual freedom'; a bit later, he claimed that 'a true revolutionary is not ashamed of declaring that he is not fighting merely for wages ... The revolution of our epoch will, for the first time, conquer spiritual freedom for humanity.'[22] And, as late as March 1945, Roy is holding forth the co-existent ideals of 'material and spiritual emancipation',

20 Swami Vivekananda, *The Complete Works*, 8 vols. (Calcutta: Advaita Ashrama, 1955–1963), Vol. 5 (1959), p. 419. Hereafter *Works*.

21 Roy, 'National Freedom', *Independent India*, 4 April 1937.

22 Roy, *India's Message*, p. 307, and *Scientific Politics*, p. 313.

although the emphasis at this time is clearly on political and economic rather than 'spiritual' or moral freedom. The decisive change in his thought was yet to occur.

In May 1946, the RDP met in Dehradun for perhaps the most critical 'political study camp' of Roy's career. For Roy and his Radical Democratic Party were meeting in the wake of two crucial events. The first was the complete defeat of the RDP in the 1946 Spring elections. The party had clearly been consigned to the political wilderness for at least the rest of Roy's life. The second event revolved around the direction of the world Communist movement in India, Russia and Eastern Europe. In his own country, Roy had long been under fierce attack from the Indian Communist Party; abroad, the ruthless ambitions of Stalin's dictatorship had become abundantly clear, and the result was Roy's profound disillusionment with Communism. The deep impact which the election experience and the direction of world Communism had upon Roy's thinking is amply illustrated throughout his lectures at the study camp. His indictment of the Indian election as 'fascist' is not surprising. What is noteworthy is that Communism is now grouped with fascism: they 'both sacrifice the individual on the altar of the collective ego'. 'Therefore, Communism has ceased to be an ideal which can inspire us and guide our steps in the march towards freedom.'[23] While Roy does distinguish between Communist practice and Marxist theory, the association between them remains, and it is not long before Roy drops the distinction and develops the association.

In his lectures at this political study camp, Roy delivered a series of original lectures published in two books, entitled *Problem of Freedom*[24] and *New Orientation*. Both represented his latest thinking on the idea of freedom. The first of these announced in the Preface that 'an analysis of the concept of freedom is the central theme of the book' and it would

---

23 Roy, *New Orientation*, pp. 142–43.

24 Ibid., pp. 26–27.

differ from previous writings on the subject. True to this promise, the opening chapter presents a strikingly original idea, expressed for the first time in Indian thought, around the phrase 'fear of freedom'. Erich Fromm had already in 1941 laid the basis for this idea in his text, first published in the US under the title *Escape from Freedom* and then a year later in Britain as *The Fear of Freedom*. Roy does not acknowledge the influence of Fromm or any other author in his book, but the analysis follows Fromm's in significant ways.

First, Roy avers at the outset that the issue before India 'is a conflict between an urge for freedom and fear of freedom'. But unlike Fromm, Roy employs psychosocial motives to explain the rise of Gandhian nationalism rather than European fascism. Gandhi is diagnosed not only as a neurotic himself, afflicted with delusions of saintliness, but one who has fostered a national neurosis so that 'the greatest enemy of freedom is the fear of freedom'. Following Fromm's psychoanalytical conceptual framework, now adapted to Gandhian authoritarianism, a perverse belief has spread that 'Man must realize his absolute powerlessness to have the power to be free! ... Unconditional submission is the condition for salvation and also for power. That is the appeal of authoritarianism—to the mass psychology dominated by the fear of freedom. That is also the essence of Gandhism.'[25] After an entire chapter on 'Psychoanalysis of Gandhism', Roy introduces another new phrase of 'spiritual freedom'. This is soon to be developed in *New Orientation*, as well as in his subsequent works.

Roy sets this forth at length as among the core concepts of his Radical Humanism:

Freedom is not a beautiful castle built in the air of imagination. It rests on the triple pillar of humanism, individualism and

---

25 Roy, *Problem of Freedom* (Calcutta, Renaissance Publication, 1945), pp. 3, 5, 7–8.

rationalism ... Freedom is the condition for the self-realisation of life. The supreme importance of the individual logically follows from the noble, liberating doctrine of Humanism ... Only on that philosophical and psychological foundation can the structure of collective freedom be raised by the continuous efforts and collective work of spiritually liberated individuals ... Therefore, the very few Indians who are spiritually liberated enough to appreciate freedom as something far greater than mere national independence—the composite Man of the Indian Renaissance—attach greater importance to modern civilization surviving the present crisis.[26]

Radical Humanists are thus charged with a heavy burden, that of uplifting their society to a level of freedom that breaks through the contemporary crisis caused by nationalism to a higher realm of universal ethics. At this point, Roy's political theory assumes a distinctiveness that he deems antithetical to the amorality of Marxism. An unprecedented way of thinking about politics, power and society becomes inextricably interwoven with a 'philosophy of freedom'. The 1946 study camp announces the advent of a 'philosophical revolution' for India, as his lectures continue with a second book aptly titled *New Orientation*.

The most striking development in Roy's thought seen in this volume of speeches does not appear with his attitude towards Communism, but rather in the unprecedented emphasis placed on the need for a 'moral philosophy', a 'philosophy of freedom', and a 'philosophical revolution' in India:

Human life must be guided by a philosophy. That philosophy may change from time to time. But there are certain values, certain principles, which transcend time and space ... A philosophy, to be a guide for all forms of human action, must have some ethics, some morals, which must recognize certain things as permanent

26 Ibid., pp. 61–65.

and abiding in humanity. And only a group of human beings—be it a political party or any other kind of organisation—primarily moved by those abiding (and I should say even permanent, as permanent as humanity itself) values, can claim to be the maker of the future ... We must know what is freedom before we can be qualified as the architects of a free world. What the world needs is a philosophy of freedom. The birth of the RDP was heralded by the declaration that India needs a philosophical revolution. Without a philosophical revolution, no social revolution is possible. We shall have to remember that.[27]

This passage suggests the nature of Roy's quest for 'permanent values' that characterized the Radical Humanist period. Marxism had now become of no help in this quest, and the extent of his departure from it is evident throughout the speeches. For example, he declares that the RDP 'must be a party not of the economic man' but rather a 'party of moral men, moved by the ideal of human freedom'. Any connection between the RDP and a particular class is repudiated. The Party's allegiance can only be to the 'abiding values' of humanity since 'ethical values are greater than economic interests'. 'Call this an idealistic deviation, if you please,' Roy tells his Party, 'I would plead guilty to the charge.'[28]

Throughout *New Orientation*, Roy extols the ideal of spiritual freedom. It has now become the ultimate value of his system, a dimension of freedom which is both primary to the attainment of political or economic liberty, and yet superior to them, existing as a supreme state of philosophical wisdom. In his subsequent elaboration of the idea, Roy seems eventually to conceive of spiritual freedom in at least two senses. These correspond to the ways in which Vivekananda,

27 Ibid., pp. 26–27.
28 Ibid., pp. 200–1, 204–5.

Aurobindo and Gandhi understand the idea as well. First, Roy posits spiritual freedom as not only the ultimate value of Radical Humanism in its hierarchy of values but also as the key motivating force of human action. 'The urge for spiritual freedom, though it has remained largely in the realm of the subconscious, has been the lever of entire human development, ever since the birth of the species.'[29]

This conception of spiritual freedom as a kind of teleological final cause may seem vague or mystical, but the idea does have firm roots in the Indian intellectual tradition. Although Vivekananda, unlike Roy, chose to identify explicitly the idea of spiritual freedom with the ancient Hindu theory of Mukti or Moksha, he fully anticipated Roy in the view of freedom as both the cause and the ultimate value or goal of human development. 'Freedom,' Vivekananda wrote, 'is the one goal of all nature ... everything is struggling towards that goal.' In this ideal is found the 'groundwork of all morality', and 'to advance oneself towards freedom, physical, mental and spiritual and help others do so, is the supreme prize of man'.[30] 'Political and social independence are well and good, but the real thing is spiritual independence—*Mukti*.'[31] The parallel with Roy is evident, but for Roy's rejection of the Vedanta and insistence that the value of spiritual freedom somehow must be grounded in a 'materialist philosophy'. This analysis of Roy's ideology will not deal with his peculiar theory of materialism since it has no logical relation to his ethical or political ideas. Rather, it seems that Roy appropriated some aspects of materialist philosophy to justify in his own mind his appeals to rationalism and modern science. This attempt did not succeed. The consequence was an incongruous conglomeration of scientism, irrationalism and moralism that vitiates the claim of

---

29 Roy, *Reason, Romanticism and Revolution*, vol. II (Calcutta: Renaissance Publication, 1955), p. 297.

30 Vivekananda, *Works*, Vol. 5 (1959), pp. 141–42.

31 Ibid., p. 458.

Radical Humanism to being a systematic philosophy. Perhaps this is a reason why Bhushan and Garfield do not include him in their book, *Minds without Fear*.

The second sense in which Roy conceived of spiritual freedom was as a prerequisite for social and political freedom. Roy often argued in his last years that 'Spiritual liberation is the condition for social and political liberation. Radical Humanism is the message of that liberation.'[32] This view of the primacy of spiritual freedom is suggested in the above passage from Vivekananda, and Gandhi wrote in similar terms, 'The outward freedom therefore that we shall attain will only be in exact proportion to the inward freedom to which we may have grown at a given moment.'[33] 'Spiritual liberation' in the sense that Roy uses it here depended upon the moral transformation of the individual in society, that is, the realization of those virtues which we shall see in a moment embodied in Roy's vision of the ideal leader. 'The burning problem of our time is the problem of morality,' Roy concluded, and for him, in this final phase, this problem had indeed become paramount.[34] The former Marxist revolutionary has thus turned moralist, preaching the goal of spiritual freedom familiar to his Indian tradition.

Roy's Conception of Power

Roy's view of power, no less than that of freedom, underwent change in that critical decade of 1937–47. As a Congressman writing in 1937, Roy repeatedly called through the columns of *Independent India* for a more effective mobilization of the masses to prepare for the great goal—

---

32 Roy, 'Radical Humanism: Theory and Practice', in *The Radical Humanist*, 9 March 1952, p. 111.

33 Gandhi, 'Freedom to the Free', *Young India*, 1 November 1928, *CWMG* 38:1–2.

34 Roy, *Reason, Romanticism and Revolution*, vol. II, p. 272.

the 'capture of power' from the British. 'Ours is not a constitutional debate,' he insisted, 'it is a political struggle for the conquest of power.' The Congress must activate the people for the coming power struggle, and no holds should be barred in dealing with the imperialists. The theory of a peaceful transfer of power was thought insipid. Such senseless faith in the British could only 'obviate the necessity of the revolutionary mass action indispensable for the conquest of power'.

If the constitutional approach was misleading, then 'the humanitarian idea of social service', with its associated moral trappings, was emasculating when applied to the revolution. Gandhism is emphatically rejected by Roy now as he had rejected it fifteen years earlier in *India in Transition*. The 'mass struggle for the capture of power ... is incompatible with the moral dogmas, religious creeds, pseudo-philosophical doctrines that have been dominating our movement for political freedom'. Gandhi talks about 'human virtues and tests of sincerity' in negotiating with the British. Here and elsewhere, he sets up impossible moral hurdles for the struggle. He should realize the hard revolutionary truth that 'anything instrumental for developing our fight for freedom should be considered proper'. The Congress effort has too often been undermined by the Gandhian insistence upon 'ethical' means. It has failed to appreciate that 'every crisis must be utilised for furthering and intensifying that decisive struggle for the capture of political power'.[35]

Once again, a decisive change of view appears in 1946 with Roy's *New Orientation*. Now Roy's attitude towards power follows from his ethical approach to politics that has been discussed above. Communists, Roy remarks, have 'vulgarised' Marxism, so that it 'can no longer give us a strong enough inspiration. We shall have to set up higher ideas and find a nobler philosophy of life. Unprincipled power-politics

---

35 Roy, *Our Problems* (editorials of *Independent India*) (Calcutta: Barendra Library, 1939), pp. 20, 38, 47–48, 66, 82, 244–45, 59.

inevitably results from the pragmatic view of history, the view that the end justifies the means.'

Thus, while a decade earlier Roy had insisted that power was the only proper concern for politics, and argued against Gandhi that any means were legitimate in the struggle for power, now he denounces power politics as 'unprincipled'. As with others in the group of seven, the means-ends theory assumes precedence. In words practically identical to those used by Gandhi, Roy writes: 'It is a fallacy to hold that the end justifies the means. The truth is that immoral means necessarily corrupt the end. This is an empirical truth.'[36] Whereas the great need in 1937 was for the mobilization of the masses in the struggle for power, Roy's desire now is for 'a decent politics, human politics [that] cannot be practised except as the expression of some higher moral urge, according to some philosophical principles'. Earlier, Roy had scorned Gandhi's talk of the 'purification of politics'. Now Roy declares that he can remain in politics only if it is purified, for 'political practice without a philosophy is a vulgar scramble for power'.[37]

The stage is set for Roy's withdrawal from politics. The obvious point might be made that he could do little else, given the hopeless political position of the RDP. Yet, to reduce Roy's view of power to this would be misleading. Roy was not merely making a virtue of necessity. He was creating a theoretical critique deeply in accord with the Indian intellectual tradition. Because the conception of power which he developed is representative of an important strand of modern Indian thinking about politics, which one political scientist has aptly called, 'The Struggle Against Power'.[38] Roy articulated this strand of thought,

---

36 Roy, *New Orientation*, p. 248.

37 Ibid., pp. 209–10 and 226.

38 Myron Weiner, 'Struggle Against Power: Notes on Indian Political Behaviour', *World Politics* 8, no. 3 (April 1956): 392–403.

with all its related assumptions about the nature of leadership, better than any of his contemporaries.

If this theme of the 'struggle against power' is analysed in the context of Roy's thought, it should be noted that Roy was not suspicious of power per se. What he feared and criticized was a craving or lust for political power. 'Power,' he observed, 'will always have a place in human society,' for 'it is precisely man's power which can make a better job of human society'. But, if the body politic is to be purged of evils like injustice, authoritarianism and corruption, then 'it must be free from the lust for power'. It is precisely the craving for power that leads to what Roy describes over and over again with disgust, the vulgar 'scramble for power'.[39] The imperative to overcome such passions connect him with Ambedkar's *The Buddha and His Dhamma* together with Gandhi and followers like J.P. Narayan.

Yet, throughout this entire discussion, Rabindranath Tagore's critique of power stands forth prominently. The first edition of this book delves much more closely into Tagore's thought than attempted here. It should be emphasized that for him, as a solid member of this group of seven, that the debate with Gandhi over uses of political power qualifies Tagore as flowing firmly within this stream of discourse.

The mad scramble for power usually culminates, according to Roy, in a concentration of power in the unworthy hands of a political party or dictatorship. This can only result in the suppression of individual freedom. Roy therefore asks for a leadership that will promote the widest possible diffusion of power in society. Since, however, the scramble and concentration of power emanate, in Roy's view, from the leader's lust for power, it follows that only a disinterested leadership, purged of normal political ambitions, can be trusted with the public welfare. Today, such men are not placed in positions of responsibility because an unenlightened public 'has been debased to the level of unthinking

---

39 Roy, *Politics, Power and Parties* (Calcutta: Renaissance Publication, 1960), pp. 72, 122, 181, 184.

beasts, to serve the purpose of power politics'. The public thereby reproduces leaders corrupted by 'hatred, greed, lust for power'.[40]

The remedy for this is to enlighten the people not only through precept but example. If the right leadership sets a high moral example, it will compel the people's respect and will be given the opportunity to transform society. This attitude towards power was best summed up by Gandhi when he explained that the ideal leadership 'does not seize power. It does not even seek power—power accrues to it.'[41] Gandhi, as the Mahatma, discovered that power often 'accrued' to him in abundance. Roy, who never developed anything like Gandhi's ingenious style of leadership, failed in his early quest for power. Yet ultimately, Roy came to share with Gandhians like J.P. Narayan (as seen in the next chapter) that conception of power which was profoundly embedded in their intellectual tradition.

Closely allied to this dark view of a selfish lust or craving that Ambedkar repeatedly condemned in the context of Buddhism, came a grim estimate of the nature of politics itself. Once again, this position was not peculiar to Roy; it had been forecast decades earlier in Bengal, and it would recur in Ambedkar's classic tales of Buddha's renunciation of political power for the cause of spiritual freedom. Once again, among members of this group of seven, Vivekananda's eloquent voice came first and as a prevailing influence. He denounced politics as 'trash', an unclean business unwisely imported from the West, and alien to the Indian tradition. 'The voice of Asia has been the voice of religion. The voice of Europe is the voice of politics.' 'Do not mix in politics' were his orders to his disciples.

At the same time, Vivekananda gave his country the apt advice that was in accord with both Hinduism and Buddhism: 'If you want to speak of politics in India, you must speak through the language of

---

40 Ibid.

41 In Mirabehn, *New and Old Gleanings* (Ahmedabad: Navajivan Publishing House, 1949), p. 15.

religion.'[42] Bengali extremists like Aurobindo had come to heed this advice by the time of Vivekananda's death in 1902. But for Aurobindo, politics soon proved to be not enough—as well as too much. Once he had followed Vivekananda's path to the seclusion and security of the ashram, he remained there until his death. From Pondicherry then came the word of 'the disease and falsehood of modern political life', the utter immorality of political leaders, and the demonic nature of the state.[43]

Unlike Aurobindo, Gandhi remained absorbed throughout most of his life in the business of politics. However, Gandhi's fundamental assumption on the nature of politics was not unlike Aurobindo's: 'If I seem to take part in politics,' Gandhi said, 'it is only because politics encircle us today like the coil of a snake from which one cannot get out, no matter how much one tries. I wish therefore to wrestle with the snake.' Until the end, Gandhi insisted that his 'work of social reform or self-purification … is a hundred times dearer to me than what is called purely political work'.[44]

As observed above, even these protestations could not exempt Gandhi from the trenchant criticism of Rabindranath Tagore. The poet's suspicion of nationalist politics led him to admonish the Mahatma: 'Power in all its forms is irrational; it is like the horse that drags the carriage blind-folded.'[45] From the ensuing Tagore–Gandhi controversy emerged the poet's overwhelming repulsion from what

---

42 Vivekananda, *Works*, Vol. 8 (1959), p. 77.

43 Sri Aurobindo, 'The Ideal of Human Unity', in *The Human Cycle: The Ideal of Human Unity, War and Self-Determination* (Pondicherry: Sri Aurobindo Ashram, 1962), pp. 388–91.

44 Gandhi, 'Neither a Saint nor a Politician', *Young India*, 12 May 1920, *CWMG* 17:406.

45 Rabindranath Tagore in R.K. Prabhu and R. Kelekar (eds.), *Truth Called Them Differently (Tagore–Gandhi Controversy)* (Ahmedabad: Navajivan Publishing House, 1961), p. 14.

M.N. Roy eventually denounced as the dominant trait of contemporary politics, the corrupting influence of power. 'All brands of politics,' Roy wrote, 'as practised today are party-politics. If party politics is bad, politics is itself bad. It is easy to see how this system is bound to lead to demoralisation.'[46] These impressions of power and politics, shared among Roy and the others, had far-reaching implications for their thinking on the problem of right leadership, the nature of the good society, and the method by which it might be achieved.

Roy on Freedom, Leadership and Revolution

> In the free state visualised by us as a practical possibility, detached individuals, modern versions of philosopher-kings—will be at the helm of public affairs. Detached individuals, that is, spiritually free men, cannot be corrupted by power. A man susceptible to corruption is not spiritually free, not detached, not a philosopher. Therefore, the doubt is not with regard to the possibility of spiritually free men to be above corruption; it is about the possibility of men ever becoming spiritually free. A Humanist philosophy does not admit of that doubt ... We maintain that, given his essential rationality, it is possible for the individual man to attain spiritual freedom, to be detached, and thus to be above corruption. Such men would not hanker after power.[47]

This critical passage from a speech of May 1947 suggests the main assumptions that Roy was to develop over the next six years, as well as the relationships which he formed among his ideas of spiritual freedom, political power and the right leadership.

Roy introduces here his conception of the ideal leader as the detached individual, the 'philosopher-king'. For one who had been so recently

---

46 Roy, *Politics, Power and Parties*, p. 70.

47 Ibid., pp. 81–82.

a Marxist and who still claimed to be a materialist, the attraction to the vision of the philosopher-king, with all its Platonic associations, may seem peculiar. Yet, Roy took not only the idea of the philosopher-king but also its association with Plato very seriously indeed. Even as a Marxist, Roy had argued that Plato's conception of the ideal state and particularly his theory of the guardian elite, 'can guide not only political thinking, but even political practice of our time'.[48]

Later, after his departure from Marxism, Roy's affection for Plato, and especially for the ideal of the philosopher-ruler, strengthened considerably. In defending Plato's *Republic* against the charge of 'fascism', Roy concludes: 'The philosopher in the Platonic sense is a person characterized by love of truth and virtue, ability for detached objective judgment, disinclination to possess or accumulate any wealth and desire to teach others.'[49] This, Roy says, is the type of leader that he wants to 'guide' his 'true democracy'. Their guidance would assume the form not of political power over others, but of 'creative and co-operative education of the common people'. Such leaders could not have 'a contempt for the unenlightened common man and seek consolation in some intellectual privacy of their own'. Rather, they would function through 'advisory councils', 'to guide and not to control social conduct'.[50] Roy's vision of a 'true democracy' guided, served and enlightened by a disinterested moral elite could find parallels with a combination of Western political thinkers. However, it can also be seen as a familiar theme of the Indian intellectual tradition, and it will be analysed here in that context.

---

48 Roy, *Nationalism, Democracy and Freedom* (Bombay: V.B. Karnik, 1943), p. 52.

49 Roy, *The Radical Humanist*, 2 December 1951, p. 556.

50 Ibid.

The anarchist ideal of a society free from the 'scramble for power', from the oppressive interference of an unwanted government, indeed from the taint of politics itself: this is implicit throughout the writings of Vivekananda, Aurobindo, Gandhi, J.P. Narayan and Roy. The Marxist Utopia represents a form of anarchism, and Roy's version might, at first glance, be identified with Marxism. This, however, would be to ignore one of the defining characteristics of Roy's ideal, a trait that establishes it clearly within the modern India context. For, while Roy's order is without government or politics, it is nonetheless a 'guided anarchy', a society directed toward righteousness by the moral example of a Karma Yoga-type elite.

In an important treatise entitled 'Practice of New Humanism' adopted by the All-India Conference of the RDP in December 1949, Roy systematically pronounced a series of fundamental principles for this political theory. These began with the critique of power politics set forth two years before in the form of '22 Theses'. Now, these basic tenets were reiterated and revised by drawing conceptual correspondences with ideas of leadership. The 1949 treatise distinguished Radical Humanism from political theories and practices on both the left and the right arguing that they had been corrupted by 'the predominance of power-politics' to the point leaders have surrendered any pretence of 'their existence as free thinking beings' as they craved 'the prize of power-politics'.

The agent of this corruption was a failure to recognize the centrality of moral means over ends:

'Engaged in a struggle for power, they tend to adopt means which contradict their profession of democracy. Striving to become popular, they tend to flatter the prejudices of the people and foster the authoritarian tradition rooted in their cultural and political backwardness ... leftist parties no less than the rightist seek to rely on totalitarian sentiments.'

This key declaration of Radical Humanist theory repeatedly emphasizes the evils of 'pursuit of power' through immoral means. Yet the prevailing theme is the quest for freedom:

> Mental freedom has necessarily been the precondition for any attempt to attain political and economic freedom … a political party striving for power cannot be the means to the attainment of freedom. A movement for freedom as visualized in the philosophy of New Humanism must be broader than a political movement, nor can it be organized and led by a political party of the traditional type. Standing outside the scramble for power, it will seek to educate people in the cultural values essential for the realization of democracy.

Finally, Roy came to the crucial conclusion:

> [Such a community must be] manned by spiritually free men and women possessed of intellectual integrity and moral detachment. It will be planned with the purpose of promoting the freedom and well-being of the individual … always be determined by the requirements of the attainment of the basic value of freedom … [ensuring that] the culture of the new society will grow in an atmosphere of individual freedom and morality … The primary task of the movement will be to bring about a cultural renaissance by propagating the philosophy of New Humanism and through its application to political, economic and other social problems.

Philosophers are responsible for making 'the people conscious of the urge for freedom'.

Just as Ambedkar concluded his Kathmandu address with a ringing call to spread the message of a spiritual transformation of society, so Roy finished these 22 Theses with a similar charge: 'The Radical Humanist Movement will provide full scope to the initiative of the individuals engaged in it who will be held together not by rules and regulations, but by the possession of a common philosophy. Radical Humanists will form a spiritual brotherhood.' In this manner, Roy and his ashramites personified in dramatic fashion what Vivekananda had characterized as 'the ideal Brahminness in which worldliness is altogether absent and true wisdom is abundantly present.'[51] That alone is true freedom.

Vivekananda's portrayal of the karmayogin as a free man, spontaneously virtuous and uniquely capable of love and compassion, is not new to the Indian tradition; as Vivekananda emphasized, Ramakrishna saw the conception in this light. The development that emerges with Vivekananda lies in his emphasis upon the free individual as a national leader, a disinterested social reformer, working in a spirit of renunciation to secure values which were often foreign to the Indian tradition. 'We must prove,' said Vivekananda, 'the truth of pure Advaitism in practical life. Shankara left this Advaita philosophy in the hills and forests, while I have come to bring it out of those places and scatter it broadcast before the work-a-day world and society.'[52] This was the role of the karmayogin: a part played by Vivekananda himself, in a social if not in a political sense. And the conceptual correspondences which he drew anticipated the emergence on the Indian political scene of a karmayogin par excellence, Mahatma Gandhi.

---

51 Roy, *Practice of New Humanism* (Bombay: Maniben Kara Publishers, 1950), pp. 3–12. These '22 Theses' were distributed as a pamphlet and the copy now in my possession was a gift from Justice V.M. Tarkunde in 1966. In the interview mentioned in my memoir (at the beginning of the book), he stressed that they were drafted by Roy, intensively discussed at the RDP All-India Conference in Calcutta on 26–29 December 1949, and constituted the essential philosophy of Radical Humanism. See also, Vivekananda, *Works*, Vol. 3 (1960), p. 197.

52 Vivekananda, *Works*, Vol. 7 (1958), p. 162.

In writing of the 'traditional ideal of the *guru* or teacher, better called "spiritual advisor"', Professor Karl Potter observed in his study of classical Indian philosophy:

> That those only are fit to guide who have gained mastery of their subject is a commonplace requirement; but the relationship of the student to his guru, an especially intimate one, requires the teacher not only to have mastered the variety of subject matters included in the 'curriculum' but also, and more important, to have such insight and superior awareness—coupled with the ability to carry out the decisions that insight dictates—as to be always cognizant of his pupil's innermost needs as well as master of the exactly appropriate ways of satisfying them. It is no wonder, with this ideal in mind, that the gifted teacher remains in contemporary India a figure highly fitted in the mind of the community to take on the added burdens of political leadership. Nor is it any wonder that, in the light of the correspondence we have noted between hero, saint, and teacher, the men who appeal to Indians as leaders have been respected and revered as being at one and the same time all three. Because of their superior understanding, such men are held to be worthy of everyone's trust and allegiance, even despite apparent external inconsistencies in their behaviour. The hero, the yogi, and the guru exemplify superior mastery of themselves and their environment; they, among men, most closely approximate the ideal of complete control or freedom.[53]

The karmayogin was indeed synonymous, in Vivekananda's view, with the classical conceptions of the hero and the guru; and it was this figure, embodying these three symbols rolled into one, surrounded with an aura of saintliness and spiritual power, that became a dominant image in modern Indian political thought. The yogin, bodhisattva or Radical

53 Karl H. Potter, *Presuppositions of India's Philosophies* (N.J.: Prentice Hall, 1963), p. 5.

Humanist had realized their respective spirituality by attaining freedom, and was thus unquestionably fitted not only to serve humanity but to lead it in all spheres of action.

A systematic theoretical statement in modern Indian thought on the theme of spiritual leadership occurs in the concluding chapters of Aurobindo's *The Life Divine* with his vision of the 'gnostic beings', a monastic type that has much in common with Roy's or Ambedkar's elites. In Aurobindo's eloquent description, one discovers the archetypal Indian leader, acting selflessly, instinctively, for the good of humanity, endowed with spiritual freedom, above the temptation of power or of political ambition, conscious of the unity of mankind, and confident of his ability to 'turn and adapt [the world] to his own truth and purpose of existence; he will mould life itself into his own spiritual image'.[54] Roy and Ambedkar express their faith that carriers of spiritual freedom will transform humanity, 'leaving the politicians to their scramble for power, very soon they will multiply themselves to be five hundred and then thousands. The contagion will spread ...'[55] Precisely the manner in which this momentum would grow was based upon a belief common to the group of seven that the moral purity of such leaders would prove irresistible. This belief is fundamental to the Indian tradition and particularly to the conceptions of power and leadership shared by those thinkers mentioned in this chapter. Gandhi expressed the belief lucidly when he remarked that the ideal government would consist of 'sages' and went on to explain:

> In modern times a 'sage' is a person who has education, a spirit of service, and the qualifications for rendering service in the largest

---

54 Aurobindo, writings on 'The gnostic being', *The Life Divine* (Pondicherry: Sri Aurobindo Ashram, 1960), p. 1163.

55 Roy, 'Preconditions for Democracy', in *The Radical Humanist*, 31 August 1952, p. 410.

measure. A man of this type will not seek power; but the people of their own desire will elect him and invest him with power, because they will realise that he is indispensable.[56]

Similar attitudes towards freedom and power that shaped the visions of Gandhi and Roy directed their more practical programmes of social reconstruction as they did Ambedkar's challenge to bhikkus. Their common suspicion of man's lust for power dictated a highly decentralized political structure, where infusion of social morality depended upon a wide diffusion of power. 'The end to be achieved,' Gandhi wrote, 'is human happiness combined with full mental and moral growth ... This end can be achieved under decentralization. Centralization as a system is inconsistent with a nonviolent structure of society.'[57] Roy espoused neither Gandhi's doctrine of nonviolence nor his aversion to industrialization, but he set forth a theory of democracy akin to Gandhi's or to Ambedkar's declaration that 'The Buddha, of course, was a great democrat'.

'Ultimately,' Roy argued, 'the problem of democratic political practice is that of decentralization.' 'Diffusion of power is the essence of democracy, because concentration of power leads to tyranny and dictatorship ...' With Gandhi, Roy looks forward to 'the foundation of a decentralized State ... laid in local republics which will combine all functions of the State as they affect the local life ... Being thus reared upon a broad foundation of direct democracies the State will be really

---

56 C.S. Shukla, *Gandhi's View of Life* (Bombay: Bharatiya Vidya Bhavan, 1956), pp. 146–47.

57 Gandhi, *Harijan*, 18 January 1942. He added: 'There is no room for power politics within the Congress ... real strengthening of the organization consists in every Congressman working the constructive program to its fullest capacity.' *CWMG* 75:239.

democratic.'[58] The village is the key unit in Roy's concept of direct democracy. Even in the early 1940s, Roy is insisting as emphatically as Gandhi on the primacy of the village for development in India.[59]

We may look back to Vivekananda once again to introduce the final point of comparison between Roy and the other Indian thinkers discussed here, that is, their theory of the right method of social change.

> ... [T]here is a class [wrote Vivekananda] which still clings on to political and social changes as the only panacea for the evils in Europe, but among the great thinkers there, other ideals are growing. They have found out that no amount of political or social manipulation of human conditions can cure the evils of life. It is a change of the soul itself for the better that alone will cure the evils of life. No amount of force, or government, or legislative cruelty will change the conditions of a race, but it is spiritual culture and ethical culture alone that can change wrong racial tendencies for the better.[60]

This marks the beginning of a prolonged Indian indictment of the Western parliamentary form of government with its alleged exclusive dependence on institutional or legislative reforms. It is a line of criticism which extends from Vivekananda through Aurobindo and Gandhi, and on to Roy and Jayaprakash Narayan. The implication was generally that expressed by Vivekananda: political changes are inevitably superficial since they leave untouched the underlying cause of social ills as well as the potential source of their correction, the moral character of the individual. 'The most drastic changes,' wrote Aurobindo, 'made by these [political] means change nothing; for the old ills exist in a

---

58 Roy, *Politics, Power and Parties*, pp. 71, 75, 77.

59 Roy, *Scientific Politics*, pp. 240–41; and chapter XIII, in *Constitution of Free India* (Delhi: V.B. Karnik, 1945), pp. 41–42.

60 Vivekananda, *Works*, Vol. 3 (1960), p. 182.

new form: the aspect of the outward environment is altered, but man remains what he was ... Only a spiritual change can make a real and effective difference.'[61] In most cases, this type of criticism was followed by a suggested remedy derived from the Indian tradition. The classic example is Gandhi's theory of satyagraha.

Roy's line of criticism on this issue is as forceful as that of any of the other thinkers. Referring to the 'crisis of modern civilisation', he says:

> Others diagnose the disease as a crisis of political theories and institutions. They recommend that the parliamentary system would be improved by various ingenious devices. It is hardly necessary to go into an examination of the mechanical remedies suggested; they are bound to fail as long as greater importance is attached to institutions than to men. The central fallacy of these political theories is to place institutions above men, to ignore that institutions are created by men. Any attempt at social reconstruction to promote economic welfare and political liberty must begin with man.[62]

Roy does not proceed to identify his theory of the right method of social change with elements of the Indian tradition. However, the similarity on this point between Roy and the others discussed here is considerable. It rests upon a common view of what constitutes genuine social change as well as on the nature of the leadership that must initiate it.

The fundamental principles of Radical Humanism, initially formulated as '22 Theses' in 1947, assumed various shapes and forms until the end, like a drumbeat of philosophical declarations: 'Society is no more than an integration of individuals, and if you want a good society, you must have good individuals. Until now, we have put the

---

61 Aurobindo, *The Life Divine*, p. 1053.

62 Roy, *New Humanism, A Manifesto* (Calcutta: Renaissance Publication, 1961), p. 85.

cart before the horse and said that we must have a good society in order to have good men.' The truth, however, is that 'Without moral men, there can be no moral society'.[63] Lasting and meaningful social change can occur only with a moral transformation of the individual in society. This approach to change, combined with Roy's views on power and politics, reinforced his belief that only a 'philosophical revolution', a fundamental reorientation of attitudes on man and society, could have the desired results. Roy not only dismissed most political agencies as ineffective, but he also subjected the party system, in particular, to scathing criticism for its lustful pursuit of power and corrosive influence upon public morality.[64]

Therefore, only a year after Gandhi had advised the Congress organization to 'disband' and 'flower into a Lok Sevak Sangh', Roy officially transformed his RDP into the Radical Humanist Movement. Writing in *The Radical Humanist* on 'The Mahatma's advice', Roy praised Gandhi's move as a sincere attempt to withdraw the Congress party 'from the scramble of power-politics and to concentrate on constructive work for the service and welfare of the people'.[65] In the years following Gandhi's death, Roy, although his attitude was ambivalent towards much of Gandhi's legacy, developed the theory of the social movement in a way that Gandhi would have approved.

In Roy's final phase, he often recalled the early inspiration of that first leader of his Calcutta youth, Jatin Mukherjee. It is in a remarkable eulogy to Jatinda that Roy indicates the nature of the reconciliation of ideals which he has finally realized:

---

63 Roy, *Politics, Power and Parties*, p. 41.

64 Ibid., p. 70.

65 Roy, 'The Mahatma's Advice', in *Radical Humanist*, 29 May 1949, pp. 247–48. Roy's praise or condemnation of Gandhi is seldom unqualified; this article is no exception.

Good men are seldom given a place in the galaxy of the great. It will continue to be so until goodness is recognised as the measure of genuine greatness. Jatinda ... did not belong to any age; his values were human and as such transcended space and time ... Like all modern educated young men of his time, he tended to accept the reformed religion preached by Swami Vivekananda—a God who would stand the test of reason and a religion which served progressive social and human purpose. He believed himself to be a Karmayogin, trying to be at any rate, and recommended the ideal to all of us. Detached from the unnecessary mystic preoccupation, Karmayogin means a humanist. He who believes that self-realisation can be attained through human action must logically also believe in man's creativeness—that man is the maker of his destiny. That is also the essence of Humanism. Jatinda was a Humanist—perhaps the first in modern India.[66]

The easy correspondence drawn here between Karma Yoga and humanism, which transforms a Hindu mystic into the first humanist of modern India, suggests where the roots of Roy's own humanism lay.

66 Roy, 'Jatin Mukherji', *Independent India*, 27 February 1949, p. 91.

Conclusion and Further Perspectives: Concepts of Freedom, Politics and Power*

J.P. Narayan

If political theory is affected, let political theorists worry; if theories of politics tumble, political life will go on as before. I believe this to be a mistaken and shortsighted view ... What the political

---

* A version of this chapter was initially published as 'The Concepts of Politics and Power in India's Ideological Tradition', in *The States of South Asia: Problems of National Integration*, ed. A.J. Wilson and Dennis Dalton (Honolulu: University of Hawaii Press, 1982), pp. 175–196. This volume is a collection of essays in honour of Professor W.H. Morris-Jones (1918–1999), a mentor during his tenure as Director of the Institute of Commonwealth Studies (1966–1983). He had served as constitutional adviser to Lord Mountbatten, as recounted in his article, 'The Transfer of Power, 1947', *Modern Asian Studies* 16, no. I (1982): 1–32. From this perspective, he was a valuable source for my study of Gandhi's Calcutta and Delhi fasts. In addition to his writings cited below, his *Government and Politics of India* (London: Hutchison University Library, 1964 and 1971) influenced this essay.

philosopher believes and teaches today will in some measure mould
what politicians believe and do tomorrow.[1]

The purpose of this final chapter is to examine how several Indian
political theorists, now including Jayaprakash Narayan, in the 'group
of seven', formed a constellation of ideas around the core concept of
freedom. It offers an extension of the comparative analysis presented in
both the Introduction and the first edition of *Indian Idea of Freedom*.
The purpose is to demonstrate a broader conceptual consensus for the
intellectual tradition in the twentieth century. This cluster, as part of a
cultural ethos, constitutes a cohesive body of thought of considerable
significance. The challenge that professor W.H. Morris-Jones poses in
the epigraph above is to appreciate the force of this Indian renaissance:
to ask if it can indeed shape how political leaders should think and act
in the twenty-first century.[2]

---

1   W.H. Morris-Jones, *Politics Mainly Indian* (Bombay: Orient Longman,
    1978), p. 9.

2   As explained in the Introduction, the 'group of seven' that constitutes
    the cluster of thinkers and ideas in this book, start with Swami
    Vivekananda or Narendranath Datta (1863–1902). See chs. 3–6
    ('The Later Nineteenth Century: Letters of Reform and Revival';
    'Liberal, Social, and Political Thought in the Late Nineteenth
    and Early Twentieth Century: The Moderates'; 'Radical Politics
    and Cultural Criticism, 1880-1914: The Extremists'; 'Mahatma
    Gandhi and Responses'), in *Sources of Indian Traditions*, ed. Rachel
    Fell McDermott et al., Third edition, Vol. 2 (New York: Columbia
    University Press, 2014). These men may appear quite dissimilar in
    terms of their styles of thought, but they exhibit a clear consensus in
    their common commitment to ideas about human nature and the good
    society, the nature of authority and the relationship of the individual
    to the state, the values of freedom and equality. Their emphasis is on
    consensus rather than conflict, cooperation rather than competition as

Why a given civilization manages to produce and clarify an intellectual tradition is uncertain, but when and where this does occur seems to be identified with two phenomena. First, in a social sense, the traditions emerge as responses to social crises which theorists perceive as fundamental challenges to established sets of values. Second, in an intellectual sense, the traditions have been clearly marked by the logical manner in which they form clusters of ideas, often centring on key concepts of freedom, politics and power. The example of India's intellectual tradition fits this pattern: it emerged in response to the crisis of values introduced by British imperialism in the nineteenth century, and it soon formed into a cohesive cluster of ideas.

Traditions of political thought have conceptualized freedom, politics and power in at least three distinct ways. First, there was the theory, best set forth by classical Greek thought, of politics as an all-embracing activity. The political community, Aristotle announced in the opening chapters of *The Politics*, is 'the most sovereign and inclusive association', 'the final and perfect association', in that it represents the natural, teleological fulfilment of all other communities and the individual may therefore achieve his highest moral attainment, the realization of law and justice, only within the political order, for 'man

---

social ideals, and on a method of change that relies on primarily moral example and suasion rather than violent revolution or legislative reform. The political concepts presented here around the idea of freedom serve to focus their agreement. But while the focus in this book is on the seven Indian thinkers, in this chapter, Vinoba Bhave's writings are also discussed. For further analysis of members of this group, see the author's 'Gandhi and Roy: The Interaction of Ideologies in India', in Sibnarayan Ray (ed.), *Gandhi India and the World* (Melbourne: The Hawthorn Press, 1970), pp. 156–70. Otherwise, B.C. Pal's and B.G. Tilak's ideas are presented in the first edition (1982).

is by nature an animal intended to live in a *polis*'.[3] This classical view
of politics was revived in modern Europe by Rousseau and Hegel, and
it remains the dominant stream of Western political theory today,
primarily found in the idea of nationalism. The classical conception
of power was allied to its view of politics. For Plato, power must be
employed in an enlightened way, by leaders with philosophical insight,
but when it is employed wisely, there are no limits on its use.[4] For
the formation of the ideal polis, then, the sovereignty and broad scope
of politics are matched by a sweeping justification of power. In his
resurrection of Plato, Rousseau argued that the legislator should apply
power and achieve 'moral freedom' in a majestic manner to inaugurate
that all-inclusive political order, the civil state.[5]

The second theory of politics and power significantly features
ideas of freedom. It has antecedents in earlier Western traditions,
but it is chiefly a modern European development that finds its best
expression in the thought of John Locke and John Stuart Mill. This
conceptualization sees society, not the state, as primary, and stresses
the sanctity of the private rather than the political sphere of human
conduct. In the defining classic, *On Liberty*, Mill meaningfully

---

3   *The Politics of Aristotle*, trans. Ernest Barker (London: Oxford
University Press, 1958), pp. 1, 4–5.

4   *The Republic of Plato*, trans. F.M. Cornford (London: Oxford University
Press, 1958). The creation of the Republic, which is 'difficult but not
impossible' (p. 208), can occur only when there will be 'power in the
hands of men who are rich, not in gold, but in ... a good and wise life'
(p. 235). These are the Guardians who will have complete command
of political power.

5   Rousseau, *Political Writings*, trans. and ed. F. Watkins (London: Nelson
Philosophical Texts, 1953), *Social Contract*, Book 1, 'On The Civil
State', pp. 150–51 and Book 2, 'On the Legislator', pp. 162–65. See
especially Rousseau's distinction between 'natural liberty' and 'civil' or
'moral liberty'.

expanded Locke's theory of liberty to warn against 'the tyranny of the majority, when society is itself the tyrant'. 'This is the liberal tradition' of political philosophy that believes in 'the minimal character of the political order'.[6] It seeks to place 'absolute' or 'inviolable' limits on the political authority of the state and its sphere of legitimate action.[7] The corresponding view of power is that if it invades the private, personal realm in the name of politics, then both politics and power will be corrupted: 'politics is a necessary and important part of human life, but it is not the whole of it, and it becomes diseased if it aspires to more than its share'.[8]

The third conception of politics and power is a logical extension of the second and a direct refutation of the first. This is the anarchist perception, systematized first by William Godwin and then developed by a wide variety of thinkers in Europe, Russia and America in the nineteenth century. It reasoned from Locke's premises about the primacy of society and the need for placing limitations on the power of the state that the best community would be purged of the excesses of political authority. However, anarchism went beyond Locke and liberalism in its vision of a social order without government and in its attack on the law. Henry Thoreau wrote:

---

6   Mill, 'On Liberty' in *Mill*, ed. Alan Ryan (N.Y.: Norton, 1997), pp.41–44 and Sheldon Wolin, *Politics and Vision: Continuity and Innovation in Western Political Thought* (London: George Allen and Unwin, 1961), p. 308. See also my 'Philosophical Background to American Values in the Western Intellectual Tradition', in *To Form a More Perfect Union: An Anthology of American Values and the Debate on Income and Wealth Disparity*, ed. Phillip Hubbart, Dennis Dalton and Charles Edelstein, (Durham, North Carolina: Carolina Academic Press, 2016), pp. 37–58.

7   Isaiah Berlin, *Four Essays on Liberty* (London: Oxford University Press, 1969), pp. 165–66.

8   Morris-Jones, *Politics Mainly Indian*, p. 26. See also pp. 25, 27–44.

I heartily accept the motto—'That government is best which
governs least'; and I should like to see it acted up to more rapidly
and systematically. Carried out, it finally amounts to this, which
also I believe—'That government is best which governs not at
all'; and when men are prepared for it, that will be the kind of
government which they will have. Government is at best but an
expedient; but most governments are usually, and all governments
are sometimes, inexpedient ... Law never made men a whit more
just; and by means of their respect for it, even the well-disposed are
daily made the agents of injustice.[9]

For Thoreau, as for all anarchists, politics and power are everywhere
suspect not merely because they may tend to 'become diseased', but
rather, they are themselves the source of the worst social disease,
authoritarianism, and so they threaten society, like a contagious virus.

Strong parallels exist between the Western anarchist and modern
Indian conceptions of freedom, politics and power. A major premise
of this book, emphasized throughout, is that these similarities begin
with Vivekananda, who, more than any other nineteenth-century
Indian theorist, shaped and inspired his country's intellectual tradition.
In each area of thought that he touched, Vivekananda placed his
indelible stamp, but nowhere more dominantly than in his teaching

---

9 Henry David Thoreau, 'Civil Disobedience', in *Walden and Civil
Disobedience* (New York: Norton and Norton, 1966), pp. 224–25.
From this point in the discussion of anarchism, and primarily the Indian
thinkers examined here who made distinctive contributions to it, see
my chapter entitled 'The Theory of Anarchism in Modern India—
An Analysis of the Political Thought of Vivekananda, Aurobindo and
Gandhi', in *Tradition and Politics in South Asia*, ed. R.J. Moore (New
Delhi: Vikas Pub., 1979), pp. 198–227. While references to the Indian
idea of anarchism occur throughout this chapter, it is not the purpose
here to present this theory as it has been in my other writings.

CONCLUSION AND FURTHER PERSPECTIVES   391

about the relation of India's freedom to politics and power. In 1897, when he returned to India from four years in America and England, he discovered that 'the nation had already accepted him as its Guru',[10] and he eagerly embraced the role. He began by making a series of conceptual distinctions that starkly separated the cultures of India and England. 'The backbone, the foundation, and the bedrock' of India's 'national life', he declared, was its spiritual genius. 'Let others talk of politics, of the glory of acquisition' or of 'the power and spread of commercialism'; these cannot inspire India. Look at 'the Western and other nations, which are now almost borne down, half-killed, and degraded by political ambitions' and the futility of that existence will be clear.[11] Anyone who knows India must understand that 'politics, power, and even intellect form a secondary consideration here. Religion, therefore, is the one consideration in India'.[12]

Vivekananda's indispensable role in the conceptualization of politics and power in modern India was to establish, with extraordinary precision, the central assumptions and lines of argument. Just as later political thinkers, from Gandhi to J.P. Narayan, would attack Western political institutions and practices, so Vivekananda, decades before them, characterized 'parliaments' as 'jokes'[13] and 'party politics' as degenerate 'fanaticism and sectarianism'.[14] Preoccupation with political power was part of a distinctly Western 'vanity', a reflection of the 'material tyranny' which tyrannized over both colonized and colonizer,

---

10 *The Life of Swami Vivekananda*, By His Eastern and Western Disciples (Calcutta: Advaita Ashrama, 1960), p. 452.

11 Swami Vivekananda, *Complete Works*, Vol. 3 (Calcutta: Advaita Ashrama, 1960), p. 148. Hereafter *Works*.

12 Ibid., p. 204.

13 Ibid., p. 158.

14 Ibid., Vol. 6 (1963), p. 8.

a terrible evil, for 'by this power, they can deluge the whole earth with blood'.[15]

One of the key premises in the Indian conceptualization of politics and power lay in its attitude towards law, especially in the relationship of law to individual morality and social change. Here, again, Vivekananda's voice was early and decisive. 'The basis of all systems, social or political,' he argued, 'rests upon the goodness of men. No nation is great or good because Parliament enacts this or that, but because its men are great and good.' The aim is to promote a sound body of individual ethics, and this must not be a political task, for 'men cannot be made virtuous by an Act of Parliament ... And that is why religion is of deeper importance than politics, since it goes to the root, and deals with the essential of conduct.'[16] Too often, the state 'tries to compel all men through rigid laws and threats of punishment to follow that path with unconditional obedience', but this is disastrous, for it means that 'the destiny of mankind becomes no better than that of a machine'.[17] The political history of India records 'a thousand years of crushing tyranny of castes and kings and foreigners',[18] but the spiritual tradition of Hinduism calls for resistance to this legalized oppression. 'The very word Sannyasin means the divine outlaw'[19] and since 'it is freedom alone that is desirable ... It is not law that we want but ability to break law. We want to be outlaws. If you are bound by laws, you will be a lump of clay.'[20] Vivekananda concludes, therefore, that 'our aim

---

15 Ibid., Vol. 3 (1960), p. 158.

16 Ibid., Vol. 5 (1959), p. 200.

17 Ibid., Vol. 4 (1955), p. 435.

18 Ibid., Vol. 3 (1960), p. 244.

19 Ibid., Vol. 5 (1959), p. 193.

20 Ibid., p. 289.

should be to allow the individual to move towards this freedom. More of goodness, less of artificial laws.'[21]

If the threat of India's contamination by political power came from the West, then the antidote is found in her own tradition, and especially in the idea of spiritual power. The Western notion of power was corrupted by an obsession with its 'material', 'external' forms, while the Indian theory of power understood the superiority of its spiritual, 'internal' aspects.[22] Vivekananda's extensive discussions of the Indian concept of spiritual power clearly anticipate Gandhi's development of the idea of 'soul-force'. Like Gandhi, Vivekananda found this approach to power a unique, special component of the Indian genius, far superior in potential to what Gandhi called the Western idea of 'brute force'.[23] 'What power is there in the hand or the sword?' Vivekananda asked. 'The power is all in the spirit.'[24]

> Political greatness or military power is never the mission of our race; it never was, and mark my words, it never will be. But there has been the other mission given to us, which is to conserve, to preserve, to accumulate, as it were, into a dynamo, all the spiritual energy of the race, and that concentrated energy is to pour forth in a deluge on the world.[25]

Finally, Vivekananda signalled a crucial and prophetic departure from his classical tradition, by arguing that this spiritual power inhered in the

---

21 Ibid., Vol. 6 (1963), p. 100.

22 Ibid., Vol. 2 (1963), p. 65.

23 M.K. Gandhi, *Collected Works of Mahatma Gandhi*, Vol.10 (Delhi: Publications Division, Government of India, 1963), pp. 42–47. Hereafter *CWMG*.

24 Vivekananda, *Works*, Vol. 2 (1963), p. 21.

25 Ibid., Vol. 3 (1960), pp. 108–9.

masses. 'All knowledge is in every soul' regardless of caste or class, 'the same power is in every man'. This means, first, that Hinduism really promotes a 'wonderful state of equality'[26] but equally important for the future of the country, that 'the only hope of India is from the masses. The upper classes are physically and morally dead'.[27] To his disciples he repeatedly urged, 'You must have a hold on the masses.' 'We must reach the masses.'[28] If only the people could unite, that would mean 'infinite power ... Therefore, to make a great future India, the whole secret lies in organization, accumulation of power, co-ordination of wills ... That is the secret of power in India.'[29] Emphatically, it was a power that could be summoned forth not from the imposition of alien forms of government and law but only from the cultivation of India's own inspired cultural and religious tradition.

In one sense, Vivekananda's ideas powerfully influenced not only the political theory but also the political practice of twentieth-century India, if one considers the application of his thought to the Indian nationalist movement for independence. His aggressive nationalism, which attacked Western culture as inferior and emphasized the need for establishing a mass base of action, with corresponding stress on social equality and reforms—all inspired the independence movement. Yet, in another sense, his conceptualization of politics and power suggested a marked divergence between main currents of Indian political theory and the practice of Indian politics after 1947. The divergence occurs between a theory that is essentially anarchist in orientation and a practice that, after independence, sought to integrate the nation under a centralized system of government. It is rather extraordinary that throughout this century, India has produced a rich body of political

---

26 Ibid., Vol. 1 (1962), p. 426.

27 Ibid., Vol. 5 (1959), p. 105.

28 Ibid., pp. 36, 114.

29 Ibid., Vol. 3 (1960), p. 299.

theory, yet not a single major theorist of centralized authority. All of India's leading political thinkers have followed Vivekananda's conceptualization of politics and power. The first to accept him was also the most systematic political philosopher of this century—Sri Aurobindo Ghose.[30]

Among Aurobindo's most influential tracts was *The Spirit and Form of Indian Polity*.[31] The ideas on politics and power set forth here follow closely those of Vivekananda. 'The master idea that has governed the life, culture, social ideals of the Indian people has been the seeking of man for his true spiritual self and the use of life.' In this quest, politics cannot perform a significant role, for it inevitably belongs to the 'imperfect', 'grosser' area of human conduct, and 'the effort at governing political action by ethics is usually a little more than a pretence'.[32] Throughout its political history, Indian polities have approached spiritual realization in only a very limited sense, but even at its worst,

Indian polity never arrived at that unwholesome substitution of the mechanical for the natural order of the life of the people which has been the disease of European civilisation, now culminating in the

---

30 Sri Aurobindo has been rightly called 'the real intellectual heir of Vivekananda'—in Romain Rolland, *Prophets of the New India*, trans. E.F. Malcolm-Smith (London: Cassell and Co., 1930), p. 499. See also my 'Swami Vivekananda's Philosophical Influence on Sri Aurobindo', in *Swami Vivekananda's Ideas and Our Times: A Retrospect on His 150th Birth Anniversary, A Commemorative Volume*, ed. Sandipan Sen et al. (Belur Math, Howrah: Ramakrishna Mission, 2015), pp. 115–62.

31 Sri Aurobindo, *The Spirit and Form of Indian Polity* (Pondicherry: Sri Aurobindo Ashram, 1966).

32 Ibid., pp. 20–21.

monstrous artificial organisation of the bureaucratic and industrial State.[33]

This kind of state comes at an 'advanced stage of corruption of the Dharma marked by the necessity of the appearance of the legislator and the formal government of the whole of life by external or written law and code and rule'.[34] The ideal society, dictated by the spirit of Indian polity, is where, 'there is no need of any political government or State or artificial construction of society, because all then live freely according to the truth of their enlightened self and God-inhabited being and therefore spontaneously according to the inner divine Dharma.'[35]

A much fuller statement of these ideas is given in Aurobindo's two major works of political philosophy, *The Human Cycle* and *The Ideal of Human Unity*. In the latter book, he vigorously attacks the idea and reality of the modern state. 'The State principle leads necessarily to uniformity, regulation, mechanisation; its inevitable end is socialism.'[36] Not only the socialist state, though, has deprived individuals of their freedom. The democratic state has failed, too, and 'we see today the democratic system of government march steadily towards such an organised annihilation of individual liberty as could not have been dreamed of in the old aristocratic and monarchical systems.'[37] The central problem lies in the very principle of the state, which in its fascist, socialist, or democratic forms promotes not merely 'tyranny of the majority', but worse, 'tyranny of the whole, of the self-hypnotised

---

33 Ibid., p. 28.

34 Ibid., p. 31.

35 Ibid., p. 30.

36 Sri Aurobindo, 'The Ideal of Human Unity', in *The Human Cycle, The Ideal of Human Unity, War and Self-Determination* (Pondicherry: Sri Aurobindo Ashram, 1962), p. 673.

37 Ibid., p. 677.

mass over its constituent groups and units',[38] usually orchestrated by a small elite of demagogic politicians. Aurobindo saw this in 'Fascist Italy and Soviet Russia'[39] alike, and in those states (like Britain and America) who claim to enjoy representative government 'legislators and administrators do not really represent their electors. The Power they represent is another, a formless and bodiless entity, which has taken the place of monarch and aristocracy, that impersonal group-being ... the huge mechanism of the modern State.'[40]

In successive chapters entitled 'The Drive Towards Economic Centralisation' and 'The Drive Towards Legislative and Social Centralisation and Uniformity', Aurobindo condemns in the 'history of the growth of the State ... the development of a central authority and of a growing uniformity in administration, legislation, social and economic life and culture.'[41] This is wrong because no centralized political authority can represent or promote the realization of individual interests. Diversity, not uniformity and over-centralization, is the 'law of life'; while order is necessary, it must be understood that 'the truest order is that which is founded on the greatest possible liberty'.[42] A society that achieves this ideal will be 'perfectly spiritualised ... as is dreamed of by the spiritual anarchist' in which 'each man will be not a law to himself, but *the* law, the divine Law ... His life will be led by the law of his own divine nature.'[43] This vision, from the ideal of an anarchist society free of state authority to the promise of spiritual

38 Ibid., p. 618.

39 Ibid.

40 Ibid., p. 679.

41 Ibid., p. 615.

42 Ibid., p. 685.

43 Sri Aurobindo, *The Human Cycle*, p. 347.

freedom that transcends the artificial regulation of politics, power and law, comes from Vivekananda.

At the same time that Aurobindo was writing, in the first quarter of this century, two other intellectual giants emerged on the national scene—Rabindranath Tagore and Mohandas Gandhi. As in the case of Vivekananda and Aurobindo, their contribution to Indian life ranged far beyond their theories of politics and power, yet their controversy over these two ideas deserves to be regarded as an unusually rich component of India's ideological tradition. Their debate was perhaps so fruitful because they shared so many basic attitudes on politics and power.

Before Gandhi had formulated his own political thought, Tagore published in 1904 an important essay entitled 'Society and State'. Tagore emulates Vivekananda's formulation, first in the sharp demarcation drawn between society and the state, and second, by associating the former with Indian civilization, and the latter with the British.

> The vital strength in different civilizations is variously embodied. The heart of a country lies wherever the people's welfare is centred. A blow aimed at that point is fatal for the whole country. In England the overthrow of the State might mean peril for the nation—that is why politics there is such a serious affair. In our country there would be danger only when the social body, samaj, becomes crippled ... England relies on the State for everything, from the relief of the destitute to the religious education of the public, whereas our country depends on the people's sense of duty. Therefore, England has to exist by keeping the State alive while we exist by preserving our social consciousness ... The government in our country has no relationship with our society and no place in the social organization, so that whatever we may seek from it must be bought at the expense of a certain freedom.[44]

---

44 Rabindranath Tagore, 'Society and State', in *Towards Universal Man* (London: Asia Publishing House, 1961), pp. 51–52.

Five years later, in *Hind Swaraj* (1909), Gandhi accepted the basic distinctions made between society and state, and India and the West, set forth by Vivekananda and Tagore. Indeed, if anything, he drew the dichotomies between the spiritual, moral fabric of Indian society, and the violent, politically corrupt nature of the European state even more dramatically than any of his predecessors. He reserved his harshest language for the English parliamentary system,[45] and described all Western political power as 'brute force'.[46] Ancient Indian society was idealized, where 'kings and swords were inferior to the sword of ethics', and people enjoyed an organic social existence in small villages independently of the abuses of political institutions.[47]

As Gandhi became increasingly involved in politics, he maintained his view of its corrupt nature in the West and often seemed ambivalent about whether it might be practised rightly in India. At best, it was an impure, threatening activity. Politics, according to him, was like a snake encircling a human being; it was not possible to get out of its clutches. So, to 'wrestle' with it was the only way out.[48]

Later, Gandhi would conclude his autobiography (1928) with his famous defence that he had been drawn into politics irresistibly in his pursuit of truth,[49] but the overriding tone in Gandhi's discussions of politics is of its subordinate, inferior status. Thus, shortly after his most successful political campaign, he could write:

---

45 *CWMG* 10:16

46 Ibid. Compare Gandhi's use of 'brute force' in 'Brute Force', pp. 42–47, with his conceptualization of 'soul-force or truth force' in 'Passive Resistance', pp. 47–53, and his identification of 'brute force' as a weapon of the extremists (p. 50). It is clear that the extremists have been infected by British methods.

47 Ibid., pp. 37–38.

48 Gandhi, *Young India*, 12 May 1920, *CWMG* 17:406.

49 Ibid., 39:401.

My work of social reform was in no way less or subordinate to political work. The fact is, when I saw that to a certain extent my social work would be impossible without the help of political work, I took to the latter and only to the extent that it helped the former. I must, therefore, confess that work of social reform or self-purification of this nature is a hundred times dearer to me than what is called purely political work.[50]

For both Gandhi and Tagore, swaraj meant more than mere political independence; it meant India's spiritual liberation through a fundamental change in each individual's moral perception. This could hardly be achieved through legislative reforms. Tagore's comment on this reflects as well his generally poor view of the potential force of law:

Our woes, we fondly imagine, can be ended by legislation, and we can become full-fledged human beings when we obtain seats in the legislature. But a nation's progress is not achieved mechanically. It cannot be achieved until we are prepared to pay the price.[51]

Politics and law were inevitably 'mechanical', 'external' and 'artificial', and usually corrupt and degraded. The 'price' for both Tagore and Gandhi must be paid in self-sacrifice, for that alone could produce the internal self-purification required for swaraj.

In all these respects, Tagore and Gandhi were in profound agreement. Their differences came over the issue of power. Gandhi believed that 'power is of two kinds'[52]—one based on physical force, the other rooted in satya and ahimsa, 'truth-force'. Tagore, conversely, argued in his classic letter to Gandhi of 12 April 1919, at the outset of the Mahatma's first national campaign in India: 'Power in all its forms

---

50 Ibid., 47:246.

51 Tagore, *Towards Universal Man*, p. 172.

52 *CWMG* 25:563.

is irrational, it is like the horse that drags the carriage blind-folded ...
The danger inherent in all force grows stronger when it is likely to gain
success, for then it becomes temptation.'[53] At the end of the letter,
Tagore grew more conciliatory by acknowledging Gandhi's struggle
against an 'overwhelming material power' that 'scoffs at the power of
the spirit' and the rightness of his attempt to 'purge [India's] present-
day politics of its feebleness'.[54]

Yet, Tagore's suspicion of politics and power increased as Gandhi
pursued his aim of independence, and at the height of Gandhi's non-
cooperation campaign of 1921, Tagore launched a salvo entitled 'The
Call of Truth', which is, perhaps, unparalleled in Indian political
literature for its eloquence. In it, Tagore concedes that 'to make the
country our own by means of our creative power is indeed a great
call'.[55] But the use of this power must be purely moral and not political,
for politics and truth will not mix. Gandhi's supreme difficulty in
responding to this charge was that he had himself set truth as his
highest goal, and had acknowledged that the practice of politics meant
to 'wrestle with [the] snake', that power can be deadly poisonous, and
even the best of men may be bitten. He could only seek to justify his
leadership with the assertion that 'my politics are not corrupt, they are
inextricably bound up with truth'.[56] It is Tagore who gets the better of
this debate, for Gandhi is arguing with not only Rabindranath, but
against a tradition, and ultimately with a part of himself.

---

53 Rabindranath Tagore in R.K. Prabhu and R. Kelkar (eds.), *Truth
   Called Them Differently (Tagore–Gandhi Controversy)* (Ahmedabad:
   Navajivan Publishing House, 1961), p. 14.

54 Ibid., p. 16.

55 Tagore, *Towards Universal Man*, p. 260.

56 Gandhi, as quoted in D.G. Tendulkar, *Mahatma: Life of Mohandas
   Karamchand Gandhi* (8 vols.), Vol. III (Delhi: Government of India,
   Publications Division, 1961), p. 113.

However, perhaps Gandhi's best response to Tagore came not within the context of this debate but rather in another aspect of his conceptualization of politics and power. This came with his development of a theory of decentralization, which his ideological tradition lacked before him. The theory was based, in part, on one main theme in the tradition, an idea that had been set forth first by Vivekananda, and then expanded by Aurobindo and Tagore. This was the concept of 'unity in diversity', which Tagore called 'the inmost creed of India'.[57] Aurobindo had explained that human communities should be formed on 'one essential principle of nature—diversity in unity',[58] and we must seek to realize the free play of interests and ideas that necessarily permeate all human relationships. Vivekananda and Aurobindo insisted that this free exchange need not give way to conflict and competition, as so often happened in the West, but could be grounded in an enlightened sense of spiritual unity. For if individuals are allowed the freedom to express and pursue their interests, they will gradually discover their identity of interests, as part of a spiritual oneness, that transcends all sense of separateness.[59]

Gandhi believed that he had discovered the essence of this principle early in his career, in South Africa, when he succeeded in resolving a legal dispute by discovering a common interest. This, he said, 'taught me to appreciate the beauty of compromise. I saw in later life that this spirit was an essential part of Satyagraha.'[60] On the basis of this insight, he constructed a theory of human nature that emphasized

---

57 Tagore, *Towards Universal Man*, p. 65.

58 Aurobindo, *Ideal of Human Unity*, p. 560.

59 Vivekananda, *Works*, Vol. 2 (1963), p. 153; Vol. 5 (1959), pp. 278, 536.

60 *CWMG* 39:122.

people's capacities for compromise and mutual aid if these are allowed to develop freely.

In agreement with others in his ideological tradition, as well as with Western anarchists like Kropotkin and Tolstoy, Gandhi argued that the state represented the greatest obstacle to our realization of both individual freedom and social harmony. 'The State represents violence in a concentrated form. The individual has a soul, but as the State is a soulless machine, it can never be weaned from violence to which it owes its very existence.'[61] In the ideal society, 'there is no political power because there is no State', but in striving towards that ideal, we may decrease the scope of violence and political power and increase the sphere of individual freedom and voluntary action by decentralizing the state's authority. Gandhi says that he views 'with the greatest fear' the increasing centralization of power in most states because this 'does the greatest harm to mankind by destroying individuality which lies at the root of all progress'.[62] Therefore, 'if India is to evolve along non-violent lines, it will have to decentralize' because 'centralization as a system is inconsistent with a non-violent structure of society'.[63] Gandhi does not delineate the precise functions that would be retained by the central government; the important point is that he advocated for independent India 'the maximum possible decentralization of the political and economic power and resources of the state'.[64] Equally important, this position places Gandhi squarely in line with the thought of Vivekananda, Aurobindo and Tagore, who share with him

---

61 Ibid., 59:318.

62 Ibid., 59:319.

63 M.K. Gandhi, *Harijan*, 18 January 1942, p. 5.

64 J. Bandyopadhyaya, *Social and Political Thought of Gandhi* (Bombay: Allied Publishers, 1969), p. 89.

suspicion of state authority and a firm desire for its decentralization based on their common attitudes towards politics and power.

Ideas of Freedom in Post-Independence India: Vinoba Bhave

In the first edition of this book, the examination of modern India's intellectual tradition was drawn from examples from the pre-independence period. From this perspective, the strong antipathy that Vivekananda, Aurobindo, Tagore and Gandhi demonstrate towards state authority might be attributed to their historical situation, that their thought understandably developed in opposition to the British Raj and the oppressive nature of that imperial authority. It is evident from their 'East vs. West' theory that this was the case.

However, as we move now to two theorists, largely of independent India, Vinoba Bhave and J.P. Narayan, and observe how they continue this intellectual tradition, it can be seen that the presence of the British is not a necessary condition for the survival of this particular line of thought. Indeed, the tradition not only survived, it also flourished for a while in independent India, enjoying the support of the country's foremost theorists since 1947. In the previous chapter on M.N. Roy, it was seen that this mode of thinking appeared in Roy's political theory of Radical Humanism as he formulated it mostly after independence. The enduring spirit and content of this tradition may be attributed, first, to the strength of its development during the nationalist period, second, to the continuing presence of a centralized state authority, and third, to the high quality and independent spirit of those theorists who have perpetuated it.

Vinayak Narahari ('Vinoba') Bhave (1895–1982) ably articulated attitudes towards freedom, politics and power that were representative of his intellectual tradition. Vinoba joined Gandhi's circle as early as 1916, but not until much later did he initiate the term 'total revolution', in the sense of a movement of change that must transform 'all aspects of life'.[65] In 1951–52, he became internationally renowned for starting his Bhoodan and Gramdan ('land and village gifts') movements. As an expansion of the theory and practice of sarvodaya ('universal uplift', a term coined by Gandhi as early as 1908), Vinoba trekked throughout India to persuade large landholders to transfer ownership to landless poor peasants. The movement reached its peak in 1969, then declined after Vinoba withdrew as its leader.

Yet, his political thought remains an important part of the tradition, especially when compared with the others in the group of seven selected here. Although grounded in religion, Vinoba's sweeping revolutionary aim was remarkably close to Roy's Radical Humanism, because the goal of each was nothing less than 'to mould a new man ... to change human life and create a new world'. For Vinoba, the departure of the British had not brought Indian society any closer to the realization of sarvodaya, and the main obstacle, as for Roy, remained the same: centralized government. 'Sarvodaya does not mean good government or majority rule, it means freedom from government, it means decentralisation of power.'[66] Gandhi had correctly defined the value of swaraj as necessary for sarvodaya. Swaraj meant 'ruling your own self', which implies 'not to allow any outside power in the world to exercise control over oneself', and 'not to exercise power over any other. These two things together make swaraj—no submission and no exploitation.' Government, with all its supposed services and benefits, inevitably violates this value of swaraj because it demands obedience. 'That is why my voice is raised in opposition to good government ... People know very well that bad government should not be allowed, and everywhere they protest against it. But what seems to me to be wrong

---

65 Vinoba Bhave, *Revolutionary Sarvodaya* (Bombay: Bharatiya Vidya Bhavan, 1964), p. 1.

66 Vinoba Bhave, *Democratic Values* (Kashi: Sarva Seva Sangh Prakashan, 1962), p. 3.

is that we should allow ourselves to be governed at all, even by a good government.'[67]

Vinoba distinguishes three theories of government to better clarify his own. The first desires the eventual 'withering away' of the state but sanctions the present use of maximum state power in order to achieve its goal. 'Those who accept this theory are totalitarians in the first stage and anarchists in the final stage.' The second theory argues that government has always existed and must remain. The best course is to organize it so that everyone will receive some benefit. The third, Vinoba's theory, shares with the first the ultimate goal of a 'stateless society', but refuses to accept its means of attaining it. 'On the contrary, we propose to proceed by decentralising administration and authority.' It may take a while to 'advance from good government to freedom from government', but it is urgently necessary to begin this movement to the 'final stage' where 'there would be no coercion but a purely moral authority'.[68] Vinoba argues further that those who advocate the second theory (e.g., those on the Indian Planning Commission) rely heavily on centralization of power. However, this leads the Indian people in the wrong direction, for 'centralised arrangements will never bring us nearer to a stateless society'; they only foster an addiction to politics and power. The immediate aim of the sarvodaya movement, therefore, is that 'production, distribution, defence, education—everything should be localised. The centre should have the least possible authority. We shall thus achieve decentralisation through regional self-sufficiency ... We must therefore start at once to introduce decentralisation, and this will be the basis of all our planning.'[69]

At the centre of Vinoba's conceptualization of freedom, politics and power lies his basic distinction between 'raj-niti', the politics of power

67 Ibid., pp. 12–13.

68 Ibid., p. 29.

69 Ibid., p. 30.

and lok-niti, 'the ethics of democracy'.[70] Vinoba believes that 'the world is at present in the clutches of centralised [state] power',[71] and people must learn that there is another source of change at their disposal, that 'nonviolence is a great power', the 'power of the Self',[72] and this can be found through pursuit of lok-niti, which strives to use 'the potential powers of the citizen'.[73] Raj-niti is enamoured of the wrong kind of power, and, in its lust for acquisition of it, there ensues 'constant struggle' among parties and politicians, elections marked by a 'ceaseless rivalry for power'. Lok-niti would abandon political parties and elections, arrive at decisions through consensus and forge an identity of interests that would ensure continuing social harmony.[74] Vinoba calls the power of lok-niti—which, following Gandhi, is necessarily nonviolent—a 'third force', distinguished from both violent coercion and 'the force of law'.[75] For Vinoba, as with others in his tradition, the impersonal force of law must be inferior to the personal influence of dedicated social workers who 'maintain the purity of their own personal lives', and shape a sarvodaya society with a 'third force' that is legitimate not because it has legal sanction, but rather because it is 'uncontaminated by any lust for [political] power'.[76]

A striking aspect of Vinoba's ideal society is the emphasis which he places on consensus rather than conflict. He repeatedly states that people must transcend 'sects, castes, parties, groups or isms' and deplores the fact that India, at present, is 'fragmented by innumerable

---

70 Ibid., p. xi.

71 Ibid., p. 117.

72 Bhave, *Revolutionary Sarvodaya*, pp. 49–50.

73 Bhave, *Democratic Values*, p. xi.

74 Ibid., pp. 86–88.

75 Ibid., pp. 212–13.

76 Ibid., p. 223.

divisions of race, caste, colour, religion and political ideologies. We need social integration if swaraj is to survive.'[77] This spirit of integration and consensus cannot be imposed by law or state power; it is attainable through the kind of voluntary effort exemplified by sarvodaya workers who encourage a genuine transformation of values. 'Every individual has to learn to put the interests of the village before his own' and hence foster an organic conception of society so integrated that 'if every limb were to function smoothly, the whole body would function properly'.[78] The aims of lok-niti can never be to 'produce conflict' but always to achieve social harmony because 'cooperation is an eternal principle of life'.[79] This argument for an organic society and social consensus runs consistently through the Indian ideological tradition. It parallels directly positions taken in the West by anarchists, such as Kropotkin and Tolstoy. But because it is essentially an anarchist conception, attacking state authority and championing natural, spontaneous forces of social harmony, it is directly opposed to the kind of political consensus advocated by apologists of a centralized state, such as Rousseau and Hegel. Like the Western anarchists, the Indian theorists connect their idea of consensus with a vision of small communities, free from coercive political institutions, precisely because people are inherently capable of organizing themselves without a strong government. It is not surprising, then, that Vinoba uses Aurobindo's term 'spiritual anarchism' to identify his political philosophy.[80]

---

77 Suresh Ram, *Vinoba and His Mission: Being an Account of the Rise and Growth of the Bhoodan Yajna Movement* (Rajghat, Kashi: Akhil Bharat Sarva Seva Sangh, 1962), p. 208.

78 Bhave, *Revolutionary Sarvodaya*, p. 45.

79 Vinoba Bhave, *Swaraj Sastra* (Rajghat, Varanasi: Sarva Seva Sangh Prakhashan, 1962), p. 63.

80 Vinoba Bhave, quoted in Vishwanath Tandon, *The Social and Political Philosophy of Sarvodaya After Gandhiji* (Rajghat, Varanasi: Sarva Seva Sangh Prakashan, 1965), p. 124.

Jayaprakash Narayan's Intellectual Journey

Jayaprakash ('JP') Narayan (1902–1979), India's most popular post-independence political figure next to Nehru, left the ruling Congress Party in 1948, then in 1954, abandoned politics altogether in favour of Gandhian 'constructive work' (sarvodaya) at the village level. His urge to spur sweeping political reforms resurfaced in the mid-1970s, and he played a major role both in precipitating Indira Gandhi's 'Emergency' of 1975 to 1977 and in leading the coalition that defeated her party in 1977. In 1979, the coalition broke apart, and soon thereafter, JP died of kidney and heart failure. His contributions to political thought won him a worldwide audience; even today, they continue to influence those who seek to infuse the economic, social and political life of the future with greater equality, justice, and respect for the individual and the local community.

JP was born in a village in eastern India, now in the state of Bihar. His father, an official superintending the operation of irrigation canals, was required by his work to move from place to place. Probably for health reasons (his eldest son died of cholera, and his eldest daughter succumbed to the plague), he left young JP in his native village with the boy's step-grandmother while the rest of the family moved away. At six, Jayaprakash started his education in the village primary school. When he was nine, his father sent him to the Collegiate School at Patna, Bihar's major city. The shy and dutiful son worked diligently and won a merit scholarship to Patna College at the age of sixteen. He had considered himself a political extremist from the age of fourteen; at nineteen, when Gandhi's non-cooperation movement arrived in Patna, Jayaprakash threw away his schoolbooks and prepared to join the movement. His father wanted him to continue studying and had him enrolled into a newly founded nationalist school called the Bihar Vidyapith.

The following year, in 1922, Gandhi suspended the non-cooperation movement, and Jayaprakash was deeply disillusioned. In addition, he found his new school insufficiently equipped with the apparatus for experiments he needed to carry on his studies in the natural sciences. A friend wrote him from the University of Iowa, urging him to complete his higher education in the United States.

In 1924, at the University of Wisconsin, he discovered the writings of Marx and was especially influenced by Marx's claim to have found the 'inevitable' solution to the problem of poverty. Jayaprakash soon became a regular reader of M.N. Roy's *New Masses* magazine and the US Communist Party's *Daily Worker*. He switched from natural science to sociology, and from Wisconsin to Ohio State, where he took his BA in 1928 and MA in 1929. He wanted to go on for a PhD, but his mother was critically ill, and so he returned home.

At once, he was drawn into the mainstream of nationalist politics: his wife took him to meet Gandhi; he met Nehru, the next Congress president, and the two became friends. Nehru invited him and his wife to live in Allahabad and help with the work of the Congress, and in 1932, when most other leaders of the Congress were in jail, he served as its general secretary until he, too, was arrested, tried and imprisoned. In 1934, he and other Leftists founded a group within the Congress that they named the Congress Socialist Party; Jayaprakash became its chief organizer and travelled all over India to recruit and teach new members. From 1936, he encouraged the newly legalized communists to enrol as Congress socialists, but by 1940 he was fed up with their manoeuvring for power and sudden changes in policy in obedience to dictates from the Soviet Union. At the same time, he was impatient with the Congress under Gandhi's moderating influence—so much so that he courted and received two successive prison sentences from 1940 to 1942 for his fiery speeches urging factory workers to start a general strike, stop paying taxes, and set up their own police, courts and government.

JP became a national hero in 1942 when he and five other prisoners climbed over the seventeen-foot-high wall of their jail on the night of Diwali (the festival of lights) and escaped capture. Undetected, he visited the major cities of India to instruct guerrilla fighters and issue proclamations urging struggle against British rule. Within a year, he was arrested at Lahore and subjected to prolonged torture in a vain attempt to make him talk about his activities. Although he was released only in 1946, a year after most of the Congress leaders, he remained determined to oust the British through a massive uprising of the people.

Thirteen years younger than Nehru, equally intellectual and even more idealistic, Jayaprakash could easily have become Nehru's right-hand man and ultimately his successor as India's prime minister. Yet he shared that part of Gandhi which could instinctively rebel against the official exercise of political power (he was never a candidate for public office). In 1948, he led his socialist followers out of the Congress, and from then on, steadily lost interest in political activity. Instead, he gravitated towards Gandhian work at the village level, beginning with Vinoba's Bhoodan movement. In 1954, he founded his own ashram in a rural part of Bihar to try to apply Gandhi's methods of village economic improvement, and by the 1960s, he was sending workers to train in Israel and Japan in order to adapt modern technology to villagers' needs.

JP never ceased to reflect and speak on his ideals for India's future. At the core of his vision lay a blend of Marx's and Gandhi's dreams: unselfish and altruistic individuals living in self-supporting communities, undisturbed by either centralized government or exploitative capitalism. He repeatedly refused opportunities to serve in the government, but his restless nature moved him to try to solve or mediate problems in one area after another—Kashmir, Nagaland, and throughout his home state of Bihar. He played the role of gadfly to both state and central governments, and attracted huge crowds of youthful sympathizers when he called for an end to corruption, police terrorism, and the misuse of power. The size of these crowds, and his vague but catchy call for 'total revolution' in 1975, provoked an

extreme clampdown by Indira Gandhi and her government that left a
scar on India's record as a liberal-democratic polity.

Because JP articulates the essential values of modern India's
intellectual tradition with exceptional clarity and directness, an
exposition of his theory may be used as a summation of that discourse,
not only with respect to its concepts of freedom, politics and power but
also to the entire cluster of ideas that it has developed. JP begins, like
all anarchists,[81] with a theory of human nature as benign: capacities for
destructive behaviour obviously exist, but if motives of compassion and
nonviolence, creativity and cooperation, are cultivated and enforced by
society, then people can unquestionably realize the essential spirit of
goodness that lies within them. With the proper example and education
to encourage them, individuals will choose to follow 'good men' and
'noble efforts'.[82] This, in turn, will lead to the evolution of the kind of
nonviolent community that Gandhi first called sarvodaya.

Methods of change commonly used by political regimes cannot
create a sarvodaya social order. JP's departure from Marxism, and the
extent of his intellectual journey, become evident with his sharp critique

81 James Joll, *The Anarchists* (London: Eyre and Spottiswoode, 1964),
    'The fundamental idea that man is by nature good and that it is
    institutions that corrupt him remains the basis of all anarchist thought'
    (p. 30). Joll is one of the few analysts of anarchist thought who includes
    recognition and comment on Indian anarchism. See his brief mention
    of Gandhi, Vinoba and JP (pp. 277–78).

82 Jayaprakash Narayan, *A Picture of Sarvodaya Social Order* (Tanjore:
    Sarvodaya Prachuralaya, 1961), p. 6. JP says: 'Man is essentially good
    and not bad.' A valuable exposition of Indian anarchism is by Geoffrey
    Ostergaard and Melville Currell, *The Gentle Anarchists: A Study of
    the Leaders of the Sarvodaya Movement for Non-Violent Revolution in
    India* (1971). This was followed by his *Nonviolent Revolution in India*
    (1985). These explore the leadership of Vinoba and JP, including their
    differences.

of Bolshevism, following the ideas of Gandhi, Roy and Ambedkar. The similarities in this instance alone are remarkable. For all three, the example of the Russian revolution and the Soviet state demonstrates the bankruptcy of violence, which only tends to 'ensure the victory of the party that is more skilled in its use', establishing an 'iron grip on the people', undermining all attempts at democracy and the attainment of social justice or equality.[83] Parliamentary democracies, on the other hand, are ineffective in their reliance on legislation. As the case of India's political system shows, legislation for the redistribution of land has failed because there has not occurred a corresponding change in moral values to enforce it. 'Law cannot come into effect without public opinion' to enforce it; 'legislation without conversion [first] is a dead letter'.[84] Echoing attitudes toward law and social change that hark back to Vivekananda, JP writes:

> It is not institutions, not laws, not political systems, not constitutions which create good people. For that you require a widespread process of education understood in the widest sense of the word. Education does not mean academic education; but the improving of human beings through service, love, examples, preaching, reasoning and argument.[85]

JP consolidates many of the ideas of his tradition in his most important work, *A Plea for Reconstruction of Indian Polity.* This book has been given close scrutiny by commentators in and outside of India,[86] and the

---

83 Ibid., pp. 4–5.

84 Ibid., p. 9.

85 Ibid., p. 151.

86 See, for example, Morris-Jones, 'The Unhappy Utopia—JP in Wonderland', in *Politics Mainly Indian*, pp. 97–106. This critique of JP's *Reconstruction* first appeared in *Economic and Political Weekly*, 25

analysis of it here will be confined to the respects that it serves to clarify or enlarge India's intellectual tradition. The treatise constitutes JP's magnum opus and, as a statement of political thought, moves much beyond Vinoba's writings and qualifies him as an important member of this group of seven. Like others in this assembly, JP is concerned with reconstituting his past, deriving enduring truths from the lessons of 'ancient Indian polity'. This was, as noted above, precisely the task that Aurobindo undertook, and JP borrows extensively and explicitly from Aurobindo's work, praising 'that extraordinary, intuitive sweep of his vision [which] has laid bare the true nature of the foundations of Indian polity'.[87] On the basis of Aurobindo's work, JP contends that in ancient India, the political order was founded on the system of the self-governing village community which lasted with remarkable 'sufficiency and solidity' until it was 'recently steamrollered out of existence by the ruthless and lifeless machinery of the British bureaucratic system'.[88] Classical India had discovered the key 'principle of an organically self-determining communal life', and today it is only 'a question of an ancient country finding its lost soul again'.[89]

Gandhi had contended in *Hind Swaraj* that Britain had seduced India into selling its soul to the demonic spirit of modern civilization, which included the false charms of parliamentary government. JP extends this line of argument, observing that independent India institutionalized a form of government that lacks both traditional sources and theoretical support from any major Indian political

---

June 1960, and prompted an exchange between William Carpenter and W.H. Morris-Jones, published in *Economic and Political Weekly*, 4 February 1961.

87 Jayaprakash Narayan, *A Plea for Reconstruction of Indian Polity* (Rajghat, Kashi: Akhil Bharat Sarva Seva Sangh, 1959), p. 22.

88 Ibid., p. 22.

89 Ibid., p. 26.

theorist. JP's condemnation of parliamentary democracy is as sweeping and categorical as any made by an anarchist, Eastern or Western. He draws from a variety of political commentators, European, American and Indian, to indict the intrinsic defects of the parliamentary system. The electoral system pretends to represent the wishes of an informed public, but instead serves only to fragment the body politic, confusing voters who are cynically 'manipulated by powerful, centrally controlled parties, with the aid of high finance and diabolically clever methods and super media.'

Consequently, only the 'forces and interests behind the parties and propaganda machines' are represented, while the masses are subjected to continuing exploitation, and the society becomes increasingly atomized. But, perhaps the most serious fault of parliamentary democracy lies in its 'inherent tendency toward centralism'. Just as Gandhi had believed that 'centralisation as a system is inconsistent with a non-violent structure of society', so JP saw centralized authority as invariably fostering vast impersonal bureaucracies and huge interest groups that made 'organic integration' impossible. The main remedy for this is to scrap the parliamentary system and replace it with a 'communitarian democracy' and decentralized political economy.[90]

In his conceptualization of this communitarian democracy, JP consistently recapitulates the central attitudes of his ideological tradition. He wants to avoid 'competitiveness' because it is necessarily exploitative, and achieve instead a 'cooperative and co-sharing', 'integrated' social order in which there would be a true 'harmonization of interests'. Only a 'deliberate and bold process of devolution and decentralization', shaping all aspects of social development, may attain this goal. It needs to be initiated by 'hundreds of thousands of voluntary workers' who understand that the basic task is one 'of moral regeneration to be brought about by example, service, sacrifice and

---

90 Ibid., pp. 66–68.

love'.'[91] Although JP is more specific about the structural organization of his decentralized system than any of his predecessors,[92] the theory that underpins it goes straight back to Vivekananda.

Among those ideas that link JP most conclusively with his Indian intellectual tradition are his preoccupations with the corrupting influence of political power and the compelling need to find a path of pure moral action. He says, for example, that he soured on Russian communism for reasons that might have been felt by Gandhi, on the one hand, or M.N. Roy, on the other. For JP, Marxism among the Soviets quickly degenerated into 'a struggle for power among the ruling class', which assumed the familiar 'pattern by which a party comes to power with high and noble ideals' and then eventually crashes into

---

91 Ibid., p. 107.

92 JP's ideas on the organization of his polity, often referred to as Panchayati Raj, are contained in various collections of his writings, including *Towards Total Revolution* (see following note) and more succinctly in *Socialism, Sarvodaya and Democracy: Selected Works of Jayaprakash Narayan*, ed. Bimla Prasad (London: Asia Publishing House, 1964), especially the essay 'Swaraj for the People', pp. 239–74. Ghanshyam Shah examined JP's Bihar Sarvodaya movement (1974–75), asking whether it was revolutionary or reformist. He concluded that 'despite the claims of being a "Total Revolution" it was essentially a protest movement, aiming at certain limited reforms of the existing order' in 'Revolution, Reform or Protest? A Study of the Bihar Movement: III', *Economic and Political Weekly* 12, no. 17 (23 April 1977): 695–702. The present author was a witness to this movement and believes that while it largely failed, interviews with JP and the examination of his writings show that the theory was revolutionary and JP's leadership exemplary, as described here and in the Memoir (see at the beginning of this book).

a state of 'demoralisation'.[93] In 1952–53, JP explained his departure from Marxism partly as a result of his 'shock' over the international experience of communism, and especially with the Soviet example. He denounced 'the totalitarian distortions of socialism in Russia', and blamed them on 'not only the heavy concentration of political but also of economic power'.[94] From his knowledge of world politics, he drew this lesson in November 1952: 'With the ghastly spectacle of the growth of totalitarianism with its leviathan state on a world scale, we realised that decentralisation and devolution of economic power must be accepted as the essential tenet of democratic socialism.'[95]

As a national leader perpetually in opposition to the Congress government throughout the 1950s, JP remained primarily concerned with the abuse of political power in India. In February 1957, on the eve of the second general election, JP issued 'an appeal to the voters', warning them that 'the most important issue this time is that of the absoluteness of Congress power'. He cited Lord Acton's dictum on power as 'one of the most profound political truths', and declared that 'concentration of every form of power must be destroyed'.[96] Eighteen years later, a month before Indira Gandhi declared the Emergency and imprisoned JP, he was still citing Lord Acton, and still convinced that 'the present all-pervading corruption has its roots in politics and power'. The chief task before the Indian people was to discover a way 'to prevent power from being corrupted in the future'.[97]

JP never saw this task as impossible. He reiterated that the worst evils of power come only when it is centralized. 'The problem,' he insisted,

---

93 J.P. Narayan, *Towards Total Revolution*, Vol. 1 of 6 vols. (Surrey: Richmond Publishing Co., 1978), p. 153.

94 Ibid., Vol. 2, pp. 218–19.

95 Ibid., p. 180.

96 Ibid., pp. 253, 255.

97 Ibid., Vol. 4, p. 127.

is always with 'concentration of too much power in the hands of a small group of persons', with 'more and more power concentrated in the hands of the executive, which in reality means one person, the Prime Minister'.[98] The first aim of the sarvodaya worker, therefore, must be to 'diffuse political and economic power and decentralise the politico-economic structure'.[99] In December 1974, during his leadership of the student movement in Bihar, he asserted that he did not advocate the disappearance of all political power but, rather, the placement of it where it belongs, in the hands of the people. The struggle for freedom depends on them. Following others in this group, however different the language, JP's thought distinguished between legitimate and illegitimate forms of power:

> What you see happening in Bihar is a struggle between 'chhatra shakti' (student power) and 'jan shakti' (people's power) on the one hand and 'rajya shakti' (state power) on the other. And the struggle is not for the capture of power ... but for the purification of government and for fashioning instruments and conditions for taming and controlling power...[100]

JP's conceptualization of power defines with commendable lucidity the attitudes of his intellectual tradition, a tradition that may surely be utopian in spirit, but its theoretical premises are at least the clearest and most consistent that India has produced in the last century. Its central concerns are familiar to Western political theory; they deal with the crucial issue of finding a legitimate basis for the exercise of power and the achievement of freedom through 'total revolution'. Like the others,

---

98   Ibid., Vol. 3, p. 79.

99   Ibid., Vol. 3, p. 79.

100 Ibid., Vol. 4, p. 110.

JP did not pretend to construct a systematic philosophy. Nor does this study of the group and its tradition of discourse make such a pretence.

Fundamental criticisms have been made of JP's thought by many of those familiar with his work, as expressed by W.H. Morris-Jones. A main concern running through Morris-Jones' critique is that there are elements in JP's thought, such as his insistence on 'systematic mass participation' and 'identification of rulers and ruled', that some political theorists have tended to 'prepare the way for totalitarianism'. In the case of Rousseau:

> Satisfied with nothing less than each man retaining his 'freedom' by taking full part in the laying down of laws he is to obey, he ends by asserting that some men will obtain their 'freedom' by being coerced; ordinary language and ordinary people both suffer when such violence is done to them.[101]

It is fair to ask if there is any explicit evidence in JP's writings that he has either defined freedom in a manner similar to Rousseau or shown himself insensitive to the dangers of totalitarianism. The answer must be 'no' on both counts. JP consistently defines freedom in this sense and that drove him away from Marxism.[102] Moreover, his writings are alive with warnings against totalitarian government. At the end of his journey, in his last eloquent yet tragic writing, *Prison Diary*, he inveighs throughout against his main foe, a prime minister who destroyed democracy, substituting for it a 'totalitarian system'.[103] Here, he argues for liberty in the fullest sense, and especially for freedom of the press.[104]

---

101 Morris-Jones, *Politics Mainly Indian*, p. 102.

102 Narayan, *Picture of Sarvodaya Social Order*, p. 112.

103 J.P. Narayan, *Prison Diary*, edited by A.B. Shah (Seattle: University of Washington Press, 1977), p. 1.

104 Ibid., pp. 105–6.

Yet Morris-Jones believes that there is an inescapable and intrinsic danger to freedom and liberal democracy in JP's ideal of mass participation:

> Men want many things from governments and they may want to be governed in certain ways, but they do not want to do the governing. The dogmatic democrat who insists that they shall do so is bound to become a tyrant—or pave the way for one.[105]

Then Morris-Jones returns to his theme of JP's parallels with Rousseau by linking his critique of the ideas of freedom and mass participation in JP's thought with his concept of consensus:

> Moreover, the stress on consensus seems to imply a peculiar view of the common good. It is thought of as something single and simple—discernible to men of insight and goodwill, attainable (as Rousseau again believed) through the silencing of particular or selfish interests.
>
> But is this really our experience? Is the position not rather that the common good is something towards which we can approximate only through a forthright expression of all relevant clashing interests and their reconciliation so far as is possible? The pretence that interests do not clash, that a common interest is somehow always present and only needs to be uncovered, is likely to yield a good that is far from common. And there is no community, however organic it may be, without different interests ... Consensus is a fair name for what could be an ugly reality.[106]

At the outset of this chapter, it was suggested that when JP and other Indians of his intellectual tradition are compared with Western political

---

105 Morris-Jones, *Politics Mainly Indian*, p. 103.

106 Ibid., p. 105.

theorists, they are allied not with the stream of thought that flows from Plato to Rousseau or Hegel, but rather with Western anarchists, and that the Indian intellectual tradition itself constitutes a significant body of anarchist thought. The central differences between the Plato–Rousseau/Hegel statists and the anarchists hinge on the concepts of politics and power.

Rousseau, following Plato, envisaged his political leaders or 'law-givers', attaining an advanced stage of consciousness, and then ruling with 'sublime reason, which is beyond the understanding of the vulgar in order to compel by divine authority those whom human prudence could not move'.[107] No anarchist, Eastern or Western, could ever justify such a conception of leadership, although we have seen how M.N. Roy found Plato's theory of Guardians appealing to some degree. Yet, even Roy could not countenance centralized state control. For Plato and Rousseau or Hegel, the unique capacity of the state was to create and nurture a life of virtue. Outside the realm of politics, justice and morality could not exist, and the role of legitimate authority was sanctified.

This is at the opposite pole from the anarchists' perception, for whom politics and power remained not only inherently suspect but also singularly incapable of producing the virtuous individual or society. If there is a 'politics' of lok-niti, it represents a kind that Plato and Rousseau would certainly regard as anaemic or impotent; they would be even less satisfied with the Indian view of the necessary limitations on law as a force in shaping human behaviour.

The emphasis which Plato and Rousseau place on the unique role of politics is decisive and nowhere more than in their view of the individual. For Rousseau, each individual 'puts in common his person and all his powers under the supreme direction of the general will', and

---

107 Rousseau, *Political Writings*, pp. 44–45.

so each becomes 'an indivisible part of the whole'.[108] The 'civil state' is thus born, with 'natural liberty' replaced by 'civil liberty'. For all of JP's stress on mass participation and the organic community, there is no language anywhere in his writings or in any of the others in his tradition that compares with Rousseau's description of the supremacy of the general will, the sovereignty of the civil state, or his contention that 'anything which breaks the unity of society is worthless'.[109]

On the contrary, the writings of those in the Indian intellectual tradition are replete with statements like Vivekananda's that 'any system which seeks to destroy individuality is in the long run disastrous'[110] or Gandhi's that 'no society can possibly be built on a denial of individual freedom'.[111] Within the context of this intellectual tradition, then, there would seem to be no theoretical justification for the creation of the 'ugly reality' that Morris-Jones fears. That sort of sanction comes from other traditions of thought, alien neither to India nor to the West, which rationalize political dictatorship.

These are not the only critical concerns that W.H. Morris-Jones has expressed about JP's thought and those theorists related to it. He levelled a major criticism at this whole line of theory, first in an essay called 'India's Political Idioms', where the idiom or language in India of 'saintly polities' was described and examined:

> ... saintly politics is important as a language of comment rather than of description or practical behaviour ... Its influence is rather

---

108 Ibid., p. 16.

109 Ibid., p. 148.

110 Vivekananda, *Works*, Vol. 4 (1955), p. 82.

111 M.K. Gandhi, 'Plain Thinking and High Living', in *Harijan*, 1 February 1942, p. 27. See also Vinoba Bhave, *Democratic Values*, p. 116: 'Every person must enjoy the fullest liberty for the propagation of his ideas.'

on the standards habitually used by the people at large for judging the performance of politicians. In men's minds, there is an ideal of disinterested selflessness by contrast with which almost all normal conduct can seem very shabby ... it contributes powerfully to several very prevalent attitudes to be found in Indian political life: to a certain withholding of full approval from even the most popular leaders; to a stronger feeling of distrust of and disgust with persons and institutions of authority; finally, to profoundly violent and desperate moods of cynicism and frustration.[112]

Morris-Jones reinforced this criticism in his new preface to his essay on JP with the comment:

Very many people in India who are far too sceptical to embrace JP's full doctrines nevertheless continue to adopt his norms, so that although they do not follow him in striving towards Utopia they use his utopian vision to look upon the functioning reality of everyday Indian politics with scorn and despair. The paradoxical consequence of the idealist is furtherance of cynicism.[113]

He concludes that it may be more constructive for a political theorist to advocate 'instead more modest versions of democracy and emphasizing some of the neglected virtues of the system, imperfect but capable of improvement, which we have with us ...'[114] This is an especially important criticism because it returns us to the view expressed in the

---

112 W.H. Morris-Jones, 'India's Political Idioms', in *Politics and Society in India*, ed. C.H. Philips (London: George Allen and Unwin, 1963), pp. 140–41. This analysis is placed in a larger context in W.H. Morris-Jones, *The Government and Politics of India*, Third revised edition (London: Hutchinson University Library, 1971), pp. 59–61.

113 Morris-Jones, *Politics Mainly Indian*, p. 97.

114 Ibid.

opening epigraph from Morris-Jones targeting the purpose and impact of political theory. Since the dawn of political philosophy, its aim has been to project a 'transcending form of vision' which meant 'thinking about the political society in its corrected fullness, not as it is but as it might be. This essential character of vision served a function for human behaviour. 'Precisely because political theory pictured society in an exaggerated, "unreal" way, it was a necessary complement to action. Precisely because action involved intervention into existing affairs, it sorely needed a perspective of tantalizing possibilities.'[115]

The Indian theorists examined here were, above all, visionaries in that they persistently posed the great Socratic question: 'Which course of life is best?' In their responses, they envisioned human nature gifted with such a panoramic range of capacities that a community based on mutual aid and nonviolence truly offered 'a perspective of tantalizing possibilities'.

It is surely debatable whether their vision is the right one, especially if it encourages, as Morris-Jones feared, cynicism, frustration and despair. Yet, India or any nation, needs a vision, and since independence, the country has been strong on power politics but weak on those ideals that this group of seven expressed. Such visions are not easy to conceive, and even then, they are easily lost. India has been markedly unable to produce any outside the group presented throughout this book. Instead, the nation has been integrated not only sans vision but against a prevailing stream of theory that has persistently called for the quality of freedom that gave its intellectual renaissance unique meaning.

Contemporary India reveals a wide gap between political practice and the outstanding theory produced during its freedom struggle. Therefore, as explicitly stated at the beginning of this chapter, and now in conclusion, the question is whether the challenges and standards posed by its formidable intellectual tradition led by the group of seven

---

115 Wolin, *Politics and Vision*, pp. 20–21.

will have a significant impact on what India's leaders and people do today.

Yet, the conclusion does not stop here by telling India what it must do. As the Introduction suggested by comparing twentieth-century India's exemplary political theory and practice with lesser mass movements, its lessons belong to the world. The Indian renaissance taught us all how liberation of self and system should be conceived. Its nexus of ideas about freedom constitutes a set of values that clarify, in the philosophy of James Tully, 'vicious and virtuous' systems of political theory that transcend Western binary thinking.

The thesis of this book is that this way of thinking about transformational politics provides the seeds to change the planet, including its environment and the well-being of its Indigenous peoples. That lives of all species matter—Gandhi's Hinduism and Ambedkar's Buddhism alike teach this vital truth. This is why we ignore Indian ideas of freedom at our peril.

APPENDIX

Gandhi on Freedom, Rights and Responsibility*

Let each do his duty. If I do my duty, that is, serve myself, I shall be able to serve others. Before I leave you, I will take the liberty of repeating:

(i)   Real swaraj is self-rule or self-control.

(ii) The way to it is passive resistance [satyagraha], that is, soul-force or love-force.

(iii) In order to exert this force, Swadeshi in every sense is necessary.

---

*   This chapter is a revised version of an essay originally published in *Gandhi Marg* 20, no. 2 (July–September 1998): 133–54. The revision extends the analysis of western ideas of freedom, especially relating to Isaiah Berlin's theory, as briefly explained in the Introduction. Here again, I am indebted to inspiring correspondence with Professor James Tully and his chapter entitled 'Two Concepts of Liberty', in *Two Concepts of Liberty: Fifty Years Later*, ed. Bruce Baum and Robert Nichols (New York: Routledge, 2013), pp. 23–51.

(iv) What we want to do should be done, not because we object
      to the English or because we want to retaliate but because it is
      our duty to do so.[1]

These concluding lines from *Hind Swaraj* are so full of meaning that
they might be called the Gandhi sutras. Connections are explicitly
drawn here among Gandhi's key ideas of freedom (swaraj), duty
(Dharma), nonviolent action (Satyagraha), and self-reliance (Swadeshi).
The focus of this chapter is on his theories of swaraj and Dharma and
the conceptual relationships that he constructed between them.

Raghavan Iyer observed:

> Gandhi equated freedom with self-rule because he wished to build
> into the concept of freedom the notion of obligation to others as
> well as to oneself while retaining the element of voluntariness that is
> the very basis of freedom. The notion of self-rule implies voluntary
> internalization of our obligation to others which will be obstructed
> by our placing ourselves at the mercy of our selfish desires.[2]

Iyer states precisely what Gandhi intended and achieved. We may
elaborate his analysis further by examining the content and implications
of this way of viewing freedom and obligation.

European and American political theory has remained split
since the seventeenth century in its conceptualization of freedom
and obligation. The philosophies of Locke and Mill on the one

---

1   M.K. Gandhi, *Hind Swaraj*, included in the *Collected Works of
    Mahatma Gandhi* (Delhi, Government of India: 1994, 100 vols.),
    10:64. Hereafter referred to as *CWMG*. See also M.K. Gandhi, *Hind
    Swaraj and Other Writings*, ed. A.J. Parel (Cambridge: Cambridge
    University Press: 1997), for its valuable introduction and notes.

2   R.N. Iyer, *The Moral and Political Thought of Mahatma Gandhi* (New
    York: Oxford University Press, 1973), p. 349.

side against Rousseau and of Hegel on the other, mark a theoretical schism related to these two concepts so deep that it suggests, in Isaiah Berlin's judgement, 'profoundly divergent and irreconcilable attitudes to the ends of life'.[3] George Sabine has argued that the philosophical differences between Locke and Rousseau on freedom and authority represent 'two democratic traditions', quite distinct from each other.[4] Attempts at reconciling these positions have been unsuccessful and American or British political theorists are sometimes reduced, in Gerald MacCallum's opinion, to making 'the facile assumption that the adherents on one side or the other are never sincere.'[5]

Perhaps Isaiah Berlin has aggravated the problem by concentrating on conflicting theories of 'negative' versus 'positive' liberty. He champions the former and treats the latter as dubious, thus: 'Everything is what it is: liberty is liberty, not equality or fairness or justice or human happiness or a quiet conscience.'[6]

British liberals, following J.S. Mill, appear to share this scepticism about positive liberty. Maurice Cranston affirms Berlin's idea of negative liberty. He defines freedom as meaning an area within which a person can do what one wants and views Rousseau's or Hegel's idea of positive liberty as a distortion.[7] Both Berlin and Cranston object

3   Isaiah Berlin, *Four Essays on Liberty* (London: Oxford University Press, l969), p. 166. See especially James Tully, '"Two Concepts of Liberty" in Context', in *Isaiah Berlin and the Politics of Freedom*, ed. Bruce Baum and Robert Nichols (N.Y.: Routledge, 2014), pp. 23–51.

4   George H. Sabine, 'The Two Democratic Traditions', *The Philosophical Review* 61, no. 4 (October 1952): 451–74.

5   Gerald C. MacCallum, Jr., 'Negative and Positive Freedom', *The Philosophical Review* 76, no. 3 (July 1967): 312–34.

6   Berlin, *Four Essays on Liberty*, p. 125.

7   Maurice Cranston, *Freedom: A New Analysis* (London: Oxford University Press, 1953), pp. 28–29.

to positive freedom because it identifies liberty with discipline. This is contradictory, whether it is self-discipline voluntarily imposed by the individual or political discipline enforced by a state. John Laird put this liberal bias bluntly thus: 'If we are seriously asked to believe that freedom means self-control under the jurisdiction of right reason, it seems clear without further argument that freedom means no such thing.'[8]

Mortimer Adler, in an encyclopaedic study of the idea of freedom, undertaken by The Institute for Philosophical Research, does not reject the concept of positive freedom because, as he observes, it has come from eminent philosophers dating back to Plato. Adler distinguishes between what he calls 'circumstantial' and 'acquired' freedom. The former 'lies in the unhampered actions by which the individual pursues his own good as he sees it and realizes his desires'.[9] It 'looks to the circumstances that affect a man's ability to carry out his wishes'.[10] Adler identifies this position with that of Locke and Mill, among many others, and it clearly corresponds with Berlin's meaning of negative freedom.

Adler offers a much more sympathetic view of positive freedom than Berlin or Cranston. The idea of 'acquired' freedom 'consists in doing as one ought to; it depends on the state of mind or character which enable a man to act in accordance with a moral law, or an ideal befitting human nature'.[11] The ability to act as one ought 'is in no sense circumstantial. The individual does not have it or lack it merely

---

8   John Laird, *On Human Freedom: Being the Forwood Lectures on the Philosophy of Religion given in the University of Liverpool in November, 1945* (London: Oxford University Press, 1947), p. 23.

9   M.J. Adler, *The Idea of Freedom: A Dialectical Examination of the Conceptions of Freedom* (London: Oxford University Press, 1958), p. 200.

10 Ibid., p. 251.

11 Ibid.

as a result of living in a favourable or unfavourable environment, but always as a result of developing his own personality, character, or mind in a certain way'.[12] Adler agrees with Berlin that these two concepts of freedom are irreconcilable. On the one hand, there is 'the acquired freedom of being able to will as one ought', and, on the other hand, 'the circumstantial freedom of being able to do as one pleases'.[13] Adler's study attempts to trace acquired freedom from the Greeks and Catholic theologians to Rousseau, Kant and Hegel. Although his catalogue of philosophers is encyclopaedic, he does not consider any Indian thinkers.

The major difficulty that Berlin, Cranston and Laird seem to have with the concept of positive or acquired freedom is not only that it distorts the meaning of freedom but also that it embraces a mode of thought friendly to authoritarianism. Berlin advocates negative liberty because it demands 'absolute barriers to the imposition of one man's will on another's. The freedom of a society is measured by the strength of these barriers and by the number and importance of the paths which they keep open.'[14] He polarizes the two schools of thought completely by contending that the difference lies not with liberty alone but includes an entire cluster of ideas, extending to how one views authority. Advocates of negative freedom, he asserts, are 'at the opposite pole from the purpose of those who believe in liberty in the positive— self-directive—sense. The former want to curb authority as such. The latter want it placed in their own hands. That is the cardinal issue.'[15] It is after making this point that he concludes that the two interpretations of liberty, as representative of contrasting intellectual traditions, 'are not two divergent interpretations of a single concept, but,' as noted

---

12 Michael Walzer, *Citizenship and Civil Society* (New Brunswick, NJ: Rutgers University Press, 1992), pp. 11–12.

13 Adler, *The Idea of Freedom*, p. 200.

14 See Berlin, *Four Essays on Liberty.*

15 Ibid.

above in the phrase that bears repetition, 'profoundly divergent and irreconcilable attitudes to the ends of life.'[16]

Berlin knew that when he gave this ringing defence of negative freedom in his inaugural address at Oxford, there were critics of the concept even among British liberals. Mill's *Liberty* had been attacked a full century before and continuously since for being muscular on individual liberties and rights but weak on reasons for political obligation or civic responsibility. The antinomies in Western political theory of negative versus positive liberty and of rights versus responsibilities were evident a hundred years ago, and in England and America, democracy has long been caught in the dilemma described by Sabine: the more individual freedom and rights, the less legitimization of civic duty and economic equality.[17]

This dilemma has been noted recently in America, especially from the critical perspective of the lack of an ethic of social responsibility and community in the United States. Michael Walzer represents this view when he comments:

We are perhaps the most individualist society that has ever existed in human history. Compared to earlier, and Old World societies, we are radically liberated, all of us. Free to plot our own course, to plan our own lives, to choose a career, to choose a partner or a succession of partners, to choose a religion or no religion, to choose a politics or an anti-politics, to choose a lifestyle—any style free to do our own thing, and this freedom energizing and exciting as it is, is also profoundly disintegrative, making it very difficult for

---

16 Ibid.

17 Sabine, 'The Two Democratic Traditions', p. 452. See my analysis of this theory in 'Philosophical Background to American Values in the Western Intellectual Tradition', in *To Form a More Perfect Union*, ed. Phillip Hubbart, Dennis Dalton and Charles Edelstein (Durham, NC: Carolina Academic Press, 2016).

individuals to find any stable communal support, very difficult for any community to count on the responsible participation of its individual members. It opens solitary men and women to the impact of a lowest common denominator, commercial culture. It works against commitment to the larger democratic union and also against the solidarity of all cultural groups that constitute our multi-culturalism.[18]

The dilemmas of the American system are perhaps worse than those that Walzer describes because he does not mention the unprecedented gross disparity of wealth that has overtaken the country since the late 1970s. This economic injustice underscores the nation's inability to assert effective civic responsibility and a spirit of mutual care. Some feminist theorists see this problem in gender terms and associate it with certain elements of a masculine mode of thought and behaviour. The most influential of this group is Carol Gilligan, who published *In a Different Voice*[19] in 1982 (first edition) as a criticism of Lawrence Kohlberg's rights theory in the field of educational psychology. Gilligan asserted that 'the morality of rights differs from the morality of responsibility in its emphasis on separation rather than connection, in its consideration of the individual rather than the relationship as primary'.[20] The dominance of the rights ethic has induced a psychology of 'winning and losing', to the point of providing a strong 'potential for violence' and a 'hierarchy of power'. American society needs an 'ethic of care' that

---

18 Walzer, *Citizenship and Civil Society*, pp. 11–12.

19 See Carol Gilligan, *In a Different Voice: Psychological Theory and Women's Development*, Second edition (Cambridge, MA: Harvard University Press, 1993).

20 Gilligan, *In a Different Voice*, pp. 19, 30, 32, 173–74. For a more developed critical analysis of individualism to nonviolence, see Judith Butler, *The Force of Non-violence: An Ethico-Political Bind* (London: Verso, 2020).

can view life 'not as opponents in a contest of rights but as members of a network of relationships on whose continuation they all depend'.[21] The virtue of such an ethic, with its code word of 'connectedness', is that it offers a mature world view or 'different voice', which will not prize 'individual autonomy' at the expense of 'relationship and responsibility'. Gilligan views with alarm the endemic social violence, particularly abuse of women, that persists in the United States. As an educationist, she believes that American society should learn to focus on 'an ethic of care which rests on the premise of nonviolence—that no one should be hurt'.[22]

The broad controversy that was sparked in the United States by Gilligan's thesis occurred in some areas of the biological sciences as well as in the social sciences and humanities. The response testified not only to the extent of her influence but more significantly to what one theorist called 'the impoverishment of political discourse' that existed in the conventional literature on rights and responsibilities. Gilligan, by becoming a popular figure in the feminist movement and advancing a critique long overdue, demonstrated that there is an urgent need in America for creative thinking about social responsibility. Sara Ruddick presents the debate on rights and duties from a feminist perspective by arguing that male and female alike should learn to

> depend on and foster conceptions of the self and 'human nature' that Carol Gilligan and others have heard in the 'different voices' associated with women. According to these conceptions, human nature is not an enemy, humans change and learn to welcome change, and responsible reconciliation is a permanent possibility. Individuals are not primarily centers of dominating and defensive activity trying to achieve a stable autonomy in threatening

---

21 Ibid.
22 Ibid.

hierarchies of strength … They are also and equally centers of care, actively desiring other selves to persist in their own lively being.[23]

This critique of social thought in America reached another point of analysis in the writings of Jean Bethke Elshtain and Mary Ann Glendon. The former contends in her *Democracy on Trial*,[24] that with the decay of a sense of civic duty in contemporary America, 'the rights-bearing individual came to stand alone—"me and my rights"—as if rights were a possession. Rights were construed increasingly in individualistic terms as their civic dimensions withered on the vine.' As legal theorist Mary Ann Glendon pointed out in her book *Rights Talk*,[25] 'the dimensions of sociality and responsibility are missing when the rights-defined self stands alone.'

Glendon presents a systematic critique of rights theory. She opens her analysis by arguing that America today utterly lacks 'the vision of a republic where citizens actively take responsibility for maintaining a vital political life'.[26] In terms of theory, the problem can be traced to British influences on American thinkers, especially to the philosophies of John Locke and even more to William Blackstone, the eighteenth-century legal philosopher, who managed to outdo even Locke in his deification of individual property rights as absolute. 'Blackstone's commentaries,' Glendon says, 'was *the* law book in the United States in the crucial years immediately preceding and following the American

---

23 See Sara Ruddick, *Maternal Thinking: Towards a Politics of Peace* (New York: Ballantine Books, 1990), pp. 182–83.

24 See Jean Bethke Elshtain, *Democracy on Trial* (New York: Basic Books, 1995), p. 15.

25 See Mary Ann Glendon, *Rights Talk: An Impoverishment of Political Discourse* (New York: Free Press, 1991). See also Elshtain, *Democracy on Trial*, p. 15.

26 See Glendon, *Rights Talk*, pp. 17, 23, 34, 45–47, 52–54.

Revolution.'[27] It proclaimed that 'there is nothing which so generally strikes the imagination and engages the affections of mankind as the right of property'.[28] Americans devoured all of this. Neither Rousseau, who wrote that 'property rights are always subordinate to the overriding claims of the community, that an owner is a kind of trustee or steward for the public good', nor Karl Marx, who warned of 'man regarded as an isolated monad, withdrawn into himself', had a chance against the appeal of British liberalism, adding now Mill to the list of most influential theorists. The consequence is that 'the exaggerated absoluteness of our American rights rhetoric is closely bound up with its other distinctive traits—a near silence concerning responsibility and a tendency to envision the rights-bearer as a lone autonomous individual'.[29] After an incisive analysis of the US Supreme Court cases, including a focus on how some key decisions have outdone Mill in glorifying 'the right to privacy, the quintessential right of individual autonomy and isolation', she asks, 'why does our rhetoric of rights so often shut out relationship and responsibility, along with reality?'[30] The theme, then, of freedom and rights versus responsibility and community, central to Western political theory for centuries, now troubles American thought. Elshtain cites Alan Wolfe, who says that Americans are 'confused when it comes to recognizing the social obligations that make freedom possible in the first place', and then she concludes that 'for all our success in modern societies, there is a sense, desperate in some cases, that all is not well that something has gone terribly awry', because the 'confusion permeates all levels, from the marketplace to the home to the academy'.[31] Berlin's negative freedom, long acclaimed by liberals as the bulwark of the free

---

27 Ibid.

28 Ibid.

29 Ibid.

30 Ibid., pp. 17, 23, 24, 45–47, 52–54, 59, 60, 72.

31 Elshtain, *Democracy on Trial*, pp. 14–15.

world against communism, now appears as flawed because it so lacks a spirit of civic duty.

What follows is an attempt to show how certain modern Indian thinkers, especially Gandhi, have discussed ideas of freedom, rights and duty. Their arguments are notably different from most American and British liberal theorists. As with all political theory, the distinctive qualities of Indian ideas are explained by their historical context, the colonial situation of British India. Generally, since Rammohun Roy (1772–1833) and particularly since Vivekananda (1863–1902), the Indian intellectual response to Western imperialism may be characterized, in Sri Aurobindo's (1872–1950) terms, as 'preservation by reconstruction'. This meant 'a synthetical restatement' which 'sought to arrive at the spirit of the ancient culture and, while respecting its forms and often preserving them to revivify, has yet not hesitated also to remould, to reject the outworn and admit whatever new motive seemed assimilable'.[32]

Bhikhu Parekh, a contemporary political theorist, observes that 'the central principles of Indian civilization' that modern thinkers beginning with Roy deemed 'sound and worth preserving' included an 'emphasis on duties rather than rights', or the regulation of life according to rules of Dharma or moral obligation.[33] But this traditional stress on Dharma had to be reconciled with the Western ideal of liberty.

Nineteenth-century India produced several prominent thinkers, but Sri Aurobindo is correct that 'Vivekananda was in his lifetime the leading exemplar and most powerful exponent of the Indian renaissance'.[34] His

---

32 Sri Aurobindo Ghose, *The Renaissance in India* (Pondicherry: Sri Aurobindo Ashram,1951), pp. 39–40.

33 Bhikhu Parekh, *Colonialism, Tradition and Reform: An Analysis of Gandhi's Political Discourse* (Newbury Park, California: Sage Publications, 1989), pp. 59–60.

34 Ghose, *The Renaissance in India*, pp. 39–40.

outstanding contribution came with how he conceived of individual freedom and social responsibility as complementary values. On the one hand, he asserted that,

> [L]iberty of thought and action is the only condition of life, of growth and well-being. Where it does not exist, the man, the race, the nation must go down. Caste or no caste, creed or no creed, any man, or class, or caste, or nation, or institution which bars the power of free thought and action of an individual—even so long as that power does not injure others—is devilish and must go down.[35]

Yet, on the other hand, he insisted that with this freedom came an obligation to 'help others' by 'attaining through unselfish work' (Karma Yoga) a stronger community.[36]

Vivekananda wrote as though his purpose was to harmonize the needs and obligations of the individual and the community:

> The individual's life is in the life of the whole, the individual happiness is in the happiness of the whole; apart from the whole, the individual's existence is inconceivable—this is an eternal truth and is the bedrock on which the universe is built. To move slowly towards the infinite whole, bearing a constant feeling of intense sympathy and sameness with it, being happy with its happiness and being distressed in its affliction, is the individual's sole duty. Not only is it his duty, but in its transgression is his death, while compliance with this great truth leads to life immortal.[37]

---

35 Swami Vivekananda, *The Complete Works*, Vol. 5 (Calcutta: Advaita Ashrama, 1959), p. 29.

36 Ibid., pp. 110, 141–42.

37 Ibid., Vol. 4 (1955), p. 463.

This, then, was the direction of thought established by the end of the nineteenth century in Bengal: a reinterpretation of personal freedom to bring it in harmony with the traditional emphasis on duty. Each person's quest for liberation must entail service to society, what Gandhi would later call the idea of sarvodaya, or uplift of all.

Vivekananda's discussion of individual freedom and social responsibility was continued and enlarged not only by Gandhi but by other Indian theorists early in this century. Aurobindo Ghose and Bipin Chandra Pal (1858–1932) conceptualized freedom around the word swaraj in ways that would become important to Gandhi. Insisting that swaraj could not be translated in Western terms of freedom or liberty, Sri Aurobindo wrote that '*Swaraj* as a sort of European idea, as political liberty for the sake of political self-assertion, will not awaken India'. An ideal of 'true *swaraj*' for India must derive from the Vedantic concept of self-liberation'.[38]

Indian philosophy, he said, leads us to the following definition of freedom:

By liberty, we mean the freedom to obey the law of our being, to grow to our natural self-fulfilment, to find out naturally and freely our harmony with our environment. The dangers and disadvantages of liberty (conceived in the limited Western sense) are indeed obvious. But they arise from the absence or defect of the sense of unity between individual and individual, between community and community, which pushes them to assert themselves at the expense of each other instead of growing by mutual help ... If a real, a spiritual, and a psychological unity were effectuated, liberty would have no perils and disadvantages; for, free individuals enamoured of unity would be compelled by themselves, by their own need, to accommodate perfectly their own growth with the growth of their fellows and would not feel themselves complete except in the free

38 See Ghose, *The Renaissance in India*.

growth of others ... Human society progresses really and vitally as law becomes the child of freedom; it will reach its perfection when, man having learned to know and become spiritually one with his fellow man, the spontaneous law of his society exists only as the outward mould of his self-governed inner liberty.[39]

B.C. Pal, writing around the same time as Aurobindo and following closely his conceptualization of freedom, agreed with him that swaraj must not be defined as liberty in the way British liberalism did, but as 'the conscious identification of the individual with the universal', suggesting 'spiritual liberation' in the traditional Hindu sense. Pal argued with that definition of swaraj as 'Home Rule' expressed by anglicized Indian liberals like Dadabhai Naoroji. He sought its true meaning 'in the *Upanishads* to indicate the highest spiritual state, wherein the individual self stands in conscious union with the Universal or the Supreme Self. When the Self sees and knows, whatever is as its own self, it attains swaraj: so says the *Chandogya Upanishad*. Pal then contrasted this Vedantic conception of swaraj with the modern European notion of freedom as he understood it, arguing as Sri Aurobindo did, the superiority of the classical Indian view:

Indeed the idea of freedom as it has gradually developed in Europe ever since old Paganism was replaced by Christianity with its essentially individualistic ethical implications and emphasis, is hardly in keeping with the new social philosophy of our age. Freedom, independence, liberty (as defined in Europe) are all essentially negative concepts. They all indicate absence of restraint, regulation and subjection. Consequently, Europe has not as yet discovered any really rational test by which to distinguish what is freedom from what is license. *Swaraj* does not mean absence

---

39 Sri Aurobindo Ghose, *The Ideal of Human Unity* (Pondicherry: Sri Aurobindo Ashram, 1962), pp. 564–66.

of restraint or regulation or dependence, but self-restraint, self-regulation, and self-dependence. A spirit of social duty or *dharma* flows from a belief in the unity of being. We are all part of one another: the self in Hindu thought, even in the individual, is a synonym for the Universal.[40]

Finally, before turning to Gandhi's thinking on these ideas, it is important to note how thinkers before him explicitly raised the issue of rights, connecting it to the basic problem of reconciling individual freedom with social responsibility. Vivekananda anticipates Gandhi when he says: 'Selflessness only, not selfishness, can solve the question. The idea of "right" is a limitation: there is really no "mine" and "thine", for I am thou and thou art I. We have "responsibility", not "rights".'[41] Sri Aurobindo then characteristically develops this idea in the context of Indian philosophy by observing: 'It was a marked feature of the Indian mind that it sought to attach a spiritual meaning and a religious sanction to all, even to the most external social political circumstances of its life, imposing on all classes and functions an ideal, not except incidentally of rights and powers, but of duties, a *dharma* with a spiritual significance.' [42]

These ideas of freedom, rights and duty flowed in the conceptual stream that Gandhi's *Hind Swaraj* dramatically widened and deepened. The unique cluster of ideas presented there soon merged with the contemporary thinking about freedom and responsibility to produce a powerful intellectual statement. There are obvious differences between

---

40 B.C. Pal, *Writings and Speeches* (Calcutta: Yugayatri Prakashan, 1958), pp. 75–77.

41 Sri Aurobindo, *Works*, Vol. 8, p. 23.

42 Sri Aurobindo Ghose, *The Spirit and Form of Indian Polity* (Pondicherry: Sri Aurobindo Ashram, 1966), pp. 7–8.

Gandhi and the Bengali thinkers mentioned above, but their thinking about swaraj and dharma is strikingly similar.

Anthony Parel argues that 'the concept of *swaraj* holds the key to Mahatma Gandhi's political philosophy' because, from the writing of *Hind Swaraj*, he develops the 'dual meaning' of swaraj connecting the self-rule of individual and nation.[43] The point to be made here is how this mode of thinking offers a way out of Berlin's 'irreconcilability' of negative and positive freedom. Vivekananda, with his interpretation of Vedanta in response to British liberalism, led others to formulate a philosophy of 'spiritual freedom' that criticized Western liberty as license. India could do much better than that with its conceptual correlates of swaraj and Dharma. The ideal was, as liberals seemed to stress, self-realization. But this could come only through awareness of human connectedness and corresponding action for humanity.

Gandhi agreed with this but insisted that freedom as swaraj could come only through acceptance of considerable personal and political obligation that involved enormous self-sacrifice and social service. No nationalist before Gandhi had embraced the responsibility of the colonized so unequivocally: 'To blame the English is useless,' Gandhi's 'Editor' (speaking in the author's voice) declared to the 'Reader', 'they will either go or change their nature only when we reform ourselves … We shall become free only through suffering.'[44] Indians must recognize this duty because '*Swaraj* has to be experienced, by each one for himself'.[45] It can be achieved only through commitment to the cause of freedom, so 'it is our duty to say exactly what we think and face the consequences'.[46]

---

43 Anthony Parel, 'The Doctrine of Swaraj in Gandhi's Philosophy', *Gandhi Marg*, 1995, pp. 57–58.

44 Ibid., pp. 63–64.

45 Ibid., p. 39.

46 Ibid., p. 64.

Hind Swaraj resounds with these challenges, demanding that if Indians want freedom, then they must sacrifice to acquire it. They have duties of disloyalty to the Raj as well as of reform of their own society. Such attainment of freedom depends wholly on the person, never on the State. When Berlin asserts that 'the cardinal issue' is authority and who holds it, that 'those who believe in liberty in the "positive"—self-directive—sense ... want it placed in their own hands', this cannot describe Gandhi's idea of freedom. His formulation of swaraj carries a large suspicion of political authority and cannot be used to legitimize arbitrary State power in the way that Berlin seems to fear.

Gandhi defies the stereotype of the positive freedom theorists as authoritarian by stressing civil liberties. The extent of his affirmation of individual rights and civil liberty should be stressed. 'Freedom of speech and civil liberty,' he asserted, 'are the very roots of *swaraj*. Without these, the foundations of *swaraj* will remain weak.'[47] This unequivocal position flowed naturally from his leadership of the nationalist movement as a champion of nonviolent resistance. Writing in early 1922 under the caption, 'Liberty of the Press', his defence of civil liberties could not be clearer.

> Liberty of speech means that it is unassailed even when the speech hurts; liberty of the Press can be said to be truly respected only when the Press can comment in the severest terms upon and even misrepresent matters, protection against misrepresentation or violence being secured not by an administrative gagging order, not by closing down the Press but by punishing the real offender, leaving the Press itself unrestricted. Freedom of association is truly respected when assemblies of people can discuss even revolutionary projects, the State relying upon the force of public opinion and the civil police, not the savage military at its disposal, to crush any actual outbreak of revolution that is designed to confound public

---

47 *CWMG* 73:22.

opinion and the State representing it ... The fight for *swaraj* means
a fight for this threefold freedom before all else.[48]

Nine years later, once again in the midst of a national campaign,
Gandhi drafted for the Congress in 1931 an extensive 'Resolution
on Fundamental Rights' that constituted the most explicit defence of
civil liberties that any modern liberal might require. Its principal aims
stated:

> Fundamental rights of the people, including freedom of association
> and combination; freedom of speech and of the Press; freedom of
> conscience and the free profession and practice of religion, subject
> to public order and morality; protection of the culture, language
> and scripts of the minorities; equal rights and obligations of all
> citizens, without any bar on account of sex; no disability to attach
> to any citizen by reason of his or her religion, caste or creed or sex in
> regard to public employment, office of power or honour and in the
> exercises of any trade or calling; equal rights to all citizens in regard
> to public roads, wells, schools and other places of public resort; ...
> religious neutrality on the part of the State; Adult suffrage; Free
> primary education; a living wage for industrial workers, limited
> hours of labour, healthy conditions of work ... Protection of
> women workers, and specially adequate provisions for leave during
> maternity period; Prohibition against employment of children of
> schoolgoing age in factories; Rights of labour to form unions to
> protect their interest...[49]

In moving this resolution before the Karachi Congress, Gandhi
stressed its extreme import, observing that it was not for legislators
but 'to indicate to the poor, inarticulate Indian the broad features of

---

48 *CWMG* 22:176–77.
49 *CWMG* 45:370–71.

swaraj by making clear precisely what the rights of citizens should constitute'. Then he proceeded to comment especially on the need to respect the rights of religious minorities and women.[50] Less than two months later, in a message to a regional Congress conference, he urged: 'The resolution on fundamental rights is the most important resolution of the Congress. It shows what kind of swaraj the Congress wants to achieve.'[51] Never content to let rest an issue that he deemed imperative, he returned that July to the connection of individual rights to democracy, asserting: 'Democracy disciplined and enlightened is the finest thing in the world. A democracy prejudiced, ignorant, superstitious will land itself in chaos and may be self-destroyed. The Fundamental Rights Resolution is not premature because Indians can use it as a strong bulwark of freedom.'[52] No rights theorist could ask for a more complete statement of liberal doctrine than this.

However, the theme of this essay is that the contribution of modern Indian political thought in general, and of Gandhi in particular, lies in how they move beyond liberal doctrine, not where they affirm it. Gandhi's position is that civil rights and liberties must be grounded in a prior sense of civic duty. If not, they may either remain dormant among an ignorant and apathetic population or assume a dangerous attitude in a democracy that Glendon deplores as 'hyperindividualism'.[53] Gandhi claimed that he yielded to no one in his defence of civil liberty, and thus he wrote:

> Liberty cannot be secured merely by proclaiming it. An atmosphere of liberty must be created within us. Liberty is one thing, and license another. Many a time we confuse license for liberty and lose

---

50 *CWMG* 45:372–73.

51 *CWMG* 46:166.

52 *CWMG* 47:346.

53 See Glendon, *Rights Talk*, p. 75.

the latter. License leads one to selfishness whereas liberty guides one to supreme good. License destroys society; liberty gives it life. In license, property is sacrificed; in liberty, it is fully cherished. Under slavery, we practice several virtues out of fear; when liberated, we practice them of our own free will.[54]

In the short period that Gandhi lived following India's independence, he repeatedly warned that 'the first lesson to be learnt' is that 'liberty never meant the license to do anything at will. Independence meant voluntary restraint and discipline…'[55]

Western rights theorists, beginning with Locke, have affirmed that freedom is not 'a liberty for everyone to do what he lists, to live as he pleases, and not be tied by laws', but it is freedom under law, and the source of civic obligation is founded in law.[56] Gandhi accepts that in an independent India, obedience comes from 'voluntary acceptance of the rule of law in the making of which the whole of India had its hand through its elected representatives'.[57] Gandhi valued highly the rule of law when derived from popular sovereignty. Yet his concept of swaraj demanded a form of social and political responsibility that Locke never required, a commitment that was much closer to Rousseau: the obligation to change oneself and one's community for the betterment of all, in a spirit of social service. This was conceived as a primary duty of citizenship, the basis for a realization of individual rights.

Raghavan Iyer observes: 'Whereas Western individualism emerged in modern urban society and is bound up with the doctrine of natural rights, Gandhi's individualism derived from the concept of *dharma* or

---

54 *CWMG* 42:380.

55 *CWMG* 89:112.

56 John Locke, *Second Treatise of Government* (Notre Dame: Hackett Publishing Company, 1980), IV, 22, p. 17.

57 *CWMG* 89:112.

natural obligations ...'[58] The centrality of Dharma to modern Indian thinkers was represented by Sri Aurobindo Ghose when he interpreted his tradition by stressing the value of Dharma or duty as being at the heart of it. But no theorist of Indian nationalism evoked the classical concept of Dharma in more ways than Gandhi. He gave the word two essential meanings, both serving his twin principles of satya (truth) and ahimsa (nonviolence).

> For me, 'there was no *dharma* higher than truth' [*Mahabharata*, Adiparvan, ch. XI, 13] and 'no *dharma* higher than the supreme duty of nonviolence'. [Shantiparvan, ch. CLXII, 24.] The word *dharma*, in my opinion, has different connotations as used in the two statements. In other words, it means that there cannot be an ideal higher than truth and there cannot be any *duty* higher than nonviolence. A man can pursue truth only by constantly adhering to this duty. There is no other means for the pursuit of truth.[59]

Whether truth or nonviolence (ahimsa paramo dharma) is the ideal, these two 'different connotations' of dharma merge, as means and ends usually do in Gandhi's writings, to translate dharma as the path of duty, 'the way of truth and nonviolence', or 'the royal road of *dharma* that leads to both earthly and spiritual bliss'.[60] Raghavan Iyer translates Gandhi's meaning of dharma as 'path of duty',[61] and R.C. Zaehner comments on Gandhi's concept of Dharma[62] as Gandhi consistently identified

---

58 Iyer, *The Moral and Political Thought of Mahatma Gandhi*, p. 115.

59 *CWMG* 62:224 (italics added).

60 *CWMG* 13:52; 72:48. See also Iyer, *The Moral and Political Writings of Mahatma Gandhi*, Vol. 2.

61 Iyer, *The Moral and Political Thought of Mahatma Gandhi*, p. 51.

62 R.C. Zaehner, *Hinduism* (London: Oxford University Press, 1962), p. 11.

dharma with truth and nonviolence or as 'religion in the highest sense of the term'.[63] Thus he says: 'We cannot commit violence in the name of *Dharma*,' and 'Violence is never an independent *Dharma*. There is only one such *Dharma*, and that is nonviolence.' 'The truth is that all activities in this world are related to *dharma* or *adharma*', and then he gives examples of pursuing either path, of morality or immorality.[64] One may of course be mistaken in one's interpretation or pursuit of *dharma* as a moral or religious duty, but the test lies in the intention to pursue the right path: 'So long as I do not see my mistakes, I must practise the *dharma* which I consider to be true.'[65]

Gandhi uses this theory of dharma to shape his idea of rights: 'Having a right surely does not mean that I should exercise that right in utter disregard of my sense of proportion … The exercise of right depends on one's sense of duty. It is my duty to follow *dharma* … I do what I consider my duty.'[66] This follows from what he had written in *Hind Swaraj*, where he argued that 'real rights are a result of performance of duty' and criticized 'in England the farce of everybody wanting and insisting on his rights, nobody thinking of his duty'.[67] He said that *Hind Swaraj* was written 'to offer a glimpse of *dharma*', to urge India and the world, and to adopt a way of life attuned to a sense of moral obligation. As he assumed leadership in India, his message consistently was that our personal and political duties are connected, part of a whole that extends even beyond the nation:

One's respective *dharma* towards one's self, family, nation and the world cannot be divided into water-tight compartments. The harm

---

63 *CWMG* 64:191.

64 *CWMG* 37:33 and 36:296.

65 *CWMG* 38:21–22.

66 *CWMG* 69:208.

67 *CWMG* 10:44.

done to oneself or one's family cannot bring about the good of the nation. Similarly, one cannot benefit the nation by acting against the world at large … Therefore, it all starts from self-purification. When the heart is pure, from moment to moment, one's duty becomes apparent effortlessly.[68]

Because cultivation of a sense of social or political duty necessarily begins with 'self-cultivation', the idea of dharma centres on Gandhi's concept of the individual as he developed it even before he wrote *Hind Swaraj*. He wrote *Ethical Religion* in early 1907 and explained there that a 'personal morality' begins with 'our duty to ourselves': '"I am responsible for this" or "this is my duty", this is a moving and wonderful thought. A mysterious, resounding voice seems to say, "To thee, individually, O man, is given this task".' Before the 'duty to have sympathy and fraternal regard for others' is 'my duty to respect myself even as I respect others'. That is, our primary duty is to develop character traits in ourselves that foster social service because 'man's highest duty in life is to serve mankind and take his share in bettering its condition. This is true worship—true prayer.' We are obligated to make a 'contribution to an ideal order of human life', and to achieve this the individual must through self-examination become 'sincere in himself, bear no malice, exploit no one, and always act with a pure mind. Such men alone can serve mankind.'[69] This is the essence of Gandhi's individualism, namely that a correct recognition of the relationship between rights and duties depends on formation of personal integrity and a strong social conscience: 'So long as one has not developed inner strength, one can never practise the *dharma* of *ahimsa*.'[70]

---

68 *CWMG* 50:360.

69 *CWMG* 6:340–41.

70 *CWMG* 28:49.

The distinctive qualities of Gandhi's mature conception of dharma defined as duty are, first, that it begins early in his writings and develops as a pervasive theme until the end, that it accentuates his individualism, and it is persistently linked with his idea of individual rights, which are always seen to flow from its performance. Near the end of his life, after independence, he dwelt in his Delhi prayer meetings on the need to acknowledge social responsibility. When he had begun the non-cooperation movement in March 1919, he had conceded that much political education would be required for Indians, to understand their duties as well as their rights.[71] In 1947, consumed with the civil war and with his own sense of failure as a leader, he directed all his thought and energy to the Hindu–Muslim conflict. At his prayer meeting in Delhi on 28 June, he stated his appeal to 'Brothers and Sisters' in these terms:

> The Constituent Assembly is discussing the rights of the citizen. That is to say that they are deliberating on what the fundamental rights should be. As a matter of fact, the proper question is not what the rights of a citizen are, but rather what constitutes the duties of a citizen. Fundamental rights can only be those rights the exercise of which is not only in the interest of the citizen but that of the whole world. Today everyone wants to know what his rights are, but if a man learns to discharge his duties right from childhood and studies the sacred books of his faith, he automatically exercises his rights too. I learnt my duties on my mother's lap. She was an unlettered village woman ... She knew my *dharma*. Thus if from my childhood we learn what our *dharma* is and try to follow it, our rights look after themselves ... The beauty of it is that the very performance of a duty secures us our right. Rights cannot be divorced from duties. This is how *satyagraha* was born, for I was always striving to decide what my duty was.[72]

---

71 *CWMG* 15:140.

72 *CWMG* 88:230.

Not satisfied with this appeal, he returned to his theme the next evening:

> Yesterday, I talked to you about duty. However, I was not able to say all that I had intended to say. Whenever a person goes anywhere, certain duties come to devolve on him. The man who neglects his duty and cares only to safeguard his rights does not know that rights that do not spring from duties done cannot be safeguarded. This applies to Hindu-Muslim relations. Whether it is the Hindus living in a place or Muslims or both, they will come to acquire rights if they do their duty. Then they do not have to demand rights … This is a paramount law and no one can change it. If Hindus consider Muslims their brothers and treat them well, Muslims too will return friendship for friendship … The duty of the Hindus is to share with the Muslims their joys and sorrows.[73]

Gandhi then talked at some length about how each person must assume responsibility for stopping the conflict and then ended his speech by returning to its main theme: 'People should not merely run after rights. He who runs after rights does not secure them. His plight is that of a dog who sees his reflection in the water and wants to attack it. His right is illusory; when you do your duty, the rights will drop into your lap.'[74]

Before independence, Gandhi had insisted that Indians must accept responsibility for colonization: they had allowed it to happen, and they could end it if they resolved to do so. Now, in the face of tragedies like the Great Calcutta killings, he demanded that people should accept responsibility for what had happened. How could they claim to enjoy their rights in a free India when they had failed in their responsibility to maintain civil peace and order? After Gandhi fasted in Calcutta for communal harmony, Dr Sarvepalli Radhakrishnan visited him and

---

73 *CWMG* 88:236–38.

74 Ibid.

then commented to the press: 'I have told Mahatmaji not to confuse between *goondas (thugs)* activities and communal violence. What had happened in Calcutta during the last few days was absolutely the work of *goondas* and nothing else.'[75]

   This was an argument that had never appealed to Gandhi. For years, Indians had blamed criminal elements in society for communal conflict as well as for other forms of urban violence. Gandhi replied: '*Goondas* do not drop from the sky, nor do they spring from the earth like evil spirits. They are the product of social disorganization and society is therefore responsible for their existence. In other words, they should be looked upon as a symptom of corruption in our body politic.'[76] That was in 1940. When in 1946 he was confronted with the Bihar riots, he again unequivocally placed the responsibility where it belonged by deploring 'the habit of procuring a moral alibi for ourselves by blaming it all on the goondas. We always put the blame on the goondas. But it is we who are responsible for their creation as well as encouragement.'[77] In September 1947, his reply to Dr Radhakrishnan was no less direct: 'The conflagration has been caused not by the goondas but by those who have become goondas. It is we who make goondas. Without our sympathy and passive support, the goondas would have no legs to stand upon ... It is time for peace-loving citizens to assert themselves and isolate goondaism.'[78]

   Until the end of his struggle for freedom, he emphasized the idea of duty that he had first announced in South Africa. After a lifetime of leadership, he sought to quench the fires of civil war with constant appeals for responsible social action by 'peace-loving citizens'. But the basic message introduced in his *Ethical Religion* and *Hind Swaraj*

---

75 Quoted in *The Statesman*, 5 September 1947, p. 8.

76 *CWMG* 72:456.

77 *CWMG* 76:76.

78 *CWMG* 89:132.

remained unchanged after the attainment of Indian Independence. Commitment to liberation of the self and of the country requires a path of dharma, not adharma. For this, satyagraha is the most effective method. As Gandhi said in one of the speeches cited above, satyagraha was born out of his 'striving to decide what my duty was'. Before independence, he translated this into 'the duty of disloyalty', the title of an article written during the Salt Satyagraha in March 1930. He argued there that to attain swaraj through satyagraha, Indians must understand their political obligation: 'It is a duty of those who have realized the awful evil of the system of Indian Government to be disloyal to it and actively and openly preach disloyalty. Indeed, loyalty to a State so corrupt is a sin, disloyalty a virtue.'[79] Civil disobedience becomes obligatory because it is the individual's 'clear duty to run any risk to achieve' swaraj. Gandhi's categorical conclusion that 'Disobedience of the law of an evil state is therefore a duty',[80] recalls Henry Thoreau, who also proclaimed that breaking the law is an obligation in an unjust polity, but he neither grounded his theory of civil resistance in a concept of dharma nor developed an ethos of nonviolence. Yet both Thoreau and Gandhi can concur with Iyer's statement that 'in the case of civil resisters, their civil disobedience is simply the performance of a duty that they owe themselves under the dictates of their conscience'.[81]

If Gandhi's theory of swaraj is related to dharma through satyagraha or, in his phrase, the 'duty of disloyalty', it is equally connected to it through his emphasis on social responsibility; that is, his ideal of the good citizen. After the colonial rule ended, Gandhi wanted his people to understand that swaraj would give them not licence to do as they wished but increased obligation to act as they should as citizens of an independent India. This is the essential distinction between 'negative'

---

79 *CWMG* 43:132–33.

80 Ibid.

81 Iyer, *The Moral and Political Thought of Mahatma Gandhi*, p. 270.

and 'positive' freedom, the latter to be acquired through insight, reflection and political education. With the goal before him of swaraj as the liberation of India, Gandhi spoke in 1939 about what 'true citizenship' meant:

> In *swaraj* based on *ahimsa* people need not know their rights (as much as) it is necessary for them to know their duties. There is no duty but creates a corresponding right, and those only are true rights which flow from a due performance of one's duties. Hence rights of true citizenship accrue only to those who serve the State to which they belong. And they alone can do justice to the rights that accrue to them. Everyone possesses the right to tell lies. But the exercise of such a right is harmful both to the exerciser and society.
>
> To him who observes truth and nonviolence comes prestige, and prestige brings rights. And people who obtain rights as a performance of duty, exercise them only for the service of society, never for themselves. *Swaraj* of a people means the sum-total of the *swaraj* (self-rule) of individuals. And such *swaraj* comes only from performance by individuals of their duty as citizens. In it, no one thinks of his rights. They come, when they are needed, for better performance of duty.[82]

Gandhi wrote this in connection with one of his many local satyagrahas, which he conceived as being more of a political education programme than a confrontation with the British. In an article written a week earlier for the same purpose, he had asked, 'Responsible government will come, but will the people be able to shoulder the burden and rise equal to the task?' He stressed his aim of 'educating the public' in the urgent need for social reform so that they should 'cultivate the spirit of corporate service', but for this, they must 'learn to be disciplined'.[83]

---

82 *CWMG* 69:62.

83 *CWMG* 69:44–45.

This was the way that he used his theory of Satyagraha to resolve contradictions between freedom and obligation, and between rights and responsibilities.

When he says, in the long passage quoted above, that swaraj does not require knowledge of rights as much as of duties, he certainly does not mean to imply an inattention to the need for the former. As noted earlier, his resolution on rights at the Karachi Congress of 1931 and subsequent commentary on it gave abundant attention then and later to individual rights. But his concept of swaraj will not permit rights to stand unattached to duties. Just as one acquires freedom through discipline and insight, so one also acquires rights by fulfilling the responsibilities of citizenship.

Gandhi explained his idea of swaraj carefully when he wrote: 'The root meaning of *swaraj* is self-rule. *Swaraj* may, therefore, be rendered as discipline rule from within ... "Independence" has no such limitation. Independence may mean license to do as you like. *Swaraj* is positive. Independence is negative ... The word *swaraj* is a sacred word, a Vedic word, meaning self-rule and self-restraint, and not freedom from all restraint which "independence" often means.'[84] He made this comment in 1931, having emphasized this interpretation of freedom since the publication of *Hind Swaraj* in 1909. His purpose was consistently to teach this hard political lesson, that freedom demands responsibility, and that rights are earned through civic service and the attainment of difficult social reforms.

Perhaps Gandhi's emphasis on social responsibility was excessive. Parekh argues that Gandhi so restricted the role of kama (sensual pleasure) and artha (property) in life that he 'thus made *dharma* the sole basis of life'.[85] From this viewpoint, his ideas can assume a dark

---

84 *CWMG* 45:263–64.

85 Bhikhu Parekh, *Gandhi's Political Philosophy: A Critical Examination*
    (Notre Dame: University of Notre Dame Press, 1989), p. 210.

colour of guilt and unnecessary suffering. On the other hand, as Parekh also observes, Gandhi's theory of obligation 'gave a new and deeper meaning' to the current conception of our political and social nature by extending a citizen's duties 'far beyond those based on consent, promise, contract, and membership of a specific community'.[86] Through his campaigns against untouchability and for Hindu–Muslim unity, 'he shamed and mobilized the Hindu masses, stirred their conscience, awakened their sense of responsibility ...'[87] Gandhi's connection of swaraj and dharma meant that India having attained independence by duty to disloyalty, could not gain full freedom without each assuming responsibility for the uplift of all.

Gandhi may be criticized from the perspective of liberal democracy as deflating human rights theory or denying natural rights doctrine by insisting that rights exist only as derivatives from performance of duty. He does have fundamental differences with liberal democracy, and these have been explained or defended by Bhikhu Parekh, Ronald Terchek, Thomas Pantham, Raghavan Iyer and Joan Bondurant.[88] This paper has tried to focus on concepts of freedom, rights and responsibility, but Gandhi's critique of liberal democracy raises other issues as well. He criticized it for being 'individualistic in the sense of stressing rights rather than duties and self-interest rather than altruism,

---

86 Ibid., p. 197.

87 Parekh, *Colonialism, Tradition and Reform*, p. 291.

88 In this connection, see the following: Bhikhu Parekh, *Gandhi's Political Philosophy*, pp. 110–14; *Colonialism, Tradition and Reform*, pp. 74 and 102; Ronald Terchek and Thomas Pantham's 'Beyond Liberal Democracy: Thinking with Mahatma Gandhi', in Thomas Pantham and Kenneth Deutsch (eds.), *Political Thought in Modern India* (New Delhi: Sage Publications, 1986), pp. 307–47; Iyer, *The Moral and Political Thought of Mahatma Gandhi*; and Joan Bondurant, *The Conquest of Violence: The Gandhian Philosophy of Conflict* (Princeton: Princeton University Press, 1958), Chapters 4 and 5.

and materialistic in the sense of being concerned solely with deriving its moral legitimacy from its ability to promote the material interests of its citizens. It lacked moral orientation and turned the state into an arena of conflict between organized groups'. This is a version of democracy gone astray.[89]

From this perspective, Gandhi's contribution to democratic thought is the way that he conceives of civic duty. He viewed the problem of democracy thus: 'We discuss political obligation as if it were a kind of moral tax extracted from us by a coercive government, rather than as an expression of our commitment to uphold and improve the quality of the shared life.'[90] Terchek makes the point that Gandhi's idea of freedom is fundamentally different from the Anglo-American liberal conception because he places such emphasis on duty that 'freedom without responsibility is a contradiction in terms'.[91]

The relationship that Gandhi establishes between swaraj and dharma is the 'different voice' of Indian political thought. Anthony Parel examines this relationship and, in explaining the idea of dharma as Gandhi conceived it, observes: '*Dharma*, he said, is not dogma; it is a "quality of the soul" through which we know "our duty in human life and our relation with other selves". We cannot know this duty unless we know the self in us. Hence, *dharma* is the means by which we can know ourselves.'[92] This interpretation of dharma places in perspective the primary role of the self in fulfilling social or political responsibility. Parel concludes his article with a quotation from a letter that Gandhi wrote to Maganlal Gandhi in 1910, which clearly makes the point of

---

89 Parekh, *Colonialism, Tradition and Reform*, p. 47.

90 Bhikhu Parekh, *The Philosophy of Political Philosophy* (Hull: University of Hull Press, 1986), p. 19.

91 Ronald Tercheck, 'Gandhi and Democratic Theory', in *Political Thought in Modern India*, ed. Pantham and Deutsch, p. 315.

92 Parel, 'The Doctrine of Swaraj in Gandhi's Political Philosophy', p. 65.

where one's duty must lie: 'Please do not carry unnecessarily on your head the burden of emancipating India. Emancipate your own self. Even that burden is very great. Apply everything to yourself. Nobility of soul consists in realizing that you are yourself India. In your emancipation is the emancipation of India.'[93]

Individualism of this variety may appear so extreme as to be irreconcilable with a firm sense of political and social responsibility. The ways that Gandhi and other Indian thinkers have interpreted swaraj and dharma to construct their conception of a right relationship of the individual to society may not appeal to most Western theorists. We cannot know how Berlin, Cranston, Adler, Elshtain, Glendon or Walzer might regard Indian thought because none of them mentions non-Western thinkers. Only Sara Ruddick, among those theorists noted in this essay, examines Gandhi seriously and values his contribution to an ethic of care.[94] I do not wish to suggest that modern Indian political thought presents a solution for the problem of the conflicting claims of individual freedom and social obligation. Yet it does offer a different voice that merits inclusion in Western political discourse. Elshtain has stated the problem precisely that 'the dimensions of sociality and responsibility are missing when the rights-defined self stands alone'. Gandhi and others of his tradition might suggest that modern theory needs to discover resources for a better conceptualization of a strong social conscience and commitment to a higher quality of civic life.

---

93 Ibid., p. 78. See also *CWMG* 10:206–7.

94 Ruddick, *Maternal Thinking*, pp. 168–71.

Afterword

JAMES TULLY

I am both honoured and humbled to be invited to say a few after words about Dennis Dalton's outstanding study of the Indian tradition of freedom from the nineteenth to the late twentieth centuries. This is an immensely rich, original and important tradition of freedom, and Dalton's careful explication and elucidation of it as a living tradition is exemplary of the craft of intellectual history at its best.

Dalton places the four theorists of the original text and the three new authors in a dialogue of reciprocal elucidation with each other of their ways of thinking about and enacting freedom. In so doing, readers are able to see the similarities and dissimilarities as they develop in response to both texts and events. Moreover, Dalton does not take a detached stance. Rather, he participates in the dialogue, clarifying aspects of texts and contexts, as well as presenting his own considered view on the criteria of freedom at issue: inner and outer, means and ends, violence and nonviolence, and so on. As a result, we come to understand the tradition as a living tradition that remains alive, well and relevant today. Moreover, the 'Memoir' and 'Introduction' show us that his dialogical method was developed through a long and distinguished career of interviewing participants and observers of the tradition. For me, and I hope for students, this distinct method of the study of political thought is just as original and important as the tradition of freedom it brings to light. Indeed, it enacts the freedom it studies.

The philosopher R.G. Collingwood suggested that to understand a tradition of thought and practice, it is necessary to recover the shared and presupposed question to which the participants respond. As Dalton shows, the underlying question from Vivekananda to M.N. Roy is how to integrate inner and outer freedom so they bring about and co-sustain the social harmony or mutual well-being of all diverse and interdependent living beings. Very schematically, 'inner freedom' refers to the freedom humans have to cultivate themselves into ethical beings by means of practices of the self ('yoga' in its primary sense). This freedom is a dialogical relationship with oneself. 'Outer freedom' refers to the relationship one has with other human beings, with the lifeforms that comprise the biodiverse living earth, and with the spiritual dimension of life (or 'being'). The role of ethics (inner freedom) is to learn how to connect with and co-sustain the pre-existing social, ecological and spiritual relationships of interdependency with others that sustain all life (outer freedom). Inner and outer freedom are relational: freedom-with one another.

The problem they confront is twofold under modernizing conditions. The four types of 'with' relationships are increasingly disintegrated, marginalized and replaced by imposed, competitive over–under relationships to oneself, others, the living earth, and spiritual traditions. The corresponding modern worldview legitimates these relationships as the means to and of civilization and developmental progress. Humans are pictured as capable of freedom from these relationships in their private lives (freedom from); freedom to compete for comparative advantage in various social systems of power over–

under relationships (freedom to), and revolutionary freedom to overthrow them and impose a new system of relationships. This kind of anthropocentric order is imposed on what is presumed to be an unordered or primitive state of nature. The necessity of imposition is the presupposition that humans are incapable of complex cooperation without a master or ruler (the rabble hypothesis). Imposition requires war, violence, colonialism, intervention, authoritarian rule, inequality and ruthless competition. Yet, these vicious means are said to bring about virtuous ends dialectically: that is, decolonization, state-building, representative democracy, limitless development, economic well-being, and perpetual peace in future generations 'to come'. (The 'to come' clause renders this 'thesis' irrefutable and unverifiable no matter how counterfactual the present state of affairs.)

From the perspective of the modernizing tradition of freedom, the Indian tradition looks like a pre-modern worldview of an earlier stage of development. From the perspective of the Indian tradition, the modernizing tradition looks like the worldview of a people who are alienated from and destroyers of the interdependent relationships of inner and outer freedom that sustain personal, social, biological and spiritual well-being. Yet, the modernizing tradition came along with colonization and the seven Indian authors were educated in its liberal, nationalist and Marxist varieties.

Thus, in addition to the problem of conceptualizing and integrating inner and outer freedom within their tradition, they also had the problem of responding to the modernizing tradition of freedom. Should they accept it in its liberal, nationalist or Marxist forms and become moderns, either in whole or in parts? Or, should they reject it and attempt to overcome it? Dalton's meticulous approach elucidates the ways in which the authors grappled with these two problems in fascinating detail, often changing their minds as they went along in response to events and debates. His use of quotations and synopses clarify the central conceptual contests in their corresponding contexts.

I have learned an enormous amount from this great work of reconstruction of an immensely important tradition. I will leave it to others who are much more knowledgeable about this Indian tradition than I am to comment on it in detail. I would like to end by mentioning one aspect of Gandhi's contribution to this tradition and the two problems its members attempted to resolve. I came to appreciate this aspect through reading Dalton's scholarship on Gandhi and studying the works of Richard Gregg, who lived and worked with Gandhi. His major text is *The Power of Nonviolence* (1934, revised 1944 and 1959).[1]

It is well known that Gandhi initially embraced the modern tradition of freedom and then rejected it in *Hind Swaraj* (1909) and after. However, it is not as well known that the alternative he developed can be seen as a response to the two problems that his Indian tradition of freedom handed to him. Dalton shows this clearly by the way he situates Gandhi in the dialogue. I will briefly summarize the main features.

The first is Gandhi's interpretation of inner freedom as 'swaraj' in its primary sense as the nonviolent dialogical relationship of self-cultivation and self-governance that we have with ourselves in practices of ethical self-formation. It is the ground and means of the ways we interact in all other 'with' relationships. In contrast to the later Aurobindo, Gandhi insists that ethical self-formation has to be practised and integrated in relationships with others (as Dalton quotes him):

'I am here to serve no one but myself, to find my own self-realization through the service of these village folk. Man's ultimate aim is the

---

1   Richard Bartlett Gregg, *The Power of Nonviolence*, edited and introduced by James Tully (Cambridge: Cambridge University Press, 2018).

realization of God, and all his activities, social, political, religious, have to be guided by the ultimate aim of the vision of God. The immediate service of all human beings becomes a necessary part of the endeavor simply because the only way to find God is to see Him in his creation and be one with it. This can be done by service of all.'

For Gandhi, ethical self-formation in nonviolent relationships of mutual service with others takes place in the inter-faith prayer meetings in ashrams. Moreover, it also takes place in all types of outer freedom-with relationships humans co-inhabit. This links together, as tightly as possible, inner freedom (means) and outer freedom (ends) from the beginning. There is no inner 'self-realization' without its expression in outer freedom, and, conversely, no relationships of genuine mutual service without the appropriate self-formation. The reason for this is that, contrary to the modernizing tradition, means are autotelic: violence begets violence, and nonviolence begets nonviolence. As Gregg puts it:[2]

Whether we are considering the life of an individual or of society, that life is a process, a series of successive stages or steps. As long as life continues, each stage grows out of the preceding stage and uses the material and structure and method of the prior stage as the means for advance. The character of each stage forms the basis for the character of the following stage. Each successive step is the immediate goal of the preceding step. So each step is not only an accomplishment in itself, but also a means toward the immediate next stage and hence enters into the achievement of the final goal. So the character of the means qualifies and determines the end both immediately and finally.

---

2   Ibid., p. xxix.

All the social relationships that comprise Gandhi's response to the problem of integrating inner and outer freedom exhibit this combination of ethical swaraj in nonviolent relationships of cooperation, contestation, and conflict resolution with each other. Village and federal swaraj consists in relationships of participatory democracy. Sarvodaya refers to the organization of economic relationships on the basis of power-with-and-for-each-other that goes along with freedom-with-each-other. Swadeshi refers to the cyclical, co-sustaining eco-economic relationships between humans and the ecological regions in which they live and on which they depend. His Constructive Programme consists in generating these relationships of integral inner and outer freedom in various spheres of life.

These virtuous relationships of inner and outer freedom are often upset by perturbations and conflicts that appear to participants as irresolvable nonviolently. They turn to vicious and violent means, and these become systemic if not addressed. In his book *Mahatma Gandhi: Nonviolent Power in Action*, Dalton shows how satyagraha—grounded in swaraj in constructive programmes—constitutes the nonviolent means of transforming violent conflicts and vicious relationships into nonviolent practices of dialogue, negotiation, conflict resolution and reintegration into co-sustainable relationships of inner and outer freedom.

Gandhi and Gregg argue that these nonviolent relationships of cooperation, contestation and conflict resolution are more powerful than the violence-based, competitive relationships of the modernizing tradition because they reconnect humans with the symbiotic power that animates and sustains the biodiverse networks of life on earth ('unity in diversity'). Following on their work, it may be said that if humans continue to disregard these networks and remain subjects of the competitive and exploitative relationships of the modernizing tradition, they will destroy life on earth by war or ecological destruction. As Gandhi wrote: 'If love or non-violence be not the law of our being, the whole of my argument falls to pieces, and there is no escape from a periodical recrudescence of war, each succeeding one outdoing the preceding one in ferocity.'[3]

If this is a plausible summary of Gandhi's contribution to the Indian tradition of freedom, then it can be seen to be based on a simple insight into the co-sustainability conditions of life on earth. Every individual and collective subject should always sustain their own well-being in their own diverse, self-realizing ways, yet, simultaneously, always in ways that also reciprocally co-sustain the well-being of all their interdependent relatives in the webs of life. The only way this can be done is by means of nonviolent linguistic and perceptual dialogues and working, trial-and-error relationships of mutual service with and for 'all affected'. This is the ongoing, experimental integration of inner and outer freedom. In so doing, we participate freely in co-generating social, ecological and spiritual harmony. This, indeed, is the compelling and very contemporary reason why the study of the Indian tradition of freedom, as it is reconstructed by Dennis Dalton, is so important today.

---

3   Gandhi, *CWMG* 69:399–401. See also Richard B. Gregg, *Which Way Lies Hope? An Examination of Capitalism, Communism, Socialism and Gandhiji's Programme* (Ahmedabad: Navajivan Publishing House, 1952).

Acknowledgements and Bibliographical Essay

I wish to acknowledge the main influences relating to my continuing contact with Indian thought. Because I want to give ample recognition to each, there will be some repetition of what has already been noted above.

This entire project of presenting my previous and current thought, including a memoir, would have been impossible without the steadfast support and inspiration of Professor James Tully, Distinguished Professor Emeritus of Political Science, Law, Indigenous Governance and Philosophy at the University of Victoria, British Columbia, Canada, whom I have mentioned in various places because of his indispensable role in my thinking about modern political thought. This will be further explained below as starting with a workshop on Gandhi that he organized with the collaboration of the philosophy department of Reed College, Portland, Oregon. Tully is rightly renowned for his mastery of the art of dialogue, and the workshop featured this through presentations by professors Akeel Bilgrami, Karuna Mantena, Tully and myself. These are as yet unpublished, along with the extensive discussions that followed, so it is appropriate to acknowledge the major ideas that developed then, as well as from extensive correspondence afterwards with Tully. My paper at Reed College was entitled 'Gandhi at the Center of Indian Political Thought', and it attempted to integrate a spectrum of twentieth-century Indian thinkers that eventually became the 'group of seven' formulated in this book. The question I posed for the workshop was what new ideas about them had emerged from recent scholarship.

As I reviewed and analysed this subject, the following was deemed especially significant. First, Vivekananda's key role in being the first to emphasize the central theory of the means-ends relationship, as Gandhi and others recognized. Outstanding recent publications on Vivekananda are two remarkable biographies: *Guru to the World: The Life and Legacy of Vivekananda* by Ruth Harris, and *Swami Vivekananda's Vedantic Cosmopolitanism* by Swami Medhananda. Harris observes Vivekananda's evident parallels with Aurobindo but also develops significant similarities with Gandhi, including their emphasis on social service 'as well as ethical, spiritual, and political freedom'.[1] Second, the important work on Aurobindo by Peter Heehs, an American historian residing in Pondicherry (or Puducherry), whose *The Lives of Sri Aurobindo* (2008) scrupulously examined his intellectual journey. This is a uniquely definitive exposition that, more than any other work on Aurobindo, establishes his profound contribution to moral and political philosophy. As the book's title indicates, it narrates his extraordinary journey or passage from terrorist to philosopher of spiritual freedom. Third, although much

---

1   Ruth Harris, *Guru to the World: The Life and Legacy of Vivekananda* (Cambridge: Harvard University Press, 2022), pp. 421–22; see also Swami Medhananda, *Vivekananda's Vedantic Cosmopolitanism* (Cambridge, MA: Oxford University Press, 2022).

has been written on Rabindranath Tagore's literary accomplishments, not enough attention was given to the significance of his political thought and particularly his concept of nationalism. This was largely compensated by Ramachandra Guha's brilliant and erudite introduction to Tagore's *Nationalism* (2017). Guha has written a generous foreword to the present book, and his role in its publication is noted below. However, in view of the destructive chauvinism that has raged recently in both India and the US, special attention should be given to Tagore's singular critique of nationalism. Fourth, the abundant scholarship on Gandhi since the last edition of my Gandhi book in 2012 was incisively enhanced by Bilgrami and Mantena at the Reed workshop, as well as in their subsequent prolific writings and addresses that have informed this edition. Their original scholarship on Gandhi has been referenced only briefly, yet I met them at Portland for the first time, and their intellectual impact proved decisive.

However, with the exception of Tully's works (cited below), the contrast between satyagraha and duragraha and its consequences have been overlooked by virtually all Gandhi scholars. As I have asserted throughout this book, including in the memoir, Gandhians such as Nirmal Kumar Bose and Pyarelal Nayar stressed the key contrast between these two types of nonviolent theory and practice, as Gandhi reiterated from 1917 to 1947. A main purpose here is to feature this as a paradigmatic interpretation of Gandhi scholarship. Most importantly, reflections on Thomas Weber's analysis of Gene Sharp's influential work (noted below), followed by correspondence with Tully, revealed the deficiencies in recent theories set forth by Erica Chenoweth and Maria Stephan in *Why Civil Resistance Works: The Strategic Logic of Nonviolent Conflict* (N.Y.: Columbia University Press, 2011) and in *Civil Resistance: What Everyone Needs to Know* (N.Y.: Oxford University Press, 2021). Following the logic of Gene Sharp, their claims for allegedly successful cases of nonviolent action are based on the premise that numerous instances of resistance are effective, whereas subsequent events show that they have failed, e.g., Arab Spring and Myanmar. The fallacy lies in a confusion between satyagraha and duragraha: failures come from adoptions of the latter when Gandhi (and Richard Gregg), insisted on pursuit of the former, with strict standards of satyagraha and steadfast Constructive Programs serving as requisites.

Fifth, in relation to B.R. Ambedkar, my chief purpose here is to correct a serious imbalance among leading Ambedkar scholars in regard to *Annihilation of Caste* as compared to *The Buddha and His Dhamma*, even though he specifically designated the latter as his magnum opus. This relative inattention was met in part by the commendable critical edition of it published by Aakash Singh Rathore and Ajay Verma (2014). As compared to previous contributions to Ambedkar's thought, this unprecedented scholarship, with scrupulous editorial commentary, serves to place Ambedkar's cumulative wisdom as a Buddhist in proper perspective. I have accordingly concentrated on this classic edition, bringing Ambedkar's moral and social philosophy within the comparative rubric of others in the 'group of seven'.

Finally, M.N. Roy's significance as a political theorist has been a major concern since I initially wrote a Master's thesis on his Radical Humanism at the University of Chicago, supervised by professor Stephen Hay from 1961 to 1962. This was fostered by discussions about Roy and J.P. Narayan with Nirmal Bose, Pyarelal and Sushila Nayar, as well as with Royists. All of my subsequent engagement with Narayan convinced me that both he and Roy had been neglected as political thinkers. These intellectual parallels were evident in Narayan's *A Plea for Reconstruction of Indian Polity* (1959), that, as he told me, had been influenced by Roy. They were closest in their ideas about power, as evident in Roy's *Politics, Power and Parties*. Their combined critique of parliamentary democracy was as devastating as it remains prescient today. James Tully affirms this in his crucial distinction between 'power over' and 'power with', discussed in the Reed workshop and subsequently published in *James Tully: To Think and Act Differently*.[2]

First and foremost is Professor Rajeev Kadambi, whom I've already cited in connection with his article on Ambedkar. This barely conveys my indebtedness to him from before my retirement in 2008, when we consulted regularly on his PhD dissertation for Brown University on Gandhi, Ambedkar and M.N. Roy, to the present. His editorial organization of this volume was indispensable, starting with the stream of source materials that he provided, his ongoing critical analysis of views or interpretations of all this book's contents, and most of all, his personification of the dedication, 'to the force of friendship'. He has acted in ways that have reinforced my past and present relationship to India in the most personal manner, as when he twice journeyed to visit my friend, Professor Sriram Mehrotra, at the Indian Institute of Advanced Study in Shimla, once a former close colleague at SOAS from 1962–69 and after, and as a valuable guide to my research in India. This was in the last stage of Mehrotra's life, as he was still struggling, though seriously debilitated, to finish his history of the Indian National Congress. Rajeev's offer to reconnect us completed the circle of my passage to India.

Professor Ramachandra Guha inspired this book first through his definitive biography of Gandhi, where his incomparable research afforded new discoveries, and then by urging me to produce an expanded edition of my original book on Indian ideas of freedom together with a memoir. But this project all started when his son, Keshava, recommended the project, so I acknowledge him as the initial prompt. Professor Guha has read and made extensive comments on this entire book and generously written a Foreword. His recent publication, *Rebels Against the Raj: Western Fighters for India's Freedom* (2022),

---

2   Alexander Livingston (ed.), 'Integral Nonviolence', in *James Tully: To Think and Act Differently* (London: Routledge, 2022), pp. 225–41.

another superlative work, follows his definitive biography of Gandhi and includes figures whom I have also related in my memoir and carefully considered. In every instance, I have benefited from his stellar publications, too numerous to mention here. Finally, we share a strong admiration for Nirmal Kumar Bose, whose immense influence on all my writing is recounted in the memoir's opening. It is inexplicable that no major biography has been published of Bose, so I hope that this testimony may spur such a project. I've conveyed above my unbounded admiration for Bose as the most astute critic of not only Gandhi but the makers of modern Indian political thought.

Numerous contributors to shaping my ideas on this subject have already been acknowledged in my book on Gandhi (2012). There are also two other scholars, briefly named above, close friends from Canada and Australia, who have had a profound influence on my thought. The first is James Tully, leading Canadian philosopher who has made a unique contribution to a theory of 'integral nonviolence'. In Gandhian terms, this begins with his key introduction to a new edition of Richard Gregg's classic, *The Power of Nonviolence* (2018). This extends to his magnum opus, *Public Philosophy in a New Key* (2 vols., 2008, especially vol. 2, with the significant subtitle of *Imperialism and Civic Freedom*). Yet he doesn't stop here. Unlike other contemporary theorists of the subject, he relates it to a lifelong study of the Aboriginal Peoples of America, especially in his acclaimed *Strange Multiplicity: Constitutionalism in the Age of Diversity* (1995). This places nonviolence in an exciting context relating it to climate change. Its full dimensions are as yet unexplored, but there are evident conceptual correspondences of wisdom from Aboriginals to Gandhi's and Ambedkar's reverence for all being, best expressed in Buddhism.

This value is stated explicitly by Ambedkar in the crucial distinction made between karuna and maitri. This lies at the core of the common emphasis in Hinduism and Buddhism as when Ambedkar wrote, 'The Buddha did not stop with teaching karuna. Karuna is only love for human beings. Buddha went beyond and taught maitri. Maitri is love for all living beings.'[3] This has been expressed by other theorists of nonviolence, as when Gandhi wrote in 1924, 'I believe in the essential unity of man and for that matter *of all that lives*.'[4] Yet only Tully has made the key connection of this with the teachings of American Indigenous peoples. The lessons of nonviolence for our planet are as profound and original as they are urgent and relevant. My relationship with Tully ranged from a Gandhi workshop in Portland, Oregon, to having engaged in extensive correspondence where he has shared innumerable ideas and sources. Not least of his intellectual strengths is that he is a master of philosophical dialogue, as evidenced in his *On Global Citizenship: James Tully in Dialogue* (2014).

Another major influence on my thought is Thomas Weber, among the most exacting and dedicated Gandhi scholars. He has contributed to Gandhian literature and concepts of conflict resolution for decades through innumerable books and articles, perhaps the best known being *Gandhi as Disciple and Mentor* (2004). I had the pleasure to co-author with him an article on Gandhi and this increased my respect for his admirably scrupulous research; he also made valuable comments on my memoir included in this book. His most publicized article has been an essay entitled 'Gene Sharp—Nonviolence becomes a political method' (included as a chapter in the aforementioned book, a version first appearing in 2003).

Like most students of Gandhi's thought and practice, I had followed with admiration the voluminous writings of Gene Sharp since his early work about him published in 1960, then by his encyclopedic cross-cultural analysis of nonviolent campaigns in *The Politics of Nonviolent*

---

3   B.R. Ambedkar, *The Buddha and His Dhamma*, ed. Aakash Rathore and Ajay Verma (New Delhi: Oxford University Press, 2011), p. 159.

4   *Collected Works of Mahatma Gandhi* (Delhi: Government of India, 1994), Vol. 25, p. 391, 4 December 1924.

Action (1973). A major shift in Sharp's thesis about how nonviolence works became increasingly clear, yet it wasn't until Weber's essay on Sharp that the implications appeared as consequential. After tracing the development of Sharp's thought, Weber asserts with characteristic clarity that 'ultimately Sharp's life work becomes one of promoting his own brand of nonviolence, not Gandhi's or Gandhi's satyagraha'. Therefore, Sharp shifts his essential theory from what he initially entitled *Gandhi Wields the Weapon of Moral Power* (1960), to become *Gandhi As A Political Strategist* (1979). This places such an emphasis on tactics that 'Sharp more or less abandons the Mahatma'.[5] The ethical basis of satyagraha or the virtue of ahimsa is absent, and the main aim becomes 'to adopt nonviolent methods as a practical expedient, a technique that works'.[6]

This change in Sharp's thought happened during the 1960s. That is, the shift to what I see as duragraha, a concept of nonviolence lacking the philosophical ethos that Tully conceives of as 'integral nonviolence'. Weber delineates this change definitively. It was already formulated at an international conference that Sharp and I attended in Delhi on Gandhi's relevance in January 1970. Sharp was a principal speaker, and he set forth the outlines of his encyclopedic magnum opus to appear three years later. It describes nearly 200 categories of nonviolent resistance. A representative example among them is the British and American Berlin airlift, 1948–49, that Sharp insists 'does meet the criteria for classification as nonviolent action'.[7] However successful this action, it couldn't qualify in Gandhian terms as satyagraha. In a review article of Sharp's book in 1974, I argued that the main flaw in his

---

5   Thomas Weber, *Gandhi as Disciple and Mentor* (Cambridge, New York: Cambridge University Press, 2004), p. 238.

6   Weber quoting Sharp in a 1997 lecture, in Ibid.

7   Gene Sharp, *The Politics of Nonviolent Action* (Boston: Porter Sargent Pub., 1973), pp. 408–9.

theory was a failure to recognize the numerous cases that he cited as being instances of duragraha.[8] Weber's incisive analysis, following and building on the earlier conceptualizations of Pyarelal and Nirmal Bose, pointed out the significance of Sharp's shift from Gandhian satyagraha to the duragraha in nonviolent resistance.

On the subject of Gandhi, I must acknowledge the indispensable contribution to Gandhi studies of Professor K. Swaminathan and C.N. Patel, editors of *The Collected Works of Mahatma Gandhi* (1994), who allowed me to work with them. They produced a monumental opus as they shared their knowledge with an unfailing generosity, openness and sharing spirit. They led a team of scholars totally committed to the highest standards of excellence. I am especially pleased now to be in continuing contact with Ms Dina Patel, CN's daughter. Her utterly selfless dedication is married to solid technical expertise as she carries on her father's work. In a letter of 3 March 2020, she wrote: 'The *CWMG* has been our lifeblood, as I have witnessed the ceaseless toil and determination over the decades. It is an inseparable part of my existence.' Gandhi was a magnetic force that drew an amazing talent and devotion throughout his life, as this book portrays in only a small part. Now the magnetism continues to attract such total commitment as an enduring testament to his spirit.

Regarding B.R. Ambedkar's thought, the analysis of his theory of means-ends and in the essay on his idea of freedom, the subject has been especially challenging. This was because I had written about him before only in *Sources of Indian Traditions*.[9] While working with the inspiring

---

8 Dennis Dalton, 'Forms of Nonviolence: Lessons from Gandhi's Method', *South Asian Review* 7, no. 2 (1974) 145–51.

9 Rachel Fell McDermott et al. (eds), 'Mahatma Gandhi and Responses', in *Sources of Indian Traditions: Modern India, Pakistan and Bangladesh*, Vol. 2, Third edition (New York: Columbia University Press, 2014), pp. 338–451.

team of scholars led by professor Rachel McDermott on this volume that I've referenced frequently in the text above as a fundamental guide, I received assistance from Frances W. Pritchett, Ambedkar scholar and Professor Emerita of modern Indic languages in the department of Middle Eastern, South Asian and African Studies at Columbia University. Since she served with me as among the five editors of this edition, I was able to benefit from her superlative website.[10] The source of the text for the electronic version of *The Buddha and His Dhamma* was from his *Writings and Speeches*, vol.11 (1992). This also contains an Unpublished Preface by Ambedkar (6 April 1956), the text provided by Eleanor Zelliot and Vasant Moon. Professor Pritchett comments at the outset of her editor's introduction that 'It remains a testament to its author's love not only for the figure of the Buddha, but for social justice, humane values, and a clear-eyed honesty in looking at life.'[11] Although I have relied principally on the edition of *The Buddha and His Dhamma* by Aakash Singh Rathore and Ajay Verma (2014) as cited throughout on Ambedkar, the edition by Pritchett has also been consulted as an essential reference.

Aakash Singh Rathore's *Indian Political Theory: Laying the Groundwork for Svaraj* (2017) contains an outstanding chapter entitled 'Gandhi and Ambedkar'[12] that is essential reading for this comparison. It concludes that 'we should be content to bring these two great men into a *constellation*' (his italics). I have used the term 'group' of seven but sometimes referred to them as a 'constellation' as well. The terms are not synonymous, and Rathore does not extend the comparison

---

10 See www.columbia.edu/itc/mealac/pritchett/00ambedkar/ambedkar_buddha/00_fwp.html 12/31/2014.

11 See p. 1.

12 Aakash Singh Rathore, 'Gandhi and Ambedkar', in *Indian Political Theory: Laying the Groundwork for Svaraj* (London, New York: Routledge, 2017), pp. 168–91.

beyond Gandhi and Ambedkar, but his correspondence with me about this use of language has been extremely helpful.

In pursuit of other Ambedkar scholars, I have also been in direct and recent correspondence with Professor Scott R. Stroud, Program Director of Media Ethics and editor of *Media Ethics* in the Moody College of Communication at the University of Texas at Austin and author of *The Evolution of Pragmatism in India: Ambedkar, Dewey, and the Rhetoric of Reconstruction* (University of Chicago Press, 2023). He generously provided me with a series of his articles on Ambedkar. These include 'Force, Nonviolence, and Communication in the Pragmatism of Bhimrao Ambedkar' in *Journal of Speculative Philosophy* (32, no.1 [2018] pp. 112–30); 'Communication, Justice and Reconstruction. Ambedkar as an Indian Pragmatist', in *B.R. Ambedkar: The Quest for Justice*, vol. 1, ed. A.S. Rathore (2020); 'Creative Democracy, Communication, and the Uncharted Sources of Bhimrao Ambedkar's Deweyan Pragmatism', in *Education and Culture* (34, no. 1 [2018]: pp. 3–22); 'Pragmatism and the Pursuit of Social Justice in India: Bhimrao Ambedkar and the Rhetoric of Religious Reorientation', in *Rhetoric Society Quarterly* (46, no. 1 [2016]: pp. 5–27); and, most recently, 'Excessively Harsh Critique and Democratic Rhetoric: The Enigma of Bhimrao Ambedkar's *Riddles in Hinduism*', in *Journal for the History of Rhetoric* (25, no. 1 [2022]: 2–30) and 'Pragmatist Riddles' in Ambedkar's *Riddles in Hinduism* (Forward Press, June 1, 2019: pp. 1–8). The range of Stroud's scholarship is remarkable, having researched the works of John Dewey and Swami Vivekananda, publishing on them as well as on Kant. Not least, he has engaged with me in fruitful correspondence about his field studies on Ambedkar in India, unearthing rare documents from Ambedkar's personal manuscripts. It must be reiterated that I am responsible for the interpretations of Ambedkar's work presented in this book, so the commendation here of various Ambedkar scholars should not imply mutual agreement among us.

Throughout my seven years as a graduate student and then lecturer on Indian political thought, I was fortunate to study or converse with several India area specialists. Ample attribution has been given above to the decisive influence of Nirmal Kumar Bose. It should be added that by directing me to the University of Chicago, this led to the supervision of Stephen Hay, professor of history there, who was then immersed in research for his major work, *Asian Ideas of East and West: Tagore and His Critics in Japan, China and India* (Cambridge, Massachusetts: Harvard Press, 1970). After Hay served on my MA thesis (1962), we were together on panels or seminars in Mexico City, New York, Washington D.C. and Toronto, often discussing his work on Tagore (for which I wrote a review in the *Journal of Asian Studies* in 1970). Hay then recommended that I apply to the School of Oriental and African Studies (SOAS) to study Tagore further with professors T.W. Clark, longstanding expert on Bengal, and Hugh Tinker, my PhD supervisor. The latter corresponded frequently with me in 1974 while he examined resources at Visva-Bharati University (V-B, founded by Tagore) at Santiniketan. Tinker's focus was on Gandhi, C.F. Andrews and Tagore, helped by Pratul Chandra Gupta, Upacharya of V-B and Trustee of the Tagore Estate. I recall this with fondness because professor Bidyut Chakrabarty, presently Vice-Chancellor of V-B, has been an extensive expert critic of the sections on Tagore included in this volume. I look forward to serving at V-B as a Visiting Professor, thanks to his generous invitation.

Among the team of scholars who produced the latest (third) edition of *Sources of Indian Traditions* referenced above, my longest relationship has been with Professor Leonard Gordon. We were colleagues at Columbia from 1969 and afterwards in New York City, a lasting association that has greatly informed my understanding of Bengali thinkers, starting with his award-winning book, *Bengal: The Nationalist Movement 1876–1940* (1974), and culminating in his definitive biography of Subhas Chandra Bose and his brother Sarat

Chandra Bose, *Brothers Against the Raj* (1990). He made a significant contribution to my chapter titled 'Gandhi and Responses' in *Sources of Indian Traditions*. This occurred primarily with his advice on the Subhas Bose section but also with a prompt to include a brief reference there to Abdul Ghaffar Khan. This, in turn, led to researching in much greater depth Khan's ideas and leadership with the guidance of Professor Vazira Zamindar, department of history at Brown University. Her extensive knowledge of him and her study of writings by and about him led me to conclude that if the 'group of seven' presented in this book were extended to a Muslim thinker, the Badshah Khan would be first and foremost to consider.

In dozens of student and faculty seminars, I had the advantage of exchanging ideas about all of the Indian thinkers included in this volume with professors A.L. Basham, the classicist and author of the famed *Wonder That Was India* (1954, 1977), Peter Hardy, contributor on Pakistan and Islam to the first edition of *Sources of Indian Tradition* (1958), J. Duncan M. Derrett, author of several publications on Indian law and comparisons of Christianity and Buddhism, especially *Religion, Law and the State in India* (1968). I am especially indebted to David Friedman, eminent Dutch Buddhologist and author of *Buddhism in Life,* whose classes on Buddhism at SOAS enriched my knowledge of that subject, and who generously read and discussed my PhD thesis, making important contributions, as noted in the text.

I have already mentioned professor Sibnarayan Ray in connection with M.N. Roy, but he was also among those who informed my study of Tagore. His edited work, *Gandhi, India and the World: An International Symposium* (1970), referenced above, includes essays by Nirmal Kumar Bose, Hugh Tinker, Amlan Datta, Amiya Chakravarty, Philip Spratt, Agehananda Bharati, Hugh Owen, J.P. Narayan and A.L. Basham. Ray wrote an introduction and contributed a chapter entitled 'Tagore–Gandhi Controversy' in the book. He did me the honour of inviting me to join these scholars, all of whom I had personally interviewed or became my colleagues. Their combined wisdom on Gandhi, Roy, Tagore and Ambedkar proved helpful for this book.

As I conclude these acknowledgements, I'm aware of scholarly associations made and unmentioned anywhere above or in this essay. For example, even before I published books on Gandhi, I met Thomas Pantham and Kenneth Deutsch, both scholars of modern Indian thought, who asked me to contribute to their excellent edition published in 1986 with esteemed academics such as Bhikhu Parekh, Partha Chatterjee, Radharaman Chakrabarti, Sudipta Kaviraj, Ronald Terchek and Ashis Nandy; together with the two editors, most have since gained prominence by writing on many of the seven thinkers included here. In our brief meeting at Barnard, Pantham impressed me with his knowledge of Gandhi, and Deutsch with Aurobindo.

Finally, I know no person more reliable as a source on the entire classical and modern Indian intellectual tradition than Professor Richard H. Davis of Bard College. This scholar of ancient and contemporary Indian religions and culture possesses such a reservoir of knowledge about all things India that I count on him for information on any subject of South Asia. Only he could write a new edition to supersede A.L. Basham's renowned tome. His unique work, *The Biography of the Gita* (2014), is a testament to his range, discussing almost all major thinkers with a typically incisive comparison of Gandhi and Ambedkar.

I am indebted to my sons, Kevin and Shaun Dalton, the former for his intellectual persistence in making fine distinctions among the following terms: group, school, constellation and genre. As an English instructor who has researched and taught T.W. Adorno, Walter Benjamin and Adrian Fowler, he was consulted for terminology, choosing 'group' more than others. Shaun showed indefatigable assistance with technical work on the manuscript.

In India, Ms Akshata Satluri provided outstanding editorial expertise, prompt, efficient and flawless. I have been extremely impressed by her exceptional skill and reliability. Also, Ms Rinita Banerjee, Senior Editor

(Literary), of HarperCollins, must rank first among the several editors of my various publications. Her exemplary service defines the essential expertise of her profession, scrupulous, skilled, and conscientious to a fault. All authors should have the privilege and benefit of having her outstanding assistance. I am immensely grateful for her dedication.

When Aristotle wrote his classic commendation of friendship in his *Ethics*, analysing the 'kinds' and 'grounds' as a human necessity (chapters 8, 9), he definitely did not overstate its inestimable virtue. He and others, from the ancient Greeks and Romans to Martin Luther King, Jr., have distinguished between *philia* for friendship and *eros* as romantic love. Only one person has combined these two qualities in my life for over sixty years, Sharron Scheline Dalton, who leads this book's dedication. Together we shared, often with our children, many passages to India.

Glossary

Advaita Vedanta:	one school of classical Indian thought which teaches that the sole reality is Brahman, the impersonal World Soul; hence, a doctrine of monism.
ahimsa:	Nonviolence, not merely non-killing or avoidance of harm, but, in a broader sense, positive dimensions of love.
Arthasastra:	The literature of 'wealth' and, more particularly, politics.
atma or atman:	the Self or soul of the individual.
bhakti:	devotion to God; bhakta, the devotee.
brahmacharya:	continence.
Brahmos:	members of the Brahmo Samaj.
dhamma:	righteousness, meaning right relations among people in all spheres of life.
dharma:	a complex term, but generally, as used here, 'sacred law'.
Dharmasastra:	the literature of dharma; religious texts.

duragraha:	Biased nonviolent resistance to attain a selfish goal that may inflict lasting detrimental consequences. Although an act of duragraha will not involve physical violence, it harbours 'violence of the spirit' in the form of anger, greed or hatred. Like 'passive resistance', as both are at the opposite pole from satyagraha.
guru:	spiritual teacher.
Indian Renaissance:	characterization of the modern Indian intellectual tradition, introduced by Sri Aurobindo in 1916, who saw it as inspired mainly by Vivekananda.
Kali Yuga:	Dark Age, the era of universal decay, which is the present age.
karma:	action or work; Karma Yoga, the yoga of action.
karuna:	loving kindness to human beings.
khaddar:	cloth made of homespun yarn.
Khilafat:	variation of Caliphate.
Lok Sevak Sangh:	people's service organization.
Lokamanya:	'Honoured by the people'; title given to B.G. Tilak.
Maharshi:	great sage or saint.
Mahatma:	great soul.
maitri/metta:	fellow feeling for all beings, friend and foe alike.
maya:	illusion.
moksha or mukti:	spiritual freedom or liberation of the spirit.
nibbana:	the goal of happiness and bliss of the Buddhist. Associated with nonviolence and love, freedom from anger or hatred.
panchama:	an untouchable or Dalit (downtrodden).
panchayat:	an organ of government, comparable on a local level to a town or village council.

Patanjali:	ancient Indian philosopher of Yoga.
Ram Rajya:	an ideal society; a reign of righteousness, patterned after the legendary rule of Ram.
sadhu (sahdu):	Hindu holy man.
Sanatana Dharma:	the Eternal Religion.
sannyasa:	renunciation; sannyasin, one who has renounced material for spiritual pursuits.
sarvodaya:	'the welfare of all'.
satya:	Truth.
satyagraha:	'adherence to the Truth'; truth or soul-force, coined by Gandhi to express the power of nonviolence.
Satyayuga:	Age of Truth; legendary Indian Golden Age.
shlok:	Sanskrit couplet or stanza.
shraddha ceremony:	that of the customary Hindu post-funeral rites.
Shvetaketu:	the name of a young seeker in the *Chandogya Upanishad*.
swadeshi:	one's own country; as a movement, the use of goods produced within one's own country.
swaraj or swarajya:	self-rule or self-control, used both in the political (national) and moral (individual) sense.
tapasya:	penance, the self-discipline associated with asceticism.
tat tvam asi:	'Thou art That'; the Upanishadic maxim asserting the identity of the individual soul with the Absolute.
Vaishya:	one of the four traditional divisions of Indian society; a caste of merchants and traders.
varnashrama dharma:	the theoretical social order of ancient India, used in Hinduism as a model for an ideal society.
yajna:	religious sacrifice.

Bibliography to the 1982 Edition

Books

Swami Vivekananda (Narendra Nath Datta)
The Complete Works of Swami Vivekananda, 8 vols. (Calcutta, 1955–1963).

Sri Aurobindo (A.A. Ghosh or Ghose)
Essays on the Gita, First Series (Calcutta, 1937).

Essays on the Gita, Second Series (Calcutta, 1949).

The Foundations of Indian Culture (Pondicherry, 1959).

The Human Cycle, The Ideal of Human Unity, War and Self-Determination (Pondicherry, 1962).

Letters, First Series, Second edition (Bombay, 1950).

Letters, Second Series (Bombay, 1949).

Letters, Fourth Series (Bombay, 1951).

The Life Divine (Pondicherry, 1960).

Sri Aurobindo On Himself and On the Mother (Pondicherry, 1959).

The Synthesis of Yoga (Madras, 1948).

M.K. Gandhi

An Autobiography, The Story of My Experiments with Truth, translated by Mahadev Desai (Boston, 1960).

Collected Works, 100 vols. (Delhi, 1958–1994).

Constructive Programme: Its Meaning and Place, Second edition (Ahmedabad, 1948).

Gandhiji's Correspondence with Government, 1942–44, Second edition (Ahmedabad, 1945).

Gandhiji's Correspondence with Government, 1944–47 (Ahmedabad, 1959).

Hind Swaraj or Indian Home Rule (Ahmedabad, 1938).

Letters to a Disciple (Mirabehn) (New York, 1950).

Letters to Rajkumari Amrit Kaur (Ahmedabad, 1961).

Satyagraha in South Africa (Ahmedabad, 1961).

Rabindranath Tagore

Collected Poems and Plays of Rabindranath Tagore (London, 1958).

Creative Unity (London, 1922).

The Diary of a Westward Voyage, translated by Indu Dutt (London, 1962).

Gitanjali (Song Offerings) (London, 1920).

Four Chapters (Calcutta, 1950).

Gora (London, 1949).

The Home and the World, translated by Surendranath Tagore (London, 1919).

Letters to a Friend, edited by C.F. Andrews (London, 1928).

Nationalism (London, 1950).

Personality, Lectures Delivered in America (London, 1917).

Red Oleanders (London, 1925).

The Religion of Man (London, 1931).

Reminiscences (London, 1920).

Sadhana, The Realisation of Life (London, 1913).
Towards Universal Man (London, 1961).

Periodicals, Compilations and Speeches

Sri Aurobindo

Indu Prakash:

'New Lamps for Old', in Haridas Mukherjee and Uma Mukherjee, *Sri Aurobindo's Political Thought*, 1893–1908 (Calcutta, 1958).

Bande Mataram:

Mukherjee, Haridas, and Uma Mukherjee, *Bande Mataram and Indian Nationalism* (1906–1908) (Calcutta, 1957).
The Doctrine of Passive Resistance (Pondicherry, 1952).

Karmayogin:

The Ideal of the Karmayogin (Pondicherry, 1950).
Speeches (Pondicherry, 1952).

Arya:

Evolution (Pondicherry, 1964).
Ideals and Progress (Pondicherry, 1951).
The Renaissance in India (Pondicherry, 1951).
The Superman, Fourth edition (Pondicherry, 1950).
Bankim-Tilak Dayananda (Pondicherry, 1955).
Gandhi and Tagore: A Study in Comparison (Madras, 1922).

M.K. Gandhi

Selections from *Young India* and *Harijan* in:
Young India, 1919–1922, I (Madras, 1922). [Selections]
Young India, 1924–1926, II (Madras. 1927). [Selections]
Young India, 1927–1928, III (Madras, 1935). [Selections]

Democracy: Real and Deceptive (Ahmedabad, 1961).

Hindu Dharma (Ahmedabad, 1950).

India of My Dreams (Ahmedabad, 1959).

Sarvodaya (The Welfare of All) (Ahmedabad, 1958).

Satyagraha (Non-Violent Resistance) (Ahmedabad, 1951).

Selections from Gandhi (Ahmedabad, 1948).

Socialism of My Conception (Bombay, 1957).

Towards Non-Violent Socialism (Ahmedabad, 1951).

Truth Is God (Ahmedabad, 1955).

Speeches and Writings of Mahatma Gandhi, Fourth edition (Madras, 1938).

Rabindranath Tagore

A Vision of India's History (Calcutta, 1951).

Salutation to Sri Aurobindo (Pondicherry, 1949).

Truth Called Them Differently (Tagore–Gandhi Controversy), edited by R.K. Prabhu and Ravindra Kelekar (Ahmedabad, 1961).

Biographies and Critical Analysis

Vivekananda

By His Eastern and Western Disciples, *The Life of Swami Vivekananda* (Calcutta, 1960).

Datta, Bhupendranath, *Swami Vivekananda, Patriot-Prophet* (Calcutta, 1954).

Rolland, Romain, *The Life of Vivekananda and the Universal Gospel*, translated by E.F. Malcolm-Smith (Calcutta, 1960).

———, *The Life of Ramakrishna*, translated by E.F. Malcolm-Smith (Calcutta, 1960).

Schweitzer, Albert, *Indian Thought and Its Development* (London, 1956).

Varma, V.P., *Modern Indian Political Thought* (Agra, 1961).

Sri Aurobindo

Chaudhuri, Haridas, and Frederic Spiegelberg, *The Integral Philosophy of Sri Aurobindo* (London, 1960).

Purani, A.B., *The Life of Sri Aurobindo* (Pondicherry, 1960).

Singh, Karan, *Prophet of Indian Nationalism: A Study of the Political Thought of Sri Aurobindo Ghose, 1893–1910* (London, 1963).

Varma, V.P., *The Political Philosophy of Sri Aurobindo* (London, 1960).

M.K. Gandhi

Andrews, C.F., *Mahatma Gandhi's Ideas, Including Selections from his Writings* (London, 1931).

Bose, Nirmal Kumar, *My Days with Gandhi* (Calcutta, 1953).

——, *Studies in Gandhism* (Calcutta, 1947).

Desai, Mahadev, *The Gospel of Selfless Action or The Gita According to Gandhi* (Ahmedabad, 1956).

Dhawan, Gopinath, *The Political Philosophy of Mahatma Gandhi* (Ahmedabad, 1957).

Doctor, Adi H., *Anarchist Thought in India* (London, 1964).

Fischer, Louis, *The Life of Mahatma Gandhi* (London, 1951).

——, *A Week with Gandhi* (London, 1943).

Kripalani, K.R., *Gandhi, Tagore, and Nehru* (Bombay, 1949).

Majumdar, Biman Bihari (ed.), *Gandhian Concepts of State* (Calcutta, 1957).

Majumdar, R.C., *Three Phases of India's Struggle for Freedom* (Bombay, 1961).

Nanda, B.R., *Mahatma Gandhi, A Biography* (London, 1958).

Mallik, Gurdial, *Gandhi and Tagore* (Ahmedabad, 1961).

Namboodiripad, E.M.S., *The Mahatma and The Ism* (New Delhi, 1959).

Pyarelal, *Mahatma Gandhi, The Last Phase*, 2 vols. (Ahmedabad, 1958).

Rothermund, Indira, *The Philosophy of Restraint* (Bombay, 1963).

Sheean, Vincent, *Lead, Kindly Light* (New York, 1949).

Shukla, Chandrashanker, *Gandhi's View of Life* (Bombay, 1956).

Tendulkar, D.G., *Mahatma: Life of Mohandas Karamchand Gandhi*, 8 vols., revised edition (Delhi, 1960–1963).

Varma, V.P., *The Political Philosophy of Mahatma Gandhi and Sarvodaya* (Agra, 1959).

Rabindranath Tagore

Andrews, C.F., and Dwijendranath Tagore, *Ethics of Destruction* (Madras, 1921).

Aronson, A., *Rabindranath Through Western Eyes* (Allahabad, 1943).

Ghose, Sisirkumar, *The Later Poems of Tagore* (Bombay, 1961).

Gupta, Atulchandra (ed.), *Studies in the Bengal Renaissance* (Calcutta, 1958).

Sen Gupta, S.C., *The Great Sentinel: A Study of Rabindranath Tagore* (Calcutta, 1948).

Kripalani, Krishna, *Rabindranath Tagore: A Biography* (London, 1962).

Radhakrishnan, S., *The Philosophy of Rabindranath Tagore* (London, 1918).

Sen, Sachin, *The Political Thought of Tagore* (Calcutta, 1947).

Contemporary Writings

Chatterjee, Bankimchandra, *The Abbey of Bliss (Anandamath)*, translated by Nares Chandra Sen-Gupta, Fifth edition (Calcutta, 1906).

Das, Bhagavan, *Ancient versus Modern Scientific Socialism or Theosophy and Capitalism, Fascism and Communism* (Madras, 1934).

———, *The Essential Unity of All Religions* (Benares, 1947).

Das, C.R., *India for Indians* (Madras, 1918).

———, *Speeches* (Calcutta, 1919).

———, *Freedom Through Disobedience*, Presidential Address at 37th Indian National Congress (Madras, 1922).

———, *To My Countrymen* (Vellore, 1922).

————, *Outline Scheme of Swaraj*, National Convention Memoranda, No. 2 (Madras, 1923).

Gokhale, Gopal Krishna, *Speeches and Writings* (1877–1913), edited by R.P. Patwardhan and D.V. Ambedkar (Poona, 1962).

Naoroji, Dadabhai, *Speeches and Writings* (Madras, 1910).

Pal, Bipin Chandra, *The New Spirit* (Calcutta, 1907).

————, *The Spirit of Indian Nationalism* (London, 1910).

————, *Indian Nationalism: Its Principles and Personalities* (Madras, 1918).

————, *Swaraj, The Goal and The Way* (Madras, 1921).

————, *Brahmo Samaj and the Battle of Swaraj in India* (Calcutta, 1926).

————, *The Soul of India: A Constructive Study of Indian Thought and Ideals*, Third edition (Calcutta, 1940).

————, *Swadeshi and Swaraj, The Rise of New Patriotism* (Calcutta, 1954).

Rai, Lala Lajpat, *India's Will to Freedom* (Madras, 1921).

————, *Young India* (Lahore, 1927).

Ramakrishna, *Prophet of New India*, translated by Swami Nikhilananda (New York, 1951).

Ramtirth, Swami, *In Woods of God Realisation or The Complete Works of Swami Ramtirath*, vols. 1–3 (Delhi, 1912–1915).

Roy, Rammohun, *The English Works of Raja Rammohun Roy*, 3 vols., edited by Chunder Ghose (Calcutta, 1901).

Saraswati, Dayanand, *Sayings and Precepts of Swami Dayanand Saraswati*, edited by Madan Mohan Seth (Allahabad, 1917).

————, *Light of Truth or Satyarth Prakash*, translated by Chiranjiva Bharadwaja (Lahore, 1927).

Sen, Keshub Chunder, *Lectures and Tracts* (London, 1870).

————, *Keshub Chunder Sen's Lectures in India*, Part II (Calcutta, 1900).

————, *Keshub Chunder Sen's Lectures in India*, 2 Vols. (London, 1901).

————, *The New Dispensation or the Religion of Harmony* (Calcutta, 1903).

Tagore, Debendranath, *The Autobiography of Maharshi Debendranath Tagore*, translated by Satyendranath Tagore and Indira Devi (London, 1916).

Tilak, Bal Gangadhar, *His Writings and Speeches* (Madras, 1918).

PhD Theses

Argov, Daniel, *The Ideological Differences between Moderates and Extremists in the Indian National Movement, with Special Reference to*

Surendranath Banerjea and Lajpat Rai, 1883–1919, PhD Thesis, School of Oriental and African Studies, University of London, June 1964.

Ghosh, S., *The Influence of Western, Particularly English, Political Ideas on Indian Political Thought, with Special Reference to the Political Ideas of the Indian National Congress 1885–1919*, PhD Thesis, University of London,1950.

McLane, John R., *The Development of Nationalist Ideas and Tactics and the Policies of the Government of India: 1897–1905*, PhD Thesis, University of London, June 1961.

Sharma, B.S., *The Political Philosophy of Mahatma Gandhi in Relation to the English Liberal Tradition*, PhD Thesis, University of London, 1955.

Other Books

Adler, M.J., *The Idea of Freedom: A Dialectical Examination of the Conceptions of Freedom* (New York, 1958).

Aiyer, Sivaswamy, *Evolution of Hindu Moral Ideals* (Calcutta, 1935).

Barker, E., *Political Thought in England, 1848 to 1914* (London, 1959).

———, *Principles of Social and Political Theory* (London, 1961).

Basham, A.L., *The Wonder That Was India* (New York, 1954).

Berlin, Isaiah, *Two Concepts of Liberty*, An Inaugural Lecture Delivered before the University of Oxford on 31 October 1958 (Oxford, 1958).

Bhagavad Gita, The, translated and interpreted by Franklin Edgerton (New York, 1964).

Bondurant, J., *Conquest of Violence* (Princeton, 1958).

Brown, D. Mackenzie, *The White Umbrella: Indian Political Thought from Manu to Gandhi* (Berkeley, 1958).

————, *The Nationalist Movement: Indian Political Thought from Ranade to Bhave* (Berkeley, 1961).

Campbell-Johnson, A., *Mission with Mountbatten* (London, 1951).

Casey, R.G., *An Australian in India* (London, 1947).

Chaudhuri, N.C., *An Autobiography of An Unknown Indian* (London, 1951).

Chirol, V., *Indian Unrest* (London, 1910).

Coomaraswamy, A.K., *Spiritual Authority and Temporal Power in the Indian Theory of Government* (New Haven, Conn., 1942).

Congress Presidential Addresses, 1911–1934, 2nd series (Madras, 1937).

Cranston, M., *Freedom, A New Analysis* (London, 1953).

Das Gupta, J.K., *A Critical Study of the Life and Novels of Bankimchandra* (Calcutta, 1937).

Dasgupta, Surama, *Development of Moral Philosophy in India* (Bombay, 1961).

Dasgupta, Surendranath, A *History of Indian Philosophy*, 5 vols., I and II (London, 1922).

Deane, H.A., *The Political and Social Ideas of St. Augustine* (New York, 1963).

de Bary, W.T. (ed.), *Sources of Indian Tradition* (London, 1958).

Dhammapada, translated by Narada Maha Tera (Calcutta, 1952).

Ghoshal, U.N., *A History of Indian Political Ideas: The Ancient Period and the Period of Transition to the Middle Ages*, revised edition (London, 1959).

Gokhale, B.G., *Indian Thought Through the Ages* (London, 1961).

Gray, A., *The Socialist Tradition, Moses to Lenin* (London, 1963).

Griffith, Arthur, *The Sinn Fein Policy*, National Council Pamphlets—B (Dublin, 1907).

Griffiths, P., *Modern India* (London, 1957).

Hancock, W.K., *Smuts: The Sanguine Years, 1870–1919* (London, 1962).

Hiriyanna, M., *The Quest After Perfection* (Mysore, 1952).

———, *Popular Essays in Indian Philosophy* (Mysore, 1952).

Hopkins, E. Washburn, *Ethics of India* (New Haven, 1924).

Law, N.N., *Aspects of Ancient Indian Polity* (Oxford, 1921).

Lumby, E.W.R., *The Transfer of Power in India, 1945–1947* (London, 1954).

MacDonell, A.A., and A.B. Keith, *Vedic Index of Names and Subjects*, 2 vols. (London, 1912).

Majumdar, R.C. (ed.), *The History and Culture of the Indian People* (London, 1951).

———, *History of the Freedom Movement in India*, III. (Calcutta, 1963).

Manu, *Ordinances of Manu*, translated by A.C. Burnell (London, 1891).

Masani, R.P., *Britain in India, An Account of British Rule in the Indian Subcontinent* (London, 1960).

Menon, V.P., *The Transfer of Power in India* (London, 1957).

Moon, P., *Divide and Quit* (London, 1961).

Monier-Williams, M., *A Sanskrit-English Dictionary*, new edition, enlarged (Oxford, 1899).

Montagu, E.S., *An Indian Diary*, edited by Venetia Montagu (London, 1930).

Moreland, W.H., and A.C. Chatterjee, *A Short History of India*, Fourth edition (London, 1958).

Mozoomdar, P.C., *The Life and Teachings of Keshub Chunder Sen* (Calcutta, 1891).

Muller, H.J., *Freedom in the Ancient World* (London, 1961).

Nevinson, H.W., *The New Spirit in India* (London, 1963).

Panikkar, K.M., *The Foundations of New India* (London, 1953).

Philips, C.H. (ed.), *Politics and Society in India* (London, 1963).

Plamenatz, J., *Man and Society*, 2 vols. (London, 1963).

Potter, K.H., *Presuppositions of India's Philosophies* (New Jersey, 1963).

Renou, L., *Religions of Ancient India* (London, 1953).

Ruskin, J., *Unto This Last* (London, 1960).

Sabine, G.H., *A History of Political Theory*, revised edition (New York, 1956).

Shay, T.L., *The Legacy of the Lokamanya: The Political Philosophy of Bal Gangadhar Tilak* (London, 1956).

Spear, P., *India, Pakistan and the West*, Third edition (London, 1958).

————, *India, A Modern History* (Ann Arbor, 1961).

Strauss, L., and J. Cropsey (eds.), *History of Political Philosophy* (Chicago, 1963).

Strauss, L., *What is Political Philosophy? and Other Studies* (Glencoe, III., 1959).

Tahmankar, D.V., *Lokamanya Tilak: Father of Indian Unrest and Maker of Modern India* (London, 1956).

Takakhav, N.S., *The Life of Shivaji Maharaj*. Adapted from original Marathi by K.A. Keluskar (Bombay, 1921).

Thoreau, H.D., *Walden and On the Duty of Civil Disobedience* (New York, 1962).

Tolstoy, L.N., *The Kingdom of God Is Within You* (London, 1905).

Topa, I.N., *The Growth and Development of National Thought* (Hamburg, 1930).

The Thirteen Principal Upanishads, translated by Robert Ernest Hume, Second edition, revised (London, 1962).

Wolpert, S.A., *Tilak and Gokhale: Revolution and Reform in the Making of Modern India* (Berkeley, 1961).

Woodcock, G., *Anarchism* (London, 1963).

Zaehner, R.C., *Hinduism* (London, 1962).

Zimmer, H., *Philosophies of India*, edited by Joseph Campbell (New York, 1959).

Articles in Periodicals and Books

Basham, A.L., 'Some Fundamental Political Ideas of Ancient India', in *Politics and Society in India*, edited by C.H. Philips (London, 1963).

Bondurant, J.V., 'The Nonconventional Political Leader in India', in R.L. Park, and I. Tinker, *Leadership and Political Institutions in India* (Princeton, 1959).

Bose, S.C., 'Swami Vivekananda', in *Vedanta for East and West* XII, No. 6 and XIII, No. 1 (July–October 1963).

Clark, T.W., 'The Role of Bankimcandra in the Development of Nationalism', in *Historians of India, Pakistan and Ceylon,* edited by C.H. Philips (London, 1961).

Friedman, D., 'Hinduism', *The Year Book of Education* (London, 1951).

Gonda, J., 'Ancient Indian Kingship from the Religious Point of View', *Numen: International Review for the History of Religions* IV, No.1 (Leiden, 1957).

Morris-Jones, W.H., 'Mahatma Gandhi—Political Philosopher?', *Political Studies* VIII, No.1 (February 1960), Oxford.

Pradhan, G.P., and A.K. Bhagwat, 'Lokamanya Tilak, The Politician and the Reformer', *Quest* II, No.1 (August–September 1956).

Ranganathan, A., 'Thoreau's Impact on Gandhi, A Study in Kingship', *Quest* II, No.2 (October–November 1956).

Sandhya, ed. Brahmabandhab Upadhyay in *Report on Native Papers in Bengal*, 1903, 906, India Office Library Transcripts.

Sharma, R.S., 'Historiography of the Ancient Indian Social Order', in *Historians of India, Pakistan and Ceylon*, edited by C.H. Philips (London, 1961).

'Swami Vivekananda: A Moulder of the Modern World', *Vedanta for East and West* XII, No. 6 (July–August 1963).

Tinker, H.R., 'Magnificent Failure?—The Gandhian Ideal in India After Sixteen Years', *International Affairs* 40, No.2 (April 1964), Chatham House.

Venkatarao, 'The Ashram Ideal in Politics: India's Version of Classless Society', in *Quest* II, No.4 (February–March 1957).

Index

DENNIS DALTON, Professor Emeritus of Political Science, Barnard College, Columbia University, is known for his classic study, *Mahatma Gandhi: Nonviolent Power in Action* (2012). His lifelong relationship with South Asia started in 1960, living and teaching in the villages of Nepal and India, on a program coordinated by the US Department of Agriculture and local community organizations. As recounted in his memoir, included within this book, throughout this year he met several participants in the Indian independence movement, especially Nirmal Kumar Bose. At Bose's initiative, he returned to study Indian political thought, ancient and modern, at the University of Chicago, Committee on Southern Asian Studies (COSAS). His MA thesis examined M.N. Roy's Radical Humanism (1962). From there, he pursued further graduate studies at the School of Oriental and African Studies (SOAS), University of London, under the supervision of professors Hugh Tinker and W.H. Morris-Jones. His dissertation on the idea of freedom in the thought of Vivekananda, Aurobindo, Gandhi and Tagore (1965), first published in book form in 1982, is republished here in a revised version. His university teaching career began at SOAS as Lecturer in South Asian Thought from 1965 to 1969 and continued at Barnard College until retirement in 2009. During this period, he participated in an international seminar on Gandhi in Delhi (1970), researched and taught as a Senior Fellow of the American Institute of Indian Studies, supervised by Professor Bimal Prasad, and was a Senior Fulbright Scholar to Nepal (1994–95). In addition to many articles and lectures on modern Indian thought, he served as an editor of *Sources of Indian Traditions* (third edition, 2014).

RAMACHANDRA GUHA is a historian and biographer based in Bengaluru. Among his best-known books are *India After Gandhi*, *Gandhi Before India*, *Gandhi: The Years That Changed the World* and *A Corner of a Foreign Field*.

JAMES HAMILTON TULLY is Distinguished Professor Emeritus of Political Science, Law, Indigenous Governance and Philosophy at the University of Victoria, British Columbia, Canada.

30 Years *of*

 HarperCollins *Publishers* India

At HarperCollins, we believe in telling the best stories and finding the widest possible readership for our books in every format possible. We started publishing 30 years ago; a great deal has changed since then, but what has remained constant is the passion with which our authors write their books, the love with which readers receive them, and the sheer joy and excitement that we as publishers feel in being a part of the publishing process.

Over the years, we've had the pleasure of publishing some of the finest writing from the subcontinent and around the world, and some of the biggest bestsellers in India's publishing history. Our books and authors have won a phenomenal range of awards, and we ourselves have been named Publisher of the Year the greatest number of times. But nothing has meant more to us than the fact that millions of people have read the books we published, and somewhere, a book of ours might have made a difference.

As we step into our fourth decade, we go back to that one word – a word which has been a driving force for us all these years.

Read.

Harper
Collins

HARPER
PERENNIAL

HARPER
BUSINESS

HARPER
BLACK

हार्पर
हिन्दी

HarperCollins
Children'sBooks

HARPER
DESIGN

HARPER
VANTAGE

Harper
Sport